WITHDRAWN

COLD NORTH KILLERS

COLD NORTH
KILLERS

CANADIAN SERIAL MURDER

Lee Mellor

DUNDURN

DUNDURN
TORONTO

Project Editor: Michael Carroll
Copy-Editor: Shannon Whibbs
Design: Courtney Horner
Printer: Webcom

Library and Archives Canada Cataloguing in Publication

Mellor, Lee, 1982-
    Cold North killers : Canadian serial murder / by Lee Mellor.

Includes bibliographical references and index.
Also issued in electronic formats.
ISBN 978-1-4597-0124-3

    1. Serial murders--Canada--History. 2. Serial murderers--Canada--
Biography. I. Title.

HV6805.M44 2011   364.152'3092271   C2011-903824-2

1   2   3   4   5   16   15   14   13   12

 Conseil des Arts Canada Council
du Canada for the Arts

Canada

 ONTARIO ARTS COUNCIL
CONSEIL DES ARTS DE L'ONTARIO

We acknowledge the support of the **Canada Council for the Arts** and the **Ontario Arts Council** for our publishing program. We also acknowledge the financial support of the **Government of Canada** through the **Canada Book Fund** and **Livres Canada Books,** and the **Government of Ontario** through the **Ontario Book Publishing Tax Credit** and the **Ontario Media Development Corporation.**

Printed and bound in Canada.
www.dundurn.com

Dundurn	Gazelle Book Services Limited	Dundurn
3 Church Street, Suite 500	White Cross Mills	2250 Military Road
Toronto, Ontario, Canada	High Town, Lancaster, England	Tonawanda, NY
M5E 1M2	LA1 4XS	U.S.A. 14150

This book is dedicated to my mother,

who taught me the beauty of the written word.

Contents

PREFACE
Canadian Serial Murder

This book is, to my knowledge, the only work dealing exclusively with Canadian serial murderers. The closest anyone has come so far is *Canadian Crime Investigations: Hunting Down Serial Killers* by the journalist Peter Boer, in which the Bernardo, Legere, Crawford, Pickton, Jesperson, Olson, and Cream cases are discussed. However the emphasis is on police work, and, as this book will reveal, there have been numerous omissions. Doug Clark's *Dark Paths, Cold Trails* focuses more on the development of the RCMP's profiling unit and Ron McKay's ViCLAS (Violent Crime Linkage Analysis System) than it does on the killers themselves. *Cold North Killers: Canadian Serial Murder*, on the other hand, is intended to be a didactic encyclopedia of sorts; as long as there is enough reliable information available, a killer or unsolved series of murders will be included. Names that appear in bold type refer to killers discussed in the book and can be accessed in the table of contents and also the index for more specific references.

As this work is the first of its kind, I would like to begin by defining what is meant by "serial murder." The term was coined in the late seventies by FBI criminal profiler Robert Ressler to describe homicides, often sexual, committed by one or more individuals in succession. Ressler was in the pioneering stages of the FBI's Behavioral Science Unit, and was quickly becoming an expert on what were then known as "lust murders" or "stranger killings." The problem was that not all of these killers were sexually motivated and once in a while a friend or acquaintance would fall victim. While attending a week's worth of police seminars and lectures in England, Ressler noted that British law enforcement were in the habit of referring to "crimes in series" such as a series of rapes or burglaries. Applying it to murder, Ressler found the term fit like a glove. Thus the "serial killer" was born. In the years since, there has been much debate over what comprises serial murder. Until recently, the FBI clung rigidly to their original definition of "three or more separate events in three or more separate locations with an emotional "cooling-off" period between homicides."[1] This definition is problematic because it relates to the killer's success rather than his psychological intent. For the purposes of this work, I will be using the definition put forth by Dr. Katherine Ramsland in her *The Human Predator:*

> A serial killer murders at least two people in separate incidents, with the strong likelihood of killing again. There is a psychological cooling-off period between incidents, which might serve as a time of preparation for a later killing. He, she, or they also choose the modus operandi and may either move around to kill or lure successive victims to a single locale. They dehumanize potential victims into objects needed for the satisfaction of their goals, which can be anything from lust to greed to anger, and their behaviour manifests an addictive quality.[2]

Now that we have a basic understanding of "serial murder," what exactly is meant by the term "Canadian serial murder"? **Keith Jesperson**, the "Happy Face Killer," was born and spent most of his childhood in Chilliwack, British Columbia. As an adult, Jesperson lived in Oregon and made his living driving long-haul trucks across the United States. Between 1990 and 1995, he strangled at least eight prostitutes, dumping their bodies like trash by the roadside. Though Jesperson was born in Canada, all of his victims were American. Is *this* an example of Canadian serial murder? Beginning in February 1926, **Earle Nelson** raped and strangled twenty women from San Francisco to Philadelphia before finally crossing into Canada where he claimed two more victims. In this case, the killer was an American killing Canadian women on Canadian soil. Is *this* an example of Canadian serial murder? The answer to both questions is "yes." For the purposes of this book, any serial killer born in or committing murder in Canada will be included. Offenders such as Hong Kong native Charles Ng, who fled north from the United States to escape arrest, will be left out because he was neither born on Canadian soil nor did he murder within Canada. Any serial killers murdering Canadian nationals outside Canada will also be excluded, unless the perpetrator was of Canadian origin.

There have been several entries that I assume will be controversial, and will do my best here to explain my reasons for including them. One that stands out immediately is that of **Doug Moore**, who murdered two teenaged boys out of revenge and a third because he knew too much. Rather than an example of serial murder, this may be better classified as a drug or gangland killing. However, Moore was a closet homosexual with a legacy of arrests for child molestation, and would have potentially been attracted to his victims. For this reason, it is possible there may have been a sexual component to the crimes. As Moore committed suicide before going to trial, the details of his murders were not disclosed to the public. The fact that he was never found guilty in a court of law is another reason his inclusion may be controversial; as are the entries of fellow suicides **Sam Pirrera**, and **Angelo Colalillo**. As I am of the opinion that a murderer should not be able to escape exposure by offing himself, Moore, Pirrera, and Colalillo have been included in this gallery of miscreants and perverts.

Another questionable entry is that of "The Cottage Killer" **David Snow**, who killed Ian and Nancy Blackburn in a single explosion of sadism. Typically, serial killers must murder on two separate occasions with a cooling-off period between. Yet the level of professionalism shown in the Blackburn murder is indicative of somebody who has killed before; in fact, Snow is a suspect in the murders of several missing women around the Caledon area. We also know that he abducted and tortured two British Columbia women for days on end, expressing his intention to murder them before he was interrupted by police. He was finally apprehended while twisting a wire coat hanger around a middle-aged woman's neck. Even though we can't prove David Snow is a serial killer, he has the appropriate psychology, attempted to kill on several more occasions, and, when looking at the circumstantial evidence surrounding the Caroline Case murder, in all probability *is* one. In the end, his case was simply too fascinating not to include.

Allan Craig MacDonald's first murders were a desperate attempt to escape police and were different in many ways from his pre-meditated sex-slaying of Lynda Shaw. Some may feel this disqualifies MacDonald from the title of serial killer, and though I disagree, their viewpoint is certainly valid.

I have also included seven unsolved cases: Toronto's Gay Village Murders, The Highway of Tears, The Edmonton Serial killer, The Hemlock Valley Murders, The Calgary Prostitute Murders, The Prostitutes-in-the Lake Killings, and Niagara's Prostitute Murders; where no suspect has been convicted, but the presence of a multiple murderer is a reasonable certainty. Though I wished to discuss many other suspected cases of serial murder, I was unable to do so, due to spatial constraints. My apologies.

I would like to make one final clarification before we dive headfirst into the world of psychosis, psychopathy, and sadism: this book is not an attempt to glorify multiple murderers, nor to canonize their victims. Above all else, it is meant to be an educational tool. Too many Canadian families have suffered as a result of inadequate press coverage, negligence, a closed judicial system, and public forgetfulness. Had our mental health system recognized men like **Woodcock, Hamill,** and **Allan MacDonald** for the incurable psychopaths they were, perhaps Dennis Kerr and Lynda Shaw would be alive today. There was plenty of cause to lock up **Gilbert Paul Jordan** and "First Nations Killer" **John Martin Crawford** for life before they had the opportunity to become serial murderers. Instead, fourteen women lay dead.

Finally, this book is also intended to be something of an exposé. Until **Robert Pickton**, the official line was that there had only ever been one serial killer in Canadian history: **Clifford Olson**. A quick look at the Table of Contents should banish these laughable misconceptions forever.

In truth, I have identified approximately sixty different Canadian serial murderers ranging from the 1840s to present day. For some of the more highly publicized cases such as **Paul Bernardo** and **Karla Homolka**, I was faced with a mountain of information, and the challenge became separating the wheat from the chaff, so to speak. Adversely, there were so few existing sources for cases such as "The London Chambermaid Killer" **Gerald Thomas Archer**, I was only able to focus on the bare-bones aspects of their stories. With that said, I have spared you no grisly details. To do so would understate the magnitude of both the victims' suffering and the killers' depravity.

Let the lesson not be "fear," but "vigilance."

— Lee Mellor

Acknowledgements

Researching and writing *Cold North Killers: Canadian Serial Murder* has been an intellectually and spiritually exhausting process spanning almost three years. For the first part of this journey I am indebted to my mother and father, along with my second family, the Brambergers, both of whom provided love, support, meals, and a bed to sleep in during my travels across southern Ontario. Thanks also to my long-time friend and fellow connoisseur of all things dark and weird, Curtis Yateman, who helped proofread and correct the initial manuscript. Prior to searching for an agent/publisher, three terrific Canadian authors provided me with invaluable advice regarding the process: Trevor Ferguson (*The Timekeeper*), Sarah Dearing *(The Bull Is Not Killed)*, and Peter Vronsky *(Serial Killers: The Method and Madness of Monsters)*. My gratitude also goes out to Mr. Vronsky for sharing his photographs of the murderer Peter Woodcock. *Cold North Killers* would have been stillborn if not for my agent Robert Lecker, who took a chance on this unorthodox subject. Thank you for your belief in my work. I also warmly acknolwedge the efforts of Ken Browne who helped make sense of the legalese for me.

Those who deserve recognition for the second or "publishing" phase of my journey are the author Robert Hoshowsky (*The Last to Die)* who continues to assist me in navigating the bizarre waters of Canadian true crime writing, and whose *Unsolved: Canadian Cold Cases* offers a wealth of information I have drawn from. Both Robert and historical crime writer Ed Butts graciously advised me on their methods of tracking down photos. Cheers also to Warren Goulding, author of the groundbreaking *Just Another Indian: A Serial Killer and Canada's Indifference* for your correspondence and photography. Another of the many talented Canadian true crime authors I was fortunate to converse with was Jon Wells (*Vanished*, *Poison*, and *Sniper*) of the *Hamilton Spectator*. My utmost appreciation to both Jon and the *Spectator* for allowing me to include their photographs of Sam Pirrera, Sukhwinder Dhillon, and Carl Hall in this book.

When my search for mugshots was stifled by the privacy policies of various police agencies, the artistic community came to my rescue, providing illustrations of the offenders for whom I was unable to find quality photographs. I am therefore eternally grateful for the efforts and talents of Andre Kirchhoff, Kay Feely, Elizabeth Roth, Stephenie Burke, and Michelle Chan. Your varying approaches and sensibilities have resulted in a book that is much more visually interesting than originally conceived. I hope my writing lives up to your work.

Much needed support, advice, and astute proofreading was also provided by Christina FitzGerald. Thank you for so much.

Finally, an honourable mention to Carrie Butler-Grenier for unearthing those old, dusty Max Haines compendiums and inadvertently leading me to the cases of Edward H. Rulloff and Dr. Robert MacGregor.

RIGHT UNDER OUR NOSES:

Colonel Russell Williams and the Writing of this Book, Part 1

On the night of Monday November 23, 2009, as I sat researching for this book at my lakeside home in Brighton, Ontario, a masked intruder invaded the downtown residence of Corporal Marie-France Comeau, repeatedly raping her and suffocating her to death with duct tape. Oblivious to the local news, it wasn't until the January 28 abduction of Belleville native Jessica Lloyd that I became alerted to the possibility of a sexually motivated killer operating in my area. Though the revelation was disturbing and coincided eerily with the book's subject matter, I was not entirely surprised. After six months of research, the pervasiveness of serial murder throughout Canadian history had become abundantly clear, and, if anything, I wondered why the corridor of Ontario between Scarborough and Ottawa had been spared from these predators. I certainly did not expect Ms. Lloyd's body to be recovered so soon, let alone the swift apprehension of her killer. Yet miraculously, within two weeks of her disappearance, the Ontario Provincial Police announced they had charged a suspect in the Lloyd/Comeau murders, along with two sexual assaults and a series of fetish burglaries in nearby Tweed and the Ottawa suburb of Orleans. The perpetrator was none other than Colonel Russell Williams, air force commander of Trenton CFB, Canada's largest Air Force base, less than twenty kilometres from my home.

Colonel Russell Williams at CFB Trenton, January 7, 2010.

Though I was aware that serial killers like Gary Heidnik and Christopher Wilder had enjoyed great financial success, Williams's arrest was shocking in that he was arguably the most prestigious multiple murderer in recent history. Not only was he a powerful Canadian military commander, he had actually flown Prime Minister Stephen Harper and the governor general across the country, at one point being photographed with Queen Elizabeth and the Duke of Edinburgh. Intrigued, I began to delve into newspaper accounts of his life, as the trial date edged closer and closer. In the meantime, I continued to work diligently on this book, hoping that Williams's story would be revealed in full before *Cold North Killers* hit the printing press.

PART A

INTRODUCING THE CANADIAN SERIAL KILLER

CHAPTER 1

THE FIRST CANADIAN SERIAL KILLERS

If you ask a friend to name some Canadian serial killers, you'll probably get an answer that starts with **Paul Bernardo** (and his equally loathed wife **Karla Homolka**) followed by **Robert Pickton** and **Russell Williams**. If the questioned party is particularly sharp or from the west coast, they might also dredge up the name **Clifford Olson** from the early eighties, though they may not be familiar with his crimes. Are there only four serial killers in Canadian history? Are Canadians really that fortunate and morally superior to their murder-ridden British, Australian and American cousins that their society has somehow been left unblemished by the homicidal maniac? The answer is "of course not." Canada has a long history of serial murderers dating back to opportunistic shooter/ poisoner **Edward Rulloff** and ripper **Joseph LaPage** who, in the 1870s, raped and mutilated two young women south of the border.

Below is a bare-bones chronology of the serial killers covered in this book divided into one of four "cultural ages" of murder. I have used the time frame devised by British serial-killer expert David Wilson in the first chapter of his book *A History of British Serial Killing*, with one slight alteration: my chronology begins forty-five years prior to Jack the Ripper.

My primary motivation in choosing Wilson's timeline as a model was that it allowed me to directly compare his account of the history of British serial killers with my Canadian research. First, I organized the murderers in this book by Wilson's criteria (much stricter than my own). Applying Wilson's exceptions and exclusions to Canadian serial killers, I compared the two histories and came across some interesting finds. Though Wilson's criteria disqualified all Canadian murderers in the first two periods, in the postwar era, Canada produced four serial killers next to Britain's nine. Canada's average population between 1945 and 1978 however was 18.7 million, compared to Britain's 51.6 million. In other words, during the postwar period Canada had 36 percent of Britain's population, but 44 percent the number of their serial killers. The modern period (1979–present) saw Canada climb to almost 50 percent of Britain's population, with an average population of 28.9 million versus 58.7 million Brits. Yet again, Canada had 64 percent the number of serial killers that Britain had in the modern period. This means that from 1945 to the present, Canada has maintained a slightly higher rate of serial murder per capita than Britain.[1]

TABLE 1: CHRONOLOGY

Guide: Killers marked with an asterisk (*) meet Wilson's criteria, while those marked with a # meet his criteria, but were convicted after the time period in his book. The Edmonton Serial Killer has been added as an unsolved case to counterbalance Wilson's inclusion of Jack the Ripper, as Gerald Thomas Archer has for John George Haigh.

I. VICTORIAN/PRE-WAR (1843–1914)

SPAN OF KILLINGS	CASE	LOCATION OF MURDERS
1843–1870	Edward Rulloff	(New York)
1874–1875	Joseph LaPage	(New England)
1877–1892	Dr. Thomas Neill Cream	(London, Ontario; Chicago; London, United Kingdom)
1895	Theo Durrant	(San Francisco)
1909–1912	Dr. Robert MacGregor	(Michigan)

II. INTERWAR (1914–1945)

1926–1927	Earle Nelson	(United States; Winnipeg)
1928	Gordon Stewart Northcott	(California)

| 1928–1945 | Lila and William Young | (East Chester, Nova Scotia) |

III. POSTWAR (1946–1978)

1946	Michael Vescio	(Winnipeg)
1946	Donald Sherman Staley	(Vancouver, Calgary)
1946–1947	Ron Sears	(Windsor)
1956–1957	Peter Woodcock	(Toronto/Brockville)
1963	Léopold Dion	(Quebec City area)
1967	Toronto's Gay Village Murders	(Schomberg, Ontario; Balsam Lake Park, Ontario)
1967–1981	James Greenidge	(Markham area, Ontario; Vancouver)
1969–1970	Gerald Archer*	(London, Ontario)
1970	Ron West	(Gormley/Palgrave, Ontario)
1970–1971	Wayne Boden*	(Montreal; Calgary)
1973–1974	Henry Williams	(Mississauga area, Ontario)
1974–1976	Christian Magee*	(Strathroy/Mount Brydges, Ontario)
1973–1977	Russell Maurice Johnson*	(London/Guelph, Ontario)
1974, 1988	Paul Cecil Gillis	(British Columbia, Ontario)
1975	David Threinen	(Saskatoon)
1975, 1985	Allan James Sweeney	(Sault Ste. Marie/Ottawa)
1974–1978	Donald Eric Armstrong	(Mississauga/Brampton)
1978, 1988	Melvin Stanton	(Toronto)

IV. MODERN (1979–PRESENT)

1975, 1989	Allan MacDonald	(Dartmouth, Nova Scotia; Oxford County, Ontario)
1965–1988	Gilbert Paul Jordan	(Vancouver)
1979–1982	Danny Wood	(Across Canada)
1980–1981	Clifford Olson*	(Vancouver suburbs)
1977, 1991	Bruce Hamill	(Ottawa/Brockville, Ontario)
1982–1983	William Dean Christenson	(Montreal; northeastern United States)

1983–2006	Edmonton Serial Killer*	(Edmonton)
1985–1998, 2011	Michael McGray*	(Across Canada)
1986, 1989	Allan Legere*	(Miramichi area, New Brunswick)
1989–1992	Serge Archambault*	(Southern Quebec/Ste-Agathe-Des-Monts Quebec)
1989, 1993	Brian Arp	(Prince George, British Columbia)
1990–1992	Paul Bernardo* and Karla Homolka	(Port Dalhousie/St. Catharines, Ontario)
1990–1995	Keith Jesperson	(Across United States)
1991, 1999	Sam Pirrera	(Hamilton, Ontario)
1991–2005	Melissa Ann Friedrich	(Halifax; Florida)
1992	David Snow	(Caledon, Ontario)
1981, 1992–1995	John Martin Crawford*	(Lethbridge; Saskatoon)
1979–1999	William Fyfe*	(Montreal suburbs/Ste-Agathe-Des-Monts)
1993–2002	Angelo Colalillo	(Montreal)
1995	Braeden Nugent	(Thunder Bay, Ontario)
1995–1996	Sukhwinder Dhillon	(Hamilton, Ontario; Punjab, India)
1997	Michael Hector	(Thunder Bay)
???–2002	Robert Pickton*	(Port Coquitlam, British Columbia)
2000–2001	Carl Hall	(Hamilton, Ontario)
2003	Doug Moore	(Clarkson, Ontario)
2003–2005	Charles Kembo#	(Vancouver area)
2005	Joseph Laboucan and Michael Briscoe	(Edmonton)
2008–2009	Colonel Russell Williams	(Brighton/Belleville, Ontario)
1974–Present	Highway of Tears	(Highway 16 area, British Columbia)

Canada's serial killer growth was fastest between the interwar and postwar periods, rising from zero to four. Unsurprisingly, this coincided with the baby boom, although one must consider that during this period, the population of most occidental countries typically doubled. This simply does not account for the 800 percent increase in British serial murder at the time, or Canada's equally stunning growth.

In the first of many studies, we will examine the Rulloff and LaPage killings. As we progress through the chapters, additional Canadian examples will be provided to illustrate their continued presence in the Great White North.

From Crapsey's The Man of Two Lives, 1871.

Edward Rulloff
The Educated Killer
6–7 Murders
Eastern United States

"From the invisible animalcule to the leviathan of the deep, one order of creatures is constantly preying upon another, and can subsist only by doing so."

MORE BRAINS THAN SCRUPLES

Canada's first serial killer was also arguably its most intelligent. Born in 1821[2] in Hammond River, New Brunswick, just outside of Saint John, John Edward Howard Rulofson was viewed as something of a genius by everyone who had the misfortune of crossing his path. Versed in Hebrew, Greek, Latin, French, and German, he was able to converse intelligently on any number of subjects ranging from geology to art history. Perhaps even more astounding was the fact that he developed this wealth of knowledge despite the complete unavailability of formal education in the tiny New Brunswick hamlet. John did not attend school until he was twelve years old, soon growing bored and leaving to become a clerk in a Saint John law firm. Shortly after, the home of a senior partner in the firm was robbed, with several expensive suits counted among the missing items. When John was spotted parading around town in the stolen garments, the teenage genius was sentenced to two years of hard time in the local jail.

Released to find his reputation irreparably tarnished, he promptly changed his name to Edward Howard Rulloff and drifted south to Dryden, New York, where in 1842 he was taken under the roof of passenger-boat proprietor Mr. William Schutt. Within no time, Rulloff's outstanding intelligence landed him a job teaching at a small private school. The twenty-one-year-old teacher was so popular that his students actually arrived early for class, staying long after it had been dismissed. Among his pupils was Schutt's sister, Harriet, an alluring sixteen-year-old whose maturity failed to keep pace with her voluptuous body. Soon, she and Rulloff were courting.

Despite the efforts of Harriet's suspicious older brothers, William, Edward, and Ephraim, the two lovers married on New Year's Eve 1843, absconding to Ithaca, New York, where Rulloff began advertising his services as a medical doctor. In reality, he was little more than a quack. Harriet soon discovered that her husband's eloquence concealed a violent temper. Convinced that his bride was carrying on an affair with her cousin, Dr. Henry Bull, Rulloff demanded she stop customarily kissing the good doctor when they visited. On another occasion, Rulloff struck Harriet on the forehead with a pestle because she had not ground his peppercorns finely enough. Despite the beatings, in 1844, Harriet became pregnant, and the couple relocated to Lansing, New York, where Rulloff found work as a phrenologist. On April 12, 1845, their daughter Priscilla was born. The following month, a sister-in-law and child by William Schutt died under Rulloff's care when he was summoned to Ithaca to treat them. At the time, nobody suspected a thing. Then, on June 23, Rulloff asked to borrow a horse and wagon from his neighbours, the Robertsons, explaining that Harriet and baby Priscilla had gone to stay with an uncle in Motts Corners. To make room for them, the uncle had stored his possessions in a large crate at the Rulloff household, and now the "doctor" wished to transport the crate back to Motts Corners and pick up his family. The Robertsons agreed, even helping to load the heavy container onto the wagon. They were more than a little puzzled when Rulloff returned to Lansing the next day alone with the crate still in his possession. This time he seemed to have no problems carrying it into the house by himself. Returning the horse and wagon, Rulloff informed the Robertsons that he was going on a two-week vacation with his family. They never set eyes on him again.

Having neither seen nor heard from their sister in some time, the Schutt brothers contacted the police with their suspicion that Rulloff had murdered her. He was tracked to Cleveland and transported back to Ithaca, where in 1846 he was charged, tried, and found guilty of abduction. As there was no physical evidence to indicate foul play, Edward Rulloff was not charged with the deaths of his wife and infant child. Still, he spent the next ten years behind the bars of an Auburn prison. Upon his release, Rulloff was informed that he would now stand trial for the suspected murders. Though Lake Cayuga had been dragged several times without result, authorities had learned that the body of a woman and child had been sold to Geneva Medical College around the time of the disappearances. Imprisoned once again in 1857, a jury found Rulloff guilty of murdering his daughter Priscilla. While awaiting sentencing, he volunteered to tutor the undersheriff's son, Albert Jarvis. Cunningly, Rulloff also wrote a flattering biography of the boy's father, and plied his considerable charms on Albert's mother, causing her to fall madly in love with him. Though it is not known which of the Jarvis family came to Rulloff's aid, in the spring of 1857, eight locks and a chain around his ankle were mysteriously opened, allowing him to escape into the night. Rulloff took to the road, catching what little sleep he could in culverts and barns. One night it was so cold that his big toe froze, and he was forced to amputate it.

Arriving in Ohio, Rulloff landed himself a position teaching, but a former convict recognized him and contacted the police. He was apprehended and sent back to Ithaca where he was held at Auburn Penitentiary to prevent him from being lynched. The bodies of Mrs. William Schutt and child were exhumed, and a subsequent autopsy revealed traces of copper poisoning. Although this was insufficient evidence to charge Rulloff with the murders, he had already been convicted of killing baby Priscilla, for which he had been sentenced to hang. Arguing that the child's absence did not prove she had been slain,

Rulloff's attorney, Francis M. Finch, won his client a new trial in 1859. To the shock and outrage of the community, the conviction was overturned, and Edward Howard Rulloff was once again a free man.

CRIMINAL MASTERMIND

Drifting east to Brooklyn in 1864, the "genius" had evidently not learned his lesson. Fashioning himself as the leader of a small criminal triumvirate, including his old pupil Albert Jarvis and a former inmate Bill Dexter, Rulloff began to plan bank robberies. In the meantime, he passed himself off as Professor E.C. Howard, teaching English to immigrants from his office in Hoboken, New Jersey. Taking on a third identity, philologist Edward Leurio of 170 Third Avenue, Manhattan, he began to develop a universal language, receiving moderate praise from the local intelligentsia.

In the early morning hours of Wednesday August 17, 1870, two clerks named Fred Mirrick and Gilbert Burrows had fallen asleep at the Halbert Brothers silk shop in Binghamton, New York, when they awoke to the sounds of a burglary in progress.[3] Surprised to find themselves confronted by resistance, the intruders, Bill Dexter and Albert Jarvis, began to struggle with the employees. A gunshot cracked through the darkness, exploding Mirrick's head. Edward Rulloff had come to Dexter and Jarvis's rescue. Turning his revolver on Burrows next, Rulloff sent a bullet whizzing through the clerk's torso. As the trio fled, the gravely injured Burrows stumbled into the night, somehow managing to reach the chief of police's house three blocks away. He would survive the attack.

Investigators at the crime scene found a single telling clue: a man's shoe stuffed with newspaper in the space usually occupied by the big toe. Two days later, the bodies of Bill Dexter and Albert Jarvis were fished out of the Chenango River, both with soggy train tickets to Batavia in their pockets. Burrows fingered them as the burglars he had struggled with on the night of Mirrick's murder. Soon after, Edward Rulloff was linked to the Mirrick slaying by way of his deformed foot and association with Dexter and Jarvis. Similarly, he was found to have a train ticket to Batavia in his possession. Rulloff was arrested, found guilty in a court of law, and sentenced to hang. In his final days, the man the press was now referring to as "The Educated Killer" confessed to murdering his wife, weighing her down with stones,

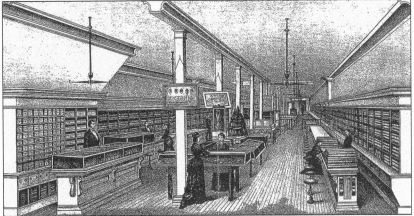

From Combination Atlas of Broome County, 1876.

Above: Halbert Brothers Shop.

Left: Rulloff fires a fatal shot at the clerk Merrick.

From The Life, Trial and Execution of Edward H Rulloff, 1871.

and dumping her body in the middle of Lake Cayuga. Rulloff claimed that on the night of June 23, 1845, the two had argued bitterly; he desired to move west to Ohio to become a lawyer or professor, while Harriet was adamant she would remain near her family. When the issue of baby Priscilla's custody arose, Rulloff flew into a rage, splitting his wife's skull with a pestle. He also admitted to killing Mrs William Schutt and her baby to exact revenge on the brother-in-law who had so fervently opposed his marriage.

Rulloff never offered any explanation as to what became of his daughter. The theory is that Priscilla was murdered and left among the murky weeds of Lake Cayuga. However, according to an article in the *New*

Rulloff attacking his wife, Harriet, with a pestle.

From *The Life, Trial and Execution of Edward H Rulloff*, 1871.

York Times, in the years following Rulloff's demise, twenty-five-year-old Priscilla Rulloff was found alive and operating a hotel in Parker's Landing. She had been raised by Rulloff's brother in Pennsylvania, and had been sent many gifts from her father, whom she believed to be her uncle.

Edward Howard Rulloff was hanged outside Binghamton Jail on May 18, 1871, having refused any religious counselling.[4] One journalist reported that his final words were "Hurry it up. I want to be in Hell in time for dinner." Despite his wish for a speedy execution, Rulloff's neck did not break, and he slowly strangled to death over the course of twenty minutes. It was the last public hanging to occur in New York State. After his body had been displayed to the public, Rulloff's corpse fell into the possession of Dr. George Burr of Geneva Medical College. Removing the brain, Burr discovered it weighed an astronomical fifty-nine ounces! Today it remains preserved in formalin and confined to a jar in a university collection.

"The Educated Killer" Edward Rulloff may have been the first Canadian serial murderer to terrorize the United States, but he certainly would not be the last.

Kay Feely.

Joseph LaPage
2 Murders
New England

BEFORE JACK, THERE WAS JOE

Jack the Ripper was a product of the Old World — a monster hatched in the overcrowded, industrialized streets of Victorian London. His predecessor, French-Canadian[5] Joseph LaPage, on the other hand, was a true butcher of the frontier.

LaPage was hired on by a Mr. Fowler, chairman of the Pembroke Board of Selectmen, to operate a threshing machine on his New Hampshire farm. Fowler found the burly, black-bearded Quebecois peculiar, but a decent worker, and kept him on indefinitely. He even allowed LaPage to dine with the family from time to time. On one such occasion, a beautiful young woman entered the dining room. Following supper, LaPage took one of Fowler's sons aside and inquired as to her identity. He learned she was the boy's sister Litia, and with further probing, LaPage discovered the path she took to school. Two days later, a local boy strolling along the same road spotted a strange figure crouched behind a patch of bushes. Assuming it was somebody waiting to play a trick on a friend, he dismissed it and carried on. Later that evening, a search party found the mutilated body of a missing young woman lying on her back in a copse four metres from the highway. Her clothing had been torn to shreds, flesh ripped and mangled, and head severed completely from her body. A post-mortem examination revealed she had been raped and her vagina was partially cut away. It wasn't until the retrieval of the head, wrapped in a blue oilcloth cape half a mile away, that the search party confirmed the identity of seventeen-year-old Josie A. Langmaid, the daughter of one of Pembroke's leading citizens, and one of Litia Fowler's best friends. The date was October 5, 1875, thirteen years before Jack the Ripper began his reign of terror.

GENESIS

Born eighty kilometres west of Montreal, probably in the 1830s, Joseph LaPagette a.k.a. LaPage was the son of an honest Quebecois farmer. At the age of twenty, he wed a woman three years his senior who bore him five children. Five years after the wedding, the LaPage family relocated to St. Beatrice, Quebec. But the marriage was not a happy one: Joseph drank heavily and, given to violent outbursts, beat his wife regularly. There were rumours circulating that he had even tried to deflower his own daughters.

In 1871, LaPage followed his sister-in-law Julienne Rousse to a pasture where, donning a buffalo robe mask to disguise his identity, he set upon her. Years later in a New Hampshire courtroom, Ms. Rousse would recount how she had torn the mask away, revealing his face, before he raped and strangled her, grinding sand in her throat and leaving her for dead. A local policeman managed to track down and arrest LaPage, but the outlaw bided his time, and when the opportunity arose, bowled his captor over and escaped. In a desperate flight from justice, he crossed the border into Vermont, far from the primitive reach of Canadian law enforcement. Within a year he settled into the sleepy community of St. Albans, where in 1871 he was joined by his wife and children. But his appetite for carnage only grew.

In 1872, LaPage returned briefly to St. Beatrice where he burned down some buildings belonging to a man who had aided in his arrest. Next, he ambushed and bludgeoned a pretty young bachelorette, causing lasting injury, and at one point attempted to lure a fourteen-year-old girl into the woods. When he tired of terrorizing the township, LaPage returned to St. Albans. On July 24, 1874, he became the chief suspect in the murder of a local schoolteacher. Miss Marietta Ball was found in a wooded area off the road she walked to school every day; her head bashed in with a rock and body hideously mutilated. There was evidence of rape. LaPage was cleared as a suspect when a witness erroneously testified that he had been berry-picking with LaPage on the afternoon in question. Hours after his release from custody, Joseph LaPage vanished.

FINAL JUDGMENT

When authorities in St. Albans learned of the Langmaid killing, they informed Pembroke police of the missing suspect in the Ball case. On October 14, LaPage was arrested in connection with the Langmaid murder. It wasn't long before mountains of evidence began to amass against him, and the two failed escape attempts in a fortnight did little to help his case.

On October 28, LaPage stood before the grand jury to plead "not guilty" to the murder of Josie Langmaid. His trial began in January 1876. Over a period of ten days, the court learned how LaPage had been spotted near the crime scene, club in hand, and how the same bloody weapon was later found shattered in three pieces a short distance from the body, along with a broken earring and comb. Forensic testing of bloodstains on LaPage's clothes revealed them to be of human origin.

Meanwhile, those willing to testify as to the nature of his character condemned him as "brutal, cruel and lustful beyond measure." LaPage remained emotionless throughout the proceedings. After two hours of deliberation, the jury returned a verdict of first-degree murder for the slaying of Josie Langmaid. However, LaPage's counsel managed to win him a new trial on the grounds that the testimony of his sister-in-law Julienne Rousse was inadmissible. The second trial commenced on February 26, 1877, but did little to improve LaPage's position. On March 9, he was reconvicted of the Langmaid murder and sentenced to hang. This time it took the jury a mere fifty minutes.

On the evening before his execution, LaPage was taken from his cell to see the warden. The two chatted amiably for several hours, with the condemned man showing no signs of apprehension. Then at nine o'clock, LaPage was returned to his cell where he was joined by two spiritual advisers: the Reverends J.E. Barry of Concord and J.B. Millette of Nashua. The men prayed for LaPage's soul, each probably suspecting it was damned to the inferno. After finishing his supper, he called for the warden. When the man arrived, LaPage became hysterical, throwing himself pitifully at his feet. Amidst a torrent of garbled tears and broken English, he confessed to the murders of Josie Langmaid and Marietta Ball, even drawing maps of the crime scenes. The warden couldn't help noting the strange serenity which seemed to follow the prisoner's confession, as if he had relieved himself of a heavy burden.

It was a cool spring morning on March 15 when Joseph LaPage mounted the gallows. Josie Langmaid's father was on hand to witness his execution — a far quicker, more humane death than LaPage had allowed his daughter. Following the mandatory reading of the death warrant, the executioner slipped a noose and black hood over the prisoner's head. At 11:08 a.m. the lever was thrown and Joseph LaPage, one of the most loathed killers in the history of New England, plummeted to his death.

––––––

Both Edward Rulloff and Joseph LaPage represent familiar serial killer types dating back through history: Rulloff, the opportunistic multiple murderer, and LaPage, the savage frenzy slayer. A precursory examination of The Educated Killer's crimes reveals a psychopath motivated by revenge, convenience, and greed. He targeted family (his wife, sister-in-law, and their infant children), accomplices (Dexter and Jarvis), and businesses (shooting the clerks in an act of spontaneity to eliminate witnesses). Taking this into consideration, Rulloff bears more psychological resemblance to a pirate or highwayman than Jack the Ripper. He is very much a murderer of the "old school."

Though the sexual attacks and mutilations of Joseph LaPage were driven by internal factors, there is ample evidence to show that these types of slayings have also occurred, albeit to a lesser extent, throughout human history. Before the age of reason, they were frequently attributed to vampires or werewolves — apparently our ancestors also found it difficult to accept that human beings could be responsible for such barbarities. Indeed, psychosis may have played a crucial role in these early lust murders, as well as the LaPage case.

Make no mistake: serial murder has increased and transformed significantly since the early twentieth century. Where materially motivated killers like Edward Rulloff were once more prevalent, the post-industrial world has seen an exponential rise in the number driven by internal needs such as deviant sexual gratification, power, or attention. Unlike the "wandering, crazy person,"[6] Joseph LaPage, who struggled to maintain a place in the communities he terrorized, these killers are cunningly adept at appearing normal. In a way, they have successfully fused the respectable social facade of Edward Rulloff with many of the urges driving "werewolves" like LaPage. The most frequently cited example of this citizen/monster dichotomy is the American killer Ted Bundy: a handsome Republican law student who publicly enjoyed skiing and exotic cuisine, privately luring beautiful co-eds to their deaths, decapitating them and returning to their dump sites to fornicate with their bodies.

There have been no shortage of theories to explain this new breed of serial killer. Author Colin Wilson has posited that as political and technological changes have more or less ensured the individual's survival in our society (he is unlikely to be without shelter or starve), the motives for serial murder have shifted away from material acquisition to issues of sexuality, socialization, and self-esteem.

Lee Mellor.

Maslow's Hierarchy of Needs.

Colin Wilson's theory is based upon psychologist Abraham Maslow's "Hierarchy of Needs," which presents a five-part order of human motivation. The individual will, for example, be mostly unconcerned with developing intimate romantic relationships if he is dying of thirst. His sole motivation will be to procure water.

That the murderers most similar to modern serial killers in history have been upper-class seems to support Wilson's theory. Gilles de Rais, a fifteenth-century French knight who fought the English alongside Joan of Arc, was one of the most evil sexual sadists of all time. A pedophile and Satanist, de Rais kidnapped, raped, tortured, and murdered as many as a hundred children in his Breton castle from 1432 until his trial in 1440. Countess Elizabeth Báthory stole the lives of an even larger number of peasant girls in late-sixteenth and- early-seventeenth-century Hungary, torturing them and forcing them to perform lesbian sex acts before slaying them and bathing in their blood.

The next two Canadian serial murderers we look at reflect the transition to the new model of killer Colin Wilson sees as emerging around the twentieth century. Saskatchewan-born Gordon Stewart Northcott lacked a castle and servants to help perpetrate his fantasies of domination. Instead, he lorded over a remote chicken ranch outside Los Angeles, browbeating his nephew and mother into aiding him. His predecessor, Theo Durrant, used his status in the San Francisco Baptist community to gain access to a killing ground. An educated and socialized necrophiliac with "no experience of women," Durrant serves as a bridge between the modern self-esteem killer and the savage werewolf. For this "Demon of the Belfry," sexual gratification was only possible if coupled with complete control over his lovers' bodies. As the first Canadian to represent Wilson's new breed of killer, in the context of this book, his crimes can be seen as a gateway between the older model of serial murderer described earlier, and a vast majority of the cases to follow.

Theo Durrant
The Demon of the Belfry

"It is not so awful to go to such a death. Such a death as mine may be the means of abolishing capital punishment in this state."

DR. DEMON

When former law student Ted Bundy stood before a Florida judge accused of the brutal necrophilist murders of over thirty women, the world expressed disbelief that such an eloquent and educated young man could be responsible. Yet eighty-four years earlier, the heinous crimes of medical student Theo Durrant had sounded alarm bells across the United States. Appearances could be fatally deceiving.

Born in Toronto on April 24, 1871, young Theo immigrated to San Francisco with his shoemaker father William and mother Isabella, where he attended a series of private schools. They were a cold, religious family. William, who suffered from manic depression, was sporatically employed and often physically or mentally absent, leaving most of the man's work around the house to the effeminite Theo. When his parents stopped sharing a bedroom, Isabella Durrant would insist that her adult son crawl into her bed because she was "scared." She reportedly flirted openly with Theo, obsessing over him. He grew to be prudish, paranoid, and given to compulsive pacing. Despite his obvious problems, the Durrants raised their son to be a paragon of courtesy, forever focused on his studies. On the surface, their approach seemed to pay off; by the time he was twenty-four years old, Theo was a respected student at Cooper Medical College, volunteering as assistant superintendent of the Sunday School program at Emmanuel Baptist Church. Undoubtedly, it was this air of success that attracted eighteen-year-old Blanche Lamont to him.

Described as dark-haired with creamy skin and a slender neck, Blanche lived with her aunt and uncle in San Francisco, where she took regular classes at Normal School. She dreamed of becoming a teacher. Instead, one afternoon in April 1895, she vanished.

Three days later, Blanche's aunt and uncle reported her disappearance to the police, and it wasn't long before suspicion fell upon Theo Durrant. On the morning of her disappearance, Blanche and Theo had been spotted flirting on a streetcar, the dapper young medical student whispering in her ear and playfully slapping at her with kid gloves. Another eyewitness reported seeing Durrant pacing nervously outside the Polk Street trolley stop at around 2:00 p.m. When Blanche approached, Durrant purportedly ran to meet her. Soon after, two additional witnesses spied the young lovers slipping in through the doorway of the Emmanuel Baptist Church. They were the last people to admit seeing Blanche Lamont alive.

The Henry Brown Collection, Whatcom Museum of History and Art.

The Henry Brown Collection, Whatcom Museum of History and Art.

Above: Blanche Lamont with her pupils in Montana.

Left: Blanche Lamont.

Three hours after Blanche and Theo entered the church, choral director George King arrived to practise his organ sonatas. Durrant suddenly appeared, looking dishevelled and pale-faced. He muttered something about attempting to repair a gas jet upstairs, and asked King if he would be kind enough to fetch some Bromo Seltzer from the pharmacy. When King returned, Durrant drank the tonic and seemed to regain his senses. Bidding the organist goodbye, he abruptly left the church. Later, he returned for the evening service and inquired about Blanche to her aunt, Mrs. Tryphena Noble. Mrs. Noble replied that she was concerned because her niece had not yet returned from school. Doing his best to reassure her, Durrant promised to drop by the house and lend Blanche a copy of William Maypeace Thackeray's *The Newcomes*. True to his word, he stopped by the next day, but upon learning that Blanche was still missing, began openly speculating that she had been kidnapped and forced into a life of prostitution. Durrant gallantly vowed to rescue her. Instead, he was later seen in the city's Tenderloin district, attempting to pawn jewellery. Shortly after, the Nobles received three rings in the mail, the envelope bearing the name of choral director George King. But King wasn't the suspect the San Francisco Police were looking at. In fact, the more they dug into Theo Durrant's past, the more convinced of his involvement they became. A fellow student and confidante admitted that Theo often claimed to have "no knowledge of women," yet following a near fatal bout with bacterial meningitis,[7] he talked about them constantly, paradoxically boasted of raping an Indian woman in a Carson City brothel. Another female attendee of Emmanuel Baptist Church reported being confronted by the nude Durrant one day while visiting the building's library.

As Easter drew near with no sign of Blanche Lamont, the dapper medical student began to turn his attentions to another young lady. Her name was Minnie Williams, and on Good Friday, April 12, 1895, she, too, would disappear.

THE BODY IN THE BELFRY

Saturday, April 13 was a busy day for the Ladies' Society of Emmanuel Baptist Church. A number had gathered at the building to clean and

Emmanuel Baptist Church.

adorn the pews with flowers for the coming Easter Sunday service. After a few hours' work, they decided to take tea in the church library. When one woman opened a cupboard to search for cups, she cried out in horror and fainted. Inside was the nude body of Minnie Williams, blood oozing from the deep slashes on her wrists. The missing twenty-one-year-old had been stabbed multiple times in the breasts with a table knife, raped after death, and stuffed into the cupboard to rot with a rag crammed down her throat. The implications of the murder were clear: if Blanche Lamont had met a similar fate, surely her body lay hidden somewhere in the church. After a thorough search of the premises revealed nothing, one member of the congregation suddenly remembered the belfry. As it had been sealed for many years, upon reaching the trap door, they surmised by the state of the rusty hinges that it had recently been forced open. They entered and were immediately assailed by flies and the stench of decaying flesh. The nude corpse of Blanche Lamont lay in the centre of the room, bloated by decomposition, her head propped between two blocks of wood — the way students were instructed to arrange a cadaver in medical school. Whoever had murdered the raven-haired beauty had taken the time to fold her arms across her chest in a crude funeral service. By now, the San Francisco police had no doubts as to who was responsible.

HANG-TIME

Having left for the bivouac on Mount Diablo as a member of the

The two faces of Theo Durrant: Medical Student and Convicted Murderer.

San Quentin Prisoner Photographs, San Quentin Mug Book Department of Corrections Record Group, California State Archives.

California Signal Corps, Theo Durrant was arrested that same day and brought back to Fisherman's Wharf where he was confronted by an angry mob. Though many in the city would have gladly killed him on the spot, the man newspapers were calling "The Demon of the Belfry" had no shortage of admirers. Like Ted Bundy, Durrant was inundated with letters and even proposals of marriage from adoring female fans. During his autumn 1895 trial, a blond woman known as "The Sweet Pea of San Francisco" arrived every morning to present him with a bouquet of flowers.

Unfortunately for Durrant, the jury would not be so enamoured. Along with the eyewitness testimonies implicating him in the murder of Blanche Lamont, there were those who claimed to have seen him arguing with Minnie Williams outside the church before her disappearance. Christian Fellowship member Mary Vogel testified that a few hours later, he arrived at her door acting peculiarly and asking to wash his hands. This cleansing ritual, like the Bromo Seltzer tonic, had seemed to calm Durrant. Immediately after, he had departed, claiming to have left something at the church. Though the defence pointed the finger at the Reverend John Gibson as the true "Demon of the Belfry," the jury took only five minutes to find Durrant guilty of both murders. He was sentenced to death by hanging. Following three years of unsuccessful appeals, Theo Durrant washed down his last meal of roast beef and fruit salad with tea, and mounted the gallows. Having recently converted to Catholicism after his Baptist minister refused to believe his innocence, he addressed those in attendance as the executioner fitted the noose around his neck: "I now go to receive the justice given to an innocent boy who has not stained his hands with the crimes that have been put upon him by the press of San Francisco ... I do not look upon people now as enemies. I forgive them as I expect to be forgiven for anything I have done ... I am innocent. I say now this day before God, to whom I now go to meet my dues, I am innocent ..." Moments later, "The Demon of the Belfry" was dead.

Gordon Stewart Northcott

Ape Man

"I suppose you are hating me for the things I have done."

Gordon Stewart Northcott in court. An attention-seeker and control freak, he insisted on conducting cross-examinations at his own trial.

FOXES IN THE HEN HOUSE

"Each of us will strike a blow," Louise Northcott's face looked ominous in the firelight. "And then if we are ever found out, we will all be equally guilty."

Later that evening, Louise, her twenty-one-year-old son Stewart, and his nephew Sanford Clark, fourteen, crept across the dusty ranch toward the henhouse. The beam from the flashlight hovered over the yard like a ghost orb, illuminating the wire mesh fences and rickety outbuildings. Inside the henhouse, nine-year-old Walter Collins was curled up asleep on a camp cot. Sanford felt a lump well up in his throat. It had been five days since his wicked uncle Stewart had snatched the boy from outside his home at 217 North Avenue 23.

Sanford knew full well what horrors he had endured. Just under two years earlier, Stewart had similarly abducted him from his home in Saskatoon promising him they were taking a trip to Vancouver. Once Sanford was out from under his parents' watchful eye, however, the older boy informed him they were going to California. Being young and timid, Sanford hadn't bothered to protest. Nor did he struggle too much when his uncle began to beat and sodomize him, lording over the Wineville chicken farm like some crazed Canadian Caligula. But now, standing in the dark henhouse with the axe weighing heavy in his hands, Sanford

Walter Collins: one of Northcott's victims.

Clark was no longer being made simply to play the victim. Instead, they were forcing him into the role of a killer. Fortunately, it seemed Stewart planned to strike first. Maybe the boy would already be dead by the time it was his turn. Hefting the axe, Stewart brought it crashing down mercilessly onto Walter's head. The boy let out a horrendous moan and toppled down to the floor as chunks of scalp and blood spattered across the cot. Stewart struck once again before he passed the axe to Sanford. When uncle, nephew, and matriarch had each contributed a stroke or two, they buried Walter under the dirt floor of the henhouse.

Two months later, Stewart lured brothers Lewis and Nelson Winslow from their model yacht club in Pomona to the ranch. As the farmhouse was in the midst of being plastered, he spent nearly a week and a half sodomizing them in the incubator house, while Sanford slept in one of the property's abandoned structures. When they weren't entertaining the Canadian pederast, the boys passed the time playing cards or drawing pictures. By now all of California was looking for the Winslows, and Stewart decided a red herring was in order. He forced the boys to write a letter to their parents telling them not to worry, that they were going to Mexico to make and sell model yachts and airplanes. Another letter postmarked May 28 claimed they were having a "wonderful adventure" travelling by night and sleeping in barns. In reality, by this time both boys had fallen victim to Stewart's axe. At first he had tried to kill Nelson with ether, convincing him to lie on the henhouse cot while he poured it through a colander over his face. Instead of quietly succumbing, the boy fell unconscious for a few minutes before waking in a fit of vomiting. The experiment abandoned, they led him back to the incubator house where they brutally hacked up both boys with the axe. That same afternoon they buried the Winslow brothers in the yard. According to Sanford Clark's testimony they were still alive and groaning when the dirt hit their faces.

A TRUE WEST COASTER

For a mid-sized Canadian city, London, Ontario, has always had a strangely disproportionate number of serial killers. It is perhaps fitting then that the seeds of one of Canada's most depraved families were sown here.

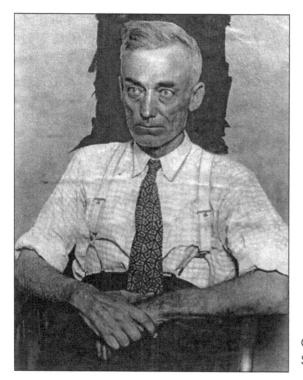

Cyrus George Northcott: Stewart's father.

On September 18, 1866, Cyrus George was born in London to farmers Augustus and Caroline Northcott. Twenty years later, he married Sarah Louise Carothorpe of Strathroy, three years his junior, who soon gave birth to a daughter Winnifred. In all she bore five children before Stewart, but only two would survive infancy. When her beloved son George died of pneumonia at age six, Louise fell into a severe depression which worsened when she discovered she was once again pregnant. At George's urging she attempted to abort the baby through various means such as continuous horse riding and jumping. As if this wasn't damaging enough to the fledgling child, one day in a drunken rage George allegedly kicked Louise in the stomach, injuring her spine.[8] By this time the family had picked up and moved west in search of better prospects. Gordon Stewart Northcott was thus born in Bladworth, Saskatchewan, on November 9, 1906. At first Louise refused to look at him, afraid of having her heart broken again.

When she finally set eyes on her newborn son, Louise became obsessed with her little Stewart, showering him with gifts and praise until he became so accustomed to having his way that any discipline or unfilled demand sent him into a towering rage.

From 1913 to 1924, the Northcott brood lived in Vancouver where Stewart developed an appreciation for classical and jazz music, particularly Beethoven and Debussy. A talented musician, he was able to earn an income leading a jazz orchestra in a Victoria cafe. When Stewart grew to manhood,

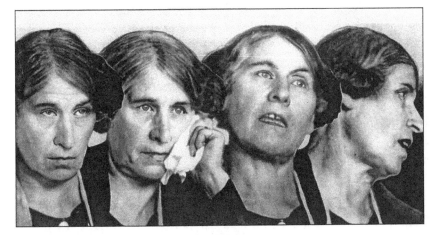

Sarah Louise Northcott: Stewart's mother and accomplice.

however, he began to demonstrate a number of peculiarities. First and foremost was the heavy carpet of body hair that appeared with puberty, causing the vain youth to spend his life seeking a cure. Later, his father George would jokingly refer to him as the "Ape Man," a moniker adopted and adapted by the press in the wake of the Wineville murders. His second, far more damning, peculiarity was his sexual predisposition toward young boys. At age fifteen he attempted to molest a ten-year-old in Kamloops.

During his time in Vancouver, Stewart contracted influenza, and accidentally struck his head on a patch of ice, causing hemorrhaging. A Dr. Grey of Edmonton suggested that his mind had been left unbalanced and that a move to California's drier clime might stabilize his condition. The Northcotts concurred, settling in Los Angeles where George found work as a contractor and builder, Louise became a laundress, and Stewart worked as a car salesman. He also attended school, befriending Claude Scott, whose younger brother he would go on to molest, though it is uncertain what consequences Stewart suffered when the child exposed him. At this time he had also earned the nickname "The Sheik of Pasadena Avenue" for his frequent use of young male prostitutes.

It soon became clear that special measures would have to be taken if Stewart was to continue his pedophile lifestyle. In the spring of 1926, he convinced his father George to purchase a three-acre chicken ranch for him in Wineville, Riverside County. Spoiled and lazy, Stewart realized he couldn't keep up the maintenance alone. At this point he made his infamous trip to the Clark homestead in Saskatoon, where he asked his sister Winnifred and her husband to allow Sanford to accompany him to Vancouver. Instead, the poor youth spent the next two years in California being abused and mistreated by his sadistic uncle.

THE MEXICAN

Gordon Stewart Northcott's premier foray into the dark realm of murder took place in February 1928. On the first day of that month, he left for Los Angeles, only to return to the ranch at noon, claiming he had killed a Mexican. When Sanford looked into the black-tar pail in the back of Stewart's Buick Roadster, he recoiled. The warm, bloody head of a dark-haired man stared blankly back at him. Aghast, Sanford asked his uncle why he had killed the man, but Stewart brushed off the question, saying that the Mexican simply "knew too much." Hours later they cremated the head along with a bundle of bloody clothing in a bonfire they built in a drained duck pond. By nightfall, only a section of blackened skull remained, which Stewart placed in a bucket and smashed to pieces with an axe. The rest of the cadaver, he claimed, had been left by the roadside in Puente. Stewart scattered the shards of skull and ashes in a nearby dump yard alongside his regular garbage. Later that evening, as he and Sanford were driving to Los Angeles to visit his parents, Stewart instructed his nephew to tell George and Louise Northcott that Stewart had caught a Mexican hired hand stealing money, and, when confronted, had been threatened with a knife. Sanford had been forced to shoot the Mexican in order to save his uncle's life, at which point Stewart had fainted. Afraid he might be the next head burning in a bonfire, Sanford agreed to corroborate his uncle's story.

Sometime around 9:00 a.m. the next morning, the headless torso was discovered. Running alongside his master's car as it drove south down Hudson Road near Puente, Lom Compton's dog began to bark excitedly. Compton peered out the window to see an arm protruding from the nearby weeds and barley. A closer look revealed a decapitated human body secreted in a sack in the ditch. Half an hour later, investigators from the Los Angeles Sheriff's Department arrived, identifying the corpse as that of a nude Mexican male between sixteen and eighteen years of age. A powder-burned bullet hole gaped through his chest. His body bore the tan marks of a recently removed bathing suit, his soft hands betraying a life unaccustomed to hard labour. A subsequent autopsy revealed no evidence of sodomy. Though the reason for the Mexican's murder would never be revealed, it set Gordon Stewart Northcott on a deadly path that would eventually lead to the end of a hangman's rope.

THE JIG IS UP

It had been two years since anyone in the Clark family had seen Sanford. Noting that his letters home showed no improvement in his writing or education, his nineteen-year-old sister Jessie began to worry about his school attendance. Determined to find out what was going on, Jessie saved her money for the long journey to California. On

Thursday, July 26, she arrived in Los Angeles and, after some difficulty in tracking down the family, went to the Wineville chicken ranch to see her brother. The first thing she noticed was that Sanford was caked in dirt and exhausted. Though obviously pleased to see his sister, he seemed timid and afraid to speak his mind. The next day he confessed to her that the letters he had written over the past two years had been dictated by Stewart, slipping her a note to mail home on his behalf. Stewart's watchful eye ensured they never had time alone, and though Jessie sensed there was more to the story than she was being told, Sanford was clearly terrified of his uncle. Later that night, when she was sure Stewart had fallen asleep, Jessie climbed into her brother's bed and began to question him. She was shocked to learn that Sanford was not only missing school altogether, but was regularly beaten, whipped, overworked, and sodomized by Stewart. Perhaps most chilling were the allegations of murder. When Jessie insisted they go back to Canada, Sanford explained that his uncle would never let him leave in case he spoke of the Wineville murders.

Jessie Clark stayed on at the ranch for a week, devising a plan to wrest her younger brother from their uncle's grip. The longer she was around, the more bizarre and brazen Stewart seemed to become. Once she saw him strike Sanford on the arm with a wrench. On another occasion he openly bragged to her of his plans to make a sex slave of local boy Steven Black, as Sanford was "getting to be a big, rough man."

On Thursday, August 2, Jessie and Sanford went to visit their grandparents' Los Angeles home accompanied, as always, by Stewart. At some point, Stewart stepped into the bathroom, leaving the siblings alone in the kitchen. Seeing her chance, Jessie instructed her brother to run, directing him to the home of a secret friend: Mrs. Svenning of 970 Menlo Avenue, Los Angeles. When Stewart returned to find his nephew missing, he flew into a panic. It became apparent that the lone eyewitness to their murders had disappeared for good, so Stewart and Louise hurried back to the chicken ranch to dispose of any remaining evidence. Sensing things were about to get bad, Jessie fled to Mrs. Svenning's house. Knowing that this was her only other contact in Los Angeles, the Northcotts arrived soon after to find Sanford also hiding at the residence. Enraged, Stewart took the boy back to the ranch immediately.

A week later, Jessie learned that Stewart had left for San Diego and, along with grandfather George Northcott, drove out to Wineville to fetch Sanford. Upon reaching the ranch, however, they ran into Louise, who was supposed to be back in Los Angeles doing laundry. The next thing they knew, Stewart returned, demanding to know what they were doing there. Jessie bravely announced she was taking Sanford home to Canada, prompting Stewart to strike her in the eye. As she lay dazed on the floor, he made her promise she would write home to tell her mother and father that Sanford was doing well at school. She promptly decided to leave for Vancouver.

On the day of her scheduled departure, Stewart and Sanford came to the city to bid her farewell. Stewart planned to stay in Los Angeles for a few days longer, but instructed Sanford to take the bus back to Wineville to sell an incubator to a potential customer. As the poor boy embraced his sister she slipped him a roll of bills and whispered for him to take the bus back from Wineville to Los Angeles. Once back in the city, he was to meet an Italian fruit vendor who would look after him until she arrived. Sanford did as she suggested, later meeting the Italian at the arranged spot. The vendor promised to buy him a bus ticket and see him safely on his way as long as Jessie could provide the fare. Nearly penniless, she approached George about providing the money and he agreed to put the boy on the bus himself. Jessie arranged to meet her brother when she changed buses in San Francisco. When she arrived at her destination, however, she was shocked to discover that Sanford was nowhere to be seen. Little did she know that on the way to the bus, George and his grandson had run into Stewart, who drove him back to the ranch, threatening to kill him.

Knowing that with Jessie gone his days of playing God at the ranch were numbered, Stewart immediately began to sell off his possessions in preparation to leave. It was a smart move — as soon as Jessie reached Vancouver she made a formal statement at the American consul, detailing how her uncle had smuggled Sanford across the border, mistreated him, and committed a series of horrific murders.

Coincidentally, while investigating Stewart in an unrelated automobile accident, members of the LAPD showed up at the Wineville ranch to question him. Assuming they were there to charge him with murder, he absconded through the fields, leaving Sanford to talk with the police. Sanford was taken to a Los Angeles juvenile home, where two days later he began to relay the details of his horrific ordeal. Looking over pictures of missing children, Sanford identified Walter Collins as one of the boys his uncle had repeatedly raped and murdered.

Over the next few months, a meticulous search of the property revealed blood-soaked soil, a cap belonging to Nelson Winslow, finger, hand, and foot bones, finger and toenails, flesh, hair, teeth, and an axe caked in blood. Warrants were immediately issued for the arrest of Gordon Stewart Northcott and his mother Louise. Canadian authorities apprehended the slippery pederast on a train heading from the Okanagan Landing in British Columbia to the United States. Louise Northcott was captured shortly after aboard a transcontinental train in Calgary, Alberta. But the show was just beginning.

MYTHS AND IMAGININGS

Over the next few months Stewart made repeated attempts to portray his niece and nephew as liars. Furthermore, the bones found at Stewart's Wineville ranch belonged to chickens. Strangely, just when Stewart had denied the murders altogether, he then did a complete about-face, admitting to the hitherto unknown slaying of nine-year-old Richard Gordon, as well as attempting to kill his father, George. In an effort to save her beloved son from the hangman's noose, Louise claimed she and Sanford were responsible for the murders, and was sentenced to life in prison. When she discovered that Stewart would still be tried for the offences, she retracted her statement.

The trial of Gordon Stewart Northcott began in a Riverside Court on Wednesday, January 2, 1929. His courtroom dramatics and maps of false burial sites sending police on wild goose chases led many to conclude he was insane. Undoubtedly this is what the fiend the press was now calling "The Ape Man" wanted, bragging that he would fool authorities into believing he was of diminished mental capacity. A true control freak, Stewart requested that he be allowed to interview and cross-examine the witnesses himself as he was privy to details his defence lawyers were not. Despite his efforts, Stewart was found guilty on three counts of first-degree murder and sentenced to death by hanging.

The Face of the 'Ape Man'

Press depictions of Stewart as a feminized "ape man."

While awaiting his execution at San Quentin's infamous prison, Stewart developed a rapport with Warden James B. Holohan and his young assistant and eventual successor, Clinton Duffy. In July 1929, believing his life was threatened by appendicitis, Stewart sent word to Duffy that he wished to make a full confession to his crimes. Over the next few hours, Duffy sat in horrified silence as Stewart detailed his rape and torture (between the end of his trial and eventual hanging, rumours began to circulate that Stewart had carved out and cut up his victims' genitals) of tens of children, only three or four of which he could remember by name. Even more appallingly, he claimed to have been a key player in southern California's child sex trade, prostituting young boys to many of the area's most respected citizens. Stewart recovered from his illness, but when pressed as to how or where he had disposed of the bodies, attempted to change the subject. In all, he would claim responsibility for the murders of up to twenty people. Then, without warning, he would change his story, asserting his innocence on all charges and begging to be helped out of his predicament. Among his many lies were that his father had died in a Canadian asylum before the trial began, even though Stewart had questioned George on the witness stand. Nor was Louise his true mother, in fact, he was the product of an incestuous relationship between his father and sister.

Despite repeated attempts to stall through false confessions and feigned madness, on Thursday October 2, 1930, a hysterical Gordon Stewart Northcott met his end at the gallows. He was the first prisoner in the history of San Quentin to be blindfolded at the time of his execution. The following year, the town of Wineville changed its name to Mira Loma, in an attempt to escape the loathsome reputation brought on by the boy from Saskatchewan. It bears the name to this day.

CHAPTER 2

NATURE, NURTURE, OR NEITHER?

One of the most pervasive questions in the identification and treatment of sexual murderers is whether they are born (the Nature argument), made (Nurture), or some combination of the two. The Nature argument points the finger purely at genetic or psychiatric deficiencies like those of "The Genesee River Cannibal" Arthur Shawcross. Born a small baby on June 6, 1945, this unusual New Yorker was plagued by abnormalities from the beginning. At the age of five he created two imaginary friends: a boy his own age, "Paul," and a nameless younger girl with whom he would converse for hours in baby talk. Shawcross would often lapse into infantile speech even as a teen, alternating it with a high-pitched, duck-like voice. He seemed constantly afraid, and was mortified by loud noises. As he grew older, Shawcross began to walk "cross-lots." Holding his body upright and swinging his arms excessively, he would trample at high speed over obstacles as if oblivious to them.[1] In his twenties, he was still secretly playing with toys. The full extent of his problems manifested when he murdered two children in Watertown, New York (though foolishly he would be released to claim a further eleven prostitutes in Rochester). Seemingly, Arthur Shawcross was the consummate natural-born killer.

Of course, bullying, the uneven discipline of his parents, and five hospitalizations for head injuries may have contributed significantly to

Shawcross's psychopathology. Nobody lives in a vacuum. It is simply not possible to exist untouched by the negative influences of the outside world. Inevitably, embryo psychopaths will run into other problems in their upbringings, making it difficult for us to separate the degree of damage done by nature from nurture.

Of the FBI's thirteen "family background characteristics" contributing to the development of a serial killer, eleven are related to nurture. We'll take a closer look at the list toward the end of the chapter. Although it hardly accounts for every serial killer, the Nurture argument adequately explains the vast majority of them. For example, one element commonly found in the background of serial killers is that they were adopted in childhood. Among the more infamous American adoptees were Ted Bundy, Kenneth Bianchi, and David Berkowitz. The trend is also marked in Canadians **Peter Woodcock**, and **Allan MacDonald**. A significant number have also received head injuries throughout their lives. Bobby Joe Long suffered a motorcycle accident that left him unable to control his sexual impulses. At the age of sixteen, John Wayne Gacy was hit in the head with a swing, causing a blood clot in his brain. Similarly, throughout this book we will see examples of Canadian killers who have suffered head injuries. Perhaps the most notable is "The Gorilla Murderer" **Earle Nelson** who was left comatose after being struck by a streetcar. Even style-conscious **Paul Bernardo** reputedly was born with minor head injuries. One nearly ubiquitous element in the childhood of a serial murder is a legacy of physical, sexual, and/or emotional abuse. John Stanley Gacy Sr. was a nasty drunk who constantly battered and berated his accident-prone son. Gacy Jr. later became the most prolific homosexual serial killer in American history. Could this have been rooted in his father's repeated whippings and assertions that his son was "stupid" and "queer"?

In the following cases, we will see examples of killers created by nature, nurture, or some combination of the two.

Kay Feely.

Russell Johnson
The Bedroom Strangler
7 Murders
London/Guelph, Ontario

"All of a sudden I am climbing balconies. I have strength way beyond me.... My mind is racing at a terrible speed. I am going hand over hand up the balconies and if I lose my grip it doesn't matter"

NATURAL CAUSES

London, Ontario. On October 18, 1973, a dark stranger slipped through the window of Mary Hicks's ground-floor apartment on Talbot Street. When his eyes adjusted to the darkness, he found the beautiful young woman asleep in bed, much the same way he had found the others. For what seemed like an eternity, he stood there watching — her chest rising and falling to the rhythm of her dreams. It gave him a tremendous feeling of power knowing that he could survey her without Mary being aware of his presence. Of course, he always liked it when they woke up; the look of horror in their eyes, their pretty mouths opening to scream only to be silenced by his massive hands. Normally he had his way with them and left back out the window. Tonight would be different.

The next morning, Mary's roommates found her tucked snugly under the covers: dead. As there were no signs of a break-in, nobody gave much thought to the pillow covering part of her face. The coroner called it "suffocation caused by a reaction to prescription drugs." The same cause of death would be given on March 4, 1974, when Eleanor Hartwick, twenty-seven, was found dead in her Westlake Street apartment, her book still lying gently by her hand. Miles away in Guelph, Ontario, similar phenomena were occurring. In November 1973, Alice Ralston had been discovered dead in her bed, ostensibly of hardened arteries. August 1974 saw forty-nine-year-old Doris Brown succumb to what was thought to be pulmonary edema, even though the pathologist found bruises and traces of blood in her mouth and rectum. Thus far, the murders had been too subtle to detect, and even if they had been noticed, they had occurred over a long time period in two separate cities. However, a look at the Brown murder reveals an escalation in the killer's violence. Soon his rage would boil over, and residents of southwestern Ontario would be forced to face a frightening truth: a serial murderer was in their midst.

REDRUM

Diane Beitz of Guelph was having one of the best times of her life. It was December 31, 1974, and on the previous day her boyfriend Jim Britton had unexpectedly proposed to her. After she had accepted, the young couple celebrated with a home-cooked lasagna supper at Diane's mother's house. They had spent the night at Diane's apartment on Drew Street, and shared a bacon-and-egg breakfast before Jim left for work. When he returned to pick Diane up for a New Year's party, he entered the apartment with his key to find it in darkness. Moving cautiously into the bedroom, he stopped short. The dark shapes of upturned furniture lay strewn about. A strange pile of covers had been arranged on the bed. Pressing down gently on them, Jim felt something hard underneath. Mustering all of his courage, he flicked on the lights and whisked the covers away. Diane Beitz lay naked on the mattress, a brassiere knotted around her neck. Behind her back, her hands were bound with pantyhose. This time there would be no strange adult "crib death" to explain away — this was murder.

Arriving on the scene, police immediately found one of Diane's slippers outside the front door and concluded she had stepped backwards out of it to avoid the killer. A second slipper was discovered by the telephone. It took them three hours to locate Diane's black cat, still cowering under the bed. The building's superintendent informed the investigators that he had glanced out of his window at 3:30 a.m. on the night of the murder and had seen a brown Buick idling by the curb. An hour later it was still there. Sure enough, police found a black patch of snow where the dirt from the exhaust had settled. Ontario's director of pathology, Dr. John Hillsdon-Smith, theorized that Diane had been carried into the bedroom, strangled, then raped and bound post-mortem. This monster was more than just a killer, he was a necrophiliac. Over the next three weeks, Guelph police interviewed two hundred people in connection with the murder. They learned that a few days before Diane was killed, a man had delivered a bouquet of flowers to her apartment. Jim knew nothing of the delivery.

It wasn't until April 1977 that the dark stranger would strike again. Luella Jeanne George was a farmer's daughter who had arrived in London to work as a cashier in the local hospital. When the twenty-three-year-old was found dead in her top-floor apartment, it was not apparent at first that she had been murdered. Like the initial four victims, still unbeknownst to the police, Luella was tucked in bed with an almost peaceful look on her face. The discovery of some of her jewellery and underwear in a garbage can a few blocks away told a grimmer tale.

Over the next two months, sightings of the man the press were calling "The Bedroom Strangler" proliferated across London, Ontario. Women awoke to find things moved around in their apartment or a shadowy intruder slipping into the night. Three survived being raped and strangled — presumably because their attacker had mistaken them for dead. Then at 11:30 on the night of July 15, a local woman answered an unexpected buzz on her apartment intercom. The man at the other end claimed to be a police officer and asked to be let in. When the woman telephoned the police to confirm, they denied knowing the officer in question. By this time, the stranger had already vanished into the shadows. If the woman had not been so cynical, she would have likely been the Bedroom Strangler's seventh victim. Instead he moved on to his most stunning prey yet: twenty-two-year-old Donna Veldboom.

A SHIFT IN THE PATTERN

It had been less than a year since Donna Veldboom had left her childhood home in New Brunswick for the "big city" of London, Ontario. The beautiful blonde with rosy cheeks and a winning smile settled into an apartment on Orchard Street and found work at a nearby gas station. On July 15, she finished her shift and spent the night in the company of a friend. Around the same time the Strangler was buzzing the apartment, Donna wished her companion good night and returned home. When she failed to show up for her shift the next morning, concerned employees at the gas station notified the police. Nobody would forget what they found. Like the others, Donna Veldboom had been strangled to death in her bed, but, in a bizarre twist, had also been slashed across the chest, leaving a gaping, bloody wound. It was clear to everyone on the scene that the Strangler's grip on reality was slowly deteriorating. Whereas after the Luella George murder he had cleaned her apartment thoroughly, this time he had actually bathed Donna's corpse!

With no promising leads to follow, investigators began to examine the building's tenants to see if any of them possessed a criminal record. One name they stumbled across was Russell Maurice Johnson. A thirty-year-old stock clerk at the Talbotville Ford Plant, Johnson was well liked by his co-workers, though he was considered a slacker. Having separated from his wife, he was now involved with a long-term girlfriend named Barb. Neither his workmates nor the women in his life had any inkling that "good ol' Russ" had once booked himself into London's psychiatric hospital where he was diagnosed as a sexual deviant. An amateur weightlifter, Johnson was handsome with a powerful physique — just the kind of man who would be capable of scaling towering apartment buildings. In fact, he had already been questioned by the police. Not only did he match the Bedroom Strangler's profile, until recently he had also lived in the same building as Luella George. When Inspector Bob Young of the London Police contacted Guelph to inform them of the suspect, he learned that at 10:30 a.m. on the morning Diane Beitz's body was discovered, Johnson had called the local police to report the theft of some luggage from his car, apparently parked around the corner from the crime scene.

Though the evidence was circumstantial, London detectives were convinced this was their man. They put Johnson under twenty-four-hour surveillance: eight detectives paired in four cars around the clock. It wasn't long before it became obvious that their suspect had profound psychological problems. Obsessed with cleanliness, Johnson washed his hands compulsively, always wearing gloves and petroleum jelly at work and the gym to prevent "contamination." He also displayed signs of psychosis, driving aimlessly for blocks before exiting his vehicle, standing on the sidewalk for a period of time, and then driving off again.

INTERROGATION

When police learned that Johnson was planning an August vacation, they made the decision to act immediately. On July 28, 1977, they knocked on the door of his basement apartment several times. Johnson finally opened it, revealing a spotlessly clean abode with gleaming floorboards. After phone calls to his lawyer and girlfriend, he passively accompanied them downtown.

Within minutes of entering the interrogation room, the Bedroom Strangler broke into a weepy confession. He claimed to experience sudden, overpowering feelings of loneliness that would drive him to scale high-rises without concern for his personal safety. If he saw a family sleeping inside he would move on because he claimed to love families and didn't "want to hurt them." His feelings toward single women were apparently a different matter. Diane Beitz had been murdered because she happened to live in the same apartment as one of Johnson's ex-girlfriends. Similarly, Donna Veldboom died because the Bedroom Strangler was a tenant in her building and had managed to bypass her lock using his plastic punch card. At first he had lain down beside her bed to feel better, but when she rose to adjust the fan he found himself strangling her.

Johnson compared strangling women to the thrill he got making tackles in football, only prolonged. Once he had strangled them and raped their corpses, however, he was overcome by remorse. So that they "wouldn't be mad" at him, he would clean their apartments — in the case of Donna Veldboom even going so far as to bathe her body. When he tucked Diane Beitz in and placed a pillow over her head it was to "make it right again," a process criminal profilers call "undoing." Johnson admitted to slashing open Donna Veldboom's chest to climb inside where it was "safe and warm." He also confessed to the hitherto unknown 1973–1974 murders of Mary Hicks, Eleanor Hartwick, Alice Ralston, and Doris Brown. After five years of terror, the Bedroom Strangler was finally off the streets.

Johnson's trial in February of 1978 further revealed the depths of his madness. Before leaving his home, the obsessive Adonis would spend as much as an hour cleaning dishes and rearranging his apartment. Psychiatrist Dr. Douglas Wickware explained that Johnson did this to create barriers for his homicidal urges, defence mechanisms that would inevitably crumble after a few drinks. Indeed, on the night of Donna Veldboom's murder, Johnson had been consuming alcohol at the Union Hall when he was suddenly overcome by his impulses. On another occasion, he picked up a woman at a local bar and took her back to his apartment. The last thing she remembered before waking to a pounding headache was Johnson forcing a pillow over her face. Another psychiatrist, Dr. R.L. Fleming, testified that Johnson's family had a history of mental illness, describing his childhood environment as the most "chaotic" and "disturbed" he had ever seen.

Classmates from Johnson's hometown of Guelph, Ontario, remembered him as a colossal, awkward kid who, despite his size, was always getting beat up by smaller children. The family lived across the street from St. Joseph's Elementary School where Russ was a student. Growing up in the shadow of his older, more intelligent brother, he seems to have taken more after his mother: a "tired" and "haggard-looking" homebody. Though he loved basketball, Johnson lacked aggression. Even when he found employment as a bouncer in his late teens, he had a reputation for being suspiciously absent whenever a customer got violent.

Ultimately, a six-man/six-woman jury found Russell Maurice Johnson not guilty by reason of insanity in the Beitz, George, and Veldboom murders. For the past thirty years he has been confined to Oak Ridge, the maximum-security wing of the Waypoint Centre for Mental Health Care (formerly known as Mental Health Centre Penetanguishene).

Andre Kirchhoff.

AK 2011

Doug Moore
3 Murders
Clarkson, Ontario

"If you phone the police, I know where you live!"

SOWING THE SEEDS OF EVIL

Douglas Donald Moore was born into an impoverished Anglophone family in Verdun, Quebec, the fifth child in as many years. A chronically underemployed lot, the Moores subsisted on welfare and the cash they gleaned from odd jobs. Although Mildred Moore was a devoted and well-meaning woman, Douglas Sr.'s drinking and hair-trigger temper cast a dark shadow over the household. Crippled by diabetes and pain in his hip, back, and legs, the native New Brunswicker had lapsed into a dependency on prescription drugs. He was not the only one in the home with health problems: Douglas Jr. was a frail, sickly boy, wracked by allergies and asthma. He had even inherited a rare blood disorder. At an early age, tubes had been inserted into his ears in an attempt to battle recurring infections. The result was permanent hearing damage. As if life hadn't dealt Douglas Jr. a hard enough hand, at the age of seven his father began to fondle his genitals. This sexual abuse lasted for roughly five years, and extended to his three older sisters. When one of the girls revealed their terrible secret to Mildred, she was devastated. Mildred sued Douglas Sr. for divorce on the grounds of adultery and mental cruelty. Shamed, he retreated to the suburbs to drink himself to death.

Doug Jr. was in grade nine. Unfortunately, the damage had already been done: rather than learning from his father's mistakes, he would follow in his footsteps. First came the drinking, weed, and hash; by the time he reached grade ten, Doug Jr. had shifted from using to dealing. He started out selling marijuana, gradually expanding to amphetamines and barbiturates, then into more powerful drugs like LSD and cocaine. By this time he had been expelled from high school for fighting.

Shortly after divorcing her husband, Mildred began a serious relationship with a younger man — a chemical factory worker named Bill. They married and in 1983 the family moved to the Clarkson district of Mississauga, Ontario, where both Mildred and Bill found jobs. The change of scenery did little to improve sixteen-year-old Doug's behaviour. Within a few months of moving to Clarkson, he established himself as the number one dealer of narcotics in the area, often driving his two-door Ford Maverick up to Montreal to restock and visit his father. Eventually the old man's repeated suicide attempts scared him away.

Though blessed with a near genius IQ, Doug dropped out of high school and struggled to hold down work as a carpenter. By now, his drinking was out of control. In the summer of 1985, Doug fell asleep at a basement party and awoke to find $400 missing from his wallet. Enraged, he grabbed a baseball bat and drove to the home of teenage boy whom he suspected of robbing him. He broke the culprit's ribs, nose, and jaw, and was later fined $200 for assault. It was a chilling glimpse of what was to come.

LIKE FATHER, LIKE SON ...

Though nobody realized it at the time, Doug had inherited his father's sexual predilections. When one of the neighbourhood mothers, Bonnie Carlson, attempted to have sex with the eighteen-year-old Moore, she found him impotent. Trudy Finch believed him to be a wonderful example to her three sons, even bringing him along on a family camping trip. Then one day her eldest child confided in her not to trust Doug because he "did things" to them. It only took a little more prying before the truth came out: Douglas Donald Moore had been sexually abusing Finch's three sons and Bonnie Carlson's twelve-year-old Johnny for the past two years.

After a brief investigation, Moore was charged with four counts of sexual assault, drug possession, and breaking and entering. As the case waited to go to trial, he repeatedly followed the Finch boys, threatening to murder them. When his day in court came, he plead guilty on all counts and was sentenced to three months in jail for breaking and entering, one month for drugs, and just a single day for the sexual assault charges! He served time at the Guelph Correctional Centre and was back out on the streets by age nineteen. Later, he was charged with mischief when Trudy Finch spotted him lurking in the shadows outside her home. She called the Peel Regional Police, who caught him an hour later driving along the lakeshore with his pants and underwear down to his ankles. Incidentally, Doug was acquitted of the mischief charge when his sister provided him with a bogus alibi. Not that it kept him out of jail. In a drunken rage, Moore broke into the office of the construction company where he worked, knocking holes in the wall and breaking windows. This earned him thirteen months in jail along with $1,300 restitution and three years' probation.

Paroled in late 1987, Moore received a telephone call from his estranged father telling him that he was "on the wagon," happily remarried, and living in Vancouver. However, he had also been diagnosed with a particularly quick-acting form of cancer and wished to share what life he had left with his son. Moore was granted permission by his probation officer to move out west as long as he identified himself to the local police upon arrival. Instead, he stole a friend's ID and used it to swindle himself a new driver's licence and credit card. He moved in with his father and set up a ring of underage drug dealers to provide him with extra cash. Much as he had done with Trudy Finch and Bonnie Carlson, he befriended another single mother and molested her twelve-year-son and his friend, Joey Jenson. The boy eventually confessed what had happened to an RCMP officer. While Moore was awaiting this next trial he crashed his motorcycle, fracturing his ribs and kneecap and breaking his nose. Things went from bad to worse for him when he was sentenced to four years in a federal penitentiary for the Jenson molestation. An additional thirty days was tacked on for fleeing the scene of the motorcycle accident.

FUGITIVE

In prison, Moore busied himself earning his grade eleven education and preparing for an eventual high school diploma. He was released on day parole to a Vancouver halfway house in June 1991, where he remained for a month before disappearing. A warrant for his arrest was issued across

Canada. Moore resurfaced around Christmas in Clarkson, intent on paying the Finch brothers back for sending him to prison. He learned that Bobby Finch was employed in the kitchen of O'Toole's Restaurant, and on the night of December 20, decided to stop in for a drink. Luckily, Finch spotted the brawny fugitive and hid in the back. As Moore sat fuelling his vengeance on a barstool, fourteen-year-old Tim Kyle walked into the restaurant. The boy's mother had sent him to the store and along the way he had decided to visit his father at O'Toole's. Moore followed Tim out onto the street and asked him if he wanted drugs or alcohol. The boy did his best to ignore him, but Moore grabbed him and threw him between two Dumpsters, threatening to hurt him if he didn't remove his pants. Sobbing, Tim complied with the man's demands, even allowing himself to be fondled. Little did Moore know that two of Tim's friends were hiding nearby. When he instructed Tim to "turn around," one of the boys came out of hiding and began to run. Moore took off after the child, giving Tim an opportunity to flee. Hearing the commotion, several men, including Tim's father, stepped outside to see what was going on. They chased Moore, knocking him to the ground and beating him until the police arrived to pull them away. Back at the station, they found a map of Mississauga and Oakville, some candy, condoms, and a container of Vaseline in Moore's duffel bag. He managed to fool police into charging and releasing him under the name Dale Sheffield before concerned locals corrected them. This time the charges included sexual assault, impersonation, assault (he had thrown his beer mug at Tim Kyle), and breaking the terms of his probation. On top of the four years for his British Columbia offences, he would now serve another four, ensuring he would remain in prison until at least 1997.

At last Moore acknowledged that he had a problem, enrolling in a prison rehabilitation program for pedophiles. Here he was determined to have made extraordinary progress and was encouraged to stay on after he finished the program to provide a positive example for others. On June 12, 1997, Douglas Moore was released into a Hamilton halfway house. By New Year's Day he was a free man.

Moore found work in a factory, making auto parts out of aluminum and moved into an apartment with his developmentally challenged brother. Once again he met a young single mother, Sandra Martin, becoming a father figure to her nine-year-old son. After Moore returned briefly to jail for carrying a concealed flick knife, he moved into a

Mississauga townhouse with Sandra. He got a new job at a Crystal Springs factory in Mississauga, setting up another ring of drug dealers based out of the Meadowvale Town Centre. Two of these young men were Robbie Grewal, twenty-two, and Joe Manchisi, twenty.

In the early morning hours of October 26, 2003, Doug Moore awoke to the sound of his patio door sliding open, but quickly drifted back to sleep. When an hour later he discovered his credit cards, marijuana supply, jewellery, and $3,800 missing, he flew into a rage. Certain that Grewal and Manchisi were responsible, Moore went out in search of vengeance. What happened next is uncertain, but police believe that on November 12 he intercepted the two at a local Tim Hortons coffee shop and tricked them into coming back to his townhouse. There he murdered them, hiding the bodies for two days in his garage. He then convinced a fourteen-year-old acquaintance to help him dismember the bodies, packing them into large plastic containers. Loading up the car, they set off east for Montreal. Along the way they would have passed Moore's boyhood home in Verdun. It was as if he were revisiting a crime scene, his very act of being there fulfilling the sad prophecy of his life. The waters of the St. Lawrence were black and impenetrable, the Champlain Bridge arching over them like a great steel stick insect on route to the south shore suburbs. Then, at long last Doug Moore found the spot he was looking for.

SLIP OF THE TONGUE

The next morning, members of the Manchisi and Grewal families filed missing persons reports with the Halton and Peel regional police. Joe Manchisi Sr. organized friends, family, and employees at his real-estate office into a kind of private investigation team. They dialled every number they could find in Joe Jr.'s personal notes, asking if the respondents had seen him and assessing them as suspects. One name kept popping up: Douglas Donald Moore. Eventually Manchisi's nephew got through to him by phone, but Moore was brusque and evasive. He denied knowing Joe and proclaimed his astonishment that they would think a man of his age would hang around with a twenty-year-old, before hanging up. At that point, Joe Manchisi was certain this man had something to do with the son's disappearance. If Moore hadn't met Joe, how did he know he was twenty? Noting him as a person of interest, the team resumed the telephone calls. But Moore's name kept coming up again and again. One youth swore he had heard Moore raving about how he was going to kill Manchisi and Grewal. When police questioned Moore, he denied any acquaintance with the missing two, but did admit to being a drug dealer.

Around this same time, a tree-cutter in Verdun, Quebec, happened across a headless, handless male torso in the bushes. The shoulder had been horribly mutilated, possibly to remove a tattoo, and consequently it would take four months to identify the corpse. Though he didn't know it yet, Doug Moore's tapestry of lies was about to unravel.

A NASTY HABIT

A month after the Manchisi-Grewal disappearance, another of Moore's drug clientele vanished into thin air. Grade ten student René Charlebois went missing sometime after leaving school on December 12, 2003. His mother filed a missing person's report at 9:00 p.m. that night. It was suspected that René knew too much about the Manchisi-Grewal disappearance and was killed to prevent him from snitching. Though Moore was a prime suspect in all three disappearances, police lacked the evidence to obtain a search warrant for his home.

Around this time, three foster children at the home of Doug's friend Linda Norton began hinting that somebody in the Caledon house was sexually abusing them. When the OPP questioned the boys they learned that Doug Moore had been fondling and sodomizing them since 2000. As some of the sexual assaults had happened in Peel Region, the Caledon OPP phoned to inform them and discovered that Peel Police were also investigating Moore in the recent disappearances.

On Friday, March 12, as social service workers showed up to remove the foster children from the Norton home, police knocked on the door of Sandra Martin's apartment looking for Moore. Little did they know that Doug and Sandra had ended their relationship in February, and that he was renting an apartment in the same building. It is believed that Martin called Moore at this point, allowing him to escape from his apartment in the same building. They caught up with him three days later at a Burlington motel, kicked his door down, and blasted him twice with a stun gun. Charged with eleven counts of sexual assault, he was imprisoned at Maplehurst Detention Centre in Milton until his trial. Four days later, a body turned up at an Orangeville area landfill. It took two weeks before DNA comparisons to hairs found on the missing boy's brushes and razors identified him as René Charlebois.

On April 1, Moore's mother came to see him in jail, where he proclaimed his innocence and promised to phone her. The next morning his lifeless body was found hanging from braided strips of bedsheet in his cell. By choosing suicide, Moore ensured he would never stand trial for the murders.

A week later, news regarding the headless corpse came down from Montreal; it had been identified as that of Robbie Grewal. He had tattooed his father's nickname "DC" on his shoulder. Joe Manchisi's remains were discovered in a park soon after. Both dumping grounds had been selected symbolically. One was located directly across the river from Moore's former Verdun home, the other near where his father had lived after the divorce. After burying their loved ones, the Manchisi and Grewal families drove up to Montreal to lay an angel where their bodies were found.

Toronto Police Service, courtesy of Peter Vronsky.

Peter Woodcock

4 Murders
Toronto/Brockville,
Ontario

"I wanted to see if Dennis had a death rattle. They really do exist. I sat next to his body for about an hour. When he died I heard something like a deep snore come from the middle of his body."

THE SCREAMING ORPHAN

The boy wouldn't stop crying — ever — not even to eat or sleep. Nobody could quite figure it out. There had been no known complications with the pregnancy or delivery. Social Services even allowed his mother, Wanita Woodcock, a nineteen-year-old unmarried prostitute, to keep him for a month to breastfeed him. Still he wailed. It was as if the very act of existing mortified him. Three years passed as screaming Peter was shuffled from one foster home to the next. It seemed nobody wanted to adopt this peculiar little boy. Families along the way were discouraged from bonding with him as inevitably he would be taken from them. This served only to separate a problematic child from any love and affection that might save him.

At twelve months Peter finally stopped crying, though he still became terrified whenever anybody drew near. By the age of two he began making "strange, whining noises" which were identified as an attempt at speech. Finally an upper-middle class foster family, the Maynards, agreed to adopt him. His new parents, Frank, an accountant, and Susan, lived near Yonge and Lawrence in an upscale area of North Toronto. They had a son ten years older than Peter, but the two boys were never close.

Susan Maynard was a short, rotund woman from a wealthy American background and she carried the class consciousness to prove it. Despite her reputation as a harsh disciplinarian and snob, her willingness to raise a troubled child betrayed a deeply compassionate nature. As the extent of Peter's psychological problems became evident, Susan gave more and more time to the baby, until he consumed her whole life. In the company of friends, she would repeatedly ask if they thought Peter was getting better. Often they would lie to avoid reducing their hostess to tears. Though it was true that Peter showed some improvement, he was still screaming the house down when anyone came near him. He had learned to walk, abnormally, swinging the same arm and leg together in a strange goose-stepping motion. People remarked that he looked like he had rickets. He also clung to his mother as if afraid for his life, and Susan responded by becoming increasingly protective of her little ward.

Finally at the age of seven, Peter stopped screaming. He began treatment for his behavioural problems at the world-renowned SickKids Hospital in Toronto. This therapy was very demanding of Susan as it required several visits a week over a period of five years. With her schedule increasingly dictated by Peter's needs, she began to neglect her husband and eldest son. Peter repaid her by vandalizing their home. The minute he was left alone he would carve up the dining room table, tear down the blinds, or shred his clothing. On one occasion he even smashed the cherished family radio. In another more insidious occurrence, Susan returned home to find her pet canary laid out dead on the piano surrounded by candles. Peter blamed the family dog.

TRAINSPOTTING

Toronto in the 1940s was something to see: taxis belching exhaust fumes, the mouth-watering smells of delicatessens wafting through the streets. The Maynards took young Peter to the Santa Claus Parade on University Avenue. Afterwards, they walked down Yonge Street where a fleet of streetcars had been idling. Peter's jaw dropped. He was awed by their tremendous physical power and efficiency, like hungry steel spiders stalking the city along strands of electrical webbing. Soon, tram drivers all over Toronto became acquainted with the strange, bespectacled boy who would sneak on to their vehicles and ride them to the end of the line. Once Peter ended up lost in Port Credit and had to call home for help. On another occasion when he failed to return, the Maynards found him cowering under some bushes. He told them that he was where God could protect him from other children.

Peter Woodcock had good cause to be afraid of his peers. Ever since his earliest school days he had been mocked and excluded for his awkwardness. Nor did he do much to help his cause. When he was allowed into a fund-raising club in his neighbourhood he slyly tried to change it to a dog and cat club and, as expected, was shot down. He calmly explained that he preferred animals to boys anyway before retreating back into his world of solitude and fantasy. Other children were unpredictable, but Peter could always depend on the streetcars.

Coincidentally, it was in the shadow of a New York City train that Susan Maynard was attacked. While she was visiting Grand Central Station, a purse snatcher pushed her down the stairs, leaving her concussed. From that moment on, Peter noted a transformation in his mother's disposition. Now whenever he misbehaved she beat him with a beaded rod.

The family moved to a large house on Lytton Boulevard when Peter was ten. Though his parents were charmed by the sun room and antique gaslights, he did not adjust well to the move. A year later, he was assessed by a Children's Aid worker and found to be intelligent, but lacking in self-control. His relationship with Susan was described as being excessively affectionate. While strolling through the Canadian National Exhibition with one social worker, Peter casually remarked that he would like to see a bomb fall on the fairground and kill all of the children.

As a result, he was sent to Sunnyside Children's Centre in Kingston. It was here that the adolescent Peter began to discover his sexuality, allegedly playing erotic games with other children. The puritanical nature of the Maynard home had left much to the imagination in the field of human anatomy and he was ever inquisitive. When he reached fourteen, the age at which most patients were discharged from Sunnyside, social workers decided that he was still not ready to be released into the regular school system. Rather than entrust him into the care of his overbearing mother, they sent him back to Waycroft in September 1954. A year later he was transferred to Lawrence Park Collegiate to begin grade nine, where he was recognized by several former classmates. Within a few weeks the other teenagers had pushed him down an embankment, ripped his Sea Cadet badges from his coat, and broken his bicycle.

He was promptly transferred to Bloordale College School where he remained until grade eleven. The previous summer, he had been given a job as a valet at Casa Loma. Impressed by his work ethic, his boss let him keep the position on weekends during the school year. To the outside world, it seemed that Peter Woodcock had progressed in leaps and bounds. Of course, nobody knew about the fantasies — those delightful images of sex and violence that he increasingly inflicted upon imaginary children in his subconscious. It didn't take many mornings of daydreaming in math class before, like a Lovecraftian god, these horrific visions crossed over into reality.

It started innocently enough: Peter would offer the children of Toronto rides on his bicycle if they took off their clothes for him. This may have been enough to sate his curiosity at first, but did little to quell his enormous rage. In February of 1956, he met a ten-year-old girl whose parents were divorcing because her father was sexually abusing her. Peter would later claim she was suicidal. They agreed that in two weeks he would return and kill her. Excited, he made plans to dissect her with his penknife. They kept their appointment, though Peter was late, and he led her down one of Toronto's many ravines. The girl lay down on the wet spring earth and Peter pressed the knife to her throat. Everything was in place, yet for some reason he couldn't bring himself to kill her. The light was already beginning to fade through the burgeoning leaves. Suddenly, the thought of thrashing through the foliage after dark troubled him. Realizing that their planning for the murder had been poor, he put the knife away and told the girl she would live. They spent the next few hours trying to find their way out of the valley. When they finally got back to the girl's house, the police were waiting for them. Peter spoke briefly with the officers before they sent him on his way. Perhaps it was the would-be victim's compliance that threw him off. Whatever the reason, his return to school the following fall was the spark that lit the powder keg.

MALLETTE, MORRIS, VOYCE

On September 16, 1956, the Mallette children of Seeley's Bay, Ontario, took a trip into the big city to see their grandparents. The home was on Empress Street in the west end of Toronto, not far from the Canadian National Exhibition ground. By fall, the area was practically deserted; the candy-coated joys of the Ex banished by the sweeping autumn wind. After visiting their grandmother, the older Mallette boys caught a streetcar for some excitement downtown. They left their youngest brother, Wayne, a blond-haired seven-year-old, happily at play in the front yard. The child was transfixed by the trains, and soon found himself wandering to the railway line that snaked through the Exhibition grounds. Obscured from the houses by trees and a chain-link fence, he came across a lanky teenager with slicked-back hair and horn-rimmed glasses. The boy introduced himself as Peter. For awhile, the two found common interest talking about trains, but when Peter tried to convince Wayne to take off his clothes, he became scared. Peter flew into a rage, battering the child to the ground with a furious array of punches and kicks. When Wayne fought back, Peter sunk his teeth ravenously into the child's leg, causing him to lose his grip. Climbing on top of him, he thrust Wayne's face into the dirt and began to suffocate him. When he heard the death rattle gurgle from the child's mouth, he felt an immense sexual thrill. Quickly, he undressed the body and stood looking over it, not knowing what to do. When he had satisfied his curiosity, he redressed the corpse and hurried off.

It took the police search party until 2:30 a.m. to locate Wayne's body, tears still glistening on his cheeks. Jack Mallette, his father, grimly confirmed the boy's identity. Strangely, the killer seemed to have defecated at the child's feet, then compulsively scattered some coins nearby. An autopsy revealed that garbage had been stuffed into Wayne's mouth, and by the dirt stains in his underwear it was clear he had been naked at some point. Witnesses reported seeing a skinny kid of about fifteen riding at top speed on a red-and-cream bicycle out through the Princes' Gates. A watchman at the CNE reported speaking to the teen earlier. Mistaking the guard for a policeman, he had asked what he would do if they found a body in the bushes. When the guard asked him if he had seen a body the boy answered, "No, but I saw a boy run out of the bushes and he looked just like me."

A description of the Toronto bicycle killer was sent out to every school in the area. Then nine days later, the police "solved" the case. Fourteen-year-old Ronald Mowatt had recently run away from home, and was therefore an ideal suspect in the minds of a prejudiced Toronto police department. Meanwhile, the real killer continued to scour the streets for children to molest and murder.

Three weeks later, Peter Woodcock was ready to kill again. This time he pre-selected a murder site: the inviting-sounding Cherry Beach. In reality, it was a ramshackle industrial port in Toronto's east end, abandoned by all but the seagulls. Woodcock cycled to the St. Lawrence Market where he picked out nine-year-old Gary Morris move up. The Sackville Street resident was spellbound by Woodcock's bike and must have felt on top of the world when the boy asked if he would like to go for a ride. Gary was an adventurous sort who had run away from home on several occasions and dreamed of going to America to join the circus. With Gary balanced precariously on the crossbar, the two rode for a mile together down to Cherry Beach. They came to a deserted waterfront at the foot of Commissioners Street. Woodcock seized Gary abruptly around the neck and strangled him into unconsciousness. As he had done three weeks earlier, he removed the child's clothes and stood hovering over him like a lecherous buzzard. Then he unleashed his fury, viciously kicking and punching the helpless little boy until his liver ruptured. He bit savagely into the child's neck, leaving pronounced tooth marks, before disappearing back into the city.

For some time, Gary's parents assumed he had simply run off to join the circus again. Just over a week later he was discovered hidden in some tall grass, a cache of paper clips sprinkled nearby. As with Wayne Mallette, he had been undressed and redressed after death. Eyewitnesses claimed they had seen Gary riding on the sidebar of a red-and-cream bicycle with an older bespectacled boy. Unfortunately, at this time police departments jealously guarded their information from one another, so no detective could connect the biting, scattering, undressing, or bicycle to the Mallette murder.

At 3:30 p.m. on January 19, 1957, four-year-olds Johnny Auld and Carole Voyce were playing outside Auld's Danforth Avenue apartment when a teenage boy with glasses pulled up alongside them on a bicycle. He asked the children their age and if they liked his bike. When they said that they did, he asked them if they wanted to go for a ride. Unfortunately, he could only take one of them. He chose Carole. Beaming from ear to ear, the brown-haired cherub took his hand and together they walked the bicycle in the direction of the ravines. Johnny stood by the roadside, sulking as he watched them shrink into the distance, the dark blue of the boy's jacket beating against the winter wind.

When they were a few blocks from the apartment, Peter Woodcock helped the little girl in the grey snowsuit onto his handlebars, and they took off through the icy streets. Eventually, they came to a ravine. Peter convinced Carole to lead the way down the hillside. Partway down, he suddenly seized her around the neck, choking her until she passed out. With the toddler now at his mercy, he gouged at her eyes with his fingers to see what happened. This time when he undressed her, he wanted to do more than just look. Snatching up a branch from the forest floor, he jammed it into the child's vagina — a blow that would kill her. He didn't bother to redress her before he left. After a few futile attempts to scramble up the oozing clay slope, Peter came back and aimed a frustrated kick at Carole's head. Getting his bearings, he walked his bicycle down to the closest road and fled. This time multiple people would remember seeing him, including a student in his own class. He even cryptically remarked to one passerby that if there was a murder the police would think he did it.

A few minutes after Peter Woodcock had whisked the four-year-old away, Carole Voyce's mother stepped outside, looking for her. When

Jimmy explained that she had gone for a bike ride with a high-school boy, she immediately telephoned the police. Two officers showed up at the house and an alert with the missing girl's description was broadcast across Toronto. The community came out in droves to search for her, with off-duty police officers pouring in from nearby divisions. At 11:09 p.m., the search was over. Constable Ernie Booth had found Carole's frozen, half-naked body not far from the Bloor Viaduct. Her father Ray Voyce tearfully confirmed the identification.

JUSTICE

Two days after the murder of Carole Voyce, Peter Woodcock was finally apprehended. The policemen who had spoken with him in March 1956 recognized him from a composite drawing and decided to look into his file. Once they had him at the police station, he confessed in full to all three murders, along with a string of sexual assaults upon children. It wasn't until four months after Woodcock's arrest that Ronald Mowatt was finally set free, lucky in those days to get an apology, let alone compensation.

Later in the year, in Court Room C of Old City Hall, Woodcock plead not guilty by reason of insanity to the murder of Carole Voyce. The jury agreed and he was sentenced to life at Oak Ridge maximum security in Penetanguishene. From there he kept up a correspondence with his foster mother until the late sixties, when it gradually tapered off. His foster father Frank Maynard never spoke to him again. Day by day, the world slowly forgot about the strange little screaming baby. Woodcock legally changed his name to David Michael Krueger in 1982.

Then one day, after thirty-five years of electroshock therapy, LSD, and homosexual favours at Penetanguishene, Peter Woodcock was back in the headlines again. On July 13, 1991, while out on his first escorted day pass at the Brockville facility, Woodcock and former Penetanguishene inmate **Bruce Hamill** attacked and murdered patient Dennis Kerr, raping his corpse before Woodcock turned them in.

Having grown to be a persuasive and manipulative psychopath, he had initiated Hamill, while still a patient, into "The Brotherhood," a strange Woodcock-based cult peculiar to Penetanguishene. Woodcock promised the severely mentally ill Hamill the resurrection of his dead

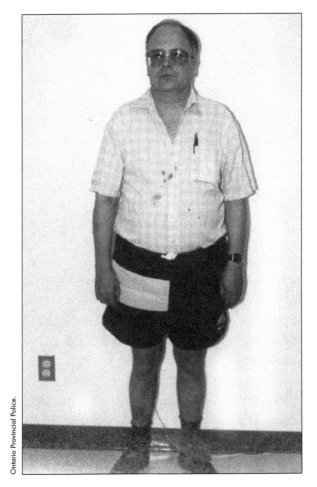

Ontario Provincial Police.

Woodcock, now calling himself David Michael Krueger, spattered in blood after the murder of Dennis Kerr.

father, a cure to all of his psychiatric malfunctions, and a place on a starship arriving in 2011, if he helped him in the bloodthirsty deed. The Toronto Bicycle Killer would not live to claim his place on the flying saucer — on March 5, 2010, he died at Oak Ridge Hospital. It was his seventy-first birthday.

To learn more about the murder of Dennis Kerr, please refer to Bruce Hamill's profile in Chapter 6.

Kay Feely.

Clifford Olson
The Beast of B.C.
11+ Murders
Vancouver Suburbs

"If I gave a shit about the parents, I wouldn't have killed the kids!"

THE FIRST TO FALL

It was another rainy Christmas in the Lower Mainland — the unlit bulbs festooning the subdivision houses doing little to brighten the spirits. For one man, the holidays were an opportunity to get some fresh air and exercise. While walking his dog behind a dump north of River Road, he noticed the animal was leading him toward a shallow pit. As they drew nearer, the cool December air became putrid and noxious — almost unbreathable. Sickened, but overcome by curiosity, the man glanced into the hole. Minutes later, the sleepy avenues of Burnaby burst into light and police sirens punctured the holy silence.

The remains were those of twelve-year-old Surrey native Christine Weller, a tomboy and habitual runaway. Besides having her throat slashed twice, she had also suffered a total of ten stab wounds. The presence of a belt looped around her neck seemed to indicate that before death she had been tortured, and there was some evidence of sexual assault. A month earlier, Christine had vanished while bicycling home from the mall. Because of her history of truancy, her family had not reported her missing until six days later on November 25, 1980; nor did the police take the news of her disappearance seriously.

Months passed and spring gradually returned to the west coast, chasing off the cold. Somehow, the winter winds seemed to sweep Colleen Daigneault away with them. On April 15, 1981, the energetic thirteen-year-old Surrey girl went missing. Six days later, as Colleen's grandmother was reporting her disappearance, sixteen-year-old Daryn

Todd Johnsrude accepted a ride from an affable stranger who offered him a high-paying job and shared a beer with him. Two weeks later, Johnsrude's naked body was hauled out of a dike in Deroche. He had been sexually assaulted and bludgeoned to death with a hammer.

With the RCMP yet to link the three cases, children and youths continued to vanish from the Vancouver area. The next to disappear was Sandra Wolfsteiner, sixteen, last seen closing her savings account at a Royal Bank in Langley. Like Christine Weller, she was filed away under the "runaway" category and immediately forgotten. But when Ada Court, also sixteen, was reported missing a month later, there was no denying that something sinister was going on. A popular Burnaby student with stand-out grades and a good reputation, Ada was seen by others as both stable and reliable. On June 20, she finished babysitting her two nieces and left to meet her boyfriend. He waited and waited, but Ada never arrived.

July 2 saw the disappearance of nine-year-old Surrey native Simon Partington. As in some of the other cases, he had left on his bike to meet a friend and failed to reach his destination. At long last, some members of the RCMP began to grudgingly wake up to the awful truth: Vancouver had its first serial killer.

A SUSPECT EMERGES

Friday the third was one of the hottest days in July and Sandra Docker and Rose Smythe had wisely opted to spend it in the air-conditioned Lougheed Mall. The two teens were hanging around outside the Lectro Fun arcade when they were approached by a swarthy man with a friendly grin. He told them he was in construction and looking for some hard workers to clean a nearby apartment complex. When he mentioned his $10/hour wages, they agreed to drive with him to check out the work site. They hopped into his silver Ford Pinto and he drove them a few blocks to the corner of Cameron and Erickson where he indicated a construction site. Excited, the girls agreed to meet him at 7:30 Monday morning to begin work. Their new boss insisted they have a beer on it.

True to his word, three days later he picked them up outside the arcade. They stopped at Nuffy's Doughnuts for coffee before heading to the construction site. However, when they arrived, their boss claimed the apartment wasn't ready yet so he drove them to a second property in Coquitlam. Unfortunately, it was the same story. Returning the girls to Lectro Fun without having done a minute of the work he had promised, he explained that there was only enough for Sandra today and that Rose should try her luck again tomorrow. Disappointed, Rose left for home while Sandra and the man continued in his Pinto back to Coquitlam. They stopped at another apartment and the man disappeared inside. He re-emerged carrying a paper bag full of beer, and passed a bottle to Sandra, who was probably starting to believe he was the best boss in the world. The next stop was a downtown photo shop, and then to Surrey, where he bought a bottle of whiskey at the liquor store and changed the Pinto for a green Ford Granada at a local car lot. By this time, Sandra was starting to feel the effects of the whiskey and beer, and also a little uneasy. Over the past hour, her boss's temperament had become darker, and, despite her protestations, he continued to feed her alcohol. When they finally pulled into a secluded area near the latest "job site," the last vestiges of her employer's mask slipped. Dark eyes blazing, he forced Sandra into the backseat and attempted to rape her. The sobbing teenager resisted so fervently that eventually he gave up. After angrily informing her that she was fired, he dropped her back off outside the arcade. The minute she was out of the car, she raced toward the road and flagged down a passing RCMP cruiser. The officer put out an alert for a green Ford Granada, license JBH 616, heading east on Cameron. Seconds later, a Constable Ewart radioed in to confirm that he had stopped the vehicle in question and needed back-up.

The driver, who identified himself as Clifford Olson, was arrested for sexual assault and DUI and taken to the RCMP lock-up. Colonel Les Forsythe of the Burnaby RCMP immediately suspected there was more to Olson than was being revealed. Both Daryn Johnsrude and Ada Court had been last seen in the vicinity of the Lectro arcade. Forsythe decided to question Olson. He was a strange, craggy-faced man with dark tangles of brown hair and eyes like cigarette burns. Forsythe would later remark that he seemed to be oozing with evil. The conversation began with Olson pointedly reminding Forsythe that he had helped the RCMP by testifying against child killer Gary Marcoux. This only made the policeman more suspicious; Olson was talking far too much for an innocent man. When Forsythe realized that Olson's apartment was directly across the street from where Ada Court was babysitting, he knew he had found her killer. Unfortunately, Sandra Docker's testimony was as good as useless, her inebriated state at the time doing little to help her credibility. They decided not to charge Olson with sexual assault. Instead, they would watch him closely.

THE PLOT THICKENS

Later that week, the case of the missing mainland children began to take some bizarre and unexpected turns. Stephen Partington received a phone call from a man demanding a ransom for his son's safe return. When he complied and dropped off the money at a BC Hydro box, two boys showed up to claim the ransom. Their little moment of victory was soon cut short by a police ambush. Eventually they were determined to be uncompassionate opportunists and therefore ruled out as suspects in the disappearance.

A second, more disturbing, phone call was placed to the office of a New Westminster apartment manager. The woman answered to hear what sounded like the crying, whimpering, and moaning of fourteen-year-old Judy Kozma, a tenant in her building. When she checked in with Kozma's parents she learned that the girl had not been seen since July 9 — four days prior. They were under the impression that she had taken the bus to Richmond with a friend.

On July 15, members of the Vancouver and New Westminster police as well as the RCMP met in Burnaby to discuss the Lower Mainland disappearances. It was an opportunity for Les Forsythe to present a five-page profile on his suspect Clifford Olson, including his past crimes and MO of offering young people non-existent jobs. At the end of the meeting it was mutually agreed to consider Olson a strong suspect.

BAD TO THE BONE

It was New Year's Day 1940 when Clifford Robert Olson Jr. first made the newspapers. Born at St. Paul's Hospital in Vancouver just after 10:00 p.m., he was among the last of the treasured New Year's babies. Although the major prizes had all been taken, his parents received a baby book and gift from Cunningham Drug Store. For Clifford and Leona Olson, the real treasure was staring into their newborn's big brown eyes. After his birth, the family left Vancouver for Edmonton, eventually returning to British Columbia and settling into a one-storey government-built home in Richmond when Clifford Jr. was five. Two younger brothers and a sister soon followed. Clifford Sr. eked out a hard, but honest living on one of Canada's last horse-drawn milk carts while his wife worked her fingers to the bone at the local fish cannery.

It was obvious from the get-go that Clifford Jr. wanted no part in such drudgery. Even at a young age he was devising scams to make a quick buck. When he wasn't travelling door to door trying to con his neighbours into buying expired lottery tickets, he was stealing the money they left for the milkman. It was no secret around Gilmore Crescent that "the Olson boy" got his kicks torturing animals, in fact, there was a rumour he had smothered two pet rabbits to death. At Bridgeport Elementary School, he was a rebel and bully, frequently disrupting the class or beating up other children. British author Carol Anne Davis has suggested that this may have stemmed from an underlying inferiority complex owing to Olson's slightly below-average intelligence and near-dyslexic English skills. He began to skip school at the age of ten, usually to shoplift or burgle houses. The unruly behaviour, which Clifford Sr. and Leona Olson had first written off as a phase, now began to take on fouler proportions. By fifteen, he had already failed his grade several times, dropping out completely a year later. For a short period, he was employed at a local racetrack before he forged and cashed his boss's cheque and was subsequently fired. In July 1957, he was finally arrested. Convicted of breaking and entering, he was sentenced to nine months in a Burnaby jail. Ever the bad boy, he briefly escaped, but was reapprehended and sentenced to an additional three months. Further charges followed and Olson faced an additional two years behind bars. Instead, he was paroled in April 1959 after serving twenty-one months. It took him only three before he was rearrested for breaking and entering in Surrey, and his parole was revoked. More convictions came in the summer of 1961 for theft, breaking and entering, possessing a firearm, false pretenses, and escaping from Saskatchewan's Prince Albert Penitentiary. This string of petty crimes, parole violation, and prison-breaking continued until 1974 when Olson was sentenced to four years for forgery, theft, and false pretenses.

NATURE, NURTURE, OR NEITHER?

Whether it was some dark demon that possessed him or the realization that he would be spending the next four years in prison, at this point Clifford Olson made the turn from bad to unforgivable: he raped a seventeen-year-old male inmate. Olson had also garnered a reputation as a "fink," or prison informant, and in 1976 was stabbed seven times in Saskatchewan Penitentiary. Placed in protective custody, he managed to convince fellow prisoner Gary Marcoux to talk about his murder of a nine-year-old girl in Mission, British Columbia. The next time Marcoux saw him, Olson was appearing at his trial testifying on behalf of the prosecution.

Perhaps inspired by the man he betrayed, on August 3, 1978, Clifford Olson was charged with indecently assaulting a seven-year-old girl in Sydney, Nova Scotia. However, he conned his way out of police custody and disappeared. When the authorities finally located him, he was serving time in a west coast penitentiary, and they decided it was too expensive to prosecute him for the Nova Scotia charges. Olson slipped the law again, counting his blessings and resolving to leave no witnesses next time.

MORE MISSING

Like Daryn Johnsrude, fifteen-year-old Raymond King was desperate for work. It was already halfway through the summer and his window of opportunity was closing. He mounted his bicycle on July 23, 1981, and set out to the New Westminster branch of Canada Manpower where he was sure to find a job. His bike was later discovered abandoned outside the building. King's name was added to the missing list along with German backpacker Sigrun Arnd, who had disappeared in Coquitlam on July 24. The following day, the Kozma family's worst fears were confirmed when Judy's decomposing body was discovered in the proximity of Weaver Lake, stabbed multiple times. Whoever was claiming the children of the Lower Mainland was accelerating his bloodlust. July 27, 1981, saw the disappearance of fifteen-year-old Terri Lyn Carson, last spotted leaving the house at eight that morning. Three days later, French-Canadian waitress Louise Chartrand, seventeen, failed to show up for her 8:00 p.m. shift at Bino's Restaurant. The following morning, her sister reported her disappearance to the RCMP.

On July 31, a special task force headed by RCMP Superintendent Bruce Northrop met to discuss the case of the Lower Mainland children. They drew up two lists: the first was comprised of all potential missing children, and the second detailed the three strongest suspects. Clifford Olson's name was at the top. Finally, the task force received permission to place him under "Special O" surveillance.

Approximately 125 kilometres to the north, in Whistler, police recovered Louise Chartrand's brassiere from the roadside. Her dress pants and shirt would follow three days later. Then on August 5, a police dog located the missing body of Raymond King, 1.5 kilometres from the Kozma dump site. Instead of finding a job, the fifteen-year-old had been beaten until he died from multiple skull fractures. A nine-centimetre nail hammered into his head was not the cause of death — merely a cruel appetizer.

Coincidentally, Clifford Olson returned to the province on the following day and was immediately placed under surveillance. Over the next five days, the RCMP watched him change cars in Coquitlam and drive around constantly, scouting for prey. At one point he even briefly tailed an undercover police officer. They continued to watch patiently on August 11 as Olson burglarized three Vancouver area homes, and another two in Victoria on August 12. Later, he stopped to pick up two female hitchhikers in Nanaimo. The trio pulled over in Tofino to share a drink as investigators watched nervously from the trees. Suddenly, Olson began yelling at one of the girls to get out of his car. Sensing that rape and murder were imminent, the task force moved in and arrested him for impaired driving. Fortunately, this time a search of the vehicle yielded a crucial piece of evidence: Olson had written Judy Kozma's name in his address book. The following morning he was transported to Burnaby where he was charged with two counts of burglary.

It was now vital that the investigating officers obtain a confession, but after four days of interrogation, Olson showed no signs of cracking. On August 8, he appeared in a Burnaby courtroom where he learned he would face three more sexual assault charges. Then the RCMP's ace card showed up. Police located one Randy Ludlow, eighteen, who confirmed he had been with Olson on July 9, the day Judy Kozma vanished. The murderer had picked Judy up shortly before dropping Ludlow at his home. Ludlow also revealed he had been drugged and raped by Olson later that same month.

Just moments after learning this information, Olson calmly pointed to a poster of the missing Lower Mainland children and began indicating the eleven he had murdered. He offered Superintendent Northrop information in exchange for a guarantee he would serve out his sentence in a psychiatric hospital. Northrop rejected the offer outright. On August 20, Olson proposed another self-serving deal: he would reveal all eleven bodies to the police (or the missing possessions of those that had already been recovered) for $100,000. At ten grand a head, he slyly presented the first one as a "freebie." With few options, this time Northrop agreed.

The deal was signed by Olson on August 26, with the $100,000 going in trust for his wife Joan. At 3:00 p.m. the same day, Olson led a team of police to the remains of Louise Chartrand in Whistler. Like Johnsrude and King, his last victim had been bludgeoned to death with a hammer. The strangled bodies of Simon Partington, Ada Court, and Terri Lyn Carson were recovered the next day, along with some of Judy Kozma's personal items. The remains of an unidentified female were weighted to a rock not far from Partington's corpse. On August 28, the hammered corpse of German tourist Sigrun Arnd was located 450 metres from the Partington site. It took some time to locate the body of Colleen Daigneault, but on August 31, she was found. Olson confessed to trying to kill her by injecting air bubbles into her bloodstream, but when this failed, defaulted to his trusty hammer.

After thirty years of imprisonment, on September 30, 2011, Clifford Olson died of cancer at the Health Care Centre of the Archambault Institution near Sainte-Anne-des-Plaines, Quebec. He was seventy-one years old. Throughout his incarceration, he had continually taunted the families of his victims, sending them graphic letters that detailed their childrens' deaths.

NEITHER

In a period of twenty-four years from 1959 to 1983, Clifford Olson enjoyed approximately four years of freedom. Seven escape attempts had all resulted in recapture. As a career criminal, he was an abysmal failure. It wasn't until he drove a knife through Christine Weller's ribs that he found his true calling as one of Canada's most despised murderers. Yet there are no signs that the original "Beast of B.C." endured any trauma during his childhood. Whereas most killers have a legacy of head injuries, sexual, emotional and/or physical abuse, and mistreatment, Olson seems to have actually enjoyed a rather happy upbringing. In the case of Russell Johnson, it was possible to trace a genetic predisposition to mental illness through his mother. However, the rest of Olson's family were responsible, law-abiding adults, casting doubt on any genetic explanations for his miscreancy.[2] Still, those who knew Olson growing up are adamant: whatever evil he possessed had been with him since birth. He was a true "embryo psychopath." Perhaps this is a question of a nature-based deviancy that we cannot yet detect. The only other possible explanation is that, at a very young age, he simply made an unprovoked, rational decision to become evil. This poses another fascinating question: if so, would Olson's be a case of nature, nurture, or neither?

––––––

Below is a list of thirteen developmental problems from the FBI's "High Risk Register," which contribute to becoming a serial killer.[3]

1. Alcohol abuse
2. Drug abuse
3. Psychiatric history
4. Criminal history
5. Sexual problems
6. Physical abuse
7. Psychological abuse
8/9. Dominant father figure aligned with a negative relationship with male caretakers
10. Negative relationships with both birth and/or adopted mother
11. Treated unfairly
12. Head trauma
13. Demon seed

We've observed examples of these thirteen precursors in this chapter's case studies of Woodcock, Johnson, Olson, and Moore. A teen when arrested, Peter Woodcock did not use alcohol or drugs. Clifford Olson, on the other hand, drank more or less twenty-four hours a day, and drug and alcohol problems were so central to Doug Moore's being that they dictated his life. To a lesser extent, alcohol acted as a "facilitator" for Russ Johnson's crimes. Whereas Moore and Olson were plain old psychopaths, Woodcock and Johnson were also plagued by psychiatric problems. All the candidates, with the exception of Woodcock, had criminal histories, though Johnson's pales in comparison to Olson's and Moore's. To our knowledge, Olson and Johnson never experienced sexual problems, and none of the killers in this chapter were psychologically abused. Beaten sporadically with a beaded rod, Woodcock endured mild physical abuse when compared to Doug Moore Sr.'s repeated sexual attacks on his son. The smothering presence of Woodcock's mother almost certainly contributed to his confusion, as did that of Johnson's; while Moore's bad relations were confined to his father. Excluded by his peers and deprived of any affection for the first three years of his life, nobody would claim Peter Woodcock had been treated fairly. Meanwhile, we find evidence of head trauma in Moore's history. Finally, we can observe traces of the demon seed in Peter Woodcock, who exhibited antisocial behaviour from birth and was born to a prostitute mother.[4] Ultimately, Doug Moore had the highest probability of becoming a serial killer at 62 percent, Johnson following with 54 percent, and Woodcock third with 46 percent. Clifford Olson, of all people, had a mere 15 percent chance!

CHAPTER 3

MODUS OPERANDI AND SIGNATURE

Having looked at the changing tide of murder over Canadian history, along with the social and biological forces that lead to a serial killer's development, we will now put their behaviour under a microscope. *What* specifically do they do to their victims, *how* do they do it, and *why*? In order to answer this last question, it is crucial to discern the difference between the killer's **Modus Operandi** and **Signature**. By analyzing his crime scene in these terms, investigators are able to link a killer's victims to one another through his thought patterns.

Modus operandi — a Latin term for "Mode of Operation" — is by no means specific to serial murderers. In fact, every criminal in history has employed one. Put simply, it is the manner in which the crime is committed. The modus operandi of **Peter Woodcock** seen in Chapter 2, for example, was to: 1) look for children on their own, 2) lure them to a secluded spot, 3) murder them, 4) sexually assault their bodies, and 5) escape by bicycle, leaving the body behind. It is of vital importance to understand that the approach to a crime is subject to the changing whims of its perpetrator. When Woodcock was let out on a day pass over thirty years later, he did not have the means to use the same MO, so he simply adapted it. Even so, his fourth victim was enticed into the woods, ambushed, and violated after death. Witchita's infamous "BTK Killer" Dennis Rader left the strangled bodies of eight of his victims in their homes, but decided to dump two others in the surrounding countryside, figuring accurately that it would throw investigators a curveball. "Co-ed Killer" Edmund Kemper III stabbed some of his victims, strangled others, shot several, and bashed his mother's head in with a hammer. For Kemper, the manner in which he killed was simply not important. Later in this chapter we will get into what *is* important to men like Rader and Kemper when we look at signature.

The following cases will focus on the crimes of "The Monster of Pont-Rouge," **Léopold Dion**, and **William Patrick Fyfe**, "The Killer Handyman." Both of these Quebec-based killers employed a modus operandi that proved successful, continuing to use it until they were caught. Dion's ruse was to pose as a photographer, offering money to boys who would model for him. Once he had isolated the children in the countryside, he would rape and strangle them before burying their bodies. Adversely, Fyfe's tastes were for women, preferably single and living alone. Pretending to be a handyman sent by their landlord, he would gain entrance to the house and viciously attack them. This rash of sex slayings will reveal the limitations of linking crimes based on modus operandi alone, opening the doorway to signature analysis.

Kay Feely.

Léopold Dion
The Monster of Pont-Rouge
4 Murders
Quebec City Area

"With my two cursed hands I made four little saints."

FROM THE BATTLEFIELD TO THE BONEYARD

April 20, 1963. For the second consecutive Saturday, twelve-year-old Guy Luckenuck left at dawn to catch a bus for the conservatory of music where he was taking lessons. By two in the afternoon, he had finished and decided to kill some time on the Plains of Abraham. Two hundred years earlier, the English General Wolfe had defeated Montcalm here, securing Lower Canada's place in the British orbit. As Guy did his best to stay amused, he was approached by a hefty man with a camera around his neck. The man explained that he was a photographer for an American magazine and that he was wondering if Guy would like to pose for him. The youngster agreed. After the photographer had snapped a few precursory pictures, he asked Guy if he would mind driving out to the country with him to take some more. Within minutes they were riding in the man's black '54 Vanguard. Somewhere between St. Augustine and St. Catherine, he pulled over and led Guy to a little sand dune a few metres from the road. There he resumed snapping pictures, but when he asked Guy to take his clothes off, the boy began to cry. He rose to flee, but the man thrust his 215-pound frame upon him and started to strangle him with his hands. After several minutes, Guy's body went limp, and the photographer placed him down on the sun-warmed earth. Retrieving a shovel from the back of the car, he dug a shallow grave and buried the body in a fetal position.

Two weeks later on a beautiful Sunday, the man met ten-year-old Michel Morel and his eight-year-old friend Alain Carrier in the shadow of Quebec's magnificent Château Frontenac. As before, the man asked the boys if they would like to pose for him, promising to pay them well in return. This time he drove them to a dilapidated cottage in Saint-Raymond de Portneuf. He told the boys he needed one of them to pretend to be a prisoner. Alain volunteered and allowed the man to tie him up inside the cottage. With the younger of the two boys secured, the man suddenly demanded that Michel pose nude. Sensing something was wrong, he turned to run, but with surprising speed, the man looped a nail-studded garrote over his neck and torqued. Michel would have felt the blood rush to his head, the petechiae bursting like fireworks on his face before lapsing into unconsciousness. When the man thought the child was dead, he slowly loosened the garrote and disengaged. He rose and stood pondering the corpse for a moment. Then he picked up a rock, and brought it down forcefully on Michel's skull, crushing it like a grape. Now that the older boy was out of the way, he was free to focus his attentions on the youngster. Retrieving a burlap sack from the car, the man entered the cottage where he found little Alain still bound and trembling with fear. The man pulled the sack over the child's head and strangled him to death with a rope before dumping both bodies into a shallow grave.

For his next crime "The Monster of Pont-Rouge" chose the scenic Anse-au-Foulon beach. Here he struck up a conversation with thirteen-year-old Pierre Marquis, who agreed to pose for photographs. The man drove him out to the country and strangled him on the same sand dune where Guy Luckenuck had died. It was Sunday May 26, 1963 — another beautiful day in Quebec.

Meanwhile, police investigating the disappearance had a major breakthrough. They had been showing mug shots of known sex offenders to a boy, hoping that he would recognize the man who had tried to lure him away weeks before. He pointed to a picture of Léopold Dion, currently on parole for raping a teacher. Quebec police tracked Dion down, arrested him, and charged him with the child murders. It took a month of interrogation before he broke down and confessed. With his psychological armour finally penetrated, he led them to the bodies of his four young victims.

On December 13, Judge Gérard Lacroix sentenced Dion to die by hanging for the murder of Pierre Marquis. Dion did not adjust well to life in prison and frequently expressed his wish to die sooner rather than later. On November 17, 1972, while waiting for the appeals process, he was stabbed to death and savagely mutilated by a fellow prisoner. His assassin, Norman Champagne, was a psychotic who claimed to be under the influence of Lawrence of Arabia. Like American cannibal-killer Jeffrey Dahmer, Léopold Dion's frenzied violence was poetically revisited on him just moments before he died. Sometimes the system works in mysterious ways.

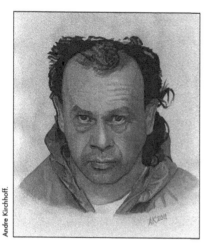

Andre Kirchhoff.

William Fyfe
The Killer Handyman
9 Murders
Montreal Suburbs/Laurentian area,
Quebec

"Why don't you just shoot me now?"

SAFE IN THE SUBURBS

They called him the "killer handyman" due to his MO of knocking on doors to offer his services. Sometimes he claimed to have been sent by the landlord — a ruse that worked particularly well because it made the women feel obliged to let him in. However, once he crossed the threshold, William Fyfe flew into a bestial rage, beating and throttling his victims into submission before raping and stabbing them repeatedly with a butcher knife. It was hardly an original MO: in the early sixties Albert DeSalvo had pretended to be a maintenance man to gain access to women's apartments and on other occasions as a talent recruit for a modelling agency. Then again, William Patrick Fyfe wasn't trying to impress anyone — he was trying to obliterate them.

Senneville, Quebec, a suburban community in Montreal's west island, was a quiet area with a noticeable absence of violent crime. It was October 14, 1999, and already the trees were going bare, shorn of their colours by an unseasonably cold wind. A collage of rain-sodden maple leaves blanketed the lawns in glistening yellow and red. At 3:00 p.m., fifty-nine-year-old Anna Yarnold backed slowly out of her driveway to take her dog Trooper to the veterinarian. She had discovered a strange lump on the animal's body and was concerned that it might damage his health. Upon meeting with the veterinarian she learned that the lump would have to be removed in an operation that was both costly and dangerous. Feeling upset, she returned home. At 5:30 p.m., Anna's daughter called to check on her and inquire about the dog's health. She would be the second-last person ever to hear her mother's voice.

The following morning, both Anna's daughter Sarah and husband Robert (who did not live with her) made a number of unanswered calls to the home. Both found it unusual that Anna would not be there to receive the calls. As darkness set in, Robert decided to drive over to Anna's to make sure she was okay. Upon arriving, he found her car in the driveway and the house lights on. He entered the home and immediately sensed something was wrong. Behind a closed bedroom door Trooper was cowering. Somebody had emptied the contents of Anna's handbag onto her bed and had rifled through her credit cards. Loose change was scattered about the place. Still there was no sign of her. Terrified of what he might find, Robert continued to search the premises. In the back garden, behind a triangular flower bed, he finally found the mother of his children: murdered. He called the police and in no time the property was swarming with crime-scene technicians. The forensic photographer found signs of bruising around Anna's neck and face, along with severe head trauma, probably caused by a heavy cement flowerpot. Discovering her eyeglasses in the sink, the police theorized that she had been suddenly attacked while in the bathroom. The carnage had spilled out into the hallway and eventually the back garden, where the attacker had choked and beat her. His homicidal gaze had fallen upon the flowerpot, and, with a series of mighty blows, he crushed Anna Yarnold's life from her body. Other than that, there was very little evidence left at the crime scene, and after questioning and clearing Robert, police soon found that all of their leads had gone cold.

Fifteen days later in the picturesque Laurentian town of Sainte-Agathe-des-Monts, workers at a local hospital were gradually becoming concerned about a missing co-worker. Forty-five-year-old Monique Gaudreau had failed to show up for her morning shift, and after a string of unanswered calls to her house, the staff telephoned her sister and informed her of the situation. Like Robert Yarnold, Monique's sister decided to investigate that evening. What she witnessed was so horrific it would never leave her. Monique Gaudreau hadn't just been stabbed; she had been stabbed fifty-five times! Police arriving on the scene were much more fortunate than their suburban colleagues — outside on the front porch they found a bloody shoe print along with several droplets of blood they correctly believed to have come from the attacker. Other than that, there were no signs of forced entry, robbery, or a murder weapon. When autopsy results confirmed that Ms. Gaudreau had been sexually assaulted, there seemed to be far too many differences to connect the two murders.

Moving into November, the winds became cruel and howling, the once-vibrant leaves turned brown and crumbled like ash into the earth. On the morning of the nineteenth when Laval police were dispatched to another absentee worker's apartment, there would have been great clouds on the horizon. Finding a stack of uncollected newspapers outside Teresa Shanahan's door, the police directed the concierge to open it. Inside they found her ravaged body covered in blood and gaping stab wounds. Later they were informed that there were thirty-two gashes in total. Right away it became clear that whoever had raped and murdered Monique Gaudreau had done the same to Teresa Shanahan. There were also several items missing from Teresa's apartment, including jewellery and bank cards. Following a hunch, police checked into her banking history and found that on the night of her murder two withdrawals of $500 had been made from her account. Security camera footage revealed a shadowy bearded figure, roughly five-foot ten and Caucasian, concealing his face behind a hood. Though they were unable to obtain an impression of the man, the detectives working the case had a lucky break when Sarah Yarnold, checking her mother's banking history, noticed that a withdrawal had also been made from Anna's account shortly after her death. Police were now able to confidently connect all three crime scenes: the Yarnold and Shanahan killings through post-mortem ATM withdrawals, and Shanahan-Gaudreau through the sexual assaults and frenzied stab wounds. What was troubling, however, was the notion that the killer now seemed to be torturing his victims for their PIN numbers.

On December 14, he claimed a fourth victim. Fifty-year-old Baie D'Urfé resident Mary Glen was found by her housekeeper the following morning, lying in a pool of blood in the living room. She had been brutally beaten, stabbed, and sexually assaulted. The crime scene was chaotic, spanning several rooms. Mary's eyeglasses were found at the bottom of the stairs, while other rooms contained clumps of hair and bloody footprints. It was obvious to every officer on the scene that she had put forth a valiant struggle. As in the other killings, there was no sign of forced entry, leading the police to conclude that the killer was using some kind of ruse to gain access to the home. Their suspicions were confirmed when neighbours told of a strange handyman who had come to their doors offering his services.

On day two of the search, they uncovered a foreign fingerprint in Mary Glen's home. Running it through the computer database, it wasn't long before detectives got a match. The prints belonged to forty-four-year-old William Patrick Fyfe, a painter and renovator who had logged arrests for breaking and entering in the seventies. In the years since, he had worked on and off as a handyman, marrying and fathering a child at one point before joining the ranks of divorcees. For years, Fyfe had lived in a small town just north of Montreal, though his current whereabouts were unknown. A former drug addict, he originally moved to the area seeking treatment, and decided to stay on as a counsellor once he was clean. Neighbours described him as generous and community-minded, though at times harshly critical of others.

Speaking with one of Fyfe's ex-girlfriends, police learned that he might be staying with his mother in Barrie, Ontario, 650 kilometres southwest of the city. Sure enough, Ontario police found his pickup truck parked outside the home and put him under twenty-four-hour surveillance. At this point, Montreal detectives decided to release Fyfe's name to the press hoping he would become desperate and incriminate himself. On December 21, Fyfe abandoned three pairs of bloodstained running shoes at a charity drop-off. By this time, officers from Montreal had arrived in Barrie and decided to make their move. They surprised him at a nearby gas station and charged him in the death of Mary Glen.

"Why don't you just shoot me now?" Fyfe grumbled.

DOWNFALL

By the time William Fyfe sat down in the interrogation room, it was apparent that he had re-evaluated his position.

"You don't got nothing!" he scoffed through a haze of smoke. In reality, he had just left them a DNA sample on his cigarette butts. When scanned, they linked him to blood evidence found on his victims' clothes. Furthermore, a search of his mother's Barrie home revealed various articles of clothing stained with Anna Yarnold's blood, a ring belonging to Teresa Shanahan, and shoes matching the prints found at the Monique Gaudreau residence.

But that wasn't all. With news of the arrest circulating the province, one of Fyfe's ex-hockey buddies came forward to suggest that investigators take another look into the unsolved murder of his mother, Hazel Scattolon. At the time of the killing, William Fyfe had been contracted to paint her house. When DNA samples from the cigarettes matched samples taken from the Scattolon crime scene, William Fyfe was implicated in his fifth homicide. At long last, the Scattolon family had a sense of closure that had eluded them for years.

Faced with insurmountable evidence, on September 21, 2001, William Fyfe plead guilty to five counts of murder and was sentenced to life with no chance of parole for twenty-five years. Months later, he confessed to a further four killings: the 1979 rape-slayings of Suzanne Bernier, fifty-five, and Nicole Raymond, twenty-six; the frenzied stabbing death of Louise Poupart-LeBlanc in 1987; and the 1989 murder of Pauline Laplante. In return, he was transferred from his Quebec prison to a psychiatric facility in Saskatchewan. Aside from suspecting him in five further murders, police are also looking at Fyfe's involvement in a series of violent rapes by a man knocking on doors pretending to be a plumber.

––––––

Today, sexual murders are analyzed not only for modus operandi, but also for signature. Unlike MO, signature is immutable: it is what the killer *has* to do in order to receive gratification from the murder. Perhaps the most perfect example of signature was the "Texas Eyeball Murderer," Charles Albright: an aging psychopath who shot prostitutes dead before carving their eyes out with an X-ACTO knife. If he wished, Albright could have changed his MO; rather than gunning down sex-trade workers he might have kidnapped women off the street. Nevertheless, he would be unable to resist the urge to take his gruesome trophies. As we saw earlier in the chapter, Dennis Rader and Edmund Kemper III certainly altered their modus operandi. However, every one of Rader's victims, including those who had already died, were intricately bound, while Kemper's were decapitated.

Many of the Canadian serial killers in this book also demonstrate clear signatures. Let's take a look at just two of them: wandering necrophiliac **Earle Leonard Nelson** and "The Butcher of St. Eustache" **Serge Archambault**, who compulsively sliced his victims to ribbons.

Winnipeg Free Press.

Earle Leonard Nelson
The Gorilla Murderer
22+ Murders
Winnipeg/Across the USA

THE DARK STRANGLER

In June 1927, Bill Patterson returned home to find his wife Emily missing. The couple were planning to sell their house and had a "For Sale" sign in the window. Typically, Mrs. Patterson would show potential buyers around the property while Bill laboured in a local department store. When Bill found his two children obliviously at play in the backyard, he immediately knew something was wrong. No matter what, Mrs. Patterson would never leave her children unsupervised. He telephoned the Winnipeg police to report her missing, and, not knowing what else to do, went about getting the children ready for bed. When he returned to his own room, he noticed the suitcase where they kept their savings had been torn open. Kneeling down to inspect, Patterson spotted what looked like his wife's coat under the bed, and reached out to retrieve it. Instead, his hand fell upon something cold and clammy. Horrified, he ran next door for help, collapsing in front of his neighbours. Minutes later, police arrived at 100 Riverton Street. They found Emily Patterson's strangled corpse wedged under the bed next to an old blue jacket and a pair of cotton trousers. She had been raped post-mortem. When Bill remarked that one of his brown suits was missing, the police deduced that the killer had shed his own ratty clothes to don something less conspicuous. Searching the pants pockets, they found newspaper clippings of local rooms for rent. Piece by piece, the evidence was pointing them in a scary direction. Had he really crossed the border? Had the notorious "Gorilla Murderer" really come to Winnipeg?

GOING APE

Earle Leonard Nelson was born in San Francisco on May 12, 1897. Even from an early age it was obvious that something was wrong with the boy. One crime writer would describe the infant as "a loose-mouthed degenerate with a vacant expression." Orphaned when both of his parents died of syphilis, he was taken in by his maternal grandmother, who proceeded to indoctrinate him with her fundamentalist Christian beliefs. To be fair, she did her best to provide a loving home for the boy, though any benefit this gave him was soon overshadowed by extreme psychiatric damage. At the age of ten, little Earle somehow managed to ride his bicycle into an oncoming streetcar and spent the rest of the week in a coma. When he emerged, his dark moods seemed to deepen and become increasingly erratic. Even as an adult, Earle's table manners were comparable to a dog's, and he was given to sudden outbursts of obscenities over dinner. Guests dropping in for coffee frequently looked on in an awkward silence as he walked around the room on his hands. He also had a strange knack for losing his clothes whenever he left the house.

At the age of fourteen, Earle dropped out of school and went on to work a series of unskilled labour jobs. What little money he earned between that and burglary was spent in the brothels of the Barbary Coast. In 1915 he was finally caught looting a house and sentenced to two years

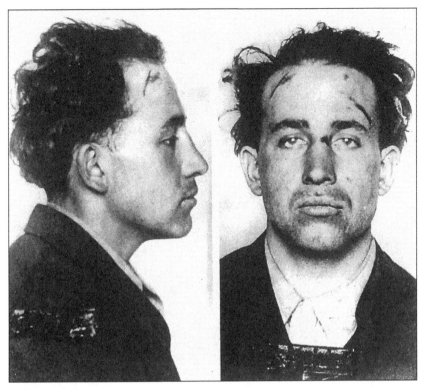

Nelson mugshot, May 1921.

in San Quentin. He emerged just as America was joining the First World War. Excited at the thought of killing Germans, he enlisted immediately. Unfortunately, Earle was so fond of violence that he spent most of the conflict in a Naval Mental Hospital. Diagnosed as a "constitutional psychopath" he was discharged in 1919.

By now he was twenty-two and looking to start a life for himself. In a bizarre union, he married a fifty-eight-year-old spinster named Mary Martin whose life he proceeded to make a living hell. When Earle wasn't spouting passages from *The Book of Revelation* or declaring himself the Messiah, he was accusing her of various imagined infidelities. Once, while Mary lay recovering from a serious illness in a hospital bed, Earle came into the room and raped her. Soon after, they were separated. A year later, Earle was recommitted to the mental hospital after attacking a twelve-year-old girl in the basement of an apartment. In 1925, he was released.

Clara Newman, Nelson's first murder victim in the United States.

Earle Nelson's first murder occurred shortly after. On February 20, 1926, under the auspices of renting a room in a boarding house, he strangled sixty-year-old Clara Newman before having sex with her corpse. February to November 1926 saw ten more landladies slaughtered in identical fashion from San Francisco to as far north as Seattle. When police coordinated a sweeping manhunt of the west coast, Earle simply moved to the interior, drifting east to commit murders in Iowa, Missouri, Michigan, and Illinois, eventually making it as far as New York and Pennsylvania. On December 28, in a display of true barbarity, he choked an eight-month-old baby to death by stuffing a rag down its throat. Thankfully, the child's mother had not been around to witness its fate; twenty-eight-year-old Germania Harpin had already been strangled to death. By the time he crossed over the Canadian border, "The Gorilla

Murderer" had claimed the lives of twenty Americans. Now he was looking to take his infamy onto a global stage. Canadian authorities would prove much more competent than he imagined.

NORTH OF THE BORDER

The day after Emily Patterson's murder, her husband Bill's brown suit showed up in a Winnipeg pawnshop. Fortunately, the owner remembered the customer well: dark-haired, with huge hands and powerful shoulders. Before leaving he had purchased a light grey suit and overcoat. A jovial fellow, he had asked to be taken to the local barber and the pawnshop owner was more than glad to assist. Armed with this information, the police sent out a cross-Canada alert describing the killer and his MO. By this time, Earle had already hitchhiked west to Regina and taken a room under the alias Henry Harcourt.

Just when Manitoba police thought they'd seen the last of Earle Nelson, another body showed up in Winnipeg. Fourteen-year-old Lola Cowan had been lured to the murderer's room with the understanding that he was going to buy flowers from her. Once she was isolated, he strangled her with his bare hands, raped her corpse, and stowed it under the bed. He absconded on June 9, neglecting to pay his rent in the process. Upon reaching Regina, he was shocked to find his description plastered all over the newspapers. Switching clothes at a local pawnshop, he left on June 13 with plans to double back to Manitoba. On Wednesday, June 15, he was sighted in the tiny hamlet of Wakopa, quenching his thirst at the local general store. Apparently the fearsome "Gorilla Murderer" was partial to cookies and soda pop. Certain that he had just served a multiple murderer, store owner Leslie Morgan played it cool until Earle had left, then immediately notified the authorities in Killarney. Nelson was arrested a few miles south of Wakopa, and by 10:40 p.m. was safely in Killarney jail. But the homicidal ape still had a few tricks up his sleeve. Within twenty minutes he had picked the lock to his cell door and hurried to Killarney Railway Station to hop a train. He hid in the shadows until 8:10 the next morning when a locomotive finally arrived. Unfortunately for Earle, it was loaded with armed police sent specifically to the area to recover him. Handcuffed, he was escorted swiftly back to Winnipeg.

Western Canada Pictorial Index

Nelson in custody at last.

Earle Nelson's trial began on November 1, 1927. To the surprise of everyone in attendance, rather than behaving like a savage animal, he remained polite and docile throughout the proceedings. Here was the Earle Nelson who charmed his way past locked doors and blended effortlessly into the population: not a bloodthirsty ape, but a cunning killer. Though his wife and aunt made the long trip from California to testify as to his mental health, he was found both guilty and sane. At 7:41 a.m. on the morning of January 13, 1928, Earle Nelson met his death at the end of a hangman's rope. In his thirty years he had claimed the lives of at least twenty-two people.

Kay Feely.

Serge Archambault

The Butcher of St. Eustache
3–6 Murders
Southern Quebec

CUTTING EDGE

January 1992. It was a crisp, clear winter day in the snowy Laurentian village of Saint-Calixte, Quebec, and Rollande Asselin-Beaucage, forty-seven, was walking her dog. Concerned about her safety, her husband Richard had bought the pet to keep her company, and the lonely housewife was quite taken with her furry protector. As she neared the end of her walk, a dark-haired, middle-aged man pulled up in his car and asked her first for directions, and then for a glass of water. A kind and trusting woman, Rollande went inside to pour him a glass of water while the stranger waited outside the front door. When she opened it to hand him his drink, he suddenly pushed his way into the house, knocking her to the floor. Sometime after, a gunshot echoed through the mountains.

Rollande Asselin-Beaucage was found that same evening by her husband. She was laying face-down in a pool of blood, hands bound behind her back, and subject to numerous mutilations. The cause of death had been quick: a .22-calibre bullet to the head. It was after he murdered his victim that the killer really went to work. Armed with a knife from Rollande's own kitchen, he carefully opened up her torso, exposing her vital organs. Next he carved up her breasts and genitals, stuffing some of the raw pieces of flesh into her mouth. Amazingly, the killer had left no evidence or witnesses.

On January 10, RCMP profiler Ron MacKay arrived at the scene. He was immediately reminded of two previous murders in the area: the 1987 death of Louise Poupart-Leblanc and the brutal slaying of Pauline Laplante in 1989. The women had been sadistically tortured, then robbed of their bank cards. Records showed the cards had been eaten at nearby ATMs after the killer repeatedly tried to exceed the daily withdrawal limit of $500. Noting many behavioural and geographic similarities, MacKay linked the three crimes. Though Asselin-Beaucage did not possess an ATM card, he saw clear indications that a sexual sadist was at work, in fact, Mackay felt the killer had escalated his violence since the last attack. He made a solemn prediction that, unless caught, the killer would strike again within a year. On this point, he was right.

STABBING, WITHDRAWING …

Eleven months later, on November 26, 1992, police descended on the scene of another horrific murder. This time the setting was the quiet middle-class town of Deux Montagnes. The victim: Chantal Brière, wife to Raymond and mother to six-year-old Jonathan. The Brières were planning to relocate and Chantal had been showing their home to potential buyers. Some days earlier she had received a telephone call from a man who was interested in the property, and wanted to view it on Thursday morning. On Thursday the 26th, Chantal awoke and drove her son Jonathan to his grandmother's as she didn't want the child to get in the way of the potential customer. When she returned to her home, she found the buyer already waiting on the front step. As they entered the house, he explained that he had taken the train from Montreal and muttered something about wanting to get his Polaroid camera. He left at just after 11:00 a.m., only to return at 12:15 p.m. Chantal and the stranger began to discuss the house when the phone rang. It was Raymond calling from work wanting to know whether or not the customer had arrived. Chantal confirmed that he had, and then passed the stranger the receiver so that he could ask Raymond some questions about the home. Within minutes of hanging up, the phone rang again: Chantal's mother. Chantal explained that she couldn't talk and ended the call. She didn't know it at the time, but Chantal's mother would never hear her daughter's voice again.

When Chantal's mother called back half an hour later, there was no answer. Over the rest of the afternoon she periodically redialled the number, but nobody seemed to be home. Concerned, she contacted her other daughter Francine and the two agreed to check on Chantal. The first thing they noticed when they pulled up to the home was that there were no lights on, only the listless flicker of a television. Immediately the hairs stood up on the back of their necks.

"We're not going in there," Chantal's mother said.

Within five minutes they were standing in the empty hallway calling Chantal's name. Moving farther inside, Francine stopped dead in her tracks. Chantal was lying face-down on the floor with her hands bound. She was naked below the waist, gagged with her brassiere, and strangled with an electrical cord. Francine called back to her mother not to come in.

The police investigation at the Brière residence revealed several items of interest. Like Rollande, Chantal had been mutilated post-mortem, but this time a sock had also been rammed down her throat. The piece of cord used to strangle her had been cut from a nearby lamp. Knowing that serial killers often kept trophies of their victims, the Sûreté du Québec took inventory of all the missing items at the scene. It was discovered that Chantal's bank card had been stolen. Contacting the bank, they learned that it had been used the previous day at a corner store in St. Eustache. The time had been 12:58 p.m.; *after* Chantal's death. Detectives immediately confiscated all garbage and security footage from the scene. The clerk explained to them that the tape was in the process of rerecording and, had they arrived eighty minutes later, the footage would have been irretrievable.

When investigators sat down to peruse the videotape, they realized to their chagrin that it contained no time code. Fortunately, it had recorded the background music from a local radio station. By contacting the station and requesting a schedule of the songs played on the day in question, police determined that at 12:58 p.m., a popular Francophone song had been spinning. When they located it on the security footage, they found themselves staring into the face of a strange balding man. At first he seemed to be standing in line to use the ATM, but when a middle-aged woman entered, he quickly left the queue and snatched up a chocolate bar. The two then conversed briefly before the woman went to use the ATM, and the balding man went to pay for his snack. They left the store together soon after. Moments later, however, the man re-entered and withdrew $300 from the ATM. At that point the Sûreté du Québec realized they were gazing upon Chantal Brière's killer.

THE BUTCHER OF ST. EUSTACHE

Half suspecting the woman at the ATM was now sliced into ribbons, police traced her name and address through banking records. When they went to question her at home, she confirmed having used the ATM at that time and location and also that the balding man was her husband. The same day, police arrested Serge Archambault, a thirty-six-year-old former butcher and packing plant manager turned travelling salesman. A search of the Archambault home revealed plentiful evidence. In the roof of a basement bedroom, police found items from Chantal Brière's house along with some of the .22-calibre shells used on Rollande Asselin-Beaucage. After a gruelling interrogation, Archambault admitted to the Asselin-Beaucage and Brière slayings. He claimed to have picked Asselin-Beaucage at random while driving north of Montreal on a business trip. Brière had likewise been selected, though in this case he had decided to torture her for her ATM PIN number. By sheer chance, he had run into his wife at the corner store half an hour later. Asselin-Beaucage and Brière were not the only women he had targeted. He told police how he had trawled the streets for prostitutes, and had picked them up on many occasions with the intention of killing them. At all times, he carried a murder-rape kit in his car consisting of knives, a gun, and various ligatures. Archambault then surprised the interrogators by confessing to a hitherto undiscovered murder: the 1989 slaughter of Anna-Maria Codina-Leva. A single mother of three living in Verdun, Codina-Leva had been having an affair with Archambault at the meat-packing plant where they both worked. She became infuriated when he broke up with her, telephoning his wife and informing her of the affair. Shortly after, Archambault contacted Codina-Leva and told her he wanted to get back together. The two arranged to meet at the plant. Despite the unusual setting, a very excited Anna-Maria took extra care readying her hair and make-up. She arrived with a surprise: a bottle of champagne. Archambault seemed pleased, and after the two had drained the bottle, told her he also had a surprise for her. Asking her to close her eyes, he led her by the hand into the nearby garage where he had secreted a knife among some wooden palettes. He told her to count to three and then open her eyes. At the exact moment she reached three, he slashed the knife viciously across her throat, leaving her to bleed out the last minutes of her life on the cold floor. When she had expired, he returned and sexually assaulted her corpse. He then dismembered it and disposed of her remains in three garbage bags. Serge Archambault's time as a butcher had certainly paid off.

LOOSE ENTRAILS

A psychiatric assessment determined that "The Butcher of St. Eustache" was mentally fit to stand trial. Though he had confessed to three murders, the court needed to determine whether they were in the first or second degree. The trial began in November 1993, with more than fifty witnesses called to testify. The defence claimed that the murders were not premeditated, and that Archambault was the victim of uncontrollable violent urges. This argument fell flat when the prosecution presented evidence of his murder kit. The trial was a harrowing experience for those involved — even the judge was seen wincing at the grisly details. After a short deliberation, on November 19, the teary-eyed jurists emerged holding hands to return a verdict of guilty on three counts of first-degree murder. Serge Archambault was sentenced to life in prison without the possibility of parole for twenty-five years.

Yet there were still loose ends. Ron MacKay, reputed as one of the best profilers in the country, remained convinced that Archambault was also responsible for the 1987 Louise Poupart-Leblanc murder and for that of Pauline Laplante in 1989. However, Archambault continued to deny involvement, and the absence of his signature mutilation or necrophilia was perplexing. William Patrick Fyfe would eventually admit to the murders. Coincidentally, the two Montreal men shared elements in their modus operandi: ATM theft and home invasion. If we consider the colder, meticulous overkill in the three Archambault slayings, a clear delineation can be drawn between his crimes and the more hot-blooded approach of William Patrick Fyfe.

A STUDY IN DISMEMBERMENT: PIRRERA VS. CHRISTENSEN

As the Canadian author Peter Vronsky points out in his masterful book *Serial Killers: The Method and Madness of Monsters*, **Paul Bernardo** and Edmund Kemper III both dismembered victims. However, Bernardo attempted this because he thought it necessary to dispose of the body carefully. When he decided it was both disgusting and a waste of time, he stopped the practice altogether. Kemper, on the other hand, dismembered his victims for a sexual thrill. The thought of quitting would have rendered his killings pointless, the gaping void in his psyche left unfulfilled.

The little-known Canadian cases of **Sam Pirrera** and **William Dean Christensen** provide respective examples of dismemberment as MO (a defensive action) and signature (a sexual act).

Gary Yokoyama, Hamilton Spectator.

Sam Pirrera
2 Murders
Hamilton, Ontario

"I'm tired of everyone fucking leaving me, so I killed someone."

TAKING OUT THE TRASH: APRIL 3, 1999

Danielle Pirrera's heart was pounding as she climbed out of her white Mercury Cougar onto the driveway of 12 Bruce Place. Her estranged husband's words kept repeating in her head like a bad dream: "I'm tired of everyone fucking leaving me, so I killed someone. I picked up a hooker, we did some crack together and then she said she wanted to leave. I told her she wasn't going anywhere." The beautiful blonde Newfoundlander had arrived earlier in the day to check Sam into the emergency psychiatric unit at St. Joseph's Hospital. The next thing she knew, he was rambling about beating a prostitute to death with a pool cue, dismembering her body, and stuffing the guts into a garbage bag around the side of the East Mountain home they once shared. Now Sam wanted Danielle to get rid of the evidence. She just prayed he was lying, as usual. Yet as she neared the garbage, she became increasingly afraid of what she would find. Sam had put her through enough already — today, she would leave this to the police. Danielle retrieved her cellphone, and with trembling fingers, began to dial. This was shaping up to be the worst Easter weekend ever.

Nine minutes later, Constable Kathy Stewart pulled into the driveway to find a nervous-looking woman standing outside. Danielle explained that she had been in the house earlier, and had noticed broken furniture and a woman's clothes. Most chillingly, the basement was spotlessly clean. Sam *never* did housework. Stewart decided to take a look at the garbage first. Danielle directed her to the side of the house where a bulky green trash bag sat atop a medium-sized cardboard box. Stewart pulled on a pair of latex gloves and hefted the bag onto the ground. It must have weighed almost four kilograms. Untying the knot, she began to rifle through empty pop bottles and plastic containers until she came across a white plastic tub. Inside the tub was a smaller bag: the kind you bought filled with soil from the garden centre. Only it didn't contain soil. Peeling back the final layer, a baby's blanket, Kathy Stewart came face to face with the horrifying truth.

"Is it a cat?" Danielle whimpered.

Stewart shook her head. "No."

"Oh my God!" Danielle Pirrera collapsed into a fit of tears. Though she had left her abusive husband six weeks ago, until this moment she hadn't realized what kind of monster she had married. If Sam was telling the truth about this murder, then what about those rambling confessions he had made three years ago? Had he really strangled his first wife? And if so, how close had Danielle herself come to being one of his victims?

WITHOUT A TRACE

Growing up together in Hamilton's rough working-class east end, Sam Pirrera and Beverly Davidson had been high-school sweethearts, marrying in May 1986 when he was nineteen and she sixteen. Two weeks later, Sam revealed his true colours by punching his beautiful bride twenty times in the head until she was unconscious. Their mutual cocaine habit only added fuel to the fire, and soon Beverly was stripping in Hamilton nightclubs to support their addictions. For his part, Sam had landed a job at his father's workplace Dofasco Steel. Though he lauded his wife's $1,000/week income, he was extremely jealous, stalking the nightclubs where she worked to ensure that nobody tried to "steal" her. Owing to his crack addiction, he became increasingly paranoid, insisting on driving Beverly home after her shift so she could not talk to anyone.

In January 1987, Beverly became pregnant, but this did little to stop the beatings; at one point Sam even kicked the expectant mother in the stomach. Thankfully, their daughter Ashlee was born premature but in good health in August 1987. The next month, Sam was caught sleeping at Dofasco, and was temporarily suspended.

By the time the couple first separated in 1988, Sam had been charged seven times with spousal abuse. On all but two occasions the charges had been dropped. They reconciled briefly, but when Beverly threatened to leave him, Sam wrapped his hands around her neck, choking her to the verge of unconsciousness. He begged her not to charge him, and she agreed on the condition that he leave her alone. Sam agreed, then filed divorce papers claiming Beverly had cheated on him with a neighbour. The ensuing custody battle for their daughter Ashlee was particularly nasty, with each parent accusing the other of abuse and drug addiction. Sam cited a failed 1986 suicide attempt as proof that Beverly was unstable. Then in 1990, they were suddenly back together again, moving into a two-bedroom townhouse on Kenora Avenue. When a baby son Matthew followed in January 1991, the Pirreras upgraded to a three-bedroom in the same housing project.

Their reunion would last until mid-May when Beverly arrived unexpectedly at her mother Lesa's home on Adams Street. She had finally had enough and was going to leave Sam for good. Soon after, he telephoned, offering to drive Beverly back to their townhouse to pick up some of her belongings. As Sam's car pulled up outside the window, the pretty young woman told her mother she would be right back. It was the last time Lesa Davidson would ever lay eyes on her daughter.

Sometime after, in a sworn affidavit to the Hamilton police, Sam Pirrera complained that Beverly had arrived at the townhouse with two men who physically assaulted him, telling him they'd be back. They never returned. Of course, Lesa wasted little time asking him why her daughter had suddenly vanished, but Sam assured her Beverly had run away to California to resume her career as a stripper. Meanwhile, he moved back in with his parents, taking their two children with him. In the summer of 1991, he filed divorce proceedings, hinting that Beverly had chosen a life of prostitution over her family.

Then one summer night while Lesa was at work, the phone rang in the Davidson house. Her daughter-in-law Lori answered the phone.

"It's Bev. Mom there?"

"She's at work," Lori frowned — the voice sounded nothing like Beverly's.

"Tell her I'm in California," the woman replied. "I'm doing okay. I'll call her later."

Within the next three months, there were two more mysterious phone calls, but never any attempt at conversation. Bewildered, Lesa tried to rationalize her daughter's behaviour. She called Sam, demanding to know what was happening, but as always he managed to deflect her suspicions. On one occasion he dropped by the Davidson home so that Lesa could see her grandchildren. He told Lesa that he had spoken to Bev recently, that she was still in California and had posted birthday presents for Ashlee and Matthew. Around this time, Ashlee began asking about pictures of Beverly on the wall. She had forgotten what her own mother looked like. Soon after, the visits to Grandma Davidson petered out.

A BLONDER REPLACEMENT

From 1991 to 1994, Tony and Lina Pirrera devoted most of their time to raising their grandchildren, while Sam drank heavily, smoked crack, and hung around strip clubs. It was through these channels that he met Danielle, an exotic dancer at Hanrahan's where Beverly had worked three years earlier. Having secured a divorce and custody of his two children, in the fall of 1994, Sam, Danielle, and the kids moved into a brand-new home in Stoney Creek. By July of the next year, they were married. Danielle was by most accounts a wonderful stepmother and attractive woman — but the demons inside Sam Pirrera were always hungry for something more. Rather than cleaning up his act, he returned to his cocaine and alcohol addictions and was soon put on medical leave at Dofasco. He began to beat his new wife, and was convicted of assaulting her in November 1998, received a year's probation, along with a thirty-day jail sentence to be served on weekends.

One day, while high on crack, Sam told his new bride something he believed would "join them forever." In 1991, he had strangled Beverly to death and pushed her down the basement stairs. There he chopped her to pieces, disposing of them later in Dofasco's steel cauldrons. If Danielle ever told anyone, Sam vowed to do the same to her.

"Nobody's looking for Bev," he warned. "Why would anyone look for you?"

Terrified and unsure of whether or not to believe him, Danielle kept his secret for years. Later she would claim to Lesa Davidson that Beverly's ghost visited her in a dream and warned her to "get out." In February 1999, Danielle finally took her ominous advice, moving out of the home with their daughter. The next time she saw her husband, he was sitting in a mess of broken dishes and furniture, rocked-up to his eyeballs on crack.

CLOSURE

Following the discovery of entrails in Sam Pirrera's garbage, the swarthy addict was arrested at St. Joseph's Hospital and charged with first-degree murder. Meanwhile, a forensics investigation team undertook a thorough search of 12 Bruce Place. With the revelation of murder at the Pirrera residence circulating, Lesa Davidson came forward to report Beverly's disappearance to the police. She had been missing for eight years. On the fifth day, they uncovered the remains of a thirty-four-year-old prostitute behind a crudely constructed false wall in the fruit cellar. Maggie Karer had been dismembered, her body parts wrapped into individual packages for disposal.

With Karer's friends threatening him at Hamilton's Barton Jail, Sam requested a transfer to Quinte Detention Centre in Napanee to await trial. There he attempted suicide by slitting his wrists and ankles, but was saved by the emergency response team. On September 27, he appeared in a Hamilton courtroom, choosing to forgo his right to a preliminary hearing because his lawyer, James Vincelli, conceded there was ample evidence to try Sam for the murder of Maggie Karer. On January 27, 2000, assistant Crown attorney Fred Campling encouraged lead detective Peter Abi-Rashed to charge him with the second-degree murder of Beverly Davidson, based on the weight of circumstantial evidence. A pre-trial plea bargain was eventually struck

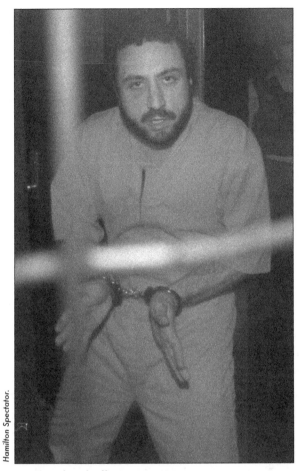

Hamilton Spectator.

Pirrera in handcuffs.

between Vincelli and the prosecutors: Sam would confess to both murders in the second degree, earning him two concurrent life sentences with the chance of parole in ten years. The date of the trial was fixed at February 18.

On February 12, Sam Pirrera committed suicide by heroin overdose at Toronto East Detention Centre, a stopover en route to Barton Jail. With a simple injection, he escaped a lifetime of torpor in the Canadian justice system, and more importantly, ever having to face the horror of his crimes. The families of Pirrera's victims, however, would not be spared this torture.

Lesa Davidson had always suspected her daughter had been murdered, but to finally hear it confirmed by a policeman brought old pain rushing back. Several days before his death, Sam had allegedly confessed to strangling Beverly, carefully dismembering her with a butcher's knife and dumping her body parts into a vat of molten steel. Her little girl had never been to California — had barely seen past the insurmountable smokestacks and strip clubs that comprised her narrow world. Somehow, Sam Pirrera had come to completely dominate Beverly's existence, and just when escape seemed imminent, had sealed the door forever.

On April 8, Lesa Davidson said goodbye to her daughter at a service held at White Chapel Memorial Gardens. There was no body to lie beneath her tombstone.

William Dean Christensen
4+ Murders
Montreal, Quebec/across eastern USA

MONTREAL

The man calling himself "Richard Owen" stepped out of the penitentiary gates, smiled, and took a long breath of the Montreal spring air. Not only had he managed to bargain down those rape charges to indecent assault, he had even fooled the Canadian authorities into incarcerating him under a false name. Now instead of transferring him back to the authorities in Maryland, they had set him free.

On April 27, 1982, a blood-curdling scream shook the walls of 105 Milton Street in the south-end of Montreal's Plateau neighbourhood. It is uncertain which mutilated segment of Trois-Rivières native Sylvie Trudel was discovered first. The twenty-seven-year-old office worker's decapitated head had been hidden in the stove, her torso bisected; the upper half stored in a pantry, and the remainder crammed into a plastic garbage bag. The apartment's tenant, a Mr. Richard Owen, had seemingly vanished into thin air.

Later that same afternoon, the remains of 26-year-old Laval woman Murielle Guay were found similarly butchered, bagged, and buried in a Mille-Îles field. At first, differences in the precision of the dismemberment led police to believe they were dealing with two different killers. By April 29, however, the cases had been linked and a warrant was issued for the arrest of "Richard Owen." Little did they know, the sinister lust killer was already back on familiar ground.

SCRANTON, TRENTON, PHILLY

After drifting aimlessly across the eastern United States for several months, the psychopath now calling himself "Stanley Holl" settled in Scranton, Pennsylvania. On September 23, 1982, he approached go-go dancer Michelle Angiers, twenty-three, in the Moonlight Inn parking lot in Dixon, stabbing her thirty times. To further degrade her, Holl placed a stuffed animal on top of her body. She was found dead at 6:30 that same morning in a puddle of congealing blood. By this time, he had already moved on in search of new victims.

Many months passed before the killer struck again, targeting two African-American men in a Trenton, New Jersey, saloon. Apparently feeling no need to act out his bizarre mutilation rituals on his male victims, he simply unloaded his gun, severely wounding them. On December 4, 1983, in Philadelphia, he treated Joseph Connelly to a repeat performance, only this time the middle-aged black man wouldn't survive. Arrested that same night, and charged under the name "Jeffrey Schrader," he was later convicted of Connelly's murder. A police search of his apartment revealed further signs of violence: a bloody mattress and hacksaw caked in hair and blood. Schrader's roommate, a local stripper, has never been located.

Meanwhile, a state trooper uncovered his connection to the slaying of Michelle Angiers in Dixon under the alias of Stanley Holl. Noting Schrader's knowledge of the criminal justice system, they had sent out a notice in a regional crime bulletin. He was transferred immediately to Lackawanna County to face charges.

While awaiting sentencing for the Connelly murder, detectives from Maryland had tracked a local sex killer named William Dean Christensen to north Philadelphia where they began to circulate pictures of him. He was quickly identified as the man arrested for the December 4 murder of Joseph Connelly. Checking police records, they realized that Christensen and Schrader were, in fact, one and the same. A native of Bethesda, Maryland, in 1969 Christensen had faced his first felony conviction at the age of twenty-four for beating and stabbing a Washington, D.C., teen. Two years later, he entered a guilty plea in the rape of a go-go dancer in Maryland and was sentenced to nine years in prison. After being paroled in 1980, he disappeared.

It wasn't until July 27, 1984, that Philadelphia police realized their forty-year-old suspect was also the Richard Owen wanted in the two Montreal slayings. The same day, Canadian Correctional Service official Michael Lauzon publicly claimed there was no record of a Richard Owen or William Dean Christensen ever having been incarcerated in Quebec. As Christensen had already drawn life without parole for the Connelly murder, Montreal authorities decided not to prosecute him for the Trudel/ Guay kilings. Both cases were permanently closed in August 1984.

On August 6, 1987, Christensen was convicted of the third-degree murder of Michelle Angiers five years earlier. He is the primary suspect in the mutilation murders of up to thirty additional female hitchhikers and go-go dancers across the eastern United States.

SIGNATURES

In the Trudel and Guay slayings, Christensen had the time and opportunity to enact his most depraved fantasies on the bodies of the victims. He chose, like Sam Pirrera many years later, to dismember them; only there was no practical reason for Christensen to do so. Rather than slicing her into three pieces, it would have been much easier for him to have hidden Sylvie Trudel's entire body in the pantry. Similarly, burying every segment of Muriel Guay's corpse in the same shallow grave did nothing to help conceal her identity (though it may have eased the transportation of the body). This is because, unlike Pirrera, Christensen's butchery was the manifestation of a sexual fantasy and not a body-disposal technique. To put it bluntly, it's what got him off. We can therefore conclude that dismemberment, an act totally unnecessary to the successful completion of Christensen's crimes, was one of his signatures. A second signature was what criminal profilers refer to as "posing." By stowing Sylvie Trudel's head in the stove and placing the stuffed animal on Michelle Angiers's body, Christensen was deriving sexual excitement by degrading his victims. Not only would they be hideously murdered, but reduced to a joke in death. In all likelihood, he gleaned immense pleasure knowing their discoverers would bear the psychological scars forever.

CHAPTER 4

VICTIMOLOGY

In his aforementioned *A History of British Serial Killing*, David Wilson identifies five victim groups most likely to fall prey to a serial murderer: prostitutes, gay men, babies/infants, the elderly, and "young people who have recently left home."[1] When comparing these five groups to known statistics of Canadian victims, we uncover both similarities and glaring discrepancies.

For instance, though prostitutes are the foremost target for serial killers in both countries, the number of sex workers murdered per capita in Canada far exceeds the British figure. This is undoubtedly owing to the vast numbers of Aboriginal streetwalkers in western Canada whose disappearances usually go uninvestigated by authorities.

Homosexual males also comprise a significant portion of victims, though unlike Britain and the United States, Canada has yet to give rise to a serial murderer who has killed in excess of ten. **Toronto's Gay Village Murders** of Richard Hovey and Eric Jones are provided as an example here, though several other predators with homosexual victims are featured in later chapters.

Wilson's inclusion of the babies/infants category is peculiar, considering his book lists only a single example of a British serial killer who has targeted them: the nefarious nurse Beverley Allitt who claimed four lives in total. This number pales in comparison to the amount of lives destroyed by Canadian baby-farmers **William and Lila Young**, whose total number may add up to over one hundred victims. That said, based upon the greater number of pedophile murderers documented in Wilson's book and my own, I have decided to broaden his category from babies/infants to children in general. Though Edward Rulloff, Gordon Northcott, Peter Woodcock, Clifford Olson, and Léopold Dion have already provided us with plenty of examples, in this chapter we will attempt a deeper examination of the psychopathology of a child predator through the lens of **Donald Sherman Staley.**

Perhaps the most significant difference between British and Canadian serial killers has been the amount of elderly victims they've claimed, with over two hundred in Britain compared to less than ten in Canada. This is attributable mainly to the pathetic existence of England's Dr. Harold Shipman, one of the world's most prolific serial killers, who murdered at least 215 geriatric patients in his care. If we dismiss Shipman as an aberration, then the numbers are more comparable (though the amount of British killers remains higher). Of the criminals featured in this book, only **Melissa Ann Friedrich** preyed solely on senior citizens. As Friedrich will be examined later as Canada's only Black Widow serial killer, here we will look at the crimes of "The Monster of Miramichi," **Allan Legere**, who, with the exception of two middle-aged female victims, beat three pensioners to death during home invasions, seriously wounding two others.

In the final "young people who have left home" category proposed by Wilson, we see a roughly comparable toll of victims between the two countries. Many of the young women who died or went missing along **The Highway of Tears** fit this criteria.

Before moving on to the case studies, it is important to note that Wilson acknowledges such victims often fit into two or more of the five categories. Particularly in Canada, "young people who have left home" often become prostitutes (as reflected in the Crawford case) or abscond because they are homosexual. Consider a young gay man who leaves an intolerant home to sell his body on the streets — he alone covers at least three of Wilson's victim types.

The most crucial thing tying the five categories together is vulnerability. A prostitute, for instance, will hop into a stranger's car within a matter of seconds, speeding off to an isolated location to engage in sexual activity. This puts them at great personal risk for several reasons: 1) They are in a remote location; 2) They have entered the killer's zone of control — his car or home; 3) They will place their bodies in compromising positions beneath the killer or with their back to him, often stripping naked; 4) Their lifestyle means they frequently travel without notifying anyone, and many have irregular or no contact with their families. Thus, a prostitute can typically disappear for extended periods before anybody notices they are missing.

As full-grown adult males, it would initially seem that gay men run a low risk of being successfully murdered. However, stigmatization of their lifestyle has historically meant they have been forced to conduct their sexual activities in secret, opening them up to many of the same vulnerabilities as prostitutes. Furthermore, homophobia has alienated many gay men from their families, forcing them into solitary lifestyles, and marking them as targets for violent bigots or self-hating homosexuals who wish to project their anger onto men of similar inclination.

While the vulnerability of children and the elderly lies in their feeble physicality and trusting nature, "young people who have left home" suffer from a mixture of this naïveté along with the frequent isolation from loved ones experienced by gay men and prostitutes.

Warren Goulding.

John Martin Crawford
The First Nations Killer
4–7 Murders
Saskatoon, SK/Lethbridge, AB

"Do her Bill. Or I'll punch the shit out of her."

STABBED

"John, for Christ's sake, what did you do?"

Bill Corrigan looked down in horror at the crumpled form of the Aboriginal woman, the gold-handled knife still jutting from her belly. If it wasn't for the stab wounds along her chest and side, he would have been sickened by the bruising. Not enough to have intervened, of course — which he didn't — but then again, he never thought his friend would go this far.

"I killed her," John Martin Crawford's double chin wobbled with each laboured breath. "She's dead. Get some branches. Help me cover her up."

Corrigan did as he was told, but made no secret that he was unhappy about it. When John had dragged the prostitute kicking and screaming out of the green Chevy Nova and began hitting her, Corrigan assumed he was just beating her up. Not wanting any part of it he had clambered inside the vehicle to warm up. Unfortunately, now he was very much a part of it. He was the only witness to a brutal sex murder, and the knife upon which the victim perished belonged to him! *What was her name again? Angie?*

After haphazardly burying the body under dead branches, the two men drove back into town. Crawford rolled the deceased woman's clothes into a ball and tossed them into a Dumpster. They stopped by the house he shared with his mother Victoria on Avenue Q north, so that he could strip out of his bloody jeans and sweater. The house wasn't the only thing they shared — every evening John borrowed her 1970s green Chevy Nova to troll for prostitutes along 20th and 21st streets. Forensic testing later determined the vehicle's interior was covered with semen stains. Corrigan watched as his friend soaked the knife in mouthwash, clouds of blood swirling in the basin like nightmares. He wondered if he would ever get a good night's sleep again. When Crawford was changed and refreshed, he drove Corrigan to a motel, then returned home to meet his 9:00 p.m. curfew. Victoria Crawford had imposed this as a punitive measure when her son was fined $250 for soliciting a prostitute. At the time, John had been twenty-eight years old.

BEATEN

Giving birth is a difficult experience for any woman, but for tiny Victoria Crawford it was particularly harrowing. Nevertheless, on March 29, 1962, John Martin Crawford arrived healthy into the world of Steinbach, Manitoba. His mother, an unwed twenty-one-year-old, married Al Crawford two years later and a brother and sister soon followed. An alcoholic taxi driver, John's stepfather regularly drank and gambled away his earnings, while Victoria Crawford struggled with her own bingo addiction. By the age of three, the child had already run away on more than one occasion.

At four years old, John severely burned his chest, neck, and arm playing with a cigarette lighter. Left with visible scarring, he was mocked mercilessly by other children. Later that same year he was molested by a babysitter — not for the last time.

When he began school at the age of five, John's moods would swing erratically from hyperactivity to withdrawal and silence. His teachers labelled him "stupid" and tried their best to get him transferred to another school. Instead he failed grade one, returning the following year, much to the annoyance of the faculty. At age seven, he was molested by a second babysitter.

Realizing their son's problems, the Crawfords uprooted to Vancouver where John could be treated for his burns and assessed by psychologists at Vancouver General Hospital. For years he suffered from horrific nightmares, and by the age of twelve was a bully and glue sniffer. This daily substance abuse usually took place in secluded parks where he would hold conversations with inanimate objects and create bizarre rituals. Sniffing glue soon led to marijuana, LSD, magic mushrooms, and the abuse of prescription medications. It didn't take long for little John to reject his Catholic faith, though he claims to have had several religious experiences, once saying he found Native systems of belief to be the most meaningful. In reality, the miracles he witnessed were probably the first signs of psychosis and if he truly had any respect for Native culture, he had a strange way of showing it.

Crawford's first consensual sexual experience came at the age of thirteen, when he and two other boys paid an eleven-year-old girl to have intercourse with them. Three years later, he began to be visited by distant voices telling him to steal, sexually assault, and kill. He decided these messages were being sent to him from outer space, enjoying how powerful and competent they made him feel. Once he hallucinated that the voices belonged to two topless green women. Though he resisted their commands, he was vulnerable while intoxicated. Unfortunately, John Martin Crawford was perpetually high. His breaking point would come in 1981, shortly after the Crawford family moved to Lethbridge, Alberta.

The Bridge Inn was a blue-collar bar in Lethbridge's skid row district, the ideal place for a sexually frustrated psychotic to meet his first victim. On the evening of December 23, 1981, Mary Jane Serloin, thirty-five, a regular at the establishment, was staggering drunk. When the nineteen-year-old Crawford offered her a cigarette, she gladly accepted, and the two gossiped about the clientele over a pitcher of draught beer. At 10:00 p.m., they left together. When Crawford returned at midnight, he was alone.

Nobody thought anything of it until next morning when Mary Jane Serloin's naked body was found beaten to death in an alcove behind the fire hall. There were savage bite marks on her neck, cheek, and breasts. Her mouth was caked in blood and vomit. A subsequent autopsy determined that at some point during her ordeal the killer had slammed a brick into her stomach, rupturing the portal vein, and causing a litre of blood to leak into her abdominal cavity. In the end she had died choking on her own vomit, murdered within a block of The Bridge Inn.

Eight hours after the gruesome discovery, police arrived at the Crawford residence to arrest John. He accompanied them to the station without incident, offering a convoluted explanation for the murder. Sure, he had beaten the life out of Mary-Jane Serloin, but only to stop her choking. As to the origin of the bite marks, he had no idea, but assumed that somebody else must have been responsible. Confident the killer was sitting in front of them, police made a wax cast of Crawford's teeth and compared them to the marks found on Serloin's body. His unique dental profile left them with no doubts: John Martin Crawford had killed Mary Jane Serloin. Police offered to reduce the charges from first-degree murder to manslaughter if he confessed, agreeing to forgo an expensive three-day trial. Crawford accepted the deal and was immediately sentenced to ten years in Drumheller, Alberta's federal institution. Terrified of prison life, he began to self-mutilate and was transferred on several occasions to mental health facilities. Here he was diagnosed as an intellectually limited dyslexic suffering from hebephrenic schizophrenia. While John was serving out his sentence, Al and Victoria Crawford divorced. Following a prison transfer to Prince Albert, Saskatchewan, Crawford's mother moved to Saskatoon to be closer to him. It was at this institution where Crawford befriended Bill Corrigan, who was also serving ten years for armed robbery.

Upon her son's release in 1989, Victoria Crawford did everything in her power to treat his problems. She took him to more than a half-dozen psychiatric centres across the province, none meeting with any success. In fact, John's mental health seemed to be worsening. In the summer of 1992, after binging for days on paint-thinner, pot, and booze, a shaky, slurring Crawford checked himself into the Royal University Hospital, complaining he was depressed and couldn't sleep.

At one point he mistook a book for a telephone. On another he picked up a surgical instrument from the emergency room table claiming he wanted to listen to music. During that same year, he strangled two local women unconscious and raped them, including a hitchhiker. Afraid of the repercussions, neither woman reported the attack, leaving Crawford free to rape again. With his mind disintegrating daily, it would not be long before "The First Nations Killer" returned to the worst of his habits.

John Martin Crawford mugshot.

Saskatoon Police Service.

STRANGLED

Sometime around September 20, 1992, John Martin Crawford murdered his third Aboriginal prostitute. He had spent the previous two days shooting Ritalin and Talwin, drinking, smoking cannabis, and popping Valium. On the night of the murder, he met pretty Eva Taysup at the Barry Hotel. They shared a beer and it wasn't long before she disclosed the fact that she was a prostitute and asked him if he wanted a date.

Crawford agreed, and after purchasing a case of beer from the hotel off-sale, drove her to an old cement factory where they continued to drink, smoke weed, and take Valium. Later in an affidavit, Crawford claimed he and Eva had consensual sex three times stopping only to buy chocolate milk and Pizza Pops. At 5:00 a.m., the sky began to pale and Eva asked to be driven back downtown. When she demanded $150 for her services, Crawford refused, instead offering $50. After all, he reminded her, he had been the one who bought all the booze. Furious, Eva allegedly threatened to accuse him of rape, prompting Crawford to strangle her to death.

"I remember just holding on to her because I didn't want to go to jail," Crawford later wrote. "I remember her hands on my arms trying to get me loose and her stomach moving up and down. I remember thinking 'She's only worth $50, I'm not going to jail. She has no right to live.'" During the trial it would be learned that Eva had suffered a broken rib and jaw. Stuffing her body into the trunk of his car, he drove ten miles to the outskirts of town where he attempted to dismember her with a saw. By the time Crawford had amputated her left arm at the elbow, he decided that it was taking too long. Besides, hard work wasn't really his thing. Instead he bundled the strangled twenty-five-year-old into a blanket, wrapping both with an extension cord, and buried her in a shallow grave. Back home, Crawford cleaned Eva's syrupy blood from the saw and fell into a deep sleep.

Less than twenty-four hours later, Crawford found himself with another mess to clean up, returning to the cement factory with twenty-two-year-old Calinda Waterhen for another round of drugs, booze, and fornication. When they had finished, Calinda allegedly threatened to tell police Crawford had abducted her unless he paid an additional $55. Enraged, he strangled her to death, driving the body out to the same place Eva Taysup lay buried, and hiding the corpse beneath a pile of leaves.

SKELETONS

The weekend of October 1, 1994, was unseasonably warm in Saskatoon and Brian Reichert was traipsing through the bush. He had decided to go deer-spotting with a friend along the South Saskatchewan River on a property owned by farmer Bill Hnatiuk. An employee at the AgPro Grain Terminal, Reichert had expected to sight a deer or mule, but certainly not a human skull! Excited, he beckoned to his friend. Nearby, the two men found more bones in the grass, along with tufts of dark human hair. Even more bizarre was the presence of colourful ribbons, tobacco pouches, and blessed cloth: traces of an Aboriginal spirit ceremony. Not wishing to get involved with the police, Reichert spent the remainder of the day debating whether or not to report his discovery. That night he telephoned the 8th Street RCMP detachment.

Early the next morning, Reichert met Constable Terry Stirling at the turn-off to the Moon Lake Golf and Country Club, and led him three kilometres to the dump site near Paradise Beach (a.k.a. "Bare Ass Beach"). Stirling photographed the remains before calling Dr. Ernie Walker, a forensic anthropologist and professor at the University of Saskatchewan. If there was anyone in the province qualified to identify a skeleton, this doctor was the man. As a true testament to his character, Walker refused to accept monetary compensation for assisting the police. On October 4, the busy doctor was finally able to examine to the dump site. Immediately he determined by the hair and scraps of soft tissue that the remains were recent rather than historical, probably belonging to a woman in her early twenties. By the end of the day, forensics had recovered 90 percent of her skeleton.

As Walker and police were busy working to uncover the identity of the victim, a second discovery was made. Fifteen kilometres west of the city, an old man thought he spotted a deer in a glade while taking his morning stroll down a gravel road. Drawing nearer, he realized to his astonishment that he had stumbled upon the nude body of a Native woman. A plastic bag pulled over her head seemed to blur her features, robbing her of face and identity. Soon after, police arrived to process the crime scene and remove the body. She was identified as mother of two, Janet Sylvestre, originally from La Roche, Saskatchewan.

Following a gut instinct, Corporal Robert Todd was searching thirty or forty metres near the Moon Lake site on October 21 when he saw something white embedded in the earth: a human skull. The RCMP now quietly suspected they may have had happened upon a mass grave. If so, it meant that Saskatoon had its first serial killer in nearly twenty years. The area was divided into three-metre strips and searched meticulously. By the end of the day, Constable John Hudak had found a third skull half-buried in the dirt. Four women now lay dead, and though the authorities couldn't say for sure who was responsible, they were certain of one thing: the perpetrator would kill again.

Eighty-five percent of the second skeleton was eventually recovered. Unlike the others, it had been left out in the open to rot. Walker identified it as belonging to a teenaged girl of First Nations descent. Of the three bodies discovered at Moon Lake, the third was the most intact. The killer had hurriedly wrapped his victim in a blanket and extension cord before burying it in a shallow grave. Her left arm had been amputated at the elbow.

When an artist's reconstruction of the three Moon Lake victims was released to the public in November, the identities of the women soon became clearer. The youngest of the three victims was Shelley Napope. Born on July 31, 1976, into the world of the One Arrow Reservation, Shelley was placed in foster care on several occasions due to her parents' excessive drinking. Her father Hubert was employed arranging jobs for Native criminals who wished to work off their fines rather than pay. It would be a profession that took its toll. One summer, the Napope family spent a month picking sugar beets in Alberta, only to find their house so badly vandalized upon returning that it was scheduled for demolition. When a year passed and no new home was built, the family moved to Saskatoon where housing was more readily available. There Shelley fell into problems at school, skipping class and resisting the authority of her teachers. Though her parents did their best to help her, Shelley's rebelliousness only worsened. At fourteen she became a ward of the social services. Two years later, she was walking the streets.

Eva Taysup had come from a strict family in Saskatchewan's Yellow Quill First Nation. The reserve was notorious for crime, and the Taysups were determined to shield their daughters from bad influences. Despite their efforts, Eva began to rebel at seventeen, running away on more than one occasion. Between 1985 and 1989 she gave birth to four children by her boyfriend Ian Gardypie. The pressures of raising such a large brood on inadequate wages led to the dissolution of the family in 1991. The children went to live with various relatives and Eva fell into a lifestyle of partying and prostitution based out of the Barry Hotel.

Eva's story bears a resemblance to Calinda Waterhen's. On October 11,

1991, the Cree woman gave birth to a baby girl, Amber, at the Pine Grove Correction Centre. A month later, mother and daughter were released into the care of Calinda's parents. Immediately, Steven Morningchild noticed a disturbing change in his daughter's personality. Calinda would sit placidly for long periods only to suddenly jump up screaming. She had even punched a hole through the wall. Steven attributed these psychological problems to her prison experimentation with a Ouija board. He believed that a malevolent spirit had followed Calinda out of captivity, and was driving his daughter to madness. Less than a week after her release, she left her baby in the loving arms of her grandparents, and drifted east to Saskatoon where she supported herself through prostitution. October 1991 would be the last time Amber Waterhen saw her mother alive.

CHASING THE DRAGON

The RCMP decided to build the case around an obese drug addict named John Martin Crawford. In July 1993, Corporal Stan Lintick had received a call from one of his most valued snitches. Normally, Lintick might have resented being interrupted on his vacation, but this time Bill Corrigan didn't want to talk about cigarette smuggling — he wanted to discuss murder. Corrigan claimed that a friend named John Martin Crawford and one "John Potter" had killed an indigenous prostitute named Angie. On August 25, 1993, he drove with Lintick, a police dog, and its handler to the dump site, but the animal failed to discover anything significant.

When the first skeletons appeared just over a year later, Lintick tracked Corrigan to Winnipeg where he was working as a crossing guard. During a heavy questioning session at a Winnipeg hotel, he gradually wore through Corrigan's shield of lies, confirming that John Potter had been a fabrication. In his subsequent statement, Corrigan implicated Crawford in the murders. A quick search of police records brought another startling revelation: Crawford's conviction for the slaying of Mary Jane Serloin in Lethbridge, Alberta. Furthermore, he had been charged on May 9, 1992, with raping an Aboriginal woman near his mother's home. The woman, who failed to appear in court, was none other than Janet Sylvestre. In August of that same year, police found a semi-comatose Crawford lying naked from the waist down at Bare Ass

Beach. He had been severely sunburned, and was running a fever of 110 degrees Fahrenheit. Pronounced dead at St. Paul's hospital, he was revived through the determination of the staff and entered into a detox program. Two months later, he spent a year in jail for nearly battering to death a man who had refused him a cigarette. According to guards at the institution, he had passed the entirety of his sentence eating and masturbating. Everyone in the RCMP agreed: John Crawford was a nut. He was placed immediately under Special O surveillance.

Within the first two days, it became alarmingly clear that Crawford was what prostitutes called "a bad trick." At 8:00 p.m. on October 11, 1994, he solicited a visibly intoxicated Native woman off the curb and drove her out to a storage lot. The surveillance vehicles followed in silent pursuit. Minutes later, Crawford sped off, leaving the battered woman struggling to see out of her swollen eyes. Despite her unbuckled pants she denied being raped when questioned. The police threw her in the drunk tank, hoping to intimidate the real story out of her, but were forced to release her the next morning. Two days later, the body of Janet Sylvestre was found, followed in a week by a third and fourth victim.

At this point in the investigation, it was decided that Bill Corrigan would go undercover. Having agreed to receive $15,000 in exchange for his total co-operation with the police, the pot-bellied informant had very little choice. Wired up with a microphone, transmitter, and audio recorder, he was able to tape Crawford admitting to the murders of Shelley Napope, Eva Taysup, and Calinda Waterhen. Interestingly, his gluttonous chum repeatedly denied any involvement in the Janet Sylvestre slaying. When Crawford expressed concern about the body he had wrapped with an extension cord and blanket, details the RCMP had intentionally withheld, the police had all the evidence they needed to make an arrest. On January 19, 1995, John Martin Crawford was apprehended driving along Avenue M south and charged with the Napope, Taysup, and Waterhen slayings.

At his subsequent trial, Crawford's defence would unsuccessfully attempt to shift the blame onto Bill Corrigan. Crawford was convicted on one count of first-degree murder for the killing of Shelley Napope, and two counts of murder in the second for Eva Taysup and Calinda Waterhen. Judge Wright condemned him to a life imprisonment with eligibility for parole in twenty-five years. Besides being the prime suspect in the smothering murder of Janet Sylvestre, Crawford has also been implicated in the disappearances of natives Shirley Lonethunder and Cynthia Baldhead.

Other Serial Killers Who Have Targeted Prostitutes:
Sam Pirrera, James Greenidge, Keith Hunter Jesperson, Dr. Thomas Neill Cream, The Edmonton Serial Killer, Robert Pickton, The Hemlock Valley Murders, The Calgary Prostitute Slayer, The Prostitutes-in-the-Lake Killings, Niagara's Prostitute Murders, Gilbert Paul Jordan

Toronto's Gay Village Murders (Unsolved)
2 Murders
Schomberg/Balsam Lake, Ontario

NAKED AND BOUND

By December 17, 1967, the Summer of Love was over, blown apart like brittle leaves in the cold gales of an Ontario winter. In Balsam Lake Provincial Park, a remote, forested area 145 kilometres north of Toronto and south of Highway 48, the skeletal remains of a male Caucasian were discovered lying nude, save for a pair of white, size-seven tennis shoes. The man's hands were bound with eleven feet of twine, leading detectives to conclude he had been the victim of foul play. Autopsy results revealed the Balsam Lake victim had lain in the spot for about six months prior to his discovery. Besides his notably small stature (five feet, three inches), there were a number of physical abnormalities that distinguished him from the norm: a thirteenth thoracic vertebra and additional thirteenth rib on his right side. Despite these oddities, the man, estimated at between fifteen and twenty-two years of age, would go unidentified for another forty-two years.

On May 15 of the following spring, a farmer plowing his field forty-one kilometres north of Toronto, near Schomberg, Ontario, noticed a sickening odour emanating from the vicinity of his septic tank. Trudging over to investigate, he stumbled upon a second decomposing body concealed in a hedgerow by a fence. Bound with shoelaces and lying prone, what little skin clung to the naked victim's scalp had dried and blackened. In an impressive feat of behavioural profiling (the practice would not become commonplace until the eighties), the Ontario Provincial Police managed to connect this body to the Balsam Lake victim. Unfortunately, like his predecessor, it would take a substantial period of time before the true identity of the Schomberg John Doe would come to light.

MAKING FACES, GETTING NAMES

In 2006, the Ontario Provincial Police decided to re-examine the murders, employing Master-Corporal Peter Thomson, a forensic artist trained at the FBI's academy in Quantico, Virginia, to mold clay reconstructions of the faces. They released details of the murders to the public, hoping that the combination of this information with photographs of the reconstructed faces would eventually pay off. This time, it did. Two east coast residents contacted the OPP independently to report that the Schomberg-area victim bore a startling resemblance to their friend and relative "Dickie" — missing for nearly forty years!

Seventeen-year-old guitarist Richard Hovey had left Marysville, New Brunswick, in 1967 to pursue his dream of becoming a rock-and-roll star in Toronto's happening Yorkville neighbourhood. He began to play regularly at a local coffee house called the Mynah Bird, his blond bangs, jackets, and turtlenecks reflecting his predilection for earlier British invasion-style bands over the increasingly popular psychedelic movement. When Dickie stopped sending letters to his parents Melvin and Phyllis, they reported his disappearance to the RCMP, though the agency ineptly failed to file a missing persons report. By the time DNA testing had confirmed the body found near Schomberg in 1968 was that of their son, both of Dickie's parents had passed away.

Another three years would elapse before the Balsam Lake victim was identified as eighteen-year-old Eric Jones of Noelville, Ontario. Born into a family of eleven children, Jones had dropped out of high school to live with his aunt in Toronto, labouring as a dishwasher in a local restaurant. The last time he had seen his family was at a sister's wedding in April 1967, where he had argued with his brother about his decision to move downtown. Like Dickie Hovey, it was an abrupt halt in the exchange of letters between

Eric and his sister that marked the time of his disappearance. Forty-two years later, in February 2009, that same sister, Pauline Latendresse, would recognize her brother's face from a clay reconstruction shown on television program *W-Five* and contact the police.

Reasonably early in the OPP's reopening of the investigation, they had begun to suspect that Richard Hovey and Eric Jones might have been involved in Toronto's gay scene. Speaking with a homosexual seniors' social club dubbed "Prime Timers" in 2006, police learned that both Eric and Dickie were last seen climbing into a light blue Corvair. The driver had been a strong-looking African Canadian, and given the choice of vehicle and terrible fate which befell his passengers, the most likely suspect was convicted serial killer **James Henry Greenidge**. Despite the startling similarities to Greenidge's crimes, officially the Toronto Gay Village Murders remain unsolved.

Other Serial Killers Who Have Targeted Gay Men:
James Henry Greenidge, Ron Sears, Michael McGray

Donald Sherman Staley
The Sex Pervert
2 Murders
Vancouver, British Columbia/Calgary, Alberta

"I am guilty, sir, but I am not responsible for my actions. I wish to be interviewed by a psychiatrist."

THE SUMMER OF 1946
It was a sunny Fourth of July in Vancouver when eight-year-old Bobby Sherman and Garry Billings, eleven, headed to Stanley Park Beach to cool off. As the two friends splashed in the cold saltwater, enjoying the first summer without war in six years, they were approached by a pleasant young soldier who offered to buy them peanuts and popcorn.

The unlikely trio spent the better part of an afternoon together, indulging in salty snacks and ice cream, even chatting amicably with an RCMP constable. The young soldier told the constable that his name was Donald Sherman Staley and that he had recently been discharged from the Scottish regiment. Before they parted ways, Staley handed the boys some money and promised to have more for them if they came back to see him at noon the following day. To Bobby Sherman and Garry Billings it must have seemed like a dream come true. In fact, they were so excited about the experience, they regaled their parents with tales of the generous man who had bought them treats and ridden partway home with them on the streetcar. Neither mentioned their plans to meet with him again. The next day Bobby showed up late to Garry's house to find that the older boy had left for the beach without him. His disappointment soon turned to concern when weeks later there was still no sign of his friend. It was as if Garry Billings had been swept away with the tide.

Nineteen days later, another innocent child disappeared on Calgary's St. George Island. Six-year-old Donnie Goss, the third of four brothers, had been playing with some other children by the swings. Within twenty-four hours, his body was located by police; beaten about the head, throat, and chest, stabbed nine times, and abandoned behind some bushes. Simultaneously, the decomposing corpse of Garry Billings was unearthed from a shallow grave in Stanley Park. Like Goss, Billings had been savagely knifed to death, his body secreted beneath some logs in a nearby grove. Perhaps most grotesquely, both boys had been sexually assaulted before and after death.

CONNECTIONS

Frank Saunders had met Donald Sherman Staley on the Île de France when they were returning to Canada to be discharged from the army. In July, the two reunited in Vancouver and decided to move into a rooming house together in Calgary. Saunders soon found a job, and whenever he returned from work, Staley would read aloud to him from the newspaper. Staley had shown a peculiar interest in the murder of Donnie Goss, his voice becoming nervous and high-pitched as he relayed the latest developments in the case. When the newspaper reported that a man named Paul had been arrested for the slaying, Staley remarked that the police were wrong in focusing on an older individual. At the time, Saunders thought nothing of it.

On August 8, Staley broke into the Diamond Cafe at 233 9th Avenue E, making off with some cigarettes and other small items. Though he would escape the wrath of Jung Tai, the iron-bar wielding tenant who lived downstairs, four days later he was arrested for the theft by Calgary detectives. Pleading guilty to shop-breaking, and with a previous record for indecency, house-breaking, and mail theft, Staley was sentenced to one year in Lethbridge jail.

Meanwhile, back in Vancouver, authorities had been building a solid case against him for the murder of Garry Billings. Identified by both Bobby Sherman and the RCMP constable who had spoken with him on July 4, they had collected Staley's photograph, fingerprints, and army record, and were waiting for him to resurface in order to make an arrest. When word came that he had been incarcerated in Lethbridge, detectives from Vancouver arrived at the jail on August 17, where they began to press him about the murder of Garry Billings. To their surprise, Staley not only confessed to the Vancouver slaying, but also to the stabbing death of Donnie Goss on St. George Island.

In the case of Billings, he had met the boy at 11:50 a.m. and walked with him around the park for an hour before enticing him into the bushes with the promise of a dollar. There he proceeded to sexually assault the eleven-year-old, choking him unconscious and stabbing him to death with a four-inch paring knife. Placing the body in a hollow, he engaged in post-mortem sex with the child's corpse before concealing it under logs and bushes.

Staley had refined certain elements of his modus operandi during the second killing. Using the same ruse to lure Donnie Goss to a remote area of the island, he struck the six-year-old with a blackjack, but failed to subdue him, bursting the weapon and scattering buckshot about the area. The two continued to struggle before Staley drove his blade into Donnie's body, rendering him helpless. With the blond-haired child lying dead before him, Staley sexually assaulted the body before leaving it to rot in the summer heat.

DEPRAVITY ON TRIAL

By the time Donald Sherman Staley went to trial in Calgary on Monday,

September 30, 1946, his story had changed dramatically. While he still accepted responsibility for the slayings, he claimed he did not intend to murder the children and had gone temporarily insane. On the afternoon of October 3, he took the stand in his own defence, revealing a troubled childhood. Donald Staley was born in Bracebridge, Ontario, on June 13, 1917. His mother died when he was three years-old, and he claimed to have no memory whatsoever of his birth father. Following his mother's passing, he was placed into an orphanage in Hespeler, Ontario, and adopted by the Ansty family two years later. He would spend half of the next six years with his new family and half at the orphanage, owing to his predisposition for theft and running away. Around the age of seven or eight, Staley had his first sexual experiences while at the orphanage. As the Anstys never spoke about the birds and the bees to their children, he was unaware of the stigma attached to these acts, slowly sowing the seeds of pedophilia deeper and deeper into his psyche. At the age of eleven, the Anstys enrolled him in Mimico Industrial School with the expectation that it would straighten him out. Staley left the institution by the age of sixteen, enlisting in the military in Vancouver eight years later on July 8, 1941. Within a month he was shipped overseas to serve.

His military record, presented as evidence at his trial, showed a history of insubordination. The first incident came on January 4, 1942, when Staley was convicted for being AWOL and sentenced to ten days' field punishment. A second reprimand for absence and theft followed on July 21, 1943, only this time he was sentenced to fifteen months' detention, 132 days of which were later remitted. During his stint in the army, Staley was treated for flat feet, then hospitalized in November 1942 for primary syphilis and gonorrhea. He was first taken into civilian custody in April 1945, and held at Winchester prison where he served eighteen months of penal servitude for a charge under the Offences Against the Person Act.

Clasping and unclasping his hands nervously from the witness stand, Staley admitted to harbouring deviant sexually sadistic desires throughout his teenage and early adult years and was always afraid that he would kill somebody (though his fears didn't stop him from carrying the paring knife which he used to commit his murders). These fantasies eventually culminated in the stabbing death of Garry Billings in Vancouver. Though Staley claimed his vision went black during the murders, the prosecution was easily able to disprove his claims of temporary insanity. Having been soaked with blood during the slaying of Garry Billings, Staley had changed his modus operandi during the Goss murder, using the child's own clothes to block the blood seeping from his wounds. This was clear evidence that he was thinking rationally.

In the end, Donald Sherman Staley was convicted by a jury of his peers and sentenced to hang. His attorney made a passionate appearance before Alberta's Supreme Court, seeking a reprieve on the basis that if his client did not meet the definition of insanity, then nobody did. Despite his efforts, on December 18, 1946, Staley was executed alongside four German prisoners of war in what was the largest public hanging in Canadian history.

Other Serial Killers Who Have Targeted Children/Infants: Edward Rulloff, Gordon Stewart Northcott, Peter Woodcock, Clifford Olson, Léopold Dion, Earle Nelson, David Threinen, Sukhwinder Dhillon, Lila and William Young, Michael McGray, Michael Vescio

Kay Feely.

Allan Legere
The Monster of Miramichi
5 Murders
Miramichi Area (New Brunswick)

"Lucifer is very powerful since nobody believes in him anymore. Only when they are scared do they pray!"

MANHUNT
On Wednesday May 3, 1989, convicted murderer Allan Legere escaped. Earlier that morning, guards had arrived to transfer him from the Atlantic

Institution in Renous, New Brunswick, to Moncton's Dumont Hospital where he would be treated for a chronic ear infection. They found the burly convict perched over the toilet. He informed them that he needed more time and they agreed. Ten minutes later, they returned, but soon after Legere was escorted from his cell he told them he had forgotten his watch and needed to go back. Again, they agreed. Astonishingly, he was then allowed to return to his cell on a second occasion, switching his slippers for sneakers and retrieving the daily newspaper and some old cigars. Of course, these activities were just a cover. Legere had slipped a folded television antennae into his rectum and was using the cigars to hide makeshift lock-picks.

When they arrived at the hospital, Legere complained that he needed to use the washroom. As was procedure, the guards escorted him inside, checked to ensure there were no other exits and then waited outside the door. Seconds later, it burst open and Allan Legere charged past them down the hospital corridor. The startled guards chased him outside into the parking lot where he was spotted by the prison van driver. The driver attempted to apprehend him, but Legere slashed out viciously with the antennae, screaming "Stay the fuck away!" Following the convict's advice, the driver ran back to his vehicle to radio for help. Another guard sprayed Legere with mace, missing his eyes. The frantic killer spotted a woman in her car waiting to pay for parking, wrenched open the driver's side door, and pushed her into the passenger seat. Taking control of the wheel, he slammed his foot hard on the accelerator and the vehicle broke through the exit barrier. Later, his hostage recalled how Legere's personality kept changing from polite and accommodating to angry and aggressive. He eventually dropped her off several blocks away, then ditched her car in the parking lot of a west end radio station. It was an area Legere was familiar with; he had been on the lam there for burglary in 1982 — not that he planned on sticking around.

CHILDHOOD

Allan Legere first drew blood on Friday February 13, 1948, when he tore through his mother Louise into the world of Chatham Head, New Brunswick. At thirteen pounds, he was a colossal baby and later in life his strength and fortitude would astound the authorities. Unfortunately, his natural intelligence and raw athleticism could not save him from a troubled childhood. Born illegitimate and into incredible poverty, Allan was the product of Louise's affair with Lionel Comeau, a violent drunk who once tried to break down the door to the family home with an axe. The true patriarch of the family, Vincent Legere, was another vicious man who had abandoned his wife and three children (Allan's older siblings) after returning from the Second World War, and was rumoured to be living in Halifax. In time, Lionel Comeau would follow suit, leaving Louise to provide for the children herself. Tragically, in 1956, Allan's older brother Freddy was killed when a car struck him from behind as he was crossing the Morrissey Bridge. The Legeres were too poor to push the case, and Freddy's killer was never convicted. As a result, the family developed a profound mistrust of the police. Allan was nine years old. Later in life, Louise would reputedly tell him that she wished he had died instead of Freddy.

Though most remember Allan Legere as a quiet, obedient boy, he was known by others to exhibit antisocial behaviour. One Chatham Head resident recalls that Allan would smile and wave, only to throw stones at her when she turned away. He also failed grade nine twice, preferring to focus his efforts on weightlifting. At sixteen, he began breaking into local homes, sometimes robbing them; mostly just to see if he could move around unseen. Legere bragged to his friends of fondling sleeping women at motels. He was arrested twice between 1964 and 1966, spending eighteen months and fifteen days in jail for theft.

Marrying a psychiatric assistant in the late sixties, Legere and his bride moved to North Bay, Ontario, where he fathered two children and found work as a machinist. By 1972, the family had returned to the Miramichi and he was hired on by the local sawmill. Unfortunately, he lost the job when he was sentenced to five months for possession of stolen goods.

Allan Legere emerged from jail with the belief that he could only survive as a criminal. Perhaps to cement his commitment to chaos and evil, he developed an interest in Satanism, demonology, and hard drugs. There is a legend that he entered a Baptist church one Sunday dressed only in cut-off jeans, announcing that he was Jesus Christ and that the congregation were damned to Hell. He also obsessed over his appearance, spending more and more time weightlifting, and showering multiple times a day. Predictably, Legere's marriage would not survive his hellraising lifestyle. In 1973 his wife moved to Ottawa, taking their son and daughter with her. This seems to have been the stressor that pushed Legere over the edge. A year later, he was questioned regarding the murder of Chatham Head resident Beatrice Mary Redmond. Returning from church, Redmond had been ambushed, stabbed eighty times, and left bleeding on her own doorstep. Legere was never charged. Around the same time, he attempted to drive a metal hook through a workmate during an altercation and had to be restrained.

For Allan Legere and four other Miramichi residents, Saturday, June 21, 1986, would be the most important night of their lives. Around 9:00 p.m., sixty-six-year-old John Glendenning and his wife Mary closed and tidied the general store they had run together for the past thirty-five years. When everything was in its place, the couple strolled across the yard to their two-storey home. After jam and biscuits, John made a few phone calls while Mary sipped tea in her rocking chair. He had just switched on the TV in the living room when three armed men came crashing through the door. One of the intruders bashed him over the head with a rock, knocking the burly senior to the floor. Another man in a stocking mask pushed Mary into the kitchen, binding her to a chair, and beating her. When he left the room, she managed to wriggle free from her poorly-knotted bonds, all the time eyeing a mysterious older intruder who stood wordlessly in the doorway. As soon as the ropes had fallen, he seized her, gagged her with a rag, and attempted to shove her into a hall closet. The younger masked intruder tore off Mary's clothes and panties and began to fondle her. Meanwhile, the man who had assaulted John demanded the combination to their safe. Hoping to spare her husband further injury, Mary volunteered to open it herself. The other two men followed her upstairs into the bedroom where the money was kept. Mary was reaching to enter the combination on the dial when she was struck twice on the back of the skull and collapsed, unconscious. She awoke with her head in the toilet bowl. The house was empty. Bruised and barely able to see, Mary crawled to the phone and called the operator. Realizing that the woman on the other end of the line might die at any minute, the operator connected her to the local RCMP. They would arrive to find the floor covered in broken glass, and blood dripping from the ceiling.

Mary Glendenning was taken to Hotel Dieu Hospital in Chatham where she was treated for numerous injuries. Nearly her entire body was bruised, her right eye swollen shut, and a three-inch laceration was carved below her left ear. Both her nose and forehead had been broken, and there were several internal injuries, including a collapsed lung. Sometime during the carnage she had been brutally raped with a blunt object. Despite her wretched condition, Mary Glendenning would survive her ordeal. Her husband had been less lucky. John Glendenning was found bound and strangled to death in the master bedroom, a light brown shirt cinched so tightly around his neck that it had fractured his Adam's apple. He had sustained a horrendous beating, leaving his nose, jaw, and cheekbone broken.

Three days after the murder of John Glendenning, authorities arrested Allan Legere, now thirty-eight years old; Scott Curtis, twenty; and Todd Matchett, eighteen, in connection with the attack. Matchett and Curtis plead guilty in court on Thursday January 8, 1987, both hinting that Legere was responsible for the brunt of the violence. Legere denied being at the crime scene, though he admitted to garnering $15,000 from the burglary. At 10:30 a.m. on Thursday, January 22, a jury found him guilty of second-degree murder and he was sentenced to life imprisonment without the possibility of parole for eighteen years. By May 3, 1989, his patience was clearly exhausted.

THE MONSTER OF MIRAMICHI

After almost a month of searching, authorities began to wonder if Allan Legere had fled the province. Then, on the morning of May 29, 1989, a pedestrian in Chatham noticed smoke billowing from the windows of Annie Flam's home. A cherished and respected local figure, Annie had opened Flam's grocery store in 1939 and for fifty years had unfailingly begun work at eight in the morning, staying behind the counter until eleven every night. At seventy-five, she was one of the few remaining members of the Miramichi's once-thriving Jewish community and her soul-warming cups of tea and sympathetic ear were legendary. Alarmed, the pedestrian alerted the police and they kicked in the back door of her brother Bernie's adjoining home to discover it in flames. There they found Bernie's wife Nina sprawled at the foot of the staircase, badly burned, but still breathing. She was immediately whisked to a hospital bed in Fredericton. Hours later, with the house reduced to ruin, Annie's body was found amongst the ashes, charred beyond recognition. At first the police thought the fire had been set to cover a robbery, but upon speaking with Nina they learned that a masked man had entered the home sometime during the night and had sexually assaulted both of them before battering them to a pulp.

It was around ten at night on Saturday, September 30, when seventy-year-old Newcastle resident Morrissey Doran came face to face with an intruder. A stocky man in a black leather jacket and ski mask met him at the top of the stairs brandishing a shotgun. Doran fought valiantly, but was shot in the back and left for dead. Fortunately, he would survive his run-in with the man newspapers were now calling "The Monster of Miramichi." So would seventy-six-year-old Sonny Russell and his wife Evangeline. The night after the Doran attack, they heard somebody attempting to get in through their basement window. Strangely, even though the man managed to remove the window, he raced around to the back door and burst into the kitchen with a shotgun. Strong in his old age, Russell wrestled the man back outside where the assailant dropped his shotgun and ran south. By the time police arrived at the Russell's, another call was already coming in from Billy Matchett's house. Apparently somebody had tried to break into the residence. Billy was father to Todd Matchett, one of the other two men convicted in the 1986 murder-robbery, and it didn't take a genius to guess who the would-be intruder was. Naturally Allan Legere had vanished back into the wilderness well before the police showed up. He wouldn't reappear again until Friday, October 13.

Forty-five-year-old Linda Daughney and her sister, Donna, shared a blue, two-storey house in a working-class area of Newcastle, New Brunswick. They had grown up in a tumultuous atmosphere centred around their alcoholic father, Charlie. Though he didn't beat his daughters, he would lock them out of the house if they came home late, and would scream at them at the slightest provocation. Every Saturday morning his wife Willa would take the children down to the sawmill where he worked to pick up his paycheque before he drank it away. Over time, migration and death had reduced the family's presence in Newcastle to just the two daughters. Linda kept a close eye on her cripplingly shy sister who did not have the social skills to cope on her own. Neither sister was married — Donna was paralyzed by timidity and Linda claimed she didn't wish to ever be treated like her mother had been.

On the morning of Saturday, October 14, 1989, a volunteer firefighter noticed smoke billowing from the Daughneys' window and immediately alerted his colleagues. Rushing into the burning Mitchell Street home without oxygen masks, they found Donna lying upstairs on her bed with Linda beside her on the floor. Though they were able to promptly extinguish the inferno, it was too late to save the Daughney sisters. Donna had been mercilessly beaten to death, while Linda had survived her battering only to succumb to smoke inhalation. Both women bore traces of sexual assault. Later it was learned that on the same night, somebody had cut the television cable at the home of a Newcastle man, probably mistaking it for the phone line. There had also been a burglary just minutes from the Daughneys' home.

In the weeks following the Daughney double-murder, RCMP presence in the Miramichi region grew astronomically. Nobody doubted that the police were seriously committed to apprehending Allan Legere, although they still were uncertain if he was responsible for the recent rash of violent crime. The media descended like a pack of vultures, pushing microphones and cameras into the faces of frightened Miramichiers. In just a few months, a sleepy community where you could normally hear a pin drop had erupted like a volcano.

Sergeant Ernie Munden called a meeting three days after the latest murders to confirm similarities between the Flam and Daughney slayings, even imploring the criminal community to help in any way they could. Munden believed that somebody local was aiding Legere. Though he asked the public not to buy guns, his pleas went unheeded. People were simply too scared.

The events of November 16 would leave them more unsettled than ever. Worshippers at the Church of the Blessed Virgin in Chatham Head had arrived for the 7:00 p.m. sermon to find the church empty and in darkness. When the always-punctual Father Smith failed to appear after ten minutes, one parishioner let himself into the rectory to see if they could locate him. Instead they found mayhem. The kitchen table lay smashed to pieces. Blood soaked the walls and floor. Not wishing to cross the threshold, the parishioner yelled back for somebody to call the police. Within minutes, two RCMP cruisers screeched up to the curb. Sergeant Jacques Ouellette entered the rectory clinging to his flashlight like a crucifix against the unholy darkness. Wandering about, he came upon the study and stopped dead in his tracks. There in the middle of the floor, the bludgeoned body of sixty-nine-year-old Father Smith lay plastered in blood. Face slashed and ribs caved inward, "Slim Jim" died choking on his own vomit. He had followed Christ in life to a torturous death.

Examining the crime scene, investigators concluded that though Smith had been killed in the early morning, his attacker had waited until evening before absconding with the priest's 1984 Oldsmobile 88 Delta. The vehicle was soon located, abandoned at Bathurst train station. The attendant recalled selling a ticket bound for Montreal to a man matching Legere's description. Authorities in Quebec were contacted, and they intercepted the train at Lévis, undertaking a thorough search. One of the passengers, identifying himself as Ferdinand Savoie, looked uncannily like Legere, but when the police discovered he had no tattoos on his right forearm, they left to look elsewhere. Little did they know that there had been an error in communications — the tattoo was on Legere's left forearm! "The Monster of Miramichi" arrived unaccosted in Montreal, but did not stay for long. He wasn't through terrorizing his community yet and the Christmas season was right around the corner.

ENSNARING THE BEAST

It was snowing heavily in Saint John, New Brunswick, on the evening of Thursday, November 23: awful weather for driving. Still, to cabbie Ron Gomke it beat shopping-mall security. The twenty-one-year-old had been driving a taxi for three weeks now, and nights like this usually brought in the big bucks. Passing by Piper's Pub, he caught sight of a clean-shaven man in a parka trying to flag him down, and stopped to let him in. Once inside, the black-haired passenger requested to be taken to Moncton. When Ron asked him for the $100 fare up front, the man suddenly produced a sawed-off rifle from his bag, poking it into the young cabbie's ribs. With little option, Ron steered the car in the direction of Moncton.

"I'm the one they're looking for. I'm Allan Legere," he calmly announced. "If your dispatcher sends anyone, the moment the cruiser pulls us over, it's over for you."

As the taxi passed through the snowy streets of Saint John, the man continued to speak. "I'll let you go if everything goes smooth. I want to go to Chatham, stay in a motel until six o'clock, then I want to go to the airport and hijack a plane to Iran," he explained. "Those cops. You have to laugh. They thought they were so close. They're so easy to elude. I lived in the woods, made friends with the chipmunks and squirrels. Hell, they ate right out of my hand. It was getting colder. I couldn't stay in the woods, I had to keep moving."

During Legere's monologue, Ron did his best to appear co-operative, but once they reached Magnetic Hill on the outskirts on Moncton, he lost control of the vehicle and it crashed into a ditch. As luck would have it, a passing vehicle slowed to pick them up. The driver, off-duty RCMP officer Michelle Mercer, offered them a ride. Legere scrambled into the front seat and Gomke got into the back. Within minutes, Legere had turned the rifle on Mercer and ordered her to drive him to Chatham. Unfortunately, she was not familiar with the area, and missed the turnoff in the heavy snow. It was close to 2:00 a.m. and the vehicle was running out of fuel. With Legere's approval, they pulled into a gas station in Sussex. He seized $20 and the keys from Mercer, pumped the gas, and disappeared inside to pay. Little did he know she had a spare set of keys. Legere exited the station in time to see his transportation speed off into the night. Skirting around the side of the building, he found Brian Golding washing the windshield of his truck. Pointing the rifle at him, Legere ordered him to get moving. Minutes later a squadron of police cars converged on the Four Corners Irving Gas Station to find them already gone.

Miles down the road, Allan Legere ordered Golding to stop just outside Chatham. When he explained his plan to hijack a plane at the local airport, the trucker informed him that the planes were propeller-driven and would not be able to reach Iran. Not knowing what else to do, Legere instructed him to keep driving. Soon after, they pulled onto a secondary road to disconnect his flatbed trailer. Noting that tractor-trailers didn't use this road, a passing trucker reported their strange activity over his CB radio. By the time Golding's orange Mac reached Barnaby River Road, a police four-wheel drive appeared behind them flashing its lights.

"Keep driving!" Legere barked.

This time the courageous Golding had a better idea. Slamming on a button that locked the brakes, the truck came to a sudden halt and he leaped out of the door with his hands in the air.

"Don't shoot! I'm not Allan Legere!" he cried.

A shadowy figure stepped out of the cab behind him, and in a calm, clear voice declared, "I'm Allan Legere." After a seven-month reign of terror, "The Monster of Miramichi" had at last been defeated.

On August 26, 1991, Allan Legere stood before a Fredericton courtroom charged with four counts of first-degree murder. Shackled to a post in the courtroom floor, he frequently interrupted the proceedings to accuse the judge and jury of prejudice. On more than one occasion he was ordered to leave the courtroom and was permitted to return only if he apologized. Two days later, a jury of six men and six women found him guilty on all four counts. Today he is safely incarcerated at the Special Handling Unit of Montreal's Sainte-Anne-des-Plaines prison. He is eligible for parole in 2014.

Other Serial Killers Who Have Targeted the Elderly:
Melissa Ann Friedrich

The Highway of Tears (Unsolved)
Potentially 33+ Murders
Highways 5, 16, and 97 Area, British Columbia

HIGHWAY TO HELL

Between Prince Rupert and Prince George runs a lonely 724-kilometre stretch of road named Highway 16, which British Columbians have dubbed "The Highway of Tears." With disparate communities and farmhouses broken up by massive tracts of wilderness, the young rely almost entirely on hitchhiking to get around. By 1995, it had become alarmingly clear that one or more sexual predators was using this isolation to their own sick advantage.

It was December 13, 1974, when the first victim went missing. Fifteen-year-old Monica Ignas disappeared near Terrace only to be found on April 6 of the following year, half-naked and strangled in a gravel pit. Police believed she had been hitchhiking to Terrace along Highway 16 from her home on the outskirts of Thornhill. Fourteen years later, Alberta Gail Williams vanished from Prince Rupert. After a frenzied search, the twenty-four-year-old's body was finally found by hikers on September 25, 1989, dumped thirty-seven kilometres east of Prince Rupert, on the Tyee overpass. Alberta Williams had come to Prince Rupert earlier in the summer to work at a local fish cannery and August 26 was her last payday. To celebrate she had gone to Popeye's Pub with a group of friends, including her sister, Claudia. When the party left the bar at 2:30 a.m., Williams started off in the direction of the Greyhound building and was never seen again.

Last spotted thumbing rides along Highway 16 from Smithers to her Telkwa home, sixteen-year-old Delphine Nikal was next to vanish on June 13, 1990. Her cousin Cecilia, though not formally considered to be a Highway of Tears victim, had also gone missing the previous year. To this day, their fates remains a mystery.

At 9:00 p.m. on June 11, 1994, Ramona Wilson, sixteen, vanished while hitchhiking from Prince Rupert to meet her friend Crystal in Smithers, 210 kilometres to the east. The two girls had been planning to attend a dance later that night. When she failed to report for work or her baseball game, Ramona's mother Matilda Wilson contacted the police. They immediately dismissed her as a runaway. Left to their own devices, Ramona's family contacted the local media, postered, started a tip line, and tried to raise funds to aid in her search. Later that year, fifteen-year-old Roxanne Thiara disappeared from Prince George, only to be found murdered six kilometres from Burns Lake on August 17, 1994. Raised in a loving foster home in Quesnel, Roxanne had become addicted to narcotics in her teens and turned to streetwalking. She had informed friends she was going to meet a client shortly before her disappearance over the July long weekend. Ramona Wilson's remains were eventually discovered in early April 1995, in the proximity of the Smithers Regional Airport. Earlier, on January 27, the RCMP had received a phone call from a man stating that her body was "behind the airport," but after searching with dogs, had come up empty-handed.

At 11:45 p.m., on the evening of December 9, three teens stumbled across the body of Alishia Germaine while taking a shortcut across Haldi Road schoolyard. Earlier the girl had attended a Christmas party at the Native Friendship Centre on George Street, but left at 8:00 p.m. and was last seen at a Holiday Inn and at JC Funland. The Aboriginal sixteen-year-old, known to turn tricks as a prostitute to support her drug habit, was repeatedly stabbed to death. She had been friends with Roxanne Thiara. A composite drawing of the man she had been seen with that night led to the identification of a suspect who was subsequently cleared. Police continue to search for the owner of a dark blue pickup truck with a homemade canopy that was seen parked on Fifth Street, where some of Alishia's personal items had been recovered. Shy forestry student Lana Derrick, nineteen, was the next to vanish on October 7, 1995. She had returned home to visit her family in Thornhill for the weekend and was last spotted at a local service station. At 3:00 a.m., Lana had called a friend and told her she was partying with some people who had a car downtown. Nobody has seen her or heard word from her since.

Seven years passed sleepily on Highway 16, and many wondered if the killer or killers had died or since moved on. This made the June 21, 2002, disappearance of Nicole Hoar all the more shocking. The twenty-five-year-old Red Deer tree planter had disappeared while hitchhiking from Prince Rupert to her sister's Smithers home to see the Midsummer Music Festival. Despite a massive search and information campaign, she has never been located. Another victim, Native Canadian Melanie Dawn Brown, thirty-one, was discovered murdered in her Prince George basement apartment on December 8, 2004.

AWAKENING

By 2005, the people residing along Highway 16 had had enough. September 17 saw the mobilization of the "Take Back the Highway" campaign in which members of the communities from Prince Rupert to Prince George gathered to march, pray, and remember the victims. Perhaps the killer was paying attention, because four days later on September 21, Tamara Chapman was swallowed up by the stretch of highway from Prince Rupert to Terrace. The twenty-two-year-old had spent the past three days partying in Prince Rupert and was last seen hitchhiking eastbound near an industrial park around 4:30 p.m. Unfortunately, Chapman's family assumed she was either visiting relatives in the Lower Mainland or hiding from one of the warrants out for her arrest. As she often disappeared for days without telling them, they didn't report her missing until November 10. When the weeks dragged by without any activity in her bank account, it became more and more clear that something had happened to her. Desperate, her family began to search along the highways, stopping to look in every culvert along the way. Yet despite their efforts and those of the ten RCMP officers assigned to the investigation, Tamara Chapman has never been located. Amnesty International Canada stated she was the thirty-third woman to disappear along the Highway of Tears. That same fall the RCMP formed Project E-Pana (the Inuit name for the goddess who cares for souls before they ascend to heaven or reincarnate), an unsolved homicide unit charged with reviewing the deaths of Alishia Germaine, Roxanne Thiara, and Ramona Wilson to see if the homicides had been perpetrated by a single individual.

In the meantime, on January 16, 2006, another woman, twenty-two-year-old Crystal Okimaw, vanished from a Prince George women's shelter, never to be seen again. Just under a month later, a passing driver found what was left of fourteen-year-old Aielah Saric-Auger at a roadside some sixteen kilometres east of Prince George. She had stayed overnight at a friend's place in the city and was last spotted climbing into a black van on February 2.

At long last, two retired RCMP investigators who had worked the case told the *Prince George Citizen* that Aielah had fallen prey to a serial killer, the same man who had murdered Ramona Wilson, Roxanne Thiara, Alishia Germaine, and, potentially, Delphine Nikal. This announcement was a complete 180-degree turn from the opinion of two FBI-trained behavioural profilers who had joined the investigation for a week in 1995 and concluded that the murders were not connected. Furthermore, the investigators of Project E-Pana decided it was prudent to expand their investigation to include any other victim who was: 1) female 2) engaged in high-risk behaviour such as hitchhiking or prostitution, etc. 3) was last seen or found murdered within one mile of Highway 16. It was eventually determined that an additional six victims fit this criteria: Monica Ignas, Alberta Williams, Delphine Nikal, Lana Derrick, Nicole Hoar, and Tamara Chapman.

PROVINCE OF TEARS?

On Thursday October 11, 2007, the RCMP doubled the number of missing and murdered Highway of Tears women on their official list from nine to eighteen. This new list had broadened its scope to encompass earlier murders taking place on connecting Highways 5 and 97. The first was that of twenty-six-year-old Gloria Moody of Williams Lake. It had been on Saturday October 25, 1969, when the mother of two and her brother Dave had ventured downtown to drink in the Lakeview, Maple Leaf, and Ranch Hotel bars. Dave eventually returned to his hotel room, certain that his sister was behind him. When he turned to speak with her, he realized she was gone. Gloria Moody's body was discovered the next morning along a cattle trail ten kilometres west of Williams Lake. She had been stripped nude, sexually assaulted, and beaten until she bled to death, her clothes found nearby. In the summer of the following year, Quebecois hitchhiker Micheline Pare was dropped off at the gates of Tompkins Ranch by another stretch of Highway 97. Her body, found twenty-one kilometres away on August 8, revealed that the twenty-one-year-old had been bludgeoned to death with a blunt object, decomposing to the point where sexual assault could only be suspected.

The October 19, 1973, disappearance of Gale Weys, nineteen, from the Clearwater service station where she was employed, marked the first victim to be linked to Highway 5. Believed to have left around 9:30 p.m. to hitchhike home to Kamloops, Weys's nude, rotting body was found in a water-filled ditch eleven kilometres south of Clearwater and just off Highway 5 on April 6, 1974. She has since been described as "wholesome" with no known involvement in drugs. Another Kamloops teenager, Pamela Darlington, went missing on November 6, 1973. At 9:00 p.m. she had informed roommates that she was going to thumb a ride to a local bar. Within twenty-four hours her partially-clad, battered body was spotted face down in the Thompson River at Pioneer Park, savaged by bite marks. Investigators later learned that a passing train crew had noticed a rusty 1950s off-white or salmon pink Chrysler exiting the park and attempting to cross the tracks. When the train beat him to it, the driver quickly sped off toward the next crossing, but was too late again, proceeding to a third, which had been closed. As the train passed, the driver switched off his headlights, presumably to avoid being seen. In

September of 1974, the body of Colleen MacMillen was located beside a logging road twenty-five kilometres south of 100 Mile House. Like so many of the other victims, Colleen had decided to hitchhike to a friend's house in Lac La Hache, six kilometres away from home, and never arrived. Detective Mel Weisgerber, an investigator into the Pamela Darlington murder, had admitted that law enforcement examined the possibility of a serial killer involved in the Weys/Darlington/MacMillen slayings, but did not comment as to whether a connection was discovered.

At twelve years of age, Monica Jack is the youngest victim to make the RCMP's official "Highway of Tears" list. On May 6, 1978, having spent the day shopping, Monica was spotted riding her bicycle home to Lake Nicola along Highway 5 by her mother Madeline Lanaro, who offered the child a ride. Monica refused, saying she wished to bike it back. The next time anybody laid eyes on her was eighteen years later when forestry workers stumbled across her skeleton off a logging road in a Swakum Mountain ravine. Her remains had been dumped twenty kilometres from her abandoned bicycle, located by a search party in 1978, shortly after her disappearance. In 1996, police acknowledged they had a suspect, but lacked sufficient evidence to charge him.

The eldest victim linked to the the Highway of Tears, thirty-three-year-old Maureen Mosie's time came on Friday May 8, 1981, while attempting to hitchhike from Salmon Arm 110 kilometres to Kamloops along Highway 1. A woman walking her dog happened upon Maureen's battered corpse the next day, sixteen kilometres east of Kamloops. She had been murdered where she was found: at the end of a run-off lane leading to Highway 97. Investigators have confirmed there was no evidence of sexual assault.

Shelly Ann Bacsu, sixteen, is the only Alberta victim to appear on the list, vanishing while walking five kilometres home from her boyfriend's trailer along Highway 16. Though her remains have never been found, the discovery of her clothes and school books by the Athabasca River, along with two eyewitness reports of seeing somebody being pushed into a van at the time and place of her disappearance, May 3, 1983, near Hinton, leave little room for optimism.

To this day women continue to disappear at an alarming rate along Highway 16.

TABLE 2: RCMP'S OFFICIAL LIST OF "HIGHWAY OF TEARS" VICTIMS

KEY: * = Highway 97 victims

          # = Highway 16 victims

          ! = Highway 5 victims

Italics — Victims not initially included on Project E-Pana's list

NAME	AGE	LAST SEEN	FOUND	DETAILS
Gloria Moody*	26	Oct. 25, 1969/ Outside Ranch hotel in Williams Lake.	Oct. 26, 1969/10 kilometres west of Williams Lake on a cattle trail.	Murdered. Beaten and sexually assaulted. Naked, clothes nearby.
Micheline Pare*	18	Summer 1970/Gates of Tompkins Ranch between Fort St. John and Hudson's Hope.	Aug. 8, 1970/21 kilometres away.	Murdered. Beaten with blunt instrument. Possible sexual assault.
Gale Weys!	19	Oct. 19, 1973/ Service station in Clearwater.	April 6, 1974/ Water-filled ditch 11 kilometres south of Clearwater.	Murdered. Nude.
Pamela Darlington*!	19	Nov. 6, 1973/ Kamloops.	Nov. 7, 1973/ Thompson River at Pioneer Park.	Murdered. Beaten. Face-down in water, partially clothed.
Colleen MacMillen*	16	Aug. 9, 1974/ Near Lac la Hache.	Sept. 1974/25 kilometres south of 100 Mile House beside a logging road.	Murdered.
Monica Ignas#	15	Dec. 13, 1974/ Thornhill.	April 6, 1975/ In dense bush six kilometres northeast of Terrace.	Murdered. Half-nude and strangled in a gravel pit.

Monica Jack!	*12*	*May 6, 1978/ Highway 5 near Lake Nicola.*	*1995/Ravine off logging road on Swakum Mountain.*	*Murdered.*
Maureen Mosie*	33	*May 8, 1981/ Salmon Arm.*	*May 9, 1981/ Run off lane from Highway 97 near Highway 1.*	*Murdered. Killed at scene. Not sexually assaulted.*
Shelly Ann Bacsu#	16	*May 3, 1983/ Hinton, Alberta.*	*Only clothing and schoolbooks found near Athabasca River.*	*Still missing.*
Alberta Williams#	24	Aug. 27, 1989/ Prince Rupert	Sept. 25, 1989/ Tyee overpass, 37 kilometres east of Prince Rupert.	Murdered. Strangled and raped.
Delphine Nikal#	16	June 13, 1990/ Between Smithers and Telkwa.	No.	Still missing.
Ramona Wilson#	16	June 11, 1994/ Near Smithers.	Early April 1995/ Near Smithers Regional Airport.	Murdered. Family has been told by an insider that she was strangled and sexually assaulted.
Roxanne Thiara#	15	July 1–4, 1994/ Prince George.	Aug. 17, 1994/ Bush along Highway 16, six kilometres from Burns Lake.	Murdered.
Alishia Germaine#	16	Dec. 9, 1994/ Prince George.	Dec. 9, 1994/ Haldi Road schoolyard.	Murdered. Stabbed multiple times.
Lana Derrick#	19	Oct. 7, 1995/ Thornhill service station.	No.	Still missing.

Nicole Hoar#	25	June 21, 2002/ Near a gas station west of Prince George.	No.	Still missing.
Tamara Chapman#	22	Sept. 21, 2005/ Between Prince Rupert and Terrace.	No.	Still missing.
Aielah Saric-Auger#	*14*	*Feb. 2, 2006/ Prince George.*	*Feb. 10, 2006/ Roadside, 17 kilometres from Prince George.*	*Murdered.*

Other Serial Killers Who Have Targeted "Young People Who Have Left Home":

Clifford Olson, James Greenidge, Wayne Boden

RIGHT UNDER OUR NOSES:

Colonel Russell Williams and the Writing of this Book, Part 2

In the shock following the arrest of Russell Williams for the murders of Marie-France Comeau and Jessica Lloyd, the Canadian media began delving into the enigmatic colonel's past. A look at his early years revealed little out of the ordinary. David Russell Williams was born on March 7, 1963, in the English Midlands town of Bromsgrove, just southwest of Birmingham. Soon after, his mother Christine gave birth to a second son, Harvey, and the family uprooted to Deep River, Ontario. There his father David, a metallurgist, found work at Canada's most reputable nuclear research lab in nearby Chalk River. Located two hundred kilometres northwest of Ottawa, from its inception, Deep River was a highly planned and structured community brimming with middle-class professionals whose activities ranged from tennis and yachting to wife-swapping. It was through these nouveau sexual experimentations that David and Christine's relationship eventually crumbled, the latter filing for divorce in October 1969, citing her husband's adulterous relationship with Marilynn, wife of his best friend Jerry Sovka. An esteemed nuclear scientist, Jerry would in turn divorce Marilynn on the same grounds.

Following the Williamses' split, Russell and Harvey relocated to Petawawa with their mother. In a bizarre twist, within four months of the divorce, Christine remarried none other than Jerry Sovka, whose surname the brothers would adopt. Jerry landed a lucrative job at

Ontario Hydro, moving his family southwest to the Toronto suburb of Scarborough. Seven-year-old Russell was enrolled in a Montessori school, and during the next few years, the Sovkas moved house several times before settling into a large bungalow on the Scarborough Bluffs, overlooking Lake Ontario. At age fifteen, Russell began attending Birchmount Park Collegiate Institute. He studied piano and became a paperboy for the *Globe and Mail* — early signs of the determined work ethic that would later earn him such glowing commendations in the military. Yet all was not right in his world. Remembered as a quiet, well-mannered child, during his teens Russell's introversion mutated into an aloof smugness, leading many of his classmates to form the opinion that he felt superior to them.

In 1979, Jerry Sovka accepted a position overseeing a nuclear reactor project in South Korea, and the adolescent Russell spent the next three years pinballing between his family in Asia and the familiar isolation of Scarborough. From 1980 to 1982, Russell remained in Toronto, boarding at the prestigious Upper Canada College, where he completed his high school education, rubbing shoulders with many of Canada's future political leaders. As a prefect, he reported to Andrew Saxton — later a Conservative MP for North Vancouver. Though by no means unpopular, he continued to be anti-social, with the exception of school activities, focusing his energies on academics and mastery of the trumpet. When he graduated in 1982, his yearbook quote read: "If you have to ask what Jazz is, you'll never know."

Choosing to study economics and politics at the University of Toronto's Scarborough campus, Russ Sovka began referring to himself as "Russell Williams" again, and seemed to crawl out of his self-imposed shell. He became affectionately known to housemates as "the drill sergeant" for his rigid assigning of chores. Williams also developed a practical joke, later to take on much darker connotations, of hiding for hours in a fellow resident's closet, only to burst out suddenly and frighten them. The game caught on, and soon every tenant in the little brown brick townhouse was joining in enthusiastically. Nearing the end of his freshman year, Williams began his first serious relationship with a Japanese exchange student named Misa, becoming infatuated with her. Though they would remain together for two years, nobody could

Elizabeth Roth.

Colonel Russell Williams — an artist's rendtition.

recall witnessing an act of physical affection pass between them. When Misa eventually told Williams she no longer wished to see him, he was devastated, breaking down in tears in front of his friends. In a last-ditch attempt to salvage the relationship, he sent her roses, which she returned with an angry clarification that they were through.

Some have speculated that this rejection may have been the spark that lit Williams's fuse. During his time at U of T Scarborough there were a number of unsolved sexual assaults on campus. On one occasion, a woman was seized in the parking lot, dragged into a nearby valley, and raped. When police realized that **Paul Bernardo** was also studying economics on campus at the same time, rumours began circulating in the press that he and Williams were once friends. Little has come of these allegations since they surfaced in February 2010.

With his romance shattered, Williams began looking for something to fill the psychological void. He found it in the 1986 blockbuster *Top Gun*. Inspired by the film, he began training to fly planes at Toronto's Buttonville Airport. Aviation became his new true love, and upon graduating from U of T in 1987, he decided to forego politics and economics in favour of a career in the Royal Canadian Air Force. Earning his wings within three years, Williams would soar through the ranks of the military at lightning speed.

While training novices in Portage la Prairie, Manitoba, on June 1, 1991, he married Mary Elizabeth Harriman, who later became an associate executive director for the Canadian Heart and Stroke Foundation. By July 2009, Williams was a colonel presiding over CFB Trenton: the largest air force base in Canada. With a new home in the Ottawa suburb of Orleans, and a cottage just north of the base in Tweed, everything seemed to be going right. Yet, by January 2010, Colonel Russell Williams was being held at Quinte Detention Centre facing two charges of murder, sexual assault, forcible confinement, and break-and-enter. On April 3, he unsuccessfully attempted suicide by jamming a cardboard toilet paper roll down his throat. What had gone wrong?

Having already researched Chapter 2: Nature, Nurture, or Neither, I decided to scan Williams's childhood for the thirteen developmental problems contributing to the psychopathology of a serial killer. The first four: drug and alcohol abuse, psychiatric history, and criminal history, I wrote off immediately. Williams was as strait-laced as they come, no doubt contributing to his unparalleled rise through the military. There had been no reports of physical abuse or head trauma in his history, and rather than finding a "demon seed" in his genes, his family are, if anything, notably successful, law-abiding citizens. It is worth mentioning that Russell reportedly became estranged from his mother and brother Harvey following Christine's 2001 divorce from Jerry Sovka. This seems to imply a reverence for his stepfather, eliminating the negative male caretaker argument.

There were four developmental factors on the list which I wasn't as ready to rule out. The first was "sexual problems." Until his first year of college, there is no mention of Williams ever having had a serious girlfriend. At first I dismissed this as the same frustrated inability to meet women that many introverted intellectual males experience in their teens. Later, while watching an interview with the colonel's best friend, Jeff Farquhar, on CBC's *The Fifth Estate*, I learned that when Williams's relationship with Misa ended, not only was the subject off-limits to his closest friends, but, alarmingly, he did not date again for another ten years! Second, in light of Williams's implication in nearly a hundred fetish burglaries, along with the knowledge that he had forced his two sexual assault victims in Tweed to model lingerie, I began to suspect that Williams might be a transvestite. "Sexual problems" thus became the first item on the list of his developmental problems where I found myself placing a firm check mark.[1] In time it would transpire that Williams had admitted to police that he had not had sex with his wife "for years." It also occurred to me that as a young man he had spent a great deal of time alone. With his parents either dragging him around the world or abandoning him to colleges and boarding schools, it seemed likely that he was unable to establish meaningful emotional connections with friends or relatives. In a way, this was a form of passive unintentional psychological abuse, and though his family's wealth gave Williams opportunities for education and social advancement unavailable to most Canadians, to say that he had been "treated unfairly" would not be inaccurate. I therefore opted to give Williams half a point each in the categories of "psychological abuse" and "treated unfairly." Finally, my uncertainty regarding Williams's childhood relationship with his mother was answered in 2011 with the publication of Timothy Appleby's *A New Kind of Monster*. According to interviews conducted with her neighbours, Christine Williams/Sovka displayed signs of being emotionally distant, prudish, cold, and controlling. With this in mind, it is possible that Russell may have developed an early sense of rejection and resentment toward the female sex. This "negative relationship" with the birth mother combined with Williams's "sexual problems" and the two half-points I attributed to him in "psychological abuse" and "treated unfairly" reveals that he stood a 23 percent chance of becoming a serial murderer. Moving beyond developmental factors, I realized that if I were to understand Williams's unique psychology, I would have to study his crimes in detail. Fortuitously, he was entering a plea of guilty on all counts, and the first day of his trial was fast approaching.

TAXONOMY OF THE CANADIAN SERIAL KILLER

In the previous section, we looked at the evolution of serial killers over Canadian history, along with the biological, psychological, and social conditions that guide their development. By contrasting modus operandi with signature we have learned to distinguish how they "get away" with the crime from how they "get off" emotionally and/or sexually.

The following chapters will examine how the world's most respected criminologists have sought to classify serial killers, beginning with the FBI's now standard Organized/Disorganized/Mixed trichotomy, and continuing through Holmes and De Burger's six categories: Visionary, Missionary, Hedonist-Comfort, Hedonist-Lust, Hedonist-Thrill, and Power/Control. Both systems have been steeped in controversy, with many critics pointing out that serial killers, like all humans, are entirely unique, often amorphous, entities. Though we may study them as individuals and draw conclusions from their behaviour, any attempt to label them is inherently flawed.

Recently, proponents of Holmes and De Burger's taxonomy have sought to remedy these obvious flaws by proposing that a killer may be a hybrid of two or more types. One of the more commonly encountered hybrids is the Visionary-Lust slayer: a serial murderer who is propelled by some combination of psychosis and sexual desire. Perhaps his confused mental state prevents him from controlling his deviant urges. Another option is that he may be a lust-motivated killer who leaves a chaotic crime scene because he also happens to be schizophrenic. Although the example of **Russell Johnson** (Chapter 2) fits this model, for the purposes of this book we will be ignoring hybrids, focusing solely on Holmes and De Burger's original six categories. First, however, we will explore examples of the FBI's Organized/Disorganized/Mixed system.

CHAPTER 5

ORGANIZED/DISORGANIZED/MIXED

When FBI behavioural science pioneers Ressler, Burgess, Douglas, and Allen compiled their popular *Crime Classification Manual*, they divided "Category 130 Sexual Homicide" into three sub-sections: Organized, Disorganized, and Mixed. After interviewing thirty-six lust murderers for *Sexual Homicide: Patterns and Motives*, Ressler and Douglas began to see a correlation between the personalities and backgrounds of the killers, and the category of sexual homicide they committed. Psychotics like Herb Mullin and Richard Chase left trails of bizarre, erratic crime scenes; whereas sane, socially competent killers often abducted, killed, and disposed of their victims in three different areas. Examples of these latter types, the "organized" serial killers of America are the infamous Ted Bundy and John Wayne Gacy, while Fred and Rosemary West, "The Moors Murderers," and Steve Wright are notable British contributions. It has been said that werewolf-like disorganized killers have been around since time immemorial (consider the crimes of **Joseph LaPage** in Chapter 1), whereas organized lust murderers are a product of the twentieth century. The following table shows typical differences in the personality and modus operandi of the organized and disorganized offender. "Mixed" category killers such as Richard Ramirez may display a combination of traits from either column.

TABLE 3: THE ORGANIZED OFFENDER VS. THE DISORGANIZED OFFENDER[1]

TRAIT/BEHAVIOUR	ORGANIZED	DISORGANIZED
Intelligence	Average or better	Low to average
Social Skills	Competent	Immature
Work History	Prefers skilled work	Poor work history
Sexual Disposition	Competent	Incompetent
Birth Order	High	Low
Father's Work History	Stable	Unstable
Childhood Discipline	Inconsistent	Harsh
Mood During Murder	Controlled	Anxious
Alcohol During Murder	Yes	No
Stressor	Yes	No
Living	With partner	Alone or with parent
Mobility	Car	Lives near crime scene
Follows Crime in Media	Yes	No
Post Crime Behaviour	May change jobs or move	No change in behaviour
Preparation	Planned	Spontaneous
Familiarity with Victim	Stranger	Known or location of crime known
Attitude Toward Victim	Personalizes. Has controlled conversation. Needs submission.	Depersonalizes. Minimal conversation. Sudden attack.
Use of Restraints	Yes	No
Sexual Assault Occurs	Prior to death	After death (necrophilia)
Body disposal	Hidden. Transports body.	In plain view where killing occurred.
Evidence at crime scene	Absent. No weapon.	Evidence and weapon present.

The necessity of including a "mixed" category has led many to question the usefulness of the organized/disorganized system. Rather than lumping a killer into one of these three groups, perhaps it is better to view him as being somewhere on a gradient between the two extremes.

With that said, the following six Canadian serial killers each provide examples from the organized, disorganized, or mixed trichotomy. Montreal sexual sadist **Angelo Colalillo**'s modus operandi was so perfectly sculpted that police hadn't even realized his first two victims had been murdered. Likewise, **David Threinen** concealed the bodies of four children so well that until he was arrested, all were being treated as disappearances.

On the opposite end of the spectrum, Thunder Bay's **Braeden Nugent** spontaneously attacked and battered two middle-aged men to death, making no effort whatsoever to cover his tracks. **Carl Hall** was in such a state of drug-induced confusion during his murders that he not only left mountains of evidence, but mixed up the details of his two crimes when questioned.

Somewhere between the two poles we find mixed offender **Donald Armstrong,** who started with sloppy, impulsive attacks on women in public places, but, after killing, calmed enough to stage the crime to look like an accident. The chapter concludes with mutilation murderer **Danny Wood**, who showed some level of organization by binding his victims and sexually assaulting them while they were still alive. On the other hand, his erratic lifestyle and single crime scene locations are more in keeping with the disorganized mindset.

Angelo Colalillo
3 Murders
Montreal, Quebec

KILL AND TELL

Rivière-des-Prairies lies in the far northeast corner of Montreal — a sleepy landscape of subdivisions, fields, and forests. Named after the Ottawa River delta that defines its northern border, it is home to a mostly Italian and Haitian population. Unlike the blue-collar Francophone areas that surround it, Rivière-des-Prairies is Liberal and anti-separatist. It was into this world that Jessica Grimard stepped on the afternoon of May 7, 2002. Pretty and blond, in recent years her body had begun to change shape, slowly blossoming into womanhood. Walking home from school, her long hair bouncing in the mid-spring sun, the fourteen-year-old would have looked radiant. Maybe this is what caught her killer's attention. Or perhaps it was her vulnerability. Whatever his reasons, the balding man managed to intercept Jessica while in sight of her home, dragging her into the trees. There he forced himself upon her, brutally raping her. That evening, when Jessica failed to return home, her father set out on foot to find her. He finally happened upon her body after dark; she had been stabbed repeatedly and dumped in a creek, her life seeping from her wounds in warm clouds of blood. Overnight, the mood in Rivière-des-Prairies turned to one of fear.

Eleven days after the Grimard murder, thirty-eight-year-old cell-phone salesman Angelo Colalillo wrote to his prison buddy Nick Paccione at Port Cartier Penitentiary. It was nothing new — he had been sending the convict letters for years now. Mostly they detailed his various ruses for luring young girls, along with some tips for removing evidence. One of his favourite tricks was to set fire to the crime scene, which, aside from making the death look like a tragic accident, also destroyed DNA. The letters contained boastful descriptions of his crimes rewritten from a third person perspective. The character of Colalillo in the stories had been thinly disguised as "Bob." When the warden at Port Cartier intercepted some of this mail containing clear references to the Grimard murder, he informed police. They confirmed that the letter contained information only the perpetrator could know. Colalillo was promptly arrested, and any previous correspondence between him and Paccione was confiscated. It soon became obvious that Jessica Grimard's murder was not the only skeleton in Angelo's closet.

ACCIDENTS HAPPEN

In February 1993, police and emergency services responded to reports of a domestic fire at the apartment of Hans and Lucie Speich. Sadly, though they arrived in time to save the structure, the Speichs' daughter Christine perished in her bed. The twelve-year-old had been up all night working on a class project, and, in a horrible stroke of luck, had stayed home from school to sleep. Faulty wiring was determined to be the cause of the blaze. The Speichs buried their child, and the incident was soon forgotten.

Two months later, twenty-year-old Anna-Lisa Cefali died under similar circumstances. This time, arson investigators believed the fire had been deliberately set, however, they attributed it to suicide. Nothing was made of Anna-Lisa's scheduled meeting with an acquaintance that morning to discuss becoming his secretary. The man's name was Angelo Colalillo.

When it was learned through the Paccione letters that Speich's and Cefali's deaths were far from accidental, police realized they had a serial killer on their hands. Nine years had passed and the news that their loved ones had not only died excruciating deaths, but had been raped, tortured, and murdered was devastating to both the Speich and Cefali families. Even more so was the knowledge that Colalillo had been imprisoned in 1987 for armed rape and had been let out, despite the fact he refused to undergo treatment for his sexual deviancy. It was during that eleven-year prison stint that Colalillo had befriended Nick Paccione. The two were released in 1998, but Paccione was soon convicted for the attempted rape of a ten-year-old girl and sent back to prison. Now Angelo Colalillo was off the streets, too — held at Rivière-des-Prairies prison less than five hundred metres from Jessica Grimard's house. But the cold-blooded killer that newspapers were comparing to **Paul Bernardo**, was not the only one writing to Nick Paccione.

SCANDAL

When police first scanned Paccione's mail they were certain they had uncovered a criminal conspiracy. Worse yet, it involved longtime corrections worker Marlene Chalfoun. In her thirty-two-letter

COLD NORTH KILLERS

correspondence, Chalfoun reportedly plotted with Paccione to have members of her own family raped and murdered. "One thing I insist on is that when he's beating her, he say: 'This is for all the bad things you've done to others … you're nothing but a whore.' Then he could do the Jack the Ripper thing," Chalfoun wrote. The "he" in question was a friend on the outside whom Paccione had suggested for the assassination. To police it seemed startlingly clear what was happening: Marlene Chalfoun was negotiating to hire Angelo Colalillo as a hitman. However, when the case went to trial, the distraught probation officer claimed she had written to Paccione purely to give an outlet to his sexual sadism. Her defence lawyer Jean-Marc Tremblay produced a further seventeen letters to support her claim. He argued that nowhere in the correspondence was a potential victim actually mentioned by name. Judge Micheline Corbeil-Laramee agreed, and the defendant was acquitted on all charges. Ultimately, Chalfoun's poor judgment cost her her career, but not her freedom. Angelo Colalillo, on the other hand, would lose everything.

TAKING ONE FOR THE FAMILY

Just days before his trial, Angelo Colalillo was found unconscious in his cell at Rivière-des-Prairies prison. He was immediately rushed to the intensive care unit at Santa Cabrini Hospital, where he died. An unusually high level of methadone was found in his system, and it was speculated that he had stolen pills from the prison infirmary. His defence attorney Mark LaBelle stated that his client had been "very, very concerned for his family" and that he may have committed suicide in order to spare them the horror of his trial. With the Paccione letters and a jailhouse informant willing to take the stand, Colalillo stood little chance of being found innocent. In secretly taped cell block conversations, he had allegedly been heard laughing as he recalled his victims' suffering.

David Threinen
4 Murders
Saskatoon, Saskatchewan

HOT AS HELL

The last time anyone saw twelve-year-old Dahrlyne Cranfield or her nine-year-old companion Robert Grubesic, the children were riding their bikes along the South Saskatchewan River. On that same day, June 15, 1975, they vanished into the summer heat. Rumours that they had drowned gained credence when local police boats were seen searching the river. Yet a month went by, and still there was no trace of them. Then in mid-July, lightning struck twice. Eight-year-old Samantha Turner and her friend Cathy Scott, seven, disappeared from an ice cream parlour at a suburban playground. With one terrifying swoop, the drowning theory was shattered and the citizens of Saskatoon were forced to come to a more sinister realization — someone was taking their children. It was a stifling hot summer, but the streets were deserted. No parent wanted to risk their child falling into the killer's clutches. With two acts, he had stolen a piece of the community's history and made it his own.

In the days before computer technology, detectives were forced to go through every sex offender file manually — a huge drain on the RCMP's resources. This time, their efforts paid off. Years earlier, west Saskatoon resident David William Threinen had been implicated in the murder of a teenage girl, but the charges were dropped. With similarities in the details of the two crimes, they decided to bring him in. While changing a tire on the highway, the twenty-seven-year-old trucker was arrested and subsequently confessed to the rape and strangulation murders of all four missing children. He led detectives to their bodies, secreted in remote fields outside the city. One officer on the case would later remark that the bodies were so well-hidden they would never have found them without Threinen's co-operation. Of the four, only Robert Grubesic was fully dressed, indicating the boy was probably killed to eliminate a witness rather than for sexual pleasure. Threinen plead guilty before a court of law, citing his inability to control his impulses. During sentencing, the judge recommended that the tattooed trucker never again be allowed on Canada's streets and roadways. Twenty-five years later, former deputy chief of police

Ken Wagner still claimed it was one of the worst crimes the city had ever witnessed. A father of two and a grandfather, Threinen was turned down for parole in 1995 and 2000 after being diagnosed a "fixated pedophile with homicidal tendencies." He refused to show up for his next hearing. Apparently, even David Threinen thinks he should remain behind bars.

Braeden Nugent
2 Murders
Thunder Bay, Ontario

GETTING HIS KICKS

According to an article written in Thunder Bay's *Chronicle-Journal*, local teen Braeden Benjamin Nugent was once described by a police investigator as "a serial killer in the making." Tragically, if we are to measure his crimes by a modern understanding of the term, at the time of his arrest he was already "made."

Nugent's bloodlust began on March 31, 1995, when he and a Pickle Lake youth followed Jean Joseph Boutin from a local bar. As they neared Hillcrest Park, the two savagely attacked, beating him to a bloody pulp and making off with his jewellery and wallet. Shortly after, they returned to find a dazed Boutin sitting up, wiping blood from his face with a Kleenex. Enraged that he had dared survive the initial onslaught, Nugent resumed kicking him in the head until he was unconscious. They left again, came back with rope and bound him so that he was fully immobile before unleashing a third flurry of kicks upon him. The next day, a woman walking her dog found Boutin's battered corpse in a lane below the park. Autopsy results revealed he had asphyxiated on his own blood.

On May 16, Nugent murdered Victor Wilson, a developmentally disabled man who communicated by grunting and humming. Confronting him in an Ambrose Street driveway, Nugent choked and beat him until his face was unrecognizable.

Nugent was arrested in December 1995 and pleaded guilty on two second-degree murder charges. He was also found guilty in separate incidents of aggravated assault, robbery, and arson — apparently he had attempted to burn down several Shuniah-area cottages. Braeden Nugent was sentenced to life in January of 1997, and incarcerated at Kingston's Collins Bay penitentiary. The Pickle Lake young offender who had participated in Boutin's murder was sentenced to a maximum term of three years in jail for manslaughter. He was released in November 1998.

Ten years after his crimes, at 8:35 p.m. on March 27, 2005, guards found Nugent laying motionless on his back in bed. When twenty-seven minutes of resuscitation failed to revive him, the doctor pronounced him officially dead. At a March 6, 2006 inquest, high levels of methadone, a narcotic used to treat pain or ease addicts off heroin, were found in his blood. Strangely, Nugent was not a known drug user, nor was he prescribed any medication.

Kay Feely.

Carl Hall
3 Murders
Hamilton, Ontario

"I did something horrible."

REDS

Carl Ernest Hall was born in Hamilton, Ontario, on November 26, 1974. For reasons unknown, throughout his childhood, his family moved back and forth between Hamilton and Hall's ancestral home of Sussex, New Brunswick. His father made a habit of beating and berating his only son, and though Carl's mother would sometimes intervene, more often than not she was out losing herself in the smoke and clamour of the local bingo halls. As he entered adolescence, Carl began to fantasize about murdering his father. On one occasion, the two were out hunting in the bush. This time the old man was particularly mean, calling his thirteen-year-old son nasty names and mocking him relentlessly. Carl decided he had had enough. Trailing casually behind, he removed the safety from his 20-gauge shotgun and fixed his father's head in its sights. Ultimately, it was his love for his mother and dog that stopped him from pulling the trigger. Two years later, Carl finally stood up to his father, and the beatings stopped. Unfortunately, the psychological damage had already been done.

Carl first ran afoul of the law at age sixteen, and was convicted for assault and breaking and entering. Taking a cue from his sister, Audrey, who had fled home at the same age, he decided to make a fresh start out west. However, his demons followed him to Edmonton, and after spending most of his time smoking hash, he was forced to flee the city to

Hamilton Spectator.

Hall partying it up.

avoid charges of drug possession and breaking and entering. He settled in Hamilton, where he met his girlfriend, Tracy, fathering a daughter by her. The relationship was a tumultuous one. On one occasion, Carl stole $1,000 from her bank account. On another, Tracy slapped him and he retaliated, leading to a January 1998 conviction for assault. Carl was sent back to Edmonton to face charges and imprisoned for eight months. Upon returning to Hamilton, he was issued a restraining order, preventing him from seeing his girlfriend or baby daughter.

With little of value left in his life, in 1999, Carl became involved with a stripper who introduced him to freebasing crack cocaine. He would later describe the experience as what he'd been looking for his whole life. It wasn't long before the sound of a crackling pipe became his sole obsession: one that he financed through constant theft. Yet rather than quell his rage, the drug distorted and displaced it. Denied visitation rights on Father's Day weekend of 2000, Carl's anger finally consumed him.

LITTLE BOY LOST

Constable Randy Carter was getting ready to finish his shift early and head home for a Father's Day barbeque when a call came over the police radio. A small boy had been sighted wandering barefoot down King Street East. It wasn't long before Carter found the toddler standing in K&M variety with a full diaper. When the clerk casually noted he had vomited on the floor, Carter decided to take the child out for some air. As he stood towering over the boy, he wondered what kind of parents would leave him to wander the streets of Hamilton alone. It wasn't long before he received an answer; two local women came rushing up to the store, explaining that the child's name was Eugene and that he lived nearby. They led the constable to a low-rise apartment building, 781 King Street East, and pointed out a second-floor unit where Eugene and his mother Charlisa Clark lived. Scaling the metal steps leading to Unit C's rear entrance, Carter pounded repeatedly on the door. No answer. He tried to force the door open, but it became lodged on something unseen. With a bad feeling in his gut, Carter radioed for backup.

The scene inside the apartment was like something from a horror movie. Inside the master bedroom, the naked body of a man lay face-down on the bed, sheet and pillows heavy with coagulated blood. The second victim, a woman, was positioned on the floor with her ankles crossed as if kneeling, her arms and head resting on the mattress. Autopsy results would later confirm the couple had succumbed to brain hemorrhaging and multiple skull fractures.

Beneath a tangle of clothing on the floor was the instrument of murder: an aluminum baseball bat lathered with blood. Its discovery came as something of a shock — the level of violence at the scene had initially led investigators to believe that the victims had been shot in the head. Lead investigator Don Forgan soon learned from a neighbour that Charlisa had borrowed it for protection, meaning the killer had not only left the murder weapon behind, but had found it at the crime scene. A palm print was later recovered from the bat, along with a bloody shoe print on the floor. Whoever had pulled off this double murder had been particularly sloppy.

With no sign of forced entry, Forgan began to suspect that the killer knew his victims. Still, there were some strange components to the crime scene that he couldn't explain. The front door, for instance, had been locked with the key inside. Forgan reasoned that the child Eugene had used this exit and had locked the door, not knowing that it was necessary to take the key with him. Certainly, he could not have left by the chain-locked back exit. Thus, Forgan determined the point of entry to be a balcony facing King Street East, with its adjoining door left open. His suspicions were confirmed when he found heavy footprints in the grass outside by an iron lamp fixture. A strong man could easily have used it as a handhold to pull himself onto the nearby balcony.

Back at the Hamilton police station, detectives were struggling to glean what had happened from their three-year-old witness. As far as they could tell, Eugene had hid in the closet during and after the murders. When the killer finally left, Eugene walked into his mother's room and attempted to wake her, misinterpreting the blood spattering the walls as red paint (Charlisa was an artist). When they wouldn't rouse, he tried to watch television, but finding it broken, had wandered outside.

The next day, fingerprint evidence identified the male victim as Charlisa's twenty-five-year-old boyfriend Pat Del Sordo. After detectives interrogated and eliminated those in the couple's inner circle, they were unable to find a motivation for the killings, and the trail soon went cold.

TEARS AND BEERS

There wasn't much in the way of company at Big Lisa's on August 19, 2001. Jackie McClean, thirty-six, arrived at the King Street East dive bar at 10:00 p.m., looking for a good time, but instead ended up sitting next to Barry — a tightly wound character with cropped hair and teardrops tattooed under his eye. She was more than a little relieved when a man with short red hair, a goatee, and a white T-shirt joined them at the table. He introduced himself as Carl and asked if he could buy her a beer. She refused. It wasn't long before Carl and Barry began badgering Jackie to score them some crack. Though she planned to enter rehab the next day, she was broke and figured she could use a boost herself.

Later that night, Jackie, Barry, and Carl relocated to Sandbar, an abandoned tavern at 193 King Street East, for a freebasing session. For unknown reasons, Jackie and Carl decided to take the party to one of the upstairs apartments. Unit 4 was a dingy room, the bare light bulbs from the ceiling exposing dried blood and graffiti along the walls. A malfunctioning lock meant that once inside, they had to push a fridge in front of the door to prevent anyone from disturbing them.

Barry Lane was downstairs smoking crack when Carl Hall returned to the room looking white as a ghost.

"The girl upstairs is dead."

"You're full of shit," Barry retaliated. Nevertheless, he felt compelled to check. Entering the doorway of Unit 4, he stopped in his tracks. A pool of blood mellowed in the centre of the room, crimson smears leading up sixteen carpeted steps to the loft level. Reaching the top of the stairs, he came upon the semi-nude body of Jackie McClean; her legs splayed as if she had been raped. Articles of clothing lay torn from her body. Barry raced down to street level, flagging down the first policeman he could find. By this time, Carl Hall was already gone.

It didn't take long for the crime scene investigators to figure out what had happened. Jackie McClean had been viciously attacked on the main floor of Unit 4, and dragged dead or unconscious to the loft where she was sexually assaulted, possibly after death. The murder weapon, a bloodstained steel bar, stood propped against the wall near the body. Interestingly, the instrument seemed to have been removed from a nearby construction site at Walnut and King. The autopsy confirmed their suspicions: Jackie had died from blunt-force trauma to the head.

ATLAS UNBURDENS

Early the next morning, Carl Hall checked into the Holmes House drug rehabilitation centre just outside Hamilton in Simcoe. During a group therapy session he met a fellow east coaster by the name of Shane Mosher, and the two soon became friends. After four days of chatting with his new pal, Carl began to open up to Shane, explaining that while growing up, his father had beaten him and that he was on the run for robbing a bank in Hamilton. Later that Thursday night, he knocked on Shane's bedroom door and asked if they could talk. For over a year he had been carrying his dark secret, and the urge to confess was unbearable. Sitting on the edge of Shane's mattress, Carl admitted that the bank robbery story was a lie. In reality, he had done something much more terrible. Roughly fourteen months ago, a drug dealer acquaintance had been harassing Carl's girlfriend Tracy, a situation that the fiery New Brunswicker decided to rectify. One night, baseball bat in hand, he had entered the dealer's apartment building to find the door blocked from the inside with a fridge.[2] Nevertheless, he managed to get inside. He found the dealer kneeling on the floor by a table and ambushed him, bashing his brains in with the bat. Then something unexpected happened: a woman entered the room. Carl hadn't wanted to kill her, but she was a witness.

"I knew what I had to do," he trembled, gripping a pillow.

Shane agreed to keep the story a secret. He was lying. Despite his cool facade, he was horrified and knew he had to tell the police. What if the guy had killed more people?

The next morning, Shane's wife Shannon arrived to drive him home for the weekend. Before leaving, he promised Carl that he would be back on Monday. He lied again.

PIPE DREAMS

Even before Shane Mosher's invaluable assistance, the net was beginning to close on Carl Hall. Detective Dave Place, assigned to head the Jackie

McClean murder investigation, had interviewed a waitress at Big Lisa's on October 25 and learned of the red-headed "Carl" seen in her company that night. Entering the name along with the suspect's physical description into the police database, he came across Carl Hall. Known as "Reds" in some circles, his last address was listed as Ferguson Avenue North. At the time, he was imprisoned in a Brantford jail for threatening an officer and obstructing police. Though he would only be incarcerated for a few more weeks, Carl was also facing assault charges against his girlfriend Crystal in Hamilton. Discovering that he was expected to enter a guilty plea, Detective Place called the prosecutor and asked that the judge demand a DNA sample as part of Hall's sentence. This could be compared to semen found on the vaginal area of McClean's body, and if matched, would be substantial evidence to charge Hall with her murder.

On October 30, the waitress positively identified Carl Hall's mugshot as the man she had seen at Big Lisa's over two months ago. Furthermore, when Detective Place eventually managed to interview his ex-girlfriend Crystal, he learned that Hall habitually beat and choked her, once stabbing her in the leg to punish her for burning supper. She had long suspected him in the Sandbar murder, and had even bumped into him later that same night stinking of crack, booze, and perfume. Crystal had tried to end their relationship, but he told her that he had done "something bad" and needed her more than ever. When she stuck to her guns, he showed his undying devotion by punching her and spitting in her face. Most tellingly, Crystal revealed that Carl got off on tearing her panties during sex, a signature enacted during the McClean murder. Detective Place had little doubt left in his mind — "Reds" had been the one responsible for the crime.

In January 2002, Shane Mosher finally informed the RCMP of Hall's confession, who in turn passed it on to Hamilton police on the condition that Mosher's identity be kept secret. On February 25, the bloody handprint found on the baseball bat was matched successfully to Carl Hall's. After twenty months of chasing false leads, Detective Dan Forgan had his man.

Fifteen days later, Carl Hall was ordered to provide a DNA sample from his jail cell. By March 15 it had been positively compared to the DNA of Jackie McClean's murderer. Within a month, Carl Hall had gone from being known as a petty thief, woman beater, and addict, to one of

Hamilton's most notorious serial killers. In two separate trials, he was convicted of the first-degree murder of Jackie McClean and the second-degree murders of Charlisa Clark and Pat Del Sordo. It was determined that in the latter case, he had broken into the apartment at King Street East planning to exact revenge against a former resident named Paul. Charlisa and her boyfriend Pat had been bludgeoned to death over a simple case of mistaken identity, exacerbated by Hall's use of crack cocaine.

Today an overweight Carl Hall sits rotting in Kingston Penitentiary. He denies any involvement in the death of Jackie McClean, claiming the two had consensual sex and that Barry Lane must have murdered her after he left. Yet the fact that there is no trace of Hall's semen on the main floor indicates the sexual assault must have happened in the upstairs loft, after she had been attacked. He also claims to find the concept of necrophilia disgusting — then again, who can trust a word Carl Hall says, when after years of drug and alcohol abuse, he can barely trust himself.

Donald Armstrong
2 Murders
Mississauga/Brampton, Ontario

MISTER FIX-IT

Rita Bayer felt a sense of relief when she saw a man with a screwdriver approaching. The seventeen-year-old's car had stalled in the parking lot of Mississauga's Square One Shopping Centre, and it was a cold November day in 1978. If she didn't get out of there soon, she figured she'd probably freeze to death. It seems that fate was truly working against Rita that day because, rather than using the tool to help her, her saviour stabbed her multiple times in the face and neck. Miraculously, she survived the attack to eventually identify the perpetrator: Halifax-born Donald Armstrong.

Armstrong was convicted of the attempted murder of Rita Bayer and possession of a dangerous weapon in April 1981, earning himself fourteen years imprisonment. A year later he was also linked to two previous murders. In May 1977, young Brampton mother Glenna Fox had been sitting in her car in the Bramalea City Centre when she was suddenly ambushed and stabbed to death with a chisel. Just under a year later, sixteen-year-old Linda Bright was selling magazine subscriptions at Frontenac Mall when Armstrong managed to abduct her. When he had finished raping and strangling Linda, he ran over her corpse with his car in a poor attempt to make the crime look like an accident. Her mauled body was found the next day on the side of the road. Though Armstrong's life sentence for the first killing meant he could not be charged with the second, it seemed certain that he would never see the light of day again. By 2003, he had been moved to Frontenac Institution in Kingston, where he allegedly had a view of the same mall where he had abducted Linda Bright. Sometime during his incarceration he married, though no further details are known.

In 2006, the Correctional Service of Canada transferred Armstrong to minimum security at Sainte-Anne-des-Plaines prison in Montreal to "create momentum" for his release, even though he had been assessed as having a 60 percent chance of reoffending. Thanks to the efforts of Linda's sister, Susan Ashley, and former Peel police chief Noel Catney, however, an internal review of CSC policies was conducted. It was subsequently learned that the board had not bothered to look into Armstrong's criminal history before transferring him. When they reviewed a mental assessment of the killer made in 1999 by Dr. John Bradford, they learned he had been diagnosed as an "incurable psychopath." The forty-six-year-old Armstrong was promptly returned to the medium-security Collins Bay Institution. He is a prime suspect in the murder of fourteen-year-old Karen Lee, who was killed near Sarnia on March 16, 1974, in a manner similar to Linda Bright. Found in a ditch along a rural road, Lee had been repeatedly run over in a failed staging attempt. She had fought her attacker so valiantly that not only was he unable to rape her, she also managed to draw blood which was later entered into the national

DNA database where it can be compared to Armstrong's. No news of a connection has been released.

Danny Wood
2–15 Murders
Across Canada

HIGHWAY TO HELL

Daniel William Wood was born in British Columbia in the mid-fifties, the son of a heroin-addicted prostitute. He left home at age ten, immediately running afoul of the law. It was the beginning of a trend that would continue for the remainder of his life. When he wasn't holed up in a drab, cramped jail cell, Wood got by through odd jobs and petty crime. By his fifteenth year, Danny's mother finally died of a heroin overdose. Wood hung around for another eight years until February 1979, when, overcome with a strange wanderlust, he caught a Greyhound bus to Calgary. Soon after, police discovered the mutilated body of a middle-aged woman in an alleyway. She had been raped and strangled to death, then stowed under a van.

By the end of the year, Danny Wood reached the town of Smiths Falls in the Ottawa area. Interestingly, a local disabled woman would report being raped by a drifter to police, though her claim was not followed up on. Meanwhile, unable to keep a job, Wood left town, resurfacing in June 1980 in the vicinity of Timmins/North Bay.

It was a pleasant July day, sunlight glittering on the shingles as Claude Oulette walked through the doorway of his North Bay home. Calling out to his girlfriend, Micheline St. Amour, twenty, he was concerned by the silence that followed. The couple had only been together for six months, but had already grown very close. Checking the house, Oulette stopped dead in his tracks as he entered the bedroom. Micheline's trousers were folded neatly on the duvet. A trail of blood led tellingly from the bed to a nearby closet. Inside he found Micheline's punctured body, blindfolded and bound at the wrists. She had been stabbed and slashed twenty-seven times, presumably after being sexually assaulted. Investigators determined that the murder had occurred no earlier than 1:00 p.m. on July 10, and that the victim had willingly let the killer into her home. They also suspected he had been aided by an accomplice. The St. Amour killing went on to become one of the few unsolved murders in North Bay's history.

New Liskeard, Ontario, lies north up Highway 11. It was from here on September 19, 1980, that eighteen-year-old Julie Fortier suddenly disappeared. Immediately police knew something was wrong; Julie was a good kid and never went anywhere without first notifying her parents. She was last seen stepping off a school bus at 8:20 a.m., her arms loaded with books. Strangely, on this occasion she seemed to have departed a few stops later than usual. Did Julie Fortier have a secret appointment she was unwilling to share with her parents?

Like a storm cloud, the evil drifted further and further up Highway 11 until it loomed over the town of Timmins, Ontario. Here it consumed Sharon McCafferty. A regular at the local bar, the thirty-two-year-old was known to prostitute herself on occasion. On October 7, her mutilated corpse was found in a cheap motel room, the scarf used to strangle her still buried in her neck. A bizarre crucifix pattern had been used to open Sharon's chest and she had been violently sexually abused. At the time, Wood had been employed cutting brush in the area and immediately fell under police scrutiny. Eventually charged with Sharon McCafferty's murder and placed under arrest, he was acquitted on September 1, 1981. OPP investigators failed to link these three cases, later admitting that a lack of communication may have hindered their abilities.

BRIGHT LIGHTS, BIG CITY

Rape and murder just seemed to follow Wood around. By the spring of 1982, he drifted south to Toronto where on May 28, nineteen-year-old Jenny Isford of North York was abducted, raped, and strangled to death. In a particularly cruel display, the killer left her body on an elderly neighbour's lawn. Less than a month later, Welsh-born Christine Prince stepped off a streetcar at 1:40 a.m. and disappeared. Her raped body was found in a wooded area along the Rouge River, not far from the Metro Toronto Zoo. Police determined she had been killed first and then rolled down a nearby embankment. A third lust murder, that of mother of four, Judy Anne Delisle, would be linked to Daniel Wood. She had been strangled, sexually mutilated, and abandoned on a side street just off Danforth Avenue. Her body was discovered on July 10. Wood was found guilty of first-degree murder and later linked to the 1980 Calgary slaying. Sometime after, he was cleared of suspicion in the Jenny Isford case when it was learned he had been incarcerated during her murder. Similarly, a drop of blood presumed to have come from Micheline St. Amour's killer was compared to a sample of Wood's, but failed to match.

In August 1982, Daniel Wood told police that fellow inmate and murderer Fernand Robinson had bragged about more than fifteen killings to him. Through Robinson's perspective, Wood provided accurate details of the crime scenes — information that only the true culprit could know. Included in the tally was the St. Amour murder. However, Robinson could not have possibly been responsible for the murders because at the time he was being treated at a psychiatric facility. Inevitably, police began to wonder how Wood could have come across this information. To many, there was only one answer.

The Micheline St. Amour case remains unsolved, with Danny Wood as its primary suspect. For ten years, Julie Fortier's status as a missing person went unchallenged despite the 1985 discovery of her school books near a New Liskeard dump. On May 8, 1990, that tragically changed. One hundred twenty-eight metres from where the books had lain, searchers found a blue sweater, gold necklace, and lower jawbone atop a mound of dirt. Dental records confirmed the news her family dreaded to hear: the remains were all that was left of Julie Fortier. Also recovered from the scene was Julie's watch — it had stopped on September 20, 1980, the day after her abduction.

For nearly thirty years, Danny Wood has remained silent regarding his suspected involvement in both the Highway 11 murders and that of Christine Prince. He may be responsible for up to fifteen slayings across western and central Canada. Today, he languishes in a Saskatchewan penitentiary, entombed with the restless ghosts of his victims.

CHAPTER 6

THE VISIONARY KILLER

Anatomy of a Visionary Killer[1]
Characteristics:
- Act-focused
- Chaotic crime scene
- Overkill
- No torture
- Body is not moved
- Victim known to killer, but not a friend, family member, or acquaintance
- Weapon left at the crime scene
- Sexual penetration by foreign object, necrophilia, or not at all
- Does not strangle victim
- Killer is male
- Cannibalism/vampirism possible

The visionary serial killer is the stereotypical foaming madman. A look at his past reveals a history of mental illness and possible institutionalization. More than likely he's only out of hospital due to a shortage of beds. He has medication, but doesn't take it. Bombarded with voices and hallucinations, he eventually succumbs to their commands. The results are horrific. With a population of 300 million, the United States has certainly had its share of visionary serial killers. Among the most memorable was "The Vampire of Sacramento," Richard Chase, a psychotic who believed that he had "soap-dish poisoning." In an interview with Robert Ressler, Chase explained his theory that everyone has a soap dish and if you lift the bar and find the underside is gooey, you have soap dish poisoning. The ailment was transforming Chase's blood to powder, which, in turn, would gradually erode his body from the inside out, destroying his "energies." Thus he had been forced to murder and drink his victims' blood and eat their brains in order to replenish his supply. Chase went on to claim that he had a Star of David birthmark on his forehead (he didn't) and that as a result Nazis were persecuting him using UFOs. These claims are of course so outrageous that they are almost humorous — until you remember poor housewife Terry Wallin, three months pregnant, gutted from neck to navel.

A few years prior to Richard Chase's frenzied home invasions, California was terrorized by the infamous Herb Mullin — a visionary killer who offered up thirteen strangers as human sacrifices in order to stop earthquakes. Philadelphia's Joseph Kallinger had visions of a disembodied head called "Charlie" who commanded him to chop off little boys' penises. He would eventually claim the lives of three people.

It is either a testament to Canada's social programs or a reflection of our low population that our nation has produced only a single visionary serial killer. The unfortunate case of **Bruce Hamill** demonstrates an offender so overwhelmed by his psychiatric problems that it was virtually impossible for him to kill without getting caught. Indeed, the only reason he became a serial killer at all was owing to the ineptitude of a psychiatric panel.

Ontario Provincial Police.

Bruce Hamill
2 Murders
Ottawa/Brockville, Ontario

"Are you here to take me? I'm ready. I've done everything you want. Where do I go? Is your vehicle here?"

Bruce Waldemar Charles Hamill, following the murder of Dennis Kerr.

STARK RAVING MAD

On November 27, 1956, Bruce Waldemar Charles Hamill was born in the Ottawa neighbourhood of New Edinburgh. Like his partner in crime, **Peter Woodcock**, it was obvious from the get-go that the child had psychiatric issues. EEG and CAT scans revealed he had been born with an abnormality in his temporal lobe that hindered his ability to control his impulses. Unfortunately, Hamill's behaviour tended toward violence and non-compliance. Not knowing what else to do, Wally and Gertrude Hamill went into denial. When news of Bruce's violent outbursts and schoolyard brawls reached them, they attributed the blame to somebody else. They figured the psychiatrist they hired was having a positive effect on him, and that Bruce's scuffles were normal for a boy of his age. Certainly he wasn't a dangerous child.

It is likely that Bruce Hamill's mental instability was exacerbated by his increasingly bizarre home life. His mother Gertrude was a paranoiac, convinced the world was out to get her family. From day one she sheltered her son from the outside world, even throwing away the pills the psychiatrist had prescribed for him. As Bruce got older and Gertrude became increasingly delusional, the two gradually switched roles until he became her protector. Of course, she wasn't the one who needed protection.

By grade ten, Bruce's violent temper had grown nearly out of control and he was working odd jobs to support a mounting drug habit. At eighteen he spent a summer in the militia where he met an emphatic and troubled young soldier named Robert Poulin. Though both would become infamous murderers, in the context of the militia they couldn't have been more different. Bored by the repetitive drills and structure, Hamill grew sulky and took to dragging his feet. On the other hand, Poulin was a model soldier known for sleeping with his rifle. Somehow the two ended up sharing a tent. When rumours that Hamill was gay began spreading, the tightly wound Poulin worried that he would be implicated, too. Tension over this and Poulin's discovery of Hamill's dirty mess tin culminated in a fistfight between the two. Later, Robert Poulin would go on to rape and murder schoolmate Kim Rabot before turning his rage against his high-school theology class. By the end of his rampage, three students lay dead. Poulin shot a second before turning the gun upon himself.

After leaving the militia, Hamill paid a visit to a homosexual friend. The two shared marijuana cigarettes and drank until his friend passed out. At once, Hamill realized that the man was completely at his mercy. Tempted, he ran a knife across his torso, deliberating whether or not to stab him. Eventually, he decided not to, but Hamill's violent urges could not be contained much longer. When a twelve-year-old insulted him shortly after Christmas, Hamill attacked the boy, nearly beating him to death. On another occasion, Hamill took offence to a jibe from a student at Lisgar Collegiate. Three days later, he confronted the boy after school, chasing him about the schoolyard with a knife before he escaped. The would-be victim had not even remembered who Hamill was. In February of the following year, Hamill stopped attending sessions with his psychiatrist. This proved to be what pushed him over the edge.

For twenty-one years, George and Betty Wentzlaff and their neighbours Wally and Gertrude Hamill had lived side by side in relative peace. The Hamills had even invited them to their twenty-fifth wedding anniversary party. Then one fateful day, Gertrude decided that she wanted to buy the Wentzlaffs's house for her daughter. When the couple politely refused, Gertrude's frustration gradually mounted into a burning obsession that she focused on Betty. She called the Wentzlaffs again on February 28, 1977, demanding they sell. Unable to convince them, Gertrude screamed in frustration before hanging up and bursting into tears. Bruce Hamill finally had the excuse he needed.

Leaving the house, he wandered the streets of New Edinburgh, his anger against Betty Wentzlaff accelerating with every step. At 5:00 a.m., Betty left for a part-time cleaning job behind her home at Chrichton Street School. She had barely stepped onto the street when suddenly Bruce Hamill vaulted over their adjoining fence and began to run at her. Fleeing, Betty made it to the side door of the school before he caught up. In a psychotic frenzy, Hamill stabbed her twenty-seven times, leaving the poor woman to soak in her own blood. The superintendent found her at 6:45 a.m. and notified the police. Two days later, Hamill was arrested. A search of the house yielded the knife he had used to kill Betty Wentzlaff. After twenty-one years of gestation, a murderer was finally born.

THE PENETANGUISHENE YEARS

Bruce Hamill arrived at Oak Ridge psychiatric hospital at Penetanguishene in the fall of 1978. Following several interviews, Dr. Russell Fleming concluded he had been sane when he knifed Betty Wentzlaff to death. On Monday, January 9, 1979, his trial began. There was little question whether he had committed the murder; the real issue was Hamill's mental capacity. Fleming was called to testify for the prosecution, as was Dr. Elliott Barker, who believed Hamill had acted logically out of loyalty to his family. On the other side of the fence was Dr. Selwyn Smith, the Royal Ottawa Hospital's head of forensic psychiatry. Smith believed Hamill had planned the murder, but had done so for illogical reasons. He then went on to describe his extensive brain damage and strange relationship with his mother. He ended by recommending that the accused be contained in a mental health facility. Consulting psychiatrist Dr. Frank Chalke concurred, noting how Hamill did not "feel" it was wrong to murder Mrs. Wentzlaff. Dr. David Bulmer saw evidence that Hamill was having an epileptic fit at the time of the killing. A day later, the jury found Bruce Hamill not guilty by reason of insanity. He was returned to Oak Ridge, where he remained until his December 1980 transfer to Brockville. He was granted day passes outside the institution and when he failed to reoffend, was eventually released. As

Hamill's crime was perpetrated while he was under the influence of severe psychosis, his criminal record was wiped clean in 1987.

STILL CRAZY AFTER ALL THESE YEARS

Saturday, July 13, 1991. The cloying humidity of an Ottawa summer made Bruce Hamill want to melt like butter in front of his fan. Unfortunately, lying around all day wasn't an option — he had serious work to do. Lately his home life had been a disaster. Days before, he had stopped talking to his wife, who correctly suspected him of carrying on a homosexual affair. The recent addition of a baby daughter to the family had only served to heighten the tension in the household. Now all the rage and frustration that had been building inside was about to find an outlet. Taking the elevator down from his eighth-floor apartment, he caught a bus to the Ottawa railway station, where he purchased a ticket for Brockville. Minutes later, he was gazing out the window of a passenger train, watching as the blond haystacks and silos of the Canadian Shield raced by. He felt a sense of comfort knowing that soon all of his problems would be similarly behind him. Recently, his lover at Brockville Psychiatric Hospital, Mike Krueger (a.k.a. Peter Woodcock, see Chapter 2), had initiated him into a secret society known as "The Brotherhood." Krueger had explained to him that as soon as their mission was accomplished, Hamill's psychiatric disorders would disappear, his father would be reincarnated, and he would be guaranteed a seat on a starship scheduled to arrive in 2011. It seemed like the answer to all of his prayers.

A few hours later, Bruce Hamill reached Brockville station. From there he limped to a Canadian Tire and picked up a hunting knife, hatchet, and sleeping bag to go with the wrench he had wrapped in newspaper. Next, Hamill bought a pack of Nytol — a non-prescription sleeping pill — at the town drug store. Sweating profusely, he carried the weapons in a plastic bag to a nearby wooded area. Packing them into his sleeping bag, he then walked ten minutes to Brockville Psychiatric Hospital. He informed the receptionist that he was Mike Krueger's supervisor and had come to collect him. Krueger arrived and Hamill signed him out for his day trip on the Brockville Hospital grounds. The two carried the sleeping bag out to the sumach grove they had selected weeks earlier and stowed their weapons in the bushes. Then they set off in search of their victim. It wasn't long before they found him: twenty-seven-year-old Dennis Kerr, a fellow patient and flutist. Krueger had arranged to lend Kerr $500 to buy drums some time earlier. He introduced Hamill and explained that they were going to get their second three-hour day pass and would meet Kerr at the sumach grove in an hour. They parted ways. After acquiring the pass, they hurried back to the grove and Krueger hid in the bush. Kerr arrived on time and was just about to ask where his money was when Krueger brought the wrench crashing down on the back of his skull.

"What did you do that for?" Kerr screamed, blood streaming from his head.

Krueger replied by striking him again in the face, knocking him to the ground. Once they were certain he was incapacitated, Krueger and Hamill retrieved the knife and hatchet from their hiding place. Together they hacked and slashed at Kerr until he was little more than a bloody pulp. This didn't stop them from sexually assaulting him. When they were done, Krueger knelt down over the body to hear the death rattle, later claiming he saw Kerr's spirit escape from his mouth. Then, Krueger and Hamill took turns sodomizing the corpse while chanting strange incantations. According to plan, after Hamill finished, he took the box of Nytol pills and dozed off on the sleeping bag. Krueger briefly considered killing him, but decided he was too tired. Instead, he walked five kilometres to the Ontario Provincial Police station and calmly confessed to the murder.

By nightfall, the humidity had broken into a heavy rain. Soaked and irritated by mosquitoes, the police search party followed Krueger back to the grove where they found a naked Bruce Hamill stumbling around in the darkness. He asked if they were here to take him. They were, but not anywhere he wanted to go. When the police ordered him to get down on his belly, Hamill ran screaming at them in a confused rage. After several minutes of fighting, they finally subdued him, locking him in the cruiser. He was taken immediately to the protective custody unit at Brockville jail to be treated for psychosis.

On December 9, 1992, Bruce Hamill and David Michael Krueger went to trial. In an Ottawa courthouse, Hamill pleaded "not guilty" to the murder of Dennis Kerr. At the time of this writing he has been safely returned to psychiatric care.

CHAPTER 7

THE MISSIONARY KILLER

Anatomy of a Missionary Killer[1]
Characteristics:
- Act-focused
- Controlled crime scene
- No overkill
- No torture
- Body usually not moved
- Victim is unknown to killer, but is a specific type (i.e., blond women, black men, etc.)
- No weapon at the crime scene
- Possible penile penetration, no necrophilia
- Does not strangle victim
- Killer is male
- No cannibalism/vampirism

Unlike the visionary, whose delusions compel him to kill seemingly at random, the missionary serial killer carefully selects and executes victims according to a personal code. Where a visionary's crime scenes appear chaotic and sloppy, the missionary's are cold, sterile, and efficient. He might, like Montana's "Unabomber" Theodore Kaczynski, target liberal intellectuals and scientists whom he perceives to be perpetuating a flawed society. Kaczynski's MO was to mail out packages personally addressed to his victims, which would explode upon opening. He also occasionally left pipe bombs in universities or polytechnic schools, seriously injuring or killing the first person to handle them. Another American missionary killer, neo-Nazi Joseph Franklin, committed as many as eighteen racially motivated murders from 1977 to 1980. From the cover of a sniper's perch, Franklin set his sights on blacks and interracial couples; in 1977 he even blew up a synagogue. Adversely, between October 1973 and April 1974 the notorious black Muslim "Death Angels" raped and killed fifteen white women in San Francisco.

We will now take a look at a case of a Canadian missionary killer: "The Slasher" Ron Sears, who targeted homosexual males.

Sears family.

Ron Sears

The Slasher
2 Murders
Windsor, Ontario

"Please forgive me but these people have destroyed my whole life."

Ronald George Sears in a mental hospital following his conviction.

HOMELESS

July 23, 1945: a warm summer's night in Windsor, Ontario. Following up on a phone call to the Windsor Police Department, Officers Ted LaPage and Bob Anderson arrived on Sandwich Street shortly after 1:30 a.m. to find the blood-soaked form of George Mannie lying half-dead in the road. Stabbed twice in the back, the dock worker was rushed immediately to Grace Hospital where it was discovered he had suffered a punctured lung. Thanks to the skill of the medical staff, Mannie would survive the attack, informing detectives that he had been knifed by two men in brown zoot suits on California Street before being pushed down an embankment toward the Detroit River. Bleeding profusely, he was able to crawl back up to Sandwich Street, where he was found by a military provost officer.

As the sun began to rise over the dreary industrial city, LaPage and Anderson returned to the crime scene to search for clues. To their amazement, they discovered a row of bushes between the street and the embankment that would have made it impossible for Mannie to have tumbled down the hill. Why was he lying? Along the riverbank were numerous empty bottles of rubbing alcohol and a straw hat flattened like a pancake. A trail of blood snaked through the grass and up the hillside toward Sandwich Street. Strangely, the evidence seemed to indicate that Mannie had been attacked at the bottom of the riverbank, not at the top as he'd claimed. Heading back to the hospital, the investigators resolved to press him for the truth. Sheepishly, Mannie admitted that on the previous night he had been drinking rubbing alcohol in some bushes by the river with two homeless men and "Pete the Swede." Eventually his companions had departed, leaving Mannie alone to sleep it off. He later awoke to find either a light-skinned Negro or tanned Caucasian of about twenty-five standing over him.

"Are you all alone pal?" the shadowy stranger asked.

Getting a weird vibe, Mannie attempted to scramble up the embankment when suddenly he felt something strike him twice in the back.

The attack was viewed as an isolated occurrence, and overshadowed by the awarding of the Victoria Cross to a local boy, was relegated to an obscure corner of the *Windsor Daily Star*. Fourteen days later, all that would change.

THE FIRST MURDERS

It was August 7 when Canadian Pacific Railway worker Earl McMaster stumbled upon the body. Climbing up an embankment away from the train tracks, he noticed a pair of feet protruding from the weeds near an old salt mine. Arriving on the scene, detectives Mahoney and Carter were baffled by what they saw. A middle-aged man in a straw hat and glasses lay dead in the undergrowth, yet none of the grass in the vicinity of the corpse was trampled. There seemed to be no way the killer could have transported the body to its final resting place. Like Mannie, the victim had been stabbed multiple times in the back, his buttocks slashed so viciously that his trousers hung from them in ribbons. The next day the victim was identified as fifty-six-year-old Windsor Bedding Company worker Frank Sciegelski. A married man, he had left Europe for greener pastures, evidently neglecting to bring his wife along for the ride. Sciegelski's landlady told police that her tenant had returned home from work on the night of August 6, changed, shaved, and left. His car was found abandoned less than a block away from the dump site. Nothing in the vehicle seemed out of the ordinary. By all appearances, Sciegelski had simply wandered off into the weeds to meet his demise.

On the same day that Frank Sciegelski's body was discovered, Sergeant Hugh Blackwood-Price stepped onto the platform of the Canadian National Station to receive his welcome-home basket. Born some forty-five years earlier in Belfast, he had fought alongside the Ulster Volunteers in the First World War before immigrating to Canada. He had settled in Windsor during the thirties, where he worked as an entertainer and astrologist, occasionally writing a column in the *Star*. By May 1940, the tee-totalling bachelor had enlisted in the Essex Scottish Regiment, returning to Europe to fight the Nazi menace. In the ten days between his return and subsequent murder, Price found work in a warehouse, spending his nights chatting with other veterans in the Active Service Club.

It was just after 1:15 a.m. on Saturday, August 18, when Ernest White noticed something out of the corner of his eye. The Crawford Avenue resident had been returning home along a trail near the abandoned salt mine, a dense scrubland overgrown with grass, wild carrot, and burdock. Beneath the tangle of weeds, he spotted what appeared to be a man's wristwatch glinting in the nearby street lamps.

Somebody seemed to have fallen asleep in the foliage. Suddenly, the realization hit him like a sledgehammer: the man wasn't asleep, he was dead! It wasn't long before flashlight beams were slicing through the darkness. White directed detectives Sam Royan and Jim Hill to the body, dumped only 140 metres from where Frank Sciegelski had been found ten days earlier. A quick search of the victim's wallet identified him as Sergeant Hugh Blackwood-Price. It was obvious that whoever had committed the Sciegelski murder was also responsible for this tragedy. Price had been stabbed twice in the back: below the shoulder blade, penetrating his chest cavity, and again through the lung. The cause of death was attributed to blood loss from a further nine stab wounds to the chest, though none were anywhere near as deep. After the killer had stood watching Blackwood-Price die over the course of five minutes, he attacked him again, stabbing him through the heart and slashing his throat. Police linked the Sciegelski and Blackwood-Price slayings to the same man. When interviewed, Ernest White admitted that he had walked through the area around 9:30–10:00 the same night, and though he was sure there had been no body, he had spotted a car idling nearby. Tire tracks fleeing the scene of the murder added credence to his story. A burly man at five feet, eight inches and 180 pounds, it would have been difficult to drag Price's body through the undergrowth, leading the detectives to speculate that his assassin was particularly strong. They theorized that Price had been killed elsewhere and his corpse was driven to the dump site at a later point.

MESSAGES FROM HELL

The brutal slaying of a respected war veteran plunged the city of Windsor into a moral panic. This was no drunken hobo or reclusive immigrant — Price's death meant that upstanding citizens like themselves could also fall prey to the Slasher's blade. Headlines in the *Windsor Star* such as, BELIEVE MANIAC IS ON RAMPAGE and reports of fictional attacks only exacerbated their apprehensions, as did one Inspector MacNab's comments to a Toronto reporter comparing the Slasher to Jack the Ripper. Witnesses swore they saw a man in army trousers stroll into a downtown café covered in blood. In another example, the operator of a local dry cleaners claimed to have been handed a bloodstained suit for cleaning. Instead of "Cowboys and Indians," the children of the west end now played "Slasher." Rubberneckers trudged ghoulishly through the weeded lot where Sciegelski and Price were found, plunging their fingers into the blood-soaked earth. At some point during the course of the summer, somebody scrawled a chilling message in the lavatory of the Detroit-Windsor tunnel:

> I'm the slasher. I've stood and talked to cops at the scene of my last killing before this. I killed a German in a camp for that I was dishonorably [*sic*] discharged from the U.S. Army. I'll kill until I'm ready to stop. I can never be caught — to all cops-... I am slasher Evans — they will never get me-... Civilian-sergent [*sic*]-sergent [*sic*] — girl next.[2]

Despite Chief Renaud's assurances that it was a hoax, the public remained convinced that a woman would be the Slasher's next victim.

In response to public demands, the largest manhunt in Windsor's history was launched. Still, most citizens believed that respectable families like their own should be free from scrutiny. Instead, police should focus their attentions on Pitt Street's notorious brothels and beer houses. Surely the madman would be found here among the dregs of society: the drunkards and vagabonds, diseased johns, and dissolute homosexuals. The socialist mayor Arthur Rheaume had clearly let Windsor descend into sin city, and many felt it was long overdue for a clean-up! Apparently many local police officers shared this opinion, filling their holding cells with all manner of "sex men" whom they vigorously interrogated. Undercover officers — ex-soldiers trained in unarmed combat — frequented parks and public washrooms at night in a vain attempt to lure the killer. The presence of "reefers" (marijuana cigarettes) on the streets of Windsor was likewise blamed for the erosion of common values. In short, anything considered abnormal was surely responsible.

As August neared its conclusion, a second message appeared on the wall of the Detroit-Windsor Tunnel: "Im [*sic*] Slasher You may think I'm through but I will strike again twice — fast — very dam [sic] soon."[3] The final, and only authentic, message from the Slasher arrived at police headquarters in March of 1946, months after the widespread fears of impending slaughter had abated. Addressed to "Police HQ in connection of murders" in red pencil was written:

> Dear sirs,
> This is a challenge to you. "I" will strike in the near future. I can not disclose this to you of course. My avenge [sic] of these people are great. Nothing shall stand in my way. I will use only the <u>knife</u> on my supposed enemies. I am not a returned soldier. This is no prank.
> THE SLASHER
> Please forgive me but these people have destroyed my whole life.[4]

Below the writing the sender had doodled the foreboding image of a knife dripping blood.

THE SLASHER RESURFACES

At 11:20 p.m. on Saturday June 22, 1946, a trim, ghostly man stumbled into Windsor Central Police Station with an awl jutting from his back. The man's companion informed on-duty officer Constable Gordon Preston that he had been driving past Government Park on Sandwich Street when he saw the victim scrambling over the embankment trying to flag him down, and had rushed him to the station. Preston and Constable George Souchuk drove the man immediately to the hospital where it was found that the awl had just missed his heart. Dr. Frank DeMarco carefully removed the instrument, and when the victim was ready to speak, summoned Preston from the waiting room. The man identified himself as Alexander Voligny, a worker at the paint and varnish plant of Canadian Industries Limited. Voligny claimed he had been walking along the riverfront to cool off and had just seated himself on a bench in Government Park when he was approached by a Caucasian man of about eighteen years and around five feet, seven inches tall. The two had lain down together on the grass, at which point his companion requested that he rolled over onto his stomach. When

Voligny turned to comply, the man suddenly plunged something twice into his back and took off in the direction of Sandwich Street.

The next day, detectives Brand and Anderson reinterviewed Voligny in the hospital. He recalled meeting the Slasher sometime around 10:00 p.m. Suspicious of entrapment, Voligny had asked him if he was a cop, to which the young man had replied, "I don't bother with the law." They had continued west to the Ambassador Bridge and then down to the riverbank where the man had pulled out Voligny's penis. The two began to masturbate each other before lying down on a slope under a tree. At this point they began to undress one another and Voligny's companion asked him to turn over so that he could sodomize him. When Voligny refused, the man pushed him over and stabbed him in the back before running away laughing. It had been a brave admission. Consenting sexual acts between adult males were still illegal in 1946, and whether he knew it or not, Voligny's statements could have landed him in jail.

Less than two weeks later, on Saturday, July 26, 1946, a couple nearing the intersection of Bridge Avenue and Sandwich Street came across the Slayer's final victim staggering down the street holding a bloody butcher's knife. Panicked, they helped him into a passing cab where the driver Lloyd Lauzon took the blade from him, promising to keep it safe. Joseph Gelencser was whisked to Grace Hospital where he was saved by plasma replacement and fourteen stitches. Speaking with police, he told them he had gone for a stroll to see the cruise ship *Noronic*. Just as he was about to cross Sandwich Street he felt somebody stab him in the back and had fallen to his knees. Unfortunately, he hadn't had the opportunity to see his attacker. When police investigated the scene, they weren't surprised to discover that Gelencser's account had been a fabrication. None of the heterosexual couples parked in a nearby lover's lane had seen a thing. However, some distance from the bridge at Campbell Avenue Park they found what appeared to be a bloodstain.

As soon as Joseph Gelencser had recovered, he was interviewed once again, this time providing a more credible account of what had happened. He had met up with a young man on Sandwich Street who had accompanied him to the Ambassador Bridge. At some point the man turned the conversation to sex, prompting Gelencser to reply that he was married and did not wish to discuss such matters. The stranger tried to convince him to sit down, and when he refused, had plunged a knife into his back.

Still not convinced that Gelencser was telling the truth, Detectives Tellier and Paget interviewed his wife along with a lodger who had roomed with the couple for the past ten years. Through these channels they learned that the stabbing victim spent a great deal of his time with a young man named Hailey Friend. Brought to the station for interrogation, Friend revealed that they had met through a mutual employer, admitting that Gelencser often paid well to perform oral sex on him. Friend had used this to his advantage, blackmailing his benefactor for exorbitant sums to keep their arrangement a secret. When the detectives confronted Gelencser about this, he fervently denied any sexual involvement with Hailey Friend. Like fellow survivor George Mannie, it was obvious Gelencser would rather risk lying to the police than exposing his sexual identity to the homophobic Windsor of the 1940s.

TRUTH AND CONSEQUENCES

Not only had The Slasher failed to kill his last two victims, he had also foolishly left his weapons at the crime scenes. Examining the butcher knife that had nearly ended Joseph Gelencser's life, police found it was missing one of the three rivets used to attach the blade to its wooden handle. When reporter Jim Yokum learned of this, he suggested that a photograph of the weapon be placed in the *Windsor Star* on the off-chance that somebody might recognize it. An hour and forty minutes after the newspaper hit the stands, Isaac Taylor arrived at the police station claiming that the knife had gone missing from a Cameron Street house where his stepdaughter Dorothy Sears lived. Married to one Donald Sears, a housing shortage had forced the couple to reside temporarily with her husband's parents and his twin brother, Ronald Sears, who had an unhealthy obsession with knives. A year earlier Dorothy had been shocked to see her brother-in-law return home one night dripping with blood. His mother Florence had washed the stains from his clothes without bothering to ask any questions. On other occasions Ron had openly bragged about the men he had murdered.

Forty-five minutes later, police descended upon 261 Cameron Street to find eighteen-year-old Ronald Sears readying himself for a wiener roast. Immediately they recognized his resemblance to descriptions of the killer. At five feet, seven inches tall, with chestnut hair and an athletic build, he was certainly capable of dragging Hugh Blackwood-Price across the CPR scrubland. Sears was arrested on the spot, and a search of his room undertaken. In the interrogation room, Sears denied any involvement in the recent knife attacks on Voligny and Gelencser, claiming that on both occasions that he had been at the Empire Theatre watching horror films. Dorothy Sears confirmed her brother-in-law's love of Dracula movies and explained to police she had once seen him viciously mutilate an old mattress. Furthermore, a German bayonet had gone missing from her father's home sometime in 1945, and was later found in Ronald's possession. Ron's sister had even been robbed of an icepick shortly before the Voligny stabbing. According to Dorothy, when Ron Sears wasn't recounting how many times he had stabbed his victims and dragged them through the fields, he hid in his room for hours holding lengthy conversations with his cat, or slashing up his pillow.

At 9:00 p.m., Ronald Sears's interrogation resumed, only now rivulets of truth began to trickle through the cracks in his facade. Sears admitted that after viewing *House of Dracula* on the night Gelencser was stabbed, he had taken a stroll down to the government dock where he encountered the forty-eight-year-old homosexual. Gelencser had talked about masturbation and asked him if he would let him "suck him off." Sears had agreed and the two men found a shadowy spot by the river. When Gelencser began to undress, Sears pulled the bread knife with the missing rivet from his inside suit pocket and jammed it into his back. Moving on to the Voligny case, Sears admitted that instead of going to the theatre he had travelled to Government Park. Voligny approached and asked him if he "had a match" — a common homosexual signal at the time. The two dined at the Arizona Lunch before venturing to the river where Sears said he "knew a nice spot." Once under cover of darkness, Voligny began to play with his penis and offered to perform fellatio on him. Sears claimed that when he refused, Voligny became enraged, prompting him to stab the man in the back with his icepick as a means of self defence.

After a short break, Sears went on to discuss the Blackwood-Price murder. He had been sitting on a bench in Government Park when the sergeant approached him and suggested they walk down by the silos. When Price offered to "suck him off" he made up his mind to kill him, and led him by the arm to a field between the railroad tracks and Crawford Avenue. They lay down in the grass where Price began to masturbate him. Sears asked him to roll over so that he could put his "cock up his rectum," and when the older man complied, stabbed him twice with a butcher knife. Sears began to flee, but noticing his victim was still alive, returned to finish the job. As he was secreting Price's corpse in the weeds, a car pulled up. His MO in the earlier Sciegelski killing was practically identical. When questioned as to his motives for the murders, Sears gave a detailed reply:

> … when I was about nine years of age a man came to our place and he was a stranger to me. He took me into the garage at the rear of the house and started to feel around me and make love to me as if I was a female. He had me jack him off and tried to put his cock in my mouth. But I wouldn't let him. I heard my mother call and didn't say anything about it because at that time I did not think it was very bad. But as I grew older it seemed to grow on me.[5]

Sears claimed he was justified in murdering Frank Sciegelski because "I knew he was a sex pervert and I knew he would probably try to get some other young boy and ruin his life."[6] By the time he was finished signing the Sciegelski statement, it was obvious to everyone in the interrogation room that Sears was on the verge of a mental and physical breakdown. Before they could offer him some respite, he collapsed onto the floor and began to vomit. The last thing Sears had said before fainting was that he was glad to be caught before he killed somebody else — a strange contradiction to his earlier statements.

The interrogation resumed the next day with Sears admitting to stabbing George Mannie when he became angry that Sears would not perform oral sex on him. The two had wrestled briefly, and when

Sears had produced the hunting knife in self defence, Mannie fled up the embankment. Enraged, Sears had followed after him, tackling him and thrusting the blade into this back. He claimed his original intent in carrying the weapon was simply to hack up some old trees, however, following this first attack, he developed his modus operandi of luring "perverts" into the shadows with promises of sex. Later that afternoon, detectives drove Sears to the area of the attacks, where he accurately identified the location of each stabbing.

Around 5:30 p.m. on Wednesday, September 18, 1946, jury foreman Grover Johnson announced to a Windsor courtroom that they had found Ronald George Sears guilty of the murder of Hugh Blackwood-Price. As required by law, Justice Dalton Courtwright Wells sentenced him to death by hanging to take place on Tuesday, December 3. Sears was immediately removed to a cell on death row to await his execution. Special guards were appointed to watch him day and night to ensure he did not attempt suicide. Under pressure from the Sears family and a homophobic public, some of whom actually saw him as a persecuted Robin Hood figure, the case was taken before the Court of Appeal. Preying on contemporary naïveté about homosexual lifestyles and mental illness, Sears's defence lawyer Arthur Martin managed to overturn the verdict. Certain that a bloodthirsty killer was about to be set free, Windsor authorities decided to charge him with attacking Joseph Gelencser. Ron Sears would not be home for Christmas after all.

On May 5, 1947, a pallid and feeble-looking Ron Sears stood before his third judge and jury. It was obvious to all on hand that jail was taking its toll. The idea that he would face a fair trial at this juncture was ludicrous — newspapers across the continent had already printed his confession to killing Hugh Blackwood-Price in full, announcing that the "Slasher panic" had finally come to its conclusion. Though the state of Sears's mind was a much more crucial component of this trial than previous ones, his defence attorney stated unequivocally that his client was perfectly sane, a fact corroborated by prison psychiatric examinations. Only one doctor, J.N. Senn of Hamilton, had the courage and acumen to disagree. He testified that he had found Sears to be "indefinite" on many issues, fitfully changing his mind in the blink of an eye and displaying signs of a "pre-psychotic personality."

The jury ruled him fit to stand trial, eventually finding him guilty of stabbing Joseph Gelencser. He was sentenced to a twelve-year term at Kingston Penitentiary.

Within months of arriving at the institution, however, it became obvious that Senn had been right on the money. Sears's crumbling mental condition prompted the commissioner of penitentiaries to transfer him to Penetanguishene Hospital in 1948, were he was diagnosed as schizophrenic. The Slasher who had terrified Windsor for two years died of pulmonary hemorrhaging brought on by tuberculosis in the spring of 1956.

CHAPTER 8

THE HEDONIST-COMFORT KILLER: BLACK WIDOWS, BLUEBEARDS, AND BABY FARMERS

Anatomy of the Hedonist-Comfort Killer[1]
Characteristics:
- Act-focused
- Controlled crime scene
- No overkill
- No torture
- Body usually not moved
- Highly specific victim, often a friend, relative, or acquaintance
- Weapon often left at the crime scene
- Usually non-sexual
- Does not strangle victim
- Killer is often female
- No cannibalism/vampirism

If there is one breed of serial killer predating the visionary in human history, it is the hedonist-comfort killer. Unlike the other offenders we have examined, he/she slays primarily for financial or material gain, dispatching their victims quickly and carefully before robbing them or collecting their insurance. Usually there is no sexual component to their crimes — in fact, comfort-motivated serial killing is one area in which there may actually be more female perpetrators than male. Californian divorcee Dorothea Puente murdered nine residents at her three-storey care home simply to collect their pensions and social security cheques.

Of course, there are plenty of male hedonist-comfort killers to go around. Englishman Donald Neilson, known as "The Black Panther" for his shadowy hood, shot and killed three postal workers in 1974 during a string of post-office holdups. His next scheme led him to kidnap heiress Lesley Whittle, seventeen, from her Shropshire home on January 14, 1975. When her family failed to come forward with the £50,000 ransom he demanded, Neilson strangled her with wire and left her body at the bottom of a sewer shaft. "The Rugley Poisoner," William Palmer, disposed of two of his creditors by way of strychnine, along with an alcoholic brother whose life he had insured for £82,000.

Unsurprisingly, Canada is no stranger to the hedonist-comfort serial killer. **Charles Kembo** chose to prey on those who knew and trusted him.

A commonly found subtype of the hedonist-comfort killer is "The Black Widow," a woman who murders her husbands, and sometimes children, for financial reasons. For example, three wealthy husbands and six insured children succumbed to America's "Queen Poisoner" Lydia Sherman from 1864 to 1871. Indiana matron Belle Gunness frequently advertised for rich bachelors to visit so they could discuss marriage. To show their honest intentions, she requested that they bring $5,000 along with them. When the Gunness farm burned down on April 28, 1908, the dismembered remains of thirteen men were found in the ashes. The money, on the other hand, was never recovered. Canada's only known Black Widow, **Melissa Ann Friedrich**, learned enough from her earlier Nova Scotia conviction to adopt more subtle methods of murder on her American victims.

Johann Otto Hoch, Henri Landru, Bela Kiss, George Smith, and George Chapman all profited as "Bluebeards," men who marry and murder several wives, usually for financial gain. They are a hedonist-comfort sub-type identical to the Black Widow in every respect but gender. **Sukhwinder Dhillon**, a Punjabi immigrant to Hamilton who offed two of his wives and a business partner for insurance and dowries, is the most vile permutation yet to be discovered on Canadian soil.

Finally, we will conclude this chapter with a look at the now extinct "Baby Farmer" subtype, a predator of the pre-legalized abortion age who targeted unwed mothers and their infants. English baby farmer Amelia Dyer was paid between £10 and £12 to adopt each of the six babies she strangled. It was simply easier for her than keeping them around. Nova Scotians **Lila** and **William Young** murdered hundreds of infants and the occasional mother through neglect in the early twentieth century.

Other Hedonist-Comfort Killers in This Book
Edward Rulloff and Dr. Robert MacGregor

Kay Feely.

Charles Kembo
4 Murders
Vancouver Area

"I am not a serial killer!"

A FAMILY AFFAIR

On November 5, 2004, maintenance worker Jesse Vetra and his boss came across a hockey bag mired in a bog near the George Massey Tunnel in Vancouver. The men were out hunting for a beaver that had felled some trees in the area, but something about the bag piqued Vetra's interest. Picking his steps carefully, he made his way through the mud until it was within his reach. He almost threw out his back trying to pull it out of the water. The thing weighed a ton! Curious to see what was inside, Vetra cut a slit in the bag with his knife. At once, the smell was overpowering. Peering inside, he recoiled at his discovery.

"I think there's a body!" he called out to his boss. But he didn't *think* there was a body; he *knew* it. The limp female arm and sweater told him as much. It wasn't long before police identified the remains of fifty-five-year-old Sui Yin Ma, missing from her Richmond home since October 22. Police suspected that Ma had been mistress to one Charles Kembo, and that he had killed her to profit from her identity. It was their belief that he used her bank card to withdraw $1,000 in cash, all of which he later spent at Costco. In 2002, Kembo and Ma first met as neighbours in Richmond, British Columbia. At the time, Kembo had been living with his common-law wife Genevieve Camara in the 7600 block on Granville Street. A tube of K-Y jelly bearing traces of his DNA was recovered in a search of Ma's apartment. In initial police interviews, Kembo denied ever knowing her, but when confronted with phone records and a credit card application from her computer, he changed his story, admitting to having had sex with her. After his arrest, Kembo allegedly confessed to her murder in a police interview. Sadly, she wouldn't be the only death linked to Charles Kembo.

ORIGINS

The son of a Presbyterian priest, Charles Gwazah grew up in poverty in Malawai. It is not known when or why he changed his surname to Kembo. When the authoritarian regime of Hastings Kamuzu Banda was on its last legs, he immigrated to Canada in September 1989 as a government-sponsored refugee. Two years later, he was convicted of theft in a Canadian court, and in late 1991 orchestrated numerous welfare scams that earned him three years in prison. He was to be deported following his 1994 parole, but somehow fell through the cracks of the system. Immigration officials would miss him a second time in 1997 when he was convicted of theft. After this last conviction, Kembo seems to have gone straight, opening a successful financial project management company and convenience store. He separated from his wife in 1999 and became involved with Margaret Yeung, an employee in his shop, who he soon married.

Margaret Yeung-Kembo was the first to vanish in January 2003. Her body has yet to be recovered. Police allege that following her disappearance, Kembo applied for five credit cards in his wife's name, making over $200,000 in twelve months. When her twenty-two-year-old daughter Rita Yeung inquired as to her mother's whereabouts, Kembo told her that she had retreated to a Buddhist monastery in China. Today he maintains that the two had enjoyed a brief relationship, but were never wed. Sometime after, Grant, Kembo's infant son by Margaret, went to live with him and his new common-law wife Genevieve Camara. On November 5 of that same year, the murdered body of Kembo's business partner and friend Ardon Bernard Samuel was unearthed from a pile of leaves in Vancouver's Quilchena Park. His penis had been severed and stuffed into his pants pocket along with four bank notes. Suspiciously, it was discovered that Kembo had taken out an $800,000 insurance plan on Samuel.

"I've known Arden a long time, since university days, a very good guy," Kembo later told a *Vancouver Sun* reporter. "The honest truth is Arden Samuel has received nothing but help from me. When he died he had been on welfare, government aid for three years. This despite my help."

Police learned that on July 23, 2005, Kembo spent nine hours driving around with Rita Yeung, stopping at a Home Hardware to pick up the garbage bags, shovel, and rope he would later use to kill her. At 1:43 a.m. on July 24, police surveillance devices in Kembo's car picked up what has been interpreted as the muffled scream of Rita Yeung. Using a GPS tracking device implanted on Kembo's car, they located this last victim on the banks of the Fraser River north of Vancouver airport. Her body, naked save for a bra, had been wrapped in plastic bags and weighed down with rocks. A diving team also retrieved a shovel from the riverbed.

Two days later on July 29, 2005, Charles Kembo was arrested while driving to Vancouver. A subsequent search yielded Kembo's personal calendar, containing a notation reading "RY Plan." Over the course of this writing, he was standing trial in Vancouver charged with four counts of first-degree murder. On Friday June 11, 2010, Kembo was convicted of each and sentenced to life in prison by judge Sunni Stromberg-Stein, who added that if she could have legally given him four consecutive life sentences, she would.

Andre Kirchhoff.

Melissa Friedrich
The Internet Black Widow
2 Murders
Halifax/Florida

"I didn't realize, but I put it in reverse instead of forward and I backed the car over him."

HATCHED

Melissa Ann Russell was born in Burnt Church, New Brunswick, a remote community north of the Miramichi region on May 16, 1938. By the age of seventeen she had met and married Russell Shephard, moving to his hometown of Montague, Prince Edward Island. Together they sired two children: a son and daughter. Melissa first ran afoul of the law in 1977 when she was sentenced to eleven months in a PEI jail for forgery. She would spend an additional five years behind bars from 1977 to 1991 for more than thirty separate attempts at fraud.

In April 1990, she married widower Gordon Russell Stewart, an ex-soldier, in Las Vegas. The couple settled in Vancouver, where Gordon soon noticed money disappearing from the $50,000 he had saved for his retirement. Around the same time, his new bride began to accuse him of beating her. Legal attempts to keep the couple apart were breached by both parties and togther they relocated to Dartmouth, Nova Scotia. On April 27, just over a year after their wedding, Melissa fed Gordon a deadly concoction of liquor, pills, and rubbing alcohol before running her car over him on a road near the Halifax International Airport. She didn't report his death until three hours later, stopping first to change clothes. At her 1992 trial, two eyewitnesses testified they had seen Melissa drive into her husband, before putting the vehicle in reverse and backing over him. Prosecutors asserted that she was trying to get access to Gordon's pension benefits. In her defence, Melissa claimed that her husband was an alcoholic who habitually abused her. Convicted of manslaughter, she was sentenced to eight years hard time at Kingston Penitentiary.

In 1994, Melissa appeared in *Why Women Kill*, a National Film Board documentary exploring battered wife syndrome. On camera she played up the image of the incompetent female driver, claiming that on the day in question Gordon had raped her and she had accidentally put the car in reverse while trying to escape. Overnight, her status changed from vile murderess to desperate victim — she was even granted money by the Ontario government to establish a women's abuse hotline. Two years into her sentence Melissa was paroled into a rapidly evolving world where the aging widow discovered the Internet.

THE WEB

By October 2001, Melissa had ensnared her third husband. Octogenarian Robert Edmund Friedrich of Bradenton, Florida, first met the younger brunette on an online dating site. When she arrived to visit him from Nova Scotia, he became enamoured. Three days later, they were engaged. Seeing Melissa for what she really was, Friedrich's son Dennis attempted to talk his father out of it. His efforts did no good. The couple eloped, marrying at a chapel in Dartmouth, Nova Scotia, before moving to Florida, where Melissa Stewart became Melissa Friedrich. It wasn't long before Robert began slurring his words and falling over. Then on December 16, 2002, he died, bequeathing all $100,000 of his assets to his wife. Unsurprisingly, his sons became highly suspicious of their stepmother, alleging to the sheriff's department that she had poisoned their father with prescription medications. As the body had been cremated, there could be no autopsy to prove their assertions. Though Melissa Friedrich was never charged with Robert's murder, she lost all but $15,000 in an ensuing court battle with her stepsons.

Less than two years after returning to Prince Edward Island, she used her Internet savvy to sucker lonely seventy-three-year-old Alexander Strategos into a relationship over a Christian dating site. Crippled with diabetes, Strategos was looking for a caring woman to make grocery runs and cook him warm meals. The sixty-nine-year-old Friedrich was only too happy to oblige. She suggested that she come to Florida to meet him, and though Strategos thought things were moving a little fast, he acquiesced. After meeting him for dinner at a Greek restaurant on Ulmerton Road, she followed him back to his condominium in Pinellas Park in her brand-new Cadillac. She moved in that night. Coincidentally, it was that very same evening that Strategos took his first of many tumbles, striking his head hard against the floor. In the following months the former Pittsburgh tax collector would continue to fall, randomly lapsing into confusion and garbling his words. As Strategos had suffered from strokes in the past, nobody thought much of it. The doting Canadian woman was a godsend, cooking for him every day and feeding him ice cream before bed. She was a snappy dresser too, in her fashionable clothes and auburn wig. Alexander Strategos soon came to believe that nobody had ever loved him like Melissa Friedrich did. He was right.

TANGLED

Despite Melissa's care, three months after her arrival, Strategos was placed in a nursing home to recover. Fortunately, the nurses weren't so trusting. Friedrich identified herself to them as his wife, but they knew better. During this period, she took over Strategos's condo, persuaded him to sign over his power of attorney, and began to suck his bank accounts dry, stealing $18,000 in total. When his son, Dean Strategos, became alerted to traces of chemicals found in Xanax and Valium in his father's bloodstream, medication Alexander wasn't prescribed, he informed the Pinellas Park Police Department.

On January 6, 2005, Melissa Friedrich was finally arrested and charged with exploitation of the elderly. Granted bail at $7,500, she was subsequently placed on hold by the Department of Homeland Security, who had learned that she had lied about her criminal record upon entering the country in 2004. Dean Strategos undertook a search of his father's condominium, and was shocked to discover not only a suitcase full of pills, but that his father's Internet homepage had suddenly changed to a Christian singles site. The "Internet Black Widow" was already trawling for her next victim!

Charges continued to amass against Melissa Friedrich for grand theft and forging cheques, though amazingly there was not enough medical evidence to pursue her for attempted murder. Back at home in Canada, the RCMP were also beginning to take a closer look at Friedrich. On February 1, a warrant for her arrest was issued for defrauding the Canadian government. From July 1997 to October 2003, Friedrich had employed two different social security numbers under the names Melissa Shephard and Melissa Stewart to leech an extra $30,348 in Old Age Security payments.

Pleading guilty to three counts of grand theft from a person over sixty-five, two counts of forgery, and two counts of using a forged document, Friedrich was sentenced to five years in a Florida jail. Soon after she stopped paying him visits, Alexander Strategos began to recover. On April 5, 2009, Melissa Friedrich was released and deported to Canada where she was confronted with fraud charges.

Hamilton Spectator.

Sukhwinder Dhillon

5 Murders
Hamilton, Ontario/Punjab, India

"Here they can't touch you!
They're not allowed to."

TO LOVE, HONOUR, AND DIE

Whenever Parvesh Dhillon's boor of a husband wasn't making her life a living hell, it was those damn headaches! On January 30, 1995, the elegant Sikh woman had found the migraines particularly excruciating, but for once, Sukhwinder or "Jodha" as they called him, was actually showing some concern for her condition. He had even given her a pill to help alleviate the pain.

Minutes later, she was writhing on the living room rug — the pale skin that had long marked her beauty in Punjabi culture was taut and burning against her bones. Unseen hands wrenched her spine upwards to the ceiling, her muscles clenching in painful protest as surges of electricity wracked her fragile body. All around she could hear the panicked voices of friends and family gradually being eclipsed by a moan that hurtled from her chest like an oncoming train.

"I am dying!"

And then a blinding white light. Was this heaven, or the supreme manifestation of human agony? Parvesh was slipping in and out of consciousness. Soon her ordeal would be over and peace would return. Her gums peeled back over her teeth, facial muscles locking in a blood-curdling grin from the strychnine pumping through her veins. What had Jodha given her? Whatever would become of her children?

Four days later, Parvesh Dhillon lay twitching on life support in Hamilton General Hospital. The paramedics had done everything in their power to revive her: chest compressions, electric shocks, even administered massive doses of Valium. In the end, Sukhwinder gave his permission to take her off the ventilator. At last, Parvesh Dhillon had the peace that had been so absent in her tumultuous life, and he had her $200,000 insurance policy. As far as "Jodha" was concerned, it was a win-win situation.

JODHA

It had been eleven years since Gobind Kaur Dhillon had been with child. So when little Sukhwinder Singh pushed his way into the world on May 9, 1959, in the city of Ludhiana, India, he instantly became the centre of her universe. At an early age, it was apparent that the Dhillons's youngest son was a hyperactive troublemaker, prompting his father to nickname him "Jodha" — "brave warrior." Fagun Dhillon, a dairy farmer who owned his own land, had once been a police officer, but had left the force following Jodha's birth. His family attributes this career change to Fagun's disgust at the wanton corruption he witnessed; other accounts say he was fired for being part of the problem. Whatever the reasons, Fagun died soon after of a heart attack, leaving the spoiled five-year-old with no paternal figure to instill discipline. Jodha eschewed his Sikh faith, refusing to wear the traditional turban and committed blasphemy by cutting his hair. As his father's demise had already bequeathed them land and servants, little Jodha saw no reason why he should attend school. On this issue, his mother did not relent, each morning sending him out to earn an education. When Jodha realized that skipping one day of school meant getting spanked on the next, he simply stopped attending altogether. Instead, he left every morning to play in the market, returning in the late afternoon with lies about his classes for his mother. When she eventually learned of his truancy, she hired a tutor. Still, Jodha showed a complete lack of interest in education. By the end of his teens he was barely literate, having spent his life in a realm of fantasy with every need met by his family's relative wealth. He had, however, developed a remarkable talent for lying, along with a ferocious sense of entitlement.

In 1981, Jodha became engaged to a beautiful Sikh woman named Parvesh Kaur Grewal. Word had spread that the twenty-two-year-old and his mother were immigrating to Canada, a place where Parvesh's parents hoped one day to live. Meanwhile, Jodha and his mother settled in a two-storey brick house owned by his older brother Sukhbir in Hamilton, Ontario. He returned to Ludhiana in 1983 to wed Parvesh. Back in Canada, the newlyweds found work on a mushroom farm. Jodha tried several higher-paying positions at a cheese factory, foundry, and as a cab driver, but lacked the work ethic to keep them. In September 1986, he finally settled at J.I. Case, a factory that manufactured farming equipment. His increased wages enabled him to purchase a house on Berkindale Drive in nearby Stoney Creek. As in his schooldays, he was a habitual truant, often feigning illness to get out of work. On February 18, 1991, he claimed to have injured his back falling from a moving trolley on the painting line. From that day on, he lived off Worker's Compensation, netting $18,838 in 1991, $19,000 in 1992, and as much as $22,554 in 1993. He also learned to collect insurance by purposely crashing used cars, averaging $18,000 a year in payouts.

Jodha's revenues from the government dropped to half in 1994 when he began to deal used cars — the perfect trade for an accomplished swindler. Working out of his home, a corner lot where he kept as many as eight automobiles at a time, he incorporated his business as Aman Auto.

His favourite trick was to buy high-mileage cars at auctions, replace their odometers, and sell them off at inflated prices.

Despite the financial success of his various scams, Jodha quickly developed a reputation in the East Indian community as something of a joke. Unlike most of Hamilton's educated Sikh population, he barely spoke Punjabi, let alone English. At the same time, he never seemed to shut up. A consummate attention-seeker, he boasted of colossal feats of strength and of having once been a wrestling champion back in Ludhiana. For a laugh, his colleagues frequently used his narcissism against him, demanding he prove his strength by doing push-ups and sit-ups. Unfailingly, he would drop to the floor and begin his exercise routines, somehow never cluing in when they burst into hysterics. A classic bully, he took to ridiculing a fellow East Indian worker at J.I. Case for marrying a white woman, bragging of how he would one day beat the man up. When the two finally came to blows, Dhillon was reputedly floored with one punch, at which point he screamed at Parvesh to "call his brothers" so they could kill him. At other times, he was seen applying black oil to his beard with a toothbrush: a crude attempt at hiding the grey spots.

TAKING CARE OF BUSINESS

Ranjit Khela had arrived in Canada on October 23, 1992, when he was twenty-one years old. It had always been his dream to join his aunt, uncle, and grandparents in Hamilton, Ontario, and the arranged marriage to his wife Lakhwinder was the perfect ticket out of India. While living in an apartment in Hamilton's east end, Ranjit was introduced to a used car salesman nicknamed "Jodha" and immediately was in awe of the older man. With his stunning wife, children, house, and lucrative career, Jodha seemed a portrait of Indian success in the New World. Better yet, he was only too happy to take Ranjit on as his apprentice. When Jodha travelled back to Punjab following the unexpected death of his wife Parvesh, he entrusted Ranjit to look after the house for him. By May 8, 1996, the two men had become so close that they visited a small insurance outlet on Barton Street East to take out life insurance policies together. Ranjit's life was insured for $100,000 plus an additional $100,000 in case of accidental death. The beneficiary was none other than his friend Jodha.

Saturday, June 22, was to be a very special day for Ranjit Khela: not only were his parents and beloved sister flying in from India, but he had also closed a $6,500 deal to sell a used Dodge Caravan to his uncle. After registering the sale with the Ministry of Transportation, he spent the afternoon celebrating with his uncle and Jodha at Ranjit's apartment. Later, as he was driving his burly mentor home, Jodha unveiled a special surprise for his ward. For some time, Ranjit had been suffering from impotence with his overweight wife Lakhwinder, a situation that was tearing at the fabric of his young soul. Now Jodha claimed to have just the solution: a capsule of miracle medicine that guaranteed to send his sexual prowess through the roof. Having long admired Jodha's rumoured sexual conquests in India, Ranjit gladly accepted the pill. At long last, the missing piece of his Canadian dream was about to fall into place.

As he slipped between the sheets with Lakhwinder, Ranjit's body felt strong and virile, his rock-hard erection pressing into her soft skin. The two made love beneath a cloud of burning incense, then lay side by side to savour the calming flood of endorphins moving through their bodies. Only rather than feeling contentment, Ranjit was acutely aware of his muscles contracting, and wondered why his erection had yet to dissipate. His skin felt extremely sensitive to the touch, so much so that he cast aside the sheets to stop them burning against his skin. Lakhwinder Khela looked on in horror as her handsome young husband toppled and began violently jackknifing against the mattress. What on earth had Jodha given him? By the time the paramedics arrived at 88 Gainsborough Road they found Ranjit's face twisted into a hideous smile, blood gushing from his gums. He was rushed to Hamilton General Hospital where he was pronounced dead at 2:03 a.m.

THE VELVET HAMMER

Cliff Elliot was experiencing an extraordinary case of déjà vu. The smooth English insurance investigator, known in the business as "The Velvet Hammer," was sure he had been to the little house on Berkindale Drive before. He remembered the stone statues of the lion and eagle guarding the neighbours' door, the plaque commemorating Christ in Portuguese. And then there was the nonchalant Sikh man whose command of the

English language seemed to vary to suit his situation. Something strange was definitely going on. Cliff explained to Mr. Dhillon, purporting to be the deceased's uncle, that before his claim could be processed he needed the signatures of Ranjit's parents or wife on several forms. Dhillon was coy: Ranjit's mother and father were travelling in America, and his wife was nowhere to be found. In reality, they were minutes away at the Khelas' 188 Gainsborough apartment.

"How did your nephew die?"

"Ranna was watching TV," Dhillon replied casually. "Said he had a pain in his chest, then fell to the ground and died in the hospital. That was it."

Before leaving, "The Velvet Hammer" informed Dhillon that he would be checking the medical reports.

Back at the office, Cliff Elliot began to sort through the company files for any previous claims issued to Dhillon. To his astonishment, he found that just a year before, Dhillon's wife Parvesh had inexplicably died on February 3, 1995, for a total payout of $200,000. That meant two healthy young Indians had died suddenly within a year, leaving Sukhwinder Dhillon their sole beneficiary. Cliff telephoned the police first thing the next morning.

Intrigued by Elliott's suspicions, Sergeant Dave McCulloch travelled to Hamilton General Hospital that afternoon to speak with forensic pathologist Chitra Rao. Rao telephoned the Centre of Forensic Sciences and requested screening for chloroform and strychnine on samples of Ranjit Khela's tissue and blood.

It wasn't long before Detective Warren Korol, now the lead investigator on the case, received the test results from the CFS: Ranjit's blood contained a fatal strychnine level of .07 milligrams/100 millilitres of blood. Though it stood to reason that Dhillon had also poisoned his wife Parvesh, obtaining evidence in her case would be much trickier. She had died over a year and a half ago and, in accordance with Sikh tradition, been cremated. Fortunately, the pathologist at Hamilton General Hospital who had performed the autopsy on Parvesh still had minute quantities of her tissue wrapped in wax in the storage room. Korol knew that, given the time frame and dissection, any trace of poison left in the sample may have been destroyed, but he decided to chance it, driving the specimens up to the CFS in person.

On October 8, 1996, Korol and his specially assigned Punjabi-speaking partner, Kevin Dhinsa, interviewed Yog Raj Rathour, an insurance agent highly respected in the Indian community. Yog revealed a number of bizarre rumours circulating in the community pertaining to Ranjit's mysterious friend Jodha. Soon after his beautiful wife Parvesh had died suddenly in 1995, Jodha had travelled to the Punjab where he had bigamously married several other women, using them sexually, and making off with their dowry money. Though he had promised to take them to live in Canada, so far none of Jodha's brides had left the sub-continent. Worse yet, one of the women had died suddenly after her husband's last visit, in circumstances eerily similar to Parvesh Dhillon's.

That same day, Korol and Dhinsa arrived at 362 Berkindale Drive to interview Sukhwinder "Jodha" Dhillon. Not wanting to reveal the full depth of their knowledge, they decided to limit the questions to those concerning the death of Ranjit Khela. Throughout the interview, Dhillon was co-operative, but denied knowing how the poison got into Ranjit's blood, explaining that he was just an ignorant dairy farmer.

LYING AND CONNING

Putting any further interviews with Dhillon temporarily on the back burner, Korol decided to look into his suspect's record with Canadian immigration. He learned that Dhillon had completed applications to sponsor two separate wives to immigrate to Canada, the first on November 2, 1995, and another on April 15, 1996.

The next morning, Korol sent an information request to the Indian branch of Interpol regarding the women, then contacted Pierre Carrier, the Canadian High Commission's liaison officer in New Delhi. Now it was simply a matter of waiting. The fax that arrived later that afternoon nearly knocked Korol out of his seat. On April 5, 1995, Sukhwinder Dhillon had married Sarabjit Kaur Brar in India, fathering two children with her. Divorce proceedings had been filed, but not completed. Fifteen days later he wed Kushpreet Kaur Toor, who died soon after of a heart attack on January 23, 1996. Dhillon took his fourth wife Sukhwinder Kaur Dhillon, who coincidentally shared his name, on February 16 and had arranged for her to immigrate to Canada, but had been denied due to his suspicious marital circumstances. Warren Korol decided then and there to convince Dhillon to submit to a polygraph test.

Korol and Dhinsa met with Dhillon again on Wednesday, November 13, where he agreed to take the lie detector that weekend. But when the detectives arrived to pick him up at his home for their Sunday appointment, the sly Sikh was nowhere to be found. Eventually he returned in his car, and they escorted him to Oakville police station where the test was to be conducted. Once in the polygraph room however, Dhillon's English suddenly deteriorated. Frustrated, but realizing this technicality could jeopardize the test's admissibility in court, Korol decided to reschedule. Though Dhinsa spoke Punjabi, there would need to be a neutral interpreter on hand.

After days of attempting to locate Dhillon to book a new appointment, they finally got him to agree to a 10:00 a.m. date on December 8. When the day came, Dhillon called to cancel, explaining that he had been involved in a car accident and had hurt his mouth.

It was December 15 when the detectives finally managed to connect him to the polygraph. Two hours of questioning later, the test was conclusive — Sukhwinder Dhillon had lied about his involvement in the murder of Ranjit Khela.

DEVASTATING DEVELOPMENTS

Days later, an Indian immigrant in Surrey, British Columbia, contacted Korol with information implicating Dhillon in two additional murders. Gurbachan Singh, originally from the little Punjabi village of Panj Grain, had read about Dhillon's alleged crimes in a local newspaper and recognized him as the man who had married his neighbour Sarabjit. He explained that Dhillon had sired twin sons by Sarabjit, but had warned her not register their births or name them. Both infants had died mysteriously one night after their father had come to visit them — in fact, it had been the only time Dhillon had set eyes upon his newborn children. By now, Warren Korol had little doubt that Sukhwinder Dhillon was an evil man, but the thought that he could murder his own children in cold blood still seemed beyond belief.

The case against Jodha took a turn for the worse on January 2, 1997, when a representative from the CFS informed Korol that they had been unable to find strychnine in Parvesh Dhillon's tissue. Too much time had passed since her death, and the lab lacked the technology to uncover smaller traces. Unperturbed, Korol requested information from the Department of Justice on how to go about collecting evidence in India. On March 15, he also submitted an application to search Dhillon's Berkindale Drive home to the Justice of the Peace.

The application was approved and after Dhillon was seen exiting the house with his daughters on March 17, a police search team descended upon the property. Ultimately, they would turn up nothing of significance.[2]

GOING GLOBAL

The rash of bad news was countered on March 15 when Korol and Dhinsa were granted permission by the chief of police to take their investigation overseas. The detectives arrived in Chandigarh by train from New Delhi on May 1, where they met Inspector Subhash Kundu of the Central Bureau of Investigation. A competent and meticulous detective, Kundu had already spent many weeks travelling around Punjab, speaking with the relatives of Dhillon's victims.

The first item on the agenda was a visit to the little village of Tibbia where Dhillon's third wife Kushpreet had died. After two hours of battling ridiculous traffic down a dusty, pot-holed road, they arrived at the home of Rai Singh Toor. As they passed through the black gate into the courtyard, the sun was already dissolving onto the orange horizon. Korol and Dhinsa were introduced to Rai Singh Toor, a Sikh man who showed them the spot in the courtyard where his daughter had collapsed. It was getting late in the day and the three detectives arranged to interview the family at their hotel the next morning. They learned that on the night before her illness, Dhillon had given Kushpreet a pill that he said would prevent her from being pregnant when she showed up for her medical evaluation for immigrating to Canada. The next day, as she was preparing lunch, her skin began to itch and feel like it was on fire. Unable to breathe and with her flesh turning blue, she had been taken into the courtyard by her sister Sukie. As her condition worsened, her powerfully built cousin Pargat had carried her to the end of the road where a Fiat had been summoned to take her to the hospital. By now her lips had pulled back over her gums in a horrific grimace, her body spasming uncontrollably. She was unconscious by the time she reached the hospital. The doctor warned them to take her back home unless they wanted the police to get involved. That meant paying hefty bribes. Kushpreet's family piled their daughter into the back of the Fiat and started on the long return journey to Tibbia. She died along the way. With no investigation, the family concluded she had suffered a heart attack and cremated her.

Having learned the details of Kushpreet's demise, Korol and Dhinsa decided to look into purchasing strychnine, *kuchila* in Punjabi, to prove that Dhillon had access to the murder weapon. It didn't take long before they procured the toxin for ten rupees from a spice store, ostensibly to kill a rabid dog.

At the village of Panj Grain, the detectives met Dhillon's second wife Sarabjit and her father Gurjant who revealed a harrowing tale of deceit, treachery, and murder. Twenty-year-old Sarabjit had been introduced to Dhillon as a potential bride by her uncle Iqbal in March 1995 and after some negotiation the two were married in early April. Dhillon had demanded and received a particularly large dowry of 200,000 rupees, a sum that could only be raised when Sarbajit's grandfather sold half the family farm and his tractor. In return, Dhillon had promised to give her a new life in Canada, opening the door for the rest of her family to follow. However, after weeks of satisfying his repeated demands for sex, her husband suddenly disappeared from her life. Occasionally he sent word that he was arranging for her to join him in Canada, but it wasn't until she disclosed her pregnancy to him that he finally returned to her. Her twin sons Gurmeet and Gurwinder were born on Friday, December 15, 1995, roughly eight-and-a-half months after her wedding. Dhillon phoned the next day to say he was in India, and though he sounded pleased at the birth of the two boys, he demanded that neither child be given a name. Having already made her decision, Sarabjit ignored his commands and registered both names immediately. On Wednesday, December 20, Dhillon finally arrived at the hospital to see them. When he learned that she had refused his requests, he became angry and stormed off, ordering her to stay with her parents. Eight days later, he reappeared at the family home, asking to spend some time alone with his infant sons. After several hours of playing with Gurmeet and Gurwinder he promptly left, insulting his in-laws by refusing to stay for dinner. Sarabjit couldn't help but notice that it was the only time since their wedding that he had not demanded sex with her. It wasn't until later that night that the children began acting strangely. Gurwinder's cries became pained, and when Sarabjit came to comfort him, noticed that his body was convulsing and his skin turning blue. Despite the efforts of the local priests, he was dead by morning. To Sarabjit's horror, Gurmeet followed soon after. Sikh tradition holds that, as babies have not yet developed a soul, they are buried rather than cremated. For Korol and Dhinsa this meant the possibility of exhuming the corpses to undergo toxicology tests.

On May 14, 1997, Korol and Dhinsa returned to Canada, easily smuggling the strychnine through Canadian customs. It took several months of legal wrangling and paperwork before permission was finally granted to exhume the bodies of Gurmeet and Gurwinder Dhillon. Dhinsa returned to India on August 13 with renowned pediatric pathologist Dr. Charles Smith, and three days later recovered the cadavers from Panj Grain cemetery.

NO JUSTICE!

With mountains of evidence accumulating against him, Korol and Dhinsa finally arrested Dhillon at his car dealership on Wednesday, October 22, 1997. During the lengthy preliminary hearing, which began on May 5, 1998, it became clear Dhillon was using his thug friends in India to intimidate witnesses into changing their testimony. Some, including Sarabjit's brother and Kushpreet's cousin, had admitted receiving mysterious phone calls threatening their families with death. Nearly a year later, on April 11, 1999, the judge concluded that there was sufficient evidence to try Dhillon in the deaths of both Parvesh and Ranjit Khela. More good news followed on December 3 — toxicologist Dr. Frederic Rieders had reprocessed Parvesh's tissue at an American laboratory and had discovered her organs to be literally soaked with strychnine. Korol was now certain he would secure convictions on both charges of murder.

All was not sunshine and rainbows though. On December 19, 2000, Judge Glithero ruled that there would be two separate trials for the murders, meaning that evidence used in the Parvesh Dhillon slaying could not be presented at the trial of Ranjit Khela, and vice versa. Perhaps the strongest card in the prosecution's hand, the coincidence factor, was now off the table. Despite this setback, on May 17, Dhillon was found guilty of the first-degree murder of his wife Parvesh, and sentenced to life imprisonment with the possibility of parole in twenty-five years. A similar conviction in the death of Ranjit Khela followed on December 2, provoking an outraged Dhillon to repeatedly shout "no justice" in Punjabi at Judge Glithero. This time, however, Jodha's lies would fail him once and for all. Justice *had* been served, and if it continues to be, Sukhwinder Singh Dhillon, murderer of two wives, two children, and a trusted associate, will be confined to a prison cell for the rest of his pathetic life.

Elizabeth Roth.

Lila and William Young
The Butterbox Baby Killers
Hundreds of Murders
East Chester, Nova Scotia

GOOD CHRISTIANS

Born into a family of Seventh-Day Adventist fishermen in Fox Point, Nova Scotia, Lila Gladys Coolen was one of eight sons and three daughters. Early accounts of her life reveal a woman whose compassion and generosity were overshadowed by her obstinance. Though she dreamed of teaching, at age twenty-six, Lila met unordained preacher William Peach Young in Memramcook, New Brunswick, became pregnant, and married. A native of Oregon, William (born January 11, 1898) had followed his father into the Seventh-Day Adventist Church, spreading the gospel across North

America. Anticipating a career as a medical missionary, he studied at a missionary school in Oshawa, Ontario, before going on to graduate from the College of Medical Evangelists in California.

Lila's pregnancy was an excruciating ordeal, and her chronic back pain would spur William's interest in alternative medicine. Following the birth of their first child, the Youngs moved to Chicago where in December 1927 William became a licensed chiropractor while Lila graduated from the National School of Obstetrics and Midwifery. The Youngs returned to Nova Scotia and opened the "Life and Health Sanitarium" in February 1928, sixty-four kilometres southwest of Halifax in East Chester. Soon renamed the "Ideal Maternity Home and Sanitarium," in reality the four-bedroom cottage was little more than a baby farm. Lila worked as the resident midwife and managing director, while her husband took on the duties of superintendent. Between 1928 and 1933, at least seventy babies were born at the establishment. Unlike similar institutions, the Ideal Maternity Home held wide appeal as it did not discriminate on the grounds of religious faith. Beginning in the 1930s, the Youngs published advertisements in the newspaper, urging interested readers to write to them for information. Arriving in the mail, the subsequent brochures promised discreet housing for unwed expectant mothers. For roughly $150 in advance, the Ideal Maternity Home provided room and board, delivered the baby, and, if necessary, arranged an adoption. There was an additional $12 fee for diapers and supplies and a weekly charge of $2 for maintaining a baby until a suitable home could be found. Infants that did not survive the delivery or who died of crib death were buried in white pine butter boxes for a cost of fifty cents per corpse. It was not unusual for the total bill to have escalated beyond $300 by the time the women left the home. Those from poorer families were given the option to work off their debt, ensuring that the home was never in need of staff. Beyond these overt costs, patients were also obliged to sign a contract granting William power of attorney and legal authority over both babies and adoptions.

Whereas William came off as a wimp with his steel-rimmed glasses and pencil moustache, Lila has been described as having a fearsome presence. Remembered as "rough" and "immense" in stature, there seemed no one the Maritime midwife wasn't able to terrify.

Unfortunately for the Youngs, Lila's tough image would not avert the suspicions of the public health minister. When Liberal Dr. Frank Davis ascended to the position in 1933, he began to hear strange rumours about the Ideal Maternity Home. East Chester physicians claimed the mortality rate was substantially higher than other Canadian hospitals, while locals whispered of dead babies decomposing in the open air at Fox Point's Seventh Day Adventist Cemetery. When questioned, Lila dismissed this as an isolated incident where a body had been left temporarily exposed while they searched for a labourer. Though initial inspections of the home revealed nothing out of the ordinary, Davis remained suspicious, ordering the deputy registrar of births and deaths in Chester to withhold issuing burial certificates to the Youngs prior to an RCMP investigation.

Despite his efforts to expose the truth about the Youngs' sordid business practices, for the time being, Davis remained unsuccessful. Meanwhile the Ideal Maternity Home flourished with eighty reported births from 1935 to 1936. Grossing $6,000 annually during the Great Depression, the Youngs quickly became wealthy and influential citizens.

FROM THE WOMB TO THE BUTTERBOX

It wasn't until the 1936 death of Seaforth woman Eva Nieforth that the Youngs' fortunes began to change. Impregnated by a drifter, Eva had already reached her ninth month when she arrived by sleigh to the Ideal Maternity Home just over a week before Christmas 1935. She soon contracted an abdominal infection and was confined to a cot until January 28 when she went into an agonizing labour. Her child perished shortly after birth, and within a day, Eva's infection had become inflamed and there were no antibiotics on the premises to treat her. Receiving a letter from William Young, Eva's boyfriend Walter hurried to the maternity home to find her near death. When he suggested calling a physician in East Chester, William dismissed the idea, claiming that he was already a doctor. The Youngs cajoled Walter into paying $20 for the burial of the infant and $5 for a shroud, before sending him on his way. By February 1, Eva Nieforth had succumbed. Charges of manslaughter were filed against the Youngs for the deaths of both mother and child. It was believed they perished from a combination of negligence and poor sanitation at the home. During their trial, provincial pathologist Dr. Ralph Smith testified that he had performed autopsies on the victims and suspected Eva had contracted peritonitis from unsterilized obstetric instruments. The infection had slowly spread from her uterus to her perineum, causing abscesses that ruptured, resulting in a torturous death. Improper use of forceps on her newborn had loosened the scalp and broken off the occipital bone. The Youngs took the stand to deny the charges, and in May 1936 they were acquitted. Throughout the proceedings it was revealed that with 148 births and twelve deaths at the home from 1928 to 1935, the infant mortality rate was 8.1 percent, a figure 5 percent higher than the rest of the province. From then on, the RCMP made a policy of scrutinizing every death at the home. What they didn't realize was that the Youngs were only reporting a fraction of the total.

It is estimated that over a hundred other infant corpses were buried next to the Adventist cemetery in a meadow in Fox Point. It was simply more profitable that way — the Youngs charged $300 to board a child for the rest of their natural lives. By ensuring those natural lives met a most unnatural end, the Youngs racked up a small fortune in no time, expanding their original cottage to a fifty-four-room complex worth an estimated $40,000 — a colossal sum at the time.

Glen Shatford, a handyman at the Ideal Maternity Home, recalled a hot July day in 1938 when he discovered a baby's body concealed in a wash basin in the workshed. Startled, he covered it with a scrub board and continued about his work. Five days later, William wrapped the corpse in a sheet and placed it in the trunk of his blue Ford. He and Glen Shatford drove to an overgrown plot of land bordering the Seventh Day Adventist cemetery. After digging a shallow grave, William covered his face with a rag and buried the baby in a butterbox below the cold earth. As the Youngs' employee, such tasks typically fell to Glen, leaving the handyman perplexed as to why William had insisted on burying this particular infant himself.

1939 marked another strange occurrence a the Ideal Maternity Home. While patient Violet Hatt struggled to give birth, Lila suddenly declared the baby was choking on its own umbilical cord and that she had no idea what to do. To Violet's astonishment, the tearful midwife fell to her knees and began praying. Fortunately, William arrived to successfully deliver the baby — a breech birth. Days later, while the new mother recovered from her harrowing ordeal, Lila entered the room with a baby in her arms, claiming that it was Violet's and had taken ill. Strangely, she kept her distance from the bed, standing in shadows where Violet could not see the infant's face. Soon after, Lila returned with shocking news — the child was dead. Rather than accepting the story, Violet was deeply suspicious. For some time, rumours had been circulating around the home that a wealthy couple in Winnipeg were inquiring into adopting a baby girl. Violet's daughter had been the only one on the premises. Until her last breath, the unfortunate mother remained convinced the Youngs had stolen her child and sold her into adoption.

On another occasion, the Youngs' neighbour, Eleanor Marriott, accepted an offer from Lila to feed, clothe, and care for one of the babies for $3/week. However, the child arrived into her care emaciated and barely clinging to life. Horrified, Marriott contacted a physician in East Chester whose examination revealed the baby was severely malnourished. Within a week it had perished. Subsequently she learned from a cook at the maternity home that babies who were ill or not fit for adoption (the deformed, birthmarked, or non-Caucasian) were placed on starvation diets of molasses and water. Marriott's fisherman husband was also paid on occasion to bury dead infants at sea, and many recalled the noxious stench of burning frequently emanating from the Youngs' property.

By the late thirties, the Youngs' reputation had become so sordid that they were disfellowshipped from the Seventh Day Adventist Church. Now William was including a waiver with their power of attorney contract, clearing the Ideal Maternity Home of all legal culpability resulting from a child's death. For their own part, the Nova Scotia government passed the Maternity Boarding House Act in April 1940 as a first step in the battle against baby farming. The Youngs were now required to keep records of patients' names, ages, and addresses that would be subject to review by the director of child welfare. It became illegal to advertise child adoption services (though they flagrantly violated this), maternity homes were obliged to submit to routine inspections without prior warning, and the director of child welfare had to be informed of any institutional deaths within twenty-four hours. Amazingly, business continued to grow at the Ideal Maternity Home, owing chiefly to the wartime baby boom. In 1941, a second nursery was added to accomodate the surplus of children, now averaging seventy. Prices had also risen to at least $300 for the delivery and adoption of babies, and between 1941 and 1946, the Youngs were arranging fifteen to twenty adoptions monthly. The couple were now netting $60,000 annually, not including the $1,000–$10,000 they made for each baby they sold.

EXPOSED

Despite the Youngs' suspicious behaviour, it wasn't until August of 1945 that health officials finally found proof of squalid conditions at the Ideal Maternity Home. Among the infractions reported were starving infants, abysmal hygiene, inadequate ventilation, and vermin infestation. Eighty babies lay in crowded rooms swarmed by flies, some in puddles of vomit, their bodies ruddied with urine from soiled diapers. Simultaneously, changes to the 1940 Maternity Boarding House Act made licensing required for all incorporated maternity homes. Based on its horrendous reputation, the Ideal Maternity Home's application was rejected. In November 1945, the business was ordered to close, though the Youngs continued to run it unlicenced while their case went through appeals. Faced with legal fees and a collapsing enterprise, William began to drink heavily and conduct secret affairs with younger women. 1946 saw U.S. Immigration and the RCMP uncover evidence that the Youngs had smuggled babies illegally across the border. By March they had been arraigned for practising medicine without a licence and violating the Maternity Board House Act. The consequence — a paltry $150 fine. For illegally selling babies to four American couples they were fined a meagre $428.90. But Lila bit off more than she could chew when she pursued a $25,000 libel suit against Montreal newspaper, *The Standard*, which had publicized the case. Jurors took no time in rejecting the suit. The resulting trial exposed the

Ideal Maternity Home as an unethical and corrupt business, prompting its closure. Penniless, the Youngs relocated to Quebec, where William died from cancer. In 1967, Lila moved back to Nova Scotia, succumbing to leukemia two years later at the age of seventy. Seven years before her death, the Ideal Maternity Home mysteriously burned to the ground. In an interview with author Bette L. Cahill, handyman Glenn Shatford admitted burying between 100 to 125 babies in rows behind the property. If true, this could potentially make William and Lila Young the most prolific serial murderers in Canadian history.

CHAPTER 9

THE HEDONIST-LUST KILLER

Anatomy of the Hedonist-Lust Killer[1]
Characteristics:
- Process-focused
- Controlled crime scene
- Usually overkill
- Evidence of torture is possible
- Body usually moved
- Victim is unknown to killer, but is a specific type (i.e., blond woman, black man, etc.)
- No weapon at the crime scene
- Aberrant sex probable, penile and object penetration, necrophilia
- May strangle victim
- Killer is male
- Cannibalism/vampirism possible

The Hedonist-Lust Killer is compelled by deviant sexual urges for which he must kill to satisfy. This can be as simple as the need to eliminate the only witness to a rape, or it might foray into the outright ghoulish. Edmund Emil Kemper III of Santa Cruz, California, fantasized about having sex with headless corpses. He claimed he did not wish to kill his beautiful co-ed victims, however given his sexual preferences, their deaths were unavoidable. The same goes for "The Plainsfield Ghoul," Ed Gein, a Wisconsin man who, in the 1950s, dug up graves in order to fashion himself a suit of female skin. In the colder months the ground froze and forced him to kill to get the necessary materials. Gein murdered two women, gutting and skinning them like deer before he was caught. Another classic lust killer, Oregon electrician Jerry Brudos, kept the foot of his first victim in a freezer so that he could use it to model high-heeled shoes. Later in the series, he suspended his victims' bodies from a hook, photographing them wearing different outfits. He also cut off the breast of his third victim, using it as a mould for a paperweight.

The following Canadian examples of Hedonist-Lust murderers are nowhere near as extreme. **Henry Williams** is a textbook example of a sexual sadist and picquerist. As we will see in his attack on Julia Sheldon, Williams made shallow stabs to torture her while probing for her heart, deriving sexual satisfaction from the sensation of piercing her skin and watching blood ooze over her back. In the mid-seventies, "The Mad Slasher" **Christian Magee** terrorized the London area. Like Williams, he felt a strong sexual compulsion to lacerate his victims' flesh, though Magee also committed minor acts of necrophilia.

Other Hedonist-Lust Killers in This Book

Donald Sherman Staley, Danny Wood, Donald Armstrong, Earle Nelson, Serge Archambault, William Dean Christensen, Peter Woodcock, Joseph LaPage, Allan Sweeney, Melvin Stanton, Paul Cecil Gillis

Henry Williams
2 Murders
Mississauga Area, Ontario

CANADIAN HOSPITALITY

Julia Sheldon was having a wonderful time in Canada. It was August 19, 1974, and the Canadian summer was in full bloom. All that sun and clear sky made a nice change from gloomy old England. Today had also been particularly fun. The attractive sixteen-year-old had spent the better half of it at the Canadian National Exhibition, and had the stuffed teddy bear in hand as proof. She caught the mid-afternoon GO Train from Exhibition station, disembarking at Clarkson around 3:00 p.m. A friend had volunteered to pick her up, but when she called him she received no answer. Anxious to make it home in time for tea, she decided to thumb a ride — it was not considered a particularly risky activity at the time and the city transit workers were on strike. It wasn't long before a car stopped to offer her a lift. The driver was an ordinary-looking fellow of about twenty-five and any doubts she had were soon assuaged by the child's car seat in the back. She climbed into the front beside him and they took off through the Mississauga suburbs. Glancing around the vehicle, Julia spotted the name "Henry Williams" and an address on a dashboard sticker. Several minutes passed as the two made small talk when suddenly Williams cranked the wheel, cutting the vehicle across a field and toward a wooded area. Terrified, Julia reached for the door handle. The next thing she knew he was upon her. The passenger side door burst open and the two tumbled out onto the coarse, dry grass. His hands seized her around the throat. She could hear the shallow wheezing of her breath as he slowly crushed the life from her body. Once he had established control, the man bound her hands behind her back, tore off her T-shirt and jammed it into her mouth. With Julia now at his complete mercy, Williams went on to sexually assault her. When he had finished that, he produced a knife and began stabbing her in the back; not hard at first, just enough to break the skin. It was as if the act of repeatedly penetrating her with the cold steel brought him some kind of bizarre sexual gratification. Finally, when he believed he had found her heart,

Williams slowly pushed the blade into her back, hefted a nearby rock and brought it crashing down upon her head. The world seemed to cut in and out like an unplugged television. Bound, overpowered, and bleeding to death, Julia Sheldon did the only thing she could: she played dead. Slow and cool-headed, he dragged her toward the bushes and began to pile rocks and branches on top of her. She waited as he cleaned up after himself, double-checking to see if he had left any evidence behind. Then he departed. Julia waited several minutes before struggling to free herself from her rocky grave. Bleeding from several places, she was nevertheless able to stagger across the field toward Winston Churchill and College Way where, fortuitously, emergency workers had arrived at the scene of an accident. Sobbing and on the brink of collapse, she recited her ordeal to the paramedics and was taken to hospital where she was treated for, among other things, a collapsed lung, a concussion, and multiple stab wounds. She was confined to the hospital for a period of three weeks. Fortunately, Julia Sheldon survived to implicate Henry Williams in her attempted murder. A quick look at the suspect didn't reveal much out of the ordinary. Williams was a married father of two who held down a steady job as a bricklayer. When police brought him into custody, however, they recovered a wad of English currency in his possession. It was clear: he had stolen the money from Julia Sheldon.

Once in the interrogation room, Williams broke down, admitting to attacking her, along with the unsolved rape-murders of Constance Dickey on September 11, 1973, and Neda Novak on October 4, 1973. After enrolling at the University of Toronto's Erindale Campus, the nineteen-year-old Dickey had vanished, only to be found sexually assaulted and strangled with wire in a nearby wood five days later. Novak, sixteen, had lain under a pile of rubble in Streetsville until April 30 when she was finally discovered. Williams later led investigators to the exact spots where he had dumped their bodies.

Despite efforts to convince the jury he was insane, Williams was found guilty of both homicides, along with the attempted murder of Julia Sheldon, garnering three life sentences to be served concurrently at Warkworth penitentiary. Blaming his crimes on uncontrollable sexual desire, Williams signed authorization forms permitting the state to castrate him in the hopes that one day he would be released from prison. As no doctor was willing to perform the operation, the procedure never took place.

In 1984, Julia Sheldon learned that Williams was being let out of prison on escorted day passes. When she brought this to the attention of the authorities it was learned that those responsible hadn't even bothered to interview Williams first. Julia travelled to Kingston where she made a presentation to the parole board and Williams's privileges were swiftly revoked.

Intrigued by the bits and pieces of police work she had picked up during the trial, Julia joined the Ontario Provincial Police, and, along with being a wife and mother, remains an active member of the force to this day. She has lectured frequently at an Aylmer, Ontario, police college on the subject of "how to survive an attack." She is adamant that for Williams, sexual assault was secondary. The real pleasure appeared as he attempted to murder her.

Andre Kirchhoff.

Christian Magee
The Mad Slasher
3 Murders
Strathroy/Mount Brydges,
Ontario

"We ain't criminals, that's supposed to be the difference between this place and the correctional system."

THE MAD SLASHER

On March 1, 1974, nineteen-year-old Judith Barksey left a Strathroy pizza restaurant, unaware that she was being followed. It was a bone-chilling winter night, and, anxious to feel the warmth of her home, she decided to cut across the railroad tracks. Before she knew what was happening, she was seized roughly by the hair and dragged to the asphalt. She would have felt the cold steel blade only momentarily before it slashed her throat. As she lay bleeding to death in the darkness, her assailant unbuttoned her pants and fondled her genitals. Then, taking whatever money he could find on her person, he retreated into the shadows. Just before noon the next day, a man posting a letter stumbled across Judith's body bleeding around a splattered pizza box, pop bottles, and a chocolate bar.

Fifteen months later, another Strathroy woman, eighteen-year-old Rosalie Winters, was heading toward Alexandra Park when all at once she was tackled to the ground. Her long-haired assailant made clear his intentions to rape her, and when he began to squeeze her neck, she acquiesced, if only to stop the pain. As he struggled to undo her pants, the zipper suddenly broke. Frustrated, he choked her unconscious and groped her vagina, but left without killing her.

His next victim would not be so lucky. It was October 20, 1975, when nineteen-year-old Mount Brydges resident Louise Jenner received an unexpected knock on her door. She opened it to reveal Christian Magee, a handsome friend whom she invited inside. However, once the door was closed, Magee forced her to the floor and tore off her pants. He started to rape her, but inexplicably stopped and withdrew after several minutes. Terrified, the woman clambered back into her clothes, but it was too late. Magee looped a black bootlace around her neck and strangled her into unconsciousness before finishing her with a jackknife to the throat. He fled the scene, leaving her in a puddle of blood on her kitchen floor. She was found at 5:00 p.m. the same evening by her husband, Denys. Upstairs, their baby daughter Rachel lay unharmed in her crib.

Unlike the previous two attacks, police had a number of leads to pursue in this latest murder. An elderly neighbour reported seeing a young white male with shoulder-length dark hair pull into Jenner's driveway in what looked to be a yellow or cream-coloured late-model Oldsmobile. He had stood outside the doorway for several minutes before entering. Inside, photographs strewn across a chesterfield led police to believe that Louise had been showing pictures to an acquaintance. This meant the killer probably knew his victim. One suspect, Christian Magee, not only had access to a cream-coloured automobile, but also knew both Jenner and Barksey. Brought in for questioning, he denied knowing anything about the murders and was released from custody.

Despite coming under police scrutiny, Magees's bloodlust remained unsated. On November 3, he picked up nineteen-year-old hitchhiker Sylvia Holly Jennings just outside of London. Driving to an isolated Mount Brydges side road, he told her to remove her clothes, and when she hesitated, tore them off in a sexual frenzy. When the girl began to kick and scream he struck her to subdue her before brutally raping her. Choking her unconscious, he then smashed a bottle over her head, fracturing her skull. She would later awake on the roadside covered with blood.

The following summer on June 15, 1976, Magee repeated his modus operandi, offering a ride to Susan Scholes, fifteen, who was hitchhiking to her parents' cottage in Hillsboro Beach. He raped her, strangled her, stabbed her in the throat and chest, and savagely slashed at her genitals. When a farmer discovered her body at 2:15 p.m. the next afternoon, she was clad only in bikini briefs. Police noted a twenty-centimetre laceration above her vagina. Retracing Susan's final hours, they learned that at 1:00 p.m. the previous day, her brother Geoffrey had dropped her in the town of Forest to buy batteries for her portable radio. She had been spotted at 1:30 p.m., walking toward County Road 12 by a Mr. McFarlane. The fork-lift driver also reported seeing her climb into a 1975 Ford truck used locally for picking up dead animals. When Mr. John Grinsven, the owner of the Strathroy-based company, was contacted by the OPP, he revealed that on the day in question, the truck had been driven by none other than Christian Magee. Though Magee claimed to have dropped Susan safely along the roadside, an inspection of the vehicle revealed the company's filleting knife to be missing. At long last, police had the evidence they needed to charge "The Mad Slasher" with murder.

DELUSIONAL

In 1977, Christian Magee stood trial for the rape-slaying of Susan Scholes, but was found not guilty by reason of insanity and committed to Oak Ridge Maximum Security mental healthcare facility. Three years later he was found not guilty by reason of insanity on two counts of first degree murder, one count of rape, and one count of indecent assault. Magee claimed to have endured a loveless, physically and emotionally abusive childhood that left him void of self esteem. To correct his slouch, his mother had forced him to carry a broomstick behind his back, curled in his elbows. His parents repeatedly told him he would amount to nothing, while his older brother beat him mercilessly.

Dr. Philip Klassen conducted a five hour assessment of Magee in April of 2004 and concluded that the Mad Slasher suffered from a personality disorder and had fantasies of torture, necrophilia, cannibalism, and dismemberment; a mindset in keeping with classic sexual sadism.

Since his imprisonment at Oak Ridge, Magee has busied himself building baby cradles and rocking horses for various charities. Having converted to Protestantism, he claims that God has since been using him to help people and that he no longer has violent urges. In early 2006, he applied to the Ontario Court of Appeals to be moved from Oak Ridge to Toronto's Centre for Addiction and Mental Health (CAMH). This would have been a first step toward Magee's eventual release. As Magee pointed out in an interview with the *Toronto Star*: "There has to be a progression of better treatment and privileges … this place thinks all they have to do is house the person, but the courts sent people here for treatment.… We ain't criminals, that's supposed to be the difference between this place and the correctional system."[2] If need be, Magee has expressed his willingness to meet the families of the victims face to face if to give them a sense of closure. But employees at Oak Ridge voiced concern that such a move would put more distance between Magee and the jurisdiction of the Ontario Review Board. His court-appointed lawyer Daniel Brodsky argued that Magee would have been better off in a penitentiary where by now he would have been in minimum security or released. But even the prospect of transferring Magee to minimum security has raised eyebrows. The move would allow him to eventually get day passes.[3] Though it is a commonly held belief in the psychiatric community that psychopaths can never be cured, in May 1991 the Supreme Court of Canada ruled that it was a violation of human rights to incarcerate a mentally ill person indefinitely. The repercussions of this law are simple and frightening: one day, Christian Magee *must* be released. In 2006, a visitor claiming to be Magee's child posted the following message at *tocrime.blogspot.com*, a popular blog (all spelling errors belong to the author of the post):

i can say in my heart i feel this man should stay right where he is at. I am scared day after day of this man. He has tried contacting me and if he gets out ever i feel that i am in danager and so is my family. My prayers go out to those families he hurts i wish there was something i could do. I will continue fighting anyone who is tring to get him out. I ask everyone and anyone to please support me in my fight, not just for the safety of me and my family but for the saftey of yous.[4]

THE HEDONIST-THRILL KILLER

Anatomy of the Hedonist-Thrill Killer[1]
Characteristics:
- Process-focused
- Controlled crime scene
- No overkill
- Evidence of torture is probable
- Body usually moved
- Victim is unknown to killer, but is a specific type (i.e., blond woman, black man, etc.)
- No weapon at the crime scene
- Aberrant sex possible, penile and object penetration, no necrophilia
- May strangle victim
- Killer is male
- No cannibalism/vampirism

In order to understand the hedonist-thrill killer, one simply has to look to California during the sixties and seventies. From 1967 to 1978, a mysterious predator calling himself "Zodiac" murdered at least five people in and around the San Francisco area. He claimed his first three victims by creeping up on couples parked in "lover's lanes," firing his pistol through their windows. The Zodiac later switched his MO, pulling a gun on two young lovers sunbathing at a lake, and tying them up. Once they were secure in their bonds, he began to excitedly stab them, killing the woman. Finally, he shot a taxi driver in the back of the head while parked in a San Francisco subdivision. Though he tended to inflict greater trauma on his female victims, at no time did the Zodiac rape or fondle them before or after death. His sole purpose came from the thrill of inflicting pain and terror on his victims and San Francisco as a whole. That is not to say that some hedonist-thrill killers don't rape their victims. "The Hillside Stranglers," Kenneth Bianchi and Angelo Buono, spent hours sexually violating and torturing their victims, before dumping their bodies like trash by the roadside. Interestingly, the motivating force of the hedonist-thrill killer has best been described by Texas drifter Tommy Lynn Sells, a drug addict with an 80 IQ who is believed to have murdered as many as sixty people over his twenty-year killing career: "I didn't do it for the power, I didn't do it for the sex.... Like a shot of dope, I did it for the rush."

Unfortunately, Canada has had its share of angry psychopaths who value a momentary thrill over the lives of their fellow human beings. **James Greenidge** got his kicks repeatedly stabbing his victims and leaving them in remote areas to die. Like Tommy Lynn Sells, "The Homicidal Drifter" **Michael McGray** was a creature of endless variety, killing men, women, and children from coast to coast, in every way imaginable.

Other Hedonist-Thrill Killers in This Book
Michael Briscoe and Joseph Laboucan, Clifford Olson, Allan Legere

James Greenidge
2–6 Murders
Markham, Ontario/Vancouver, British Columbia

RAGE

As if being born a black man in 1940s Toronto wasn't hard enough, young James Henry Greenidge suffered from neglect and both physical and psychological abuse at the hands of his domineering aunt, giving rise to an insurmountable temper. Developing tuberculosis at the age of five, he was removed to a sanatorium where he was ordered to clean toilets. A habitual thief and runaway, Greenidge was eventually sent to reform school where he was repeatedly sexually assaulted, likely paving the way for his later sexual sadism. By age sixteen, he was a male prostitute and narcissist, viewing himself as a lone wolf and a victim of racial persecution. Growing up, his aunt had repeatedly instilled in him a fear of white women and homosexuals, and unsurprisingly it would be from these two groups that Greenidge would ultimately draw his victims.

The first to suffer at his hands was a fourteen-year-old girl carrying her bags home from the grocery store. Pouncing upon her, Greenidge tore her clothes from her body and beat her to a bloody pulp before raping and nearly choking her to death. Twenty-one days later, he was arrested at his job in a hospital laundry room and sentenced to ten years in prison. Following his parole in 1960, there is little doubt that Greenidge resumed his old habits, though it was not until 1965 that he would be caught red-handed. Spotting a man whom he believed was responsible for his incarceration, Greenidge overwhelmed him with a brutal attack, dragging him thirty metres into an alleyway. Neighbours overheard the commotion and telephoned the police, who arrived to arrest Greenidge in the process of trying to murder the man. Convicted once again, he would spend a mere six months in a reformatory before being released to commence his most savage spree of violence yet.

After picking up a young man at a movie theatre in Toronto's Gay Village, Greenidge drove them out to farmer's field north of Barrie, where his partner requested $20 for sex. Flying into a rage, Greenidge punched and kicked his victim senseless, before repeatedly driving a pen knife into his chest. Binding the man's body to prevent him from moving, Greenidge fled, leaving him to die in the field. Fortune intervened, and his victim was miraculously found and saved.

The first murder that can be confidently attributed to James Henry Greenidge is that of seventeen-year-old Robert Wayne Mortimore. The insurance clerk was reported missing by a sibling on July 11, 1967, his rotting corpse eventually discovered in a meadow northeast of Markham where he was identified through fingerprints. A portion of the deceased's birth certificate was found in Greenidge's car, along with two of his rings, a chain with a gold cross, and a pair of Mortimore's blue and white pants. By the time this evidence was discovered, Greenidge was already serving a prison term for the attempted murder of the man from the Gay Village.

Though common sense would dictate that such a dangerous individual should never be released from prison, that's exactly what happened in 1978. Changing his name to James Gordon Henry, shortly after his release he was charged with sodomizing a thirteen-year-old Winnipeg boy and attempting to strangle him with a blanket. Eventually, the charges were stayed.

Having relocated to Vancouver in 1981, Greenidge picked up prostitute Elizabeth Fells and drove her to a secluded area in the north woods, ostensibly to engage in sex. Once he had isolated the young woman, Greenidge viciously raped and stabbed her, finishing by slitting her throat and leaving her to bleed out in the dirt. Remarkably, Elizabeth Fells managed to somehow crawl to the Squamish Highway where she was discovered by a passing motorist. Eight days later, she died in a hospital bed, but not before identifying her assailant. As a result, James Henry Greenidge was convicted of her murder, and has spent the last thirty years locked in a British Columbia jail. He is described as a model prisoner with a high IQ, and has reportedly completed an "intensive sex offender program." The ability to adapt well to structured surroundings is not unusual among serial killers, and it is still likely that if the geriatric Greenidge is ever released, he will revert to his old ways. Now nearing his mid-seventies, he holds the distinction of not only being a rare bisexual thrill killer, but also the first confirmed African-Canadian serial murderer in history.

THE MARKHAM TRANSVESTITE MURDER

Aside from the likelihood that Greenidge was responsible for the **Toronto Gay Village Murders** (see Chapter 4), he is also suspected of the 1978 slaying of a John/Jane Doe in Markham. At around 8:30 p.m. on July 16, 1980, a man pulled over along a country road in Markham to urinate, wandering roughly twenty-five metres into the surrounding woods. There he came upon a set of skeletal remains, later identified as belonging to a small white man between the ages of twenty-five and forty who had likely lain in the spot for two years. Strangely, the body was found next to a pile of women's clothing including size 30 jeans, a red blouse with matching high heel shoes, white socks, and a cosmetics compact containing powder and a make-up mirror. Though police quickly deduced that the victim was transvestite or transgendered, they also concluded that he had been hit by a passing car and literally knocked out of his clothes. As incredulous as this account is, it would have also meant that the John/Jane Doe's garments had landed in the exact same spot.

On Christmas Eve 1983, the remains were interred in Toronto's Mount Pleasant Cemetery along with the clothing found at the crime scene. Four years later, York Regional Police decided to reinvestigate the case, recognizing that it was clearly murder, and exhuming the body to collect DNA. Eventually, a clay reconstruction of the face was made, though there have been no successful attempts to identify the victim.

Released into a minimum security prison in 1977, Greenidge is the number-one suspect. Not only was he regularly permitted unescorted weekend passes to Toronto to visit a friend, his crime fits the modus operandi, and he was in the right place and time to commit the murder.

Andre Kirchhoff.

Michael McGray
The Homicidal Drifter
7–17 Murders
Across Canada

"I need to kill somebody!"

MONCTON

Michael Wayne McGray was a drifter — a man who owed no allegiance and expected none in return. He knew full well what society had in store for him, the sexual abuse he had endured in group homes and reform schools had taught him that. Nor did he give a rat's ass about his only family: an angry, drunken father who mercilessly beat him and taught him to hurt animals before tossing him out of the house in his early teens. Instead of embracing his fellow man, McGray embraced the chaos and excitement of the highway.

On the evening of February 28, 1998, the thirty-four-year-old found himself in Moncton, New Brunswick, mainlining cocaine with his friend, Glen Bennett. The desire to spill blood had been building for some time, and with the coke surging through his brain, McGray felt full of energy and confidence. *Yes, tonight.* Soon he would be smelling the blood and savouring the screams of his victims. If he didn't, he thought he'd probably go crazy.

Joan Hicks, forty-eight, had moved to Moncton with her eleven-year-old daughter Nina to be closer to her imprisoned lover Aubrey Sparks. Natives of Musgrave Harbour, Newfoundland, the two had only been in Moncton for six months, initially living at a woman's shelter where they met Tammy McClain. The twenty-two-year-old had been quarrelling with her boyfriend, Mike, and Joan, a truly compassionate

245

soul, was always willing to lend a sympathetic ear. Despite their age differences, the two women quickly became friends. Tammy helped Joan and her daughter find a basement apartment in the city, and they often had her over for coffee and a game of cards. Earlier in the evening of February 28, Tammy telephoned Joan to tell her she was fighting with her boyfriend again, and asked if she could come over to get away for a while. As always, Joan welcomed her with open arms. Some time after Tammy arrived, there was a knock on the door. Joan opened it to find two dangerous-looking men standing in the early morning darkness. The scarier of the two, a moustached fellow with a stony glower, introduced himself as Tammy's boyfriend, Mike McGray. He ordered Tammy into a taxi and she obeyed. Once the vehicle had sped into the night, McGray went to use the bathroom, but found there was no toilet paper. When Joan rose to fetch it for him, he seized her suddenly around the neck, slamming her against the wall. For perhaps a minute or more the poor woman gargled and fought, but she was no match for his bestial strength. Unconscious, she slipped to the floor where he furiously beat her and slit her throat with a bread knife. The heady aroma of blood rose around him like a storm, charging him with murderous thunder. Glen Bennett looked on in helpless horror as McGray set his sights on young Nina. It was like a nightmare from which he would never awake.

Later that morning, the pale-faced Bennett walked into the Moncton police station, visibly upset and rambling about a murder. When police arrived at the basement apartment they soon understood his agitation. Joan Hicks lay sprawled near the bathroom door, the pool of blood around her body turned brown and syrupy. After a brief search, Nina was found hanging dead in the closet. A subsequent autopsy revealed she had been smothered to death before this final indignity occurred. With both a name and address to go on, the outraged police apprehended McGray at Tammy McClain's apartment where the two were playing cards.

TIP OF THE ICEBERG

Once in custody, McGray hinted at numerous other murders he had committed across Canada in the late eighties and early nineties. A plea bargain was arranged with the police, and soon he was spilling his guts.

On April 24, 1985, he had been driving with a fellow miscreant near Waymouth, Nova Scotia, when he spotted a teenaged girl thumbing at the side of the road. They stopped to offer her a ride, but once she was in the vehicle McGray demanded oral sex as payment. When she refused, he became outraged and pulled her out of the truck, knifing her to death in the dirt. Seventeen-year-old Gayle Tucker would not be found until six months later, so decomposed that she had to be identified through dental records.

Another senseless killing took place in November 1987 in Saint John, New Brunswick. McGray and two other undesirables, Norm Warren and Mark Daniel Gibbons, had been riding in a taxi on a Saturday night. When they reached their destination, they told the cabbie he was being robbed. Without warning, Gibbons plunged a knife into the cabbie's body, killing him. The three men took off into the night. Eventually Gibbons and McGray stopped for a rest, at which point the latter knifed his accomplice to death for botching the robbery. When questioned by police, McGray blamed Warren for Gibbons's murder and they believed him. Three lives were taken that day, including that of Norman Warren, who spent eleven years incarcerated for a crime he didn't commit.

McGray also claimed responsibility for the 1991 murders of two homosexuals in Montreal. Though imprisoned in a minimum-security Quebec prison at the time, he had managed to obtain a day pass for an Easter weekend outing. When he arrived in the city, he checked into a halfway house, as was required, and awoke the next day with an overwhelming urge to kill. At some point he travelled to the Gay Village where he picked up homosexual retiree Robert Assaly at a local bar. The two went back to Robert's apartment to watch TV and enjoy some more drinks. McGray fell asleep and awoke at 6:00 a.m. the next morning to the sound of his host dressing himself in a nearby bedroom. Snatching a knife from the kitchen, he confronted Robert and ordered him to lie down. When his victim burst into laughter, McGray smashed his skull in with a nearby lamp and stabbed him multiple times in the chest and throat. Pilfering a bottle of booze, he left the apartment intent on having more good times in the city. A week later, Robert Assaly was found. By that time, McGray had claimed his second homosexual victim. Unemployed salesman Gaetan Ethier had invited him over to his bachelor pad where the two watched hockey and shared a bottle of wine. When it became apparent that McGray wasn't going to warm to his advances, Ethier passed out on his bed. The next morning, McGray awoke his host by shattering a beer bottle over his head and knifing him to death. Soon after, he returned to the prison as if nothing had happened.

UNREFORMED

While being transported to the federal penitentiary in Renous, McGray offered to confess to a further eleven murders across Canada and the Pacific Northwest. In return, he wanted immunity from prosecution and medical treatment for his homicidal urges. Unsurprisingly, the deal was refused.

Over the course of a fifteen-minute media interview, McGray spoke of wandering aimlessly from Vancouver to Halifax, sticking to gay districts or the seedier parts of town frequented by prostitutes and drug addicts. These easy targets comprised the bulk of his victims. McGray seemed calm and detached, at one point claiming that he was only bothered that the killings *didn't* bother him. In 2001, he plead guilty to the first-degree murders of Nina and Joan Hicks, Robert Assaly, Gaetan Ethier, Gayle Tucker, and Mark Gibbons's second-degree murder, earning concurrent life sentences. Confined to Atlantic maximum security at Renous, McGray maintained for years that if given the opportunity, he would continue to kill. Prison guards began to take these claims more seriously when their celebrity prisoner attempted to smuggle a shiv into a meeting with his defence lawyer. Clearly, even those on Michael McGray's side risked falling prey to his deadly compulsions.

By May 2011, this lesson had long been lost on the Canadian Correctional System. While incarcerated at Mountain Institution in British Columbia's Fraser Valley, McGray battered his cellmate Jeremy Phillips unconscious with a cat-scratch post, then strangled him to death with his bedsheets. In the weeks leading up to his murder, Phillips had allegedly begged to be transferred out of concern for his personal safety.

CHAPTER 11

THE POWER/CONTROL KILLER

Anatomy of the Power/Control Killer[1]

Characteristics:

- Process-focused
- Controlled crime scene
- No overkill
- Evidence of torture is probable
- Body usually moved
- Victim is unknown to killer, but is a specific type (i.e., blond woman, black man, etc.)
- No weapon at the crime scene
- Aberrant sex possible, penile and object penetration, possible necrophilia
- May strangle victim
- Killer is male
- Possible cannibalism/vampirism

As we have seen, **hedonist-lust** killers murder exclusively for sexual reasons. Though sexual acts may be just as prevalent in the crimes of the

power/control serial killer, they are simply a means to an end. That end is ultimately possession and dominance over the victim. For one reason or another, these types of serial killers often rank among the most infamous modern sexual murderers. There is no better example of this phenomenon than Ted Bundy. Charming, handsome, and educated, Bundy used his chameleon-like abilities to abduct, rape, and murder upwards of thirty-five beautiful young women across the United States in the 1970s. The fact that he held the power to decide whether or not a woman continued to exist was, for Bundy, the supreme thrill. From 1978 to 1983, British civil servant Dennis Nilsen strangled and drowned at least fifteen teenaged boys and young men, stowing their bodies in the wardrobe and under the floorboards of his London apartment. Whenever he felt the urge, Nilsen would retrieve his human mannequins, seating them beside him to watch TV, holding bizarre one-way conversations, and engaging them in post-mortem sexual acts. For Nilsen, the bodies were little more than objects to be controlled and manipulated as he saw fit. It was only when they began to decompose that he hacked them to pieces, boiling flesh from bone, and flushing the resulting sludge and innards down his toilet.

Keith Jesperson was a Canadian-born power/control killer who targeted American victims — in this case, truck-stop prostitutes whom he introduced to his harrowing "Death Game." Jesperson was also an occasional and reluctant necrophiliac, a trait he shared with Bundy and Nilsen, who could only truly appreciate sex when their victims were totally unable to resist their demands. Ultimately the most compliant partner is a dead one. "Sunset Strip Slayer" Doug Clark, "Green River Killer" Gary Ridgway, and John Christie, "The Monster of Rillington Place," are three further examples of power/control killers who emphasized necrophilia above all else. Jesperson merely dabbled in a little post-mortem fondling.

Though power/control killers John Wayne Gacy and "BTK" Dennis Rader certainly toyed with the bodies of their dead, their focus was mostly on the bondage and torture of their victims. This latter type is evidenced in Canadian serial killer **David Snow**. Holed up in his filthy Orangeville home, this sexually sadistic antiques dealer voraciously consumed S&M pornography focusing on the subjugation of women. At some point his control fantasies bled into the real world, ruining countless lives from Ontario to British Columbia.

Other Power/Control Killers in This Book

Léopold Dion, Gilbert Paul Jordan, Paul Bernardo, Sam Pirrera, Colonel Russell Williams

Kay Feely.

David Snow
The Cottage Killer
2–12 Murders
Caledon, Ontario

"I'm going to fuck you to death."

FIRST SNOW

On October 3, 1991, Caroline Case vanished from her Toronto antiques business, The Jewelled Elephant on Bloor Street West. At approximately four o'clock that afternoon, she had telephoned her daughter to inform her that she was coming home. Somebody had other plans. Later that same month, Caroline's Mercedes station wagon was found abandoned in a ditch on a Caledon, Ontario, country road, roughly an hour north of the city. Splatters of rust-coloured blood staining the vehicle's interior painted a grim portrait of her final hours. The car was strewn with leaves, the headrests torn savagely from the back seats as if the forest had reached out to consume her. A wool blanket had been placed over the back windshield, and on the back seat, investigators found a striped tea towel. A light blue bedsheet lay tangled on the floor. It was soon determined that none of these items belonged to the missing woman. Police surmised that Case had already realized the full extent of the danger she was in, and, deciding to take a chance, veered the wheel suddenly in an attempt to throw her aggressor from the vehicle. By the time her body was discovered eleven months later, the chief suspect in her murder would already be in police custody.

AVALANCHE

Orville Osborne[2] stood at the window of his Caledon East home, staring in bewilderment at the burgundy Cadillac parked askew in the Blackburns' driveway. It didn't make any sense — the weekend was long gone, and his neighbour, Ian, a realtor, should have been back in Toronto. Concerned, he telephoned his son Jamie in the city and asked him to drop by the Blackburn residence on St. Leonards Avenue to see if anything was wrong. Outside the North Toronto home, Jamie found four days' worth of newspapers piled by the front door and their second automobile, a Chevrolet Celebrity, gleaming in the April sun. Peering through the car window, his eyes fell upon something more sinister: a bloodstained tissue lying crumpled on the front seat. Unsure of what to make of the situation, Jamie reasoned that if the Blackburns had planned on going away, they might have packed suitcases, so he decided to check the trunk. What he found inside would haunt him for the rest of his life. For years, Ian and Nancy Blackburn had awoken side by side, their arms embracing each other in affection. Now, crammed like sardines into the back of Nancy's car, the first signs of decomposition showed they would never rise again.

Toronto police did not need the autopsy results to determine that fifty-four-year-old Ian Blackburn had been brutally beaten; the dried blood around his nose and bruising on his lower lip attested to this. A post-mortem examination would attribute symmetrical abrasions on both sides of his face to repeated pressure from the muzzle of a gun. Battered and threatened, his death had come by way of ligature strangulation and asphyxiation caused by something rammed down his throat. It was suspected the killer had pulled a plastic bag over his head to finish him off. Where Ian Blackburn had been found fully clothed, the nude condition of his wife Nancy, forty-nine, seemed to indicate sexual assault. A coroner's examination would later confirm that she had been raped. Though both bodies showed bondage marks around the wrists and above the knees, injuries to Nancy's hips and shoulders revealed that the killer had hogtied her, using the rope as a handle to carry her around before strangling her to death with a ligature.

A police search of the Blackburns' Toronto home revealed little out of the ordinary, save for a basement storage cupboard that had been robbed of photography equipment. Back in Caledon, the Ontario Provincial Police, now working in conjunction with the Toronto forces, were having much better luck. A back window was discovered to be the killer's point of entry — probably jimmied open with a small screwdriver. Initially, there were no signs of a violent struggle, but when auxiliary lighting was employed, they found bloodstains later determined to belong to Nancy Blackburn. When phone records showed that two unanswered calls had been made from the Blackburns' Caledon residence to their Toronto home within an hour of Ian's arrival, and that a third call lasting several minutes had gone through just before 8:00 p.m. the same evening, the police began to construct a narrative of the couple's final hours.

Ian Blackburn left Toronto for Caledon on the morning of April 7 to prepare for the following weekend's Easter gathering. Pulling his Cadillac into the farmhouse driveway, he came face to face with a gun-wielding attacker who used a combination of physical violence and armed intimidation to overcome him. Ushering the realtor inside, his attacker bound him at the wrists and above the knees. Under threat of death, he forced Ian to call their Toronto home to lure Nancy to the cottage. The first two phone calls went unanswered. A third attempt just before eight o'clock when the honey-blond nurse had arrived home met with success. Ostensibly detecting nothing in her husband's voice to warn her of any impending danger, Nancy had been persuaded to drive to Caledon, where upon entering the home, she was immediately attacked and subdued by the intruder. Police theorized that the Blackburns had been isolated from one another in separate rooms as the killer subjected Nancy to a horrific, ritualized ordeal of rape and torture. When he had finally finished with her, he strangled her to death with the same wire and rope he had used to hogtie her, before stowing her body in the trunk of the Chevy. Bound and probably unaware that his wife had been strangled, Ian Blackburn had been forced to drive the killer to Toronto at gunpoint. Once he reached their home on St. Leonards, he too, was murdered and wedged into the trunk beside Nancy's body. All in all, it had been a cold-blooded, calculated, and highly organized double murder, and both police agencies felt a burning desire to bring the perpetrator to justice.

SNOWFLAKES

In the following days, more bizarre evidence began to surface in East Caledon. Searching the area around the crime scene, police discovered numerous bags of garbage stowed in nearby ditches. Among the food wrappers and scraps of newspaper were several disturbing contents: juice boxes and bottles filled with human urine, feces packaged methodically in containers, and lists of antiquated military equipment, mostly from the Second World War, divided into columns and given abstract values as if from a game. Peculiar as these findings were, the Caledon police had seen them before; in fact they bore a striking resemblance to those found at the scenes of "The House Hermit."

In the early months of 1992, a series of bizarre break-ins had been reported in seasonal homes around the Caledon area. Returning to their cottages after a long winter's hibernation, residents discovered that their homes had been broken into by a mysterious stranger who had lived there for weeks without managing to leave a single fingerprint. The bottles of urine and wads of excrement wrapped in newspaper were another matter. On several occasions, cottagers had actually returned to find the intruder still in their home, but it wasn't until March 18, three weeks before the Blackburn murders, that "The House Hermit" revealed his darker side. When Toronto residents, the Appeltons, found him squatting in their Midland cottage, the Hermit suddenly produced a gun and ordered them to drive him to their city home. They complied. Somewhere along Highway 400 their abductor became suddenly agitated, telling them he had been imprisoned for murdering his father, and might have to go back to jail due to theft charges in Orangeville. Halfway to the city he instructed Mr. Appelton to pull onto a side road, but the elderly man refused.

"If you want to kill us, do it right here, right now!"

This seemed to calm "The House Hermit" until they reached Toronto, where at the intersection of Yonge and Dundas he alighted, disappearing into the crowded streets.

Upon reviewing the Appelton case, it became clear to detectives that "The House Hermit" and the man the press were now calling "The Cottage Killer" were one and the same. Fortunately, they had gleaned fingerprints from the Appleton abduction along with a police sketch of an unkempt man in his mid-to-late thirties with messy hair and a long, serpentine neck. A profile describing the suspect as a "quiet, meticulous loner" exhibiting "intense, obsessive behaviour" was developed. When three months had passed with no further leads, the authorities decided to release their sketch and handwriting samples to the general public. It was to be the decision that cracked the case.

An hour north of Toronto, Orangeville artist Alison Shaw came across the military equipment lists while perusing the front page of the *Toronto Star* and felt her jaw drop. Not only did she recognize the handwriting as that of her former colleague David Snow, she had also encountered similar lists while searching his Quonset hut in October of 1991. Her husband Darris had been in business with Snow, until one day his partner had simply vanished, neglecting to pay back a substantial sum of money he owed. Determined to recoup some of his losses, Darris had traced the owner of the hut and paid him $1,200 in rent that Snow owed in order to gain access. Inside, the Shaws found a suitcase full of hardcore pornography including clippings of women cut from magazines with a razor blade. They had been catalogued by body part, with a particularly extensive section on the buttocks. Among the other peculiarities were lesbian sado-masochistic pornography; hardcore S&M videos; and a black hardcover notebook with lists of American, German, and Japanese Second World War military equipment written in Snow's handwriting. Darris figured it was related to some kind of war game. Alison had come away with a much eerier view of the find. David Snow had always been physically dirty, his rotting teeth and body odour so repulsive that being in his presence was almost unbearable. Now, after years of suspecting something was wrong with the aloof misogynist, she finally had proof: David Snow's filth emanated from his very soul.

Shaken by the revelation that he was the man responsible for murdering the Blackburns, Alison contacted the OPP and later that evening was interviewed by Detective Constable Brendan Keenoy.

Running the name David Snow through police records, detectives learned that in the past he had been charged with fraud, and although he had never appeared in court, his fingerprints were on record. When compared to those of "The House Hermit," it was discovered that they matched.

SNOWFALL

Late in the afternoon of June 29, 1992, David Snow drifted into a clothing store in Kitsilano, British Columbia, the rancid stench of body odour hovering over him like a stormcloud. He claimed to be interested in purchasing an outfit for a family member, and asked manager Rosalind Taylor to direct him to the nearest bank machine. His foulness was still lingering in the air when, as she was closing shop for the day, he suddenly returned, talking his way back inside. Once he was past the door, Snow produced a pistol and ordered her into the back room. There, he forced Taylor to strip naked before gagging her and binding her wrists with twine so tightly she would later suffer permanent nerve damage. As he penetrated her with his long, filthy fingers, an unexpected noise from the front of the store prompted him to investigate. Seizing her chance to escape, she unlocked a deadbolt on the back door and ran naked and screaming into the alleyway.

Five days later, Snow burst into a downtown Vancouver photography shop, brandishing a pistol and ordering beautiful, blond Lenore Rattray outside. With the firearm hidden in his jacket pocket, he marched the terrified employee across the half-mile-long Second Narrows Bridge in broad daylight. Once they had reached North Vancouver, Lenore was led an additional eight kilometres to a wooded area just off the Trans-Canada highway: David Snow's campsite.

For the next eight days "The Cottage Killer" kept Lenore bound and naked, subjecting her to repeated beatings and sexually assaulting her three to four times a day. These assaults ran the gamut from forced fellatio to vaginal rape and sodomy. It was only through Ms. Rattray's miraculous survival that psychologists would later learn the true extent of Snow's depravity. Over the course of a week, she was constantly threatened as her captor pressed one of three pistols to her head, boasting that his life was "more important" than hers.[3] For Snow, bondage was not merely a means of securing his victim, but a form of torture in itself. Lenore was left bound in excruciating positions for hours at a time, her breasts tied so tightly and intricately that she felt they would wither off her chest. When he wasn't punching and kicking her, Snow would spend prolonged periods rubbing her genitals until the burning sensation became nearly unbearable. At other times he pulled violently on her nipples or thrust his fingers savagely into her vagina and anus.

"Don't, it hurts!" she once pleaded with him.

Snow's expression remained unchanged. "Well, it's going to be done to you, regardless."

Throughout the ordeal, Snow seemed to lapse in and out of a fantasy world, bragging about his enormous penis (it wasn't), his wife Alison (he was unmarried), and of numerous property crimes he almost certainly hadn't committed. The sexual assault and torture itself seemed to be highly ritualized as if he were reading from a script. Snow sought to dehumanize her, telling her she could be a porn star. At one point she made him laugh and he told her he didn't wish to have sex with her now because he "respected her" for "having brains." In fact, whenever the scenario differed from Snow's idealized fantasies of ritual objectification, he would inevitably lose his erection. Along with this pronounced erectile disorder, he also displayed signs of inhibited orgasm. Apparently, whatever Snow was doing to get himself off wasn't entirely working. Perhaps he needed something more.

On the morning of July 11, 1992, "The Cottage Killer" entered a video store in a North Vancouver shopping centre. Flashing his pistol at a nineteen-year-old female employee and her male boss, he declared his intentions to rob the store and take the girl hostage. Once he had emptied the register and bound the manager with telephone cord, he led the young woman at gunpoint to her 1975 Volkswagen Beetle and ordered her to drive to his campsite. There she found a trembling Lenore Rattray still gagged and bound to a tree — a nasty indicator of what lay in store for her. Explaining that he wished to move his campsite, Snow forced the two women into the Volkswagen at gunpoint.

At this time, two particularly intelligent RCMP patrolmen who had been alerted to the latest kidnapping, reasoned that the nineteen-year-old's abductor would only have taken her with him if he planned to sexually assault her. This required a secluded area. Following their hunch, Dave Kwasnica and Reg Cardinal set out in search of such a location. At the base of Mount Seymour they discovered the missing Volkswagen and were just peering inside to investigate when a woman's scream shook the forest. Racing into the woods, weapons drawn, they came across the quivering form of the missing nineteen-year-old gagged and bound to a tree. As Cardinal hurried to untie her, a second cry led Kwasnica deeper into the forest where he found the fully clothed Lenore Rattray. David Snow was nowhere to be seen.

Within an hour, the largest manhunt in North Vancouver's history was well underway. Hundreds of officers arrived on the scene, sealing off roads and alerting the surrounding communities to the monstrous fugitive running loose in their midst It wasn't long before Snow's trail went cold. As night descended over the Mount Seymour pines, seasoned RCMP officers must have been asking themselves the inevitable question: did they have another Allan Legere on their hands?

WINTER'S END

The stars were twinkling through a canopy of summer foliage as fifty-three-year-old restaurant manager Dalia Gelineau double-checked the locks on the front door and started toward the parking lot. A one-storey log structure with twin gables and a stone-faced chimney, The Bridge House resembled more of an alpine lodge than a North Vancouver restaurant. As she passed by the arrangements of perennials adorning the front patio, she came face to face with a shadowy stranger.

"Don't move or you're dead!" he growled, jamming a pistol into her ribs. "I'm desperate, I need money and I don't care what I have to do to get it."

Forcing her back inside, he ordered her to inform the security company that the alarm had been accidentally tripped and that everything was all right. Something in her voice told the operator otherwise and they immediately contacted a local security guard and the RCMP. In the meantime, the petite grandmother put up a furious resistance as her attacker dragged her outside and shoved her to the ground, beating her so viciously that he fractured her skull. Overpowered, she continued to struggle helplessly as he tore clothing from her body, using them to bind her before stuffing a slip into her mouth.

"What do you want with me?" she choked.

"What do you think?" he sneered, stepping onto her stomach. "I'm going to fuck you to death!" He proceeded to brutally sexually assault her.

Arriving at the restaurant as quickly as possible, RCMP Officer Peter Cross circled around the back to find Dalia Gelineau face down with a plastic bag over her head and a wild-eyed David Snow twisting a wire plant hanger around her neck.

"Stop, it's the police!" he shouted, aiming his revolver.

Snow took off towards the parking lot, but Officer Cross soon closed the distance, tackling him to the ground. Though she would survive her ordeal, Dalia Gelineau would never forget the early morning hours of July 12, 1992, when she had come within thirty seconds of death.

DANGEROUS OFFENDER

On September 11, 1992, David Snow was convicted in Vancouver of sexual assault causing bodily harm, unlawful confinement, choking and strangling to assist in committing an indictable offence, and misuse of a firearm — all relating to the Dalia Gelineau attack. Amazingly, Judge Paradis found him not guilty of her attempted murder, leading to a public outcry.

Back in Ontario, on the same early November day that Snow was charged with the first-degree murders of Ian and Nancy Blackburn, the skeletal remains of Caroline Case were discovered near First Line East south of 10 Sideroad, only 500 yards from where police had located her Mercedes station wagon eleven months earlier. Though he would never be charged in connection with her death, Snow was found guilty of both first-degree Blackburn murders in July 1997.

A hearing to determine whether or not David Snow would be assigned the status of Dangerous Offender commenced on March 17, 1993. After testimonies from the Shaws and David's brother, Victor Snow, on July 12, psychiatrist Dr. Elizabeth Zoffman took the stand to give her analysis of "The Cottage Killer's" mental state. By the end of the hearing, Snow was determined to meet the criteria of a Dangerous Offender, meaning he could be incarcerated indefinitely for the protection of the Canadian public. Below are some excerpts from Zoffman's March 9, 1993, psychiatric report detailing Snow's childhood and the possible roots of his psychopathic sadism:

> David's parents were diametric opposites of one another. David's father was a very dominant personality who had many social contacts and was continually involved in community work and good works in general. David's mother is described as being an "English, stiff upper lip type of person with no emotion." She was timid, shy and generally emotionally unavailable to her children.... At the time David was born, the parents had very much wanted a daughter. They were quite disappointed.... It's also my suspicion that David's mother suffered from post-partum depression after the births of David and Carol. The importance of this fact is that the mother would then have been emotionally unavailable to him as she would have been too ill.... When David was approximately 3 1/2 to 4 years old the family moved to Orangeville. At that time his mother was very distressed by the move and became so distraught that her hair fell out.... Within two years of this move, Carol was born. This was a double blow for David's development, as his mother once again suffered post-partum depression. As well, his sister, who was a very much desired daughter, got all of the attention and David was emotionally ignored and left out ... David's father died in 1967. He passed away one Saturday morning in the presence of his sons, Brian and David. Victor recalls that the entire family was devastated. His grandparents were in a state of collapse. His mother had retreated into a world of her own and everyone was experiencing a great deal of distress. Once again David drifted in the background (this was when David was age eleven). From 1968 onward, it appears that the young boy, now age twelve,

controlled the family home. He was often noted to be abusive and verbally aggressive towards his mother and sister. It eventually got to the point where both women were terrified of him and walked around on eggshells. Carol tells of an episode where he grabbed her and physically choked her for interfering with his stamp collection. We are also told that he often raised his fist to his mother.... David dropped out of school in Grade 11 after a period of sporadic attendance. It appears that David blamed his failure to keep up in his course work and to obtain the grades that he needed on his mother for not making him attend his classes and ensure that he got the courses he wanted.... After he left school, he had numerous jobs that he couldn't keep. He would even pretend to his mother that he was going to work, but would be unemployed all the while.... Finally she left because she could not take it anymore.... We also find from secondhand information that David's mom was afraid of him and terrified whenever he would visit her. She apparently hid all of her sharp knives whenever he came around. David's work history over the next 18–20 years is very sporadic.... He was incapable of taking direction from others ...[4]

A second report prepared by Roger Sasaki focused on Snow's deviant social history:

David throughout his life has been unable to accept authority; unable to develop and maintain relationships; and unable to maintain employment. He was completely lacking in social skills and for the most part his adult life has been characterized by continual financial and personal crisis.... His view of women seemed to have been reinforced by his ongoing preoccupation with pornography.... It is also significant that David's longstanding isolation and alienation from his environment contributed to an unusual and distorted perception of himself and others.... While there is less evidence of any psychotic symptomatology and/ or major depressive symptoms, David may have been preoccupied with fantasies ...[5]

SNOW'S SHOES

Though David Snow's only murder convictions came as a result of the Blackburns, he is a suspect in ten other slayings committed in the Caledon-Albion Hills area dating back to 1977. When the OPP searched his Orangeville home in late 1992, they found a hand-drawn map with routes leading to several places where dead bodies had been found. Particularly interesting is the death of an elderly woman who perished after spending an evening in Snow's company. In an unlikely coincidence, Snow was seen in possession of her antique clock the next day, proudly displaying his latest find. A similar incident occurred involving an old man from whose estate Snow had procured a valuable red chair. After the man was mysteriously found dead one day, Snow was given the duty of clearing his house and selling off any valuables. One murder, above all others, has Snow's name written all over it. The circumstantial evidence implicating him in Caroline Case's death is nothing short of overwhelming:

1. Both Snow and Case were highly knowledgeable and involved in the antique business. It was more than likely that they had crossed paths at some point.
2. The day before Case disappeared, Snow arrived at his mother's Toronto home, where he spent the afternoon and night. Roberta Snow lived on Windermere Avenue, right around the corner from The Jewelled Elephant where Case was abducted.
3. Case's abandoned station wagon and corpse were found in Caledon, close to the Blackburn house.

Clark County Sheriff's Department.

Keith Jesperson

The Happy Face Killer
8+ Murders
Across the United States

"I thought about keeping her
as my sex slave. I wanted total
possession — no bullshit and no
back talk."

WHERE CREDIT'S DUE

If BTK needed attention, Keith Hunter Jesperson craved it like Tim Hortons coffee. Perhaps the bizarre circumstances surrounding the discovery of his first victim, Taunja Bennett, led him to develop a complex.

Portland, Oregon. On January 22, 1990, a Mount Hood Community College student cycling along a trail by the Columbia Gorge spotted the body of a young woman lying in the undergrowth. Her bra and pants had been bunched up, exposing her breasts and genitals, and a white nylon rope was cinched around her neck. Strangely, an oval section at the front of her fly had been completely removed. Nobody was surprised when autopsy results indicated rape. A police sketch artist drew up a profile of her face, which was released to the media in the hopes that she would be identified. It was a difficult task: the woman's face had been literally beaten to a pulp. Eight days later, Loretta Bennett recognized her mentally handicapped daughter Taunja on the television, and went to the morgue to confirm the identity.

Investigators spoke with staff at the B&I Tavern who claimed Taunja had patronized the bar between 1:00 and 8:00 p.m. on January 21, the day she was murdered. She had been in good spirits, chatting up two blond guys at the pool table and had asked the day bartender Carol if she wanted to go dancing after her shift. Immediately, the pool players became their number-one suspects.

Then something totally unexpected happened. Fifty-seven-year-old grandmother Laverne Pavlinac approached the police with information that her abusive partner John Sosnovske, thirty-seven, had coerced her into helping him kidnap, rape, and strangle Taunja Bennett, dumping her body at the Columbia Gorge. Amazingly, she also produced an excised section of jeans corresponding to the fly area from Bennett's pants. Sosnovske was brought in for questioning, where despite repeated denials of involvement, he failed two polygraph tests. His brown hair also bore a resemblance to samples retrieved from Bennett's body.

Driven up to the Columbia Gorge, Pavlinac misidentified the dump site by five metres. However, as the crime had been allegedly committed at night, investigators assumed she was simply confused. In fact, the total accumulation of evidence was so convincing that when Pavlinac finally admitted fabricating the entire story, nobody believed her. Despite their mutual protestations of innocence, the strange Portland couple were each sentenced to lengthy prison terms.

Months later, an enormous trucker named Keith Hunter Jesperson sat on a toilet seat at a Greyhound rest stop in Livingston, Montana. Deciding to take a gamble, he reached out with his ballpoint pen to scribble on the wall: "I killed Tanya [sic] Bennett January 21, 1990 in Portland Oregon. I beat her to death, raped her and loved it. Yes I'm sick, but I enjoy myself too. People took the blame and I'm free." He paused a moment before signing the message with a happy face.

A TYPICAL CANADIAN BOY[6]

Les Jesperson came from a long line of "warrior Danes," the son of an alcoholic Saskatchewan farmer ruined by dust storms. Having left school in grade ten, his entrepreneurial spirit and mind for machines led him to great prosperity as an inventor. Unfortunately, Les carried the dark seed of his father's alcoholism with him, getting drunk daily on rye and Pepsi, sometimes as early as 10:00 a.m. His wife, Gladys Bellamy, was a large woman from a devoutly religious Anglo-Canadian family. Raised to be ashamed of her body, nobody in the household ever saw Gladys naked, including her husband. Despite this difficulty, they somehow managed to conceive three sons and two daughters.

The most famous of the Jesperson clan, Keith, was born on April 6, 1955. Within a few years it was obvious to the rest of the family that there was something different about him. Keith was happy to play for hours in his own little world, forever dawdling on family hikes and getting lost. To the other Jespersons he was slow and laughably gullible. From a young age, he was forced to work for his room and board, apparently under the impression his brothers were bound by the same obligation. Later in life, he would discover he was the only one exempted from free accommodation. When asked about his earliest memory by author Jack Olsen, Keith recalled rolling a rock down a slide, hitting his brother in the head.

Of course, this incident was nothing compared to the frequent lashings from Les's leather belt. Keith alleged he had once been forced to scramble under the kitchen table to avoid the old man's wrath, only to be strapped across the backside. When he burst into tears, Les reportedly warned him to, "Stop crying or I'll give you something to cry about!" He showed even less sensitivity when, after learning he had beaten Keith for someone else's mistake, he refused to apologize, saying he "probably had it coming, anyway." On another occasion, Keith alleged he had seen Les tear down the bathroom door to belt his sister. By all accounts, Keith got the worst of the five siblings. His relationship with his mother was more positive, but ultimately she preferred her two daughters.

Things didn't bode any better for Keith at school. He frequently misbehaved and was beaten with a beaver tail until his hands were swollen. Other kids mocked him for his colossal size and lack of co-ordination, nicknaming him everything from "Hulk" to "Igor." A slower runner, he had no interest in team sports, already viewing himself as a lone wolf. Bullies targeted him, and he earned a reputation as a big guy who wouldn't fight back. Instead, Keith internalized his rage and resentment until it suddenly exploded in violent outbursts.

LOT LIZARDS

Keith Jesperson committed his second murder on a boiling summer's day in 1992. Lying under his truck at an I-15 checkpoint near San Bernardino, California, beads of sweat falling to the asphalt as he set his brakes, he was approached by a pretty, busty girl who introduced herself as Claudia, a self-described "throwaway woman," and asked if he could give her a ride to Phoenix. He smiled earnestly and told her to hop in the cab. After two years of fantasizing about raping and murdering another woman, he had found his ideal victim.

Later, parked outside the Burns Brothers truck stop in Coachella, Jesperson began to kiss his passenger, but found her unresponsive. She claimed that if he wanted sex he would have to pay for it. Jesperson had a better idea. Tearing her clothes from her body, he forced apart her legs and raped her.

When they reached the next truck stop, rather than making an attempt to run, Claudia asked Jesperson if he had any crank. He refused, angrily telling her that he did not allow drugs on his rig, and handed her a $20 bill. Insulted that he had paid her so little for sex, she threatened to call the cops unless he gave her the rest of his money. Deciding a third option was necessary, Jesperson overpowered her, binding her wrists and ankles with duct tape. Once she was secured, he ground his fist into her throat until she blacked out, then raped her again. At another truck stop, he repeated his sexual assault before deciding to play "The Death Game" — choking her unconscious and reviving her three times, before finally finishing her off.

On August 30, 1992, Claudia's body was found decomposing under a cover of tumbleweeds about fifteen kilometres north of Blythe, California. She had been bound with duct tape and strangled. Although police did not realize it at the time, hers was the second in a series of murders that would soon be popping up all over America. Dismissed as a case of drug overdose, the remains of Jesperson's third victim, Cynthia Lynn Rose, were found a month later off Highway 99 near Turlock, California.

Twenty-six-year-old prostitute Laurie Ann Pentland's strangled corpse was discovered next behind a Salem, Oregon, store in November 1992. July of the following year revealed the body of a Jane Doe dumped on the side of the state highway west of Santa Nella, California. Like Rose, her death was dismissed as an unintentional drug overdose. With two killings in the series misidentified as accidents, and little to connect them by way of geography, the presence of a trans-American multiple murderer remained off the police radar.

AMERICAN DREAMS

When Keith was twelve, the Jespersons uprooted 250 miles south of Chilliwhack to Selah, Washington. Les had been contracted to design machinery there for local hop growers, setting up shop in Moxee. By eighth grade, Keith's fantasy life had become more vivid and elaborate. Like American serial killer Richard Ramirez, a relative who had served in Vietnam regaled Keith with stories of torture: the pleasure of pulling out teeth with pliers and of hearing Vietnamese women scream in pain. Increasingly, Keith found himself sexually aroused by these mental images. He had also developed a strange fixation with fire, routinely starting out-of-control blazes to help himself de-stress. Using his father's machine tools, he crafted cannons and pipe bombs which he tested in the surrounding countryside.

Upon earning his driver's licence, Keith frequently drove into the Wenas Valley to shoot animals with his .22 rifle. He had already slaughtered all the stray cats in his neighbourhood, and now turned his attentions to deer, rabbits, coyotes, and muskrats. Rather than shooting to kill, however, he took a markedly sadistic approach to hunting, aiming for the animals' eyes, legs, testicles, and anuses, in order to inflict maximum pain and distress. One day he claimed to massacre sixty-eight snakes; on another he recalled shooting a cow, delighting as it lay bellowing on its side. It gave him an immense feeling of power.

FLORIDA HEAT

"You're not one of those serial killers, are you?"

At first Keith Jesperson thought the light-skinned black woman in the Spandex jumpsuit was joking, but one look at her concerned expression told him otherwise.

"You should never ask stupid questions!" he forced a laugh, trying to ignore the rage rumbling inside him like a volcano. "Do you want me to tell the truth, or lie? If you had your doubts you should have stayed the hell out."

She took the $20 bill from his hand and smiled. After they had finished having sex in the back of his sleeper-cab, she disappeared back into the truck-stop parking lot. Unlike the lot lizards, however, Jesperson's anger would not leave so quickly.

Later that night at the same truck stop in Tampa, Florida, he ran into a leggy blue-eyed blonde who introduced herself as Susanna and asked if he was heading north. She was in luck. They spent the next day riding north together, stopping for an all-you-can-eat spaghetti dinner before reaching Cairo, Georgia, by midnight. There Jesperson loaded up over twenty-five thousand kilograms of electrical conduit at a pipe yard before heading back to the Florida panhandle, where he could transfer on to the I-10 highway. At 3:00 a.m., they pulled off the interstate into a Mini Mart parking lot to catch some sleep, planning to continue west in the morning. They agreed to share the sleeper cab, though Susanna specified they had to keep their clothes on.

Some time later, Keith Jesperson awoke drenched in sweat. With the air conditioner broken and the temperature inside the sleeper cab hovering in the nineties, he turned on the dome light, intending to roll down the windows. His eyes fell upon the sleeping beauty beside him and he felt himself go rock hard. Slipping off his clothes, he lay down beside her, encircling her waist in his arms. Stirred from her slumber to find the naked trucker pressing against her body, Susanna began to scream. Panicking, Jesperson clamped his gargantuan hand over her mouth.

"You just do as I ask and everything will go easy on you," he began. "Now make love to me like we're lovers."

With little option she complied, doing her best to please him over the next few hours. When they were finished she closed her eyes and lay back down on the mattress asleep, or pretending to be. As Jesperson weighed the risks of the situation, he felt himself becoming aroused again and pulled up her skirt to rape her. Susanna screamed. This time his hands found her throat, crushing the life from her trembling body as he had already done to five women before. He hid her strangled corpse in the bushes off an Okaloosa County exit ramp, binding two fourteen-inch plastic ties around her neck in case he ever needed to prove he was the killer. By the following evening he was already in Shreveport, Louisiana, far from the suspicions of the Florida police.

LOVE AND MARRIAGE

Awkward and unable to navigate the mysterious world of the fairer sex, as a teenager, Keith's thoughts turned to rape and domination. In his senior year of high school, he met a girl who liked the fact that he was a wrestler, but she dumped him when he developed a severe limp following a rope-climbing injury. As a D Student who coasted through high school copying and cheating, Keith had few aspirations for college. Instead, he stuck around Selah working as an equipment operator for his father's construction business. It was here that Keith began to develop the passion for trucks that would permeate the rest of his working life.

Keith's fortunes with women turned around in the fall of 1974 when he met seventeen-year-old Rose Pernick. On August 2, 1975, the couple were married, though not necessarily for the right reasons: Rose wanted out of her family home, and Keith lacked the confidence to pursue other women. Around this time, he helped his father Les construct the 105-lot Silver Spur mobile home park, moving into Lot 56 with Rose. His favourite part of the job was clearing strays and unpermitted pets from the property. Among his most cherished moments were wringing the necks of cats, dousing them in gasoline, and setting them on fire, and half-decapitating a stray dog with a scythe.

Despite the hard work the Jespersons put in, continuing financial problems with the park forced them to sell it two years later. Keith became a truck driver for Muffet and Sons, and soon Rose gave birth to two children, a daughter, Melissa, and, in 1980, a son, Jason. A third child, Carrie Ann, followed in 1983. Though Keith was a good father, the marriage was compromised by the couple's incongruous sex drives. Rose's low libido was at odds with her husband's, who required sex at least once a night. It wasn't uncommon for Keith to lock himself in the bathroom to masturbate while his wife slept. Like everything else in Keith's life, his marriage to Rose eventually disintegrated, leaving him with nothing but the dark emptiness of the American highway.

ROADKILL

With her midnight black hair and penetrating blue-grey eyes, Angela Subrize drifted into the Ridpath Hotel lounge on a cloud of perfume, seating herself at a table less than ten feet away from the bar. Jesperson set his sights on her immediately.

"Mind if I join you?"

She smiled and motioned for him to sit down. The two made small talk for a time, before he pitched the idea of letting her stay in his room.

"Maybe we'll behave ourselves and maybe not. That's up to you. I never force myself on anyone," he lied.

After she had finished her beer, the couple returned to his room and settled in for a nice, long night of sex and pizza. The next morning, January 21, 1995, Jesperson slipped quietly out of the room, leaving her $30 and directions on how to contact him through his trucking company. It wasn't long until she did, asking him if he could take her to Denver to visit her father. As he would soon be passing through the city on his way to Pennsylvania, Jesperson agreed, and the two met up again in Spokane, Washington.

On the first day of their expedition, Jesperson had little time for sex — unloading railroad iron in Seattle and restocking the truck with cedar before heading east that night across the Snoqualmie Pass. After catching some shut-eye, the two made love and continued through Wyoming. They stopped off at a rest area in Fort Bridges, where Angela telephoned her father and learned that he didn't want to see her after all. Now she requested that Jesperson take her east to Indiana to reconcile with an estranged boyfriend. She explained that she was pregnant and revealed a devious plan to have sex with her old lover and claim the child was his. Jesperson agreed to take her to Indiana, but was becoming suspicious of her true intentions. What if the lover rejected her? Who would she point the finger at then?

The snow was falling heavily on the I-80 as they crossed the Nebraska state line. With a blizzard raging outside his windshield, Jesperson slowed the truck to a snail's pace. As Angela lay slumbering in the sleeper, he began to rifle through her purse. When he came across a can of pepper spray, he decided it would be best to hide it. On the dark road over Elk Mountain to Cheyenne, trucks lay jackknifed against the storm — great steel dragons slain by the undefeatable winter.

Skillfully, Jesperson navigated his rig through the blizzard, reaching the first rest station on Interstate 80 by 7:00 p.m. With the worst behind him, he decided he needed at least four hours of sleep before pressing on. To Angela, this delay was unacceptable. When she refused to let him rest, he decided enough was enough, and began to rape her. Terrified, her arm groped for her pepper spray only to find it missing. Smiling with sadistic glee, Jesperson decided to introduce his helpless prey to "The Death Game." Though utterly exhausted, the ensuing power-high flooded him with energy, allowing him to strangle and resuscitate her five times before lying down to catch some sleep beside her corpse.

Sometime after, Jesperson awoke well-rested, and set about disposing of Angela Subrize. By now such activities had become more or less routine — the only problem was that, owing to her transient lifestyle, she was probably in the police fingerprint records. Worse still, he had been with her for over a week, allowing her to use his credit card to make phone calls to her father and boyfriend. Jesperson decided that the disposal of Angela Subrize called for special measures.

After fondling her clammy breasts one last time, he drove the truck for hours past the closest way station, and pulled over to the side of the road. By now it was night — the darkness proving a valuable ally. Taping her hands in front of her, he carefully carried her body onto the roadside and bound it with a black nylon rope face-down beneath the trailer. Once he was certain that she was well-hidden and secure, Jesperson guided his truck onto the highway, dragging her body twenty kilometres before he stopped, scrambling under the trailer to see what was left. Grinding against the road had detached both of Angela's arms, a shoulder and thigh, shattered her chest and left her entrails streaming down the highway. Most importantly, it had reduced her once beautiful face to something resembling gritty hamburger meat. With no fingerprints or teeth left to identify the body, Jesperson dragged her down a grassy embankment, and left her for the crows.

THE HAPPY FACE KILLER

In 1994 a letter arrived at Clark County's Courthouse claiming to be from the real murderer of Taunja Bennett:

271

I killed Miss Bennett Jan 20, 1990 and left her 1 ½ miles east of Lateral Falls on the switchback. I used a 1/2" soft nylon rope burnt on one end — frayed cut on the other — and tied it around her neck. Her face [*sic*] her teeth protruded from her mouth. Death was caused by my right fist pushed into her throat until she quit moving. Threw her walkman away. Her purse $2.00 — I threw into the Sandy River. I cut the buttons off her jeans. I had raped her before and after her death. I left her facing downhill and her jeans down by her ankles. I did not know any of them.[7]

Though the author showed a remarkable knowledge of the details of the case, his correspondence was ultimately ignored. A second letter, sent to *The Oregonian* newspaper in April 1994, met with equal disregard:

I would like to tell my story! I am a good person at times. I always wanted to be liked. I have been married and divorced with children — I didn't really want to be married, but it happened. I have read your paper and enjoyed it a lot. I have always wanted to be noticed like Paul Harvey, Front Page, etc. So I started something I don't know how to stop. On or around January 20th 1990 I picked up Sonya [*sic*] Bennett and took her home. I raped her and beat her real bad. Her face was all broke up. Then I ended her life by pushing my fist into her throat. This turned me on. I got a high. Then panic set in. Where to put the body? I drove out to the Sandy River and threw her purse and walkman away and I drove the scenic road past the falls. I went back home and dragged her out to the car. I want to know [*sic*] that it was my crime. So I tied a 1/2" soft white rope cut on end and burned on the other — around her neck. I drove her to switchback on the scenic road and 1 1/2 miles east of Lateral Falls. Dragged her downhill. Her pants were around her knees because I had cut her buttons off. They found her the next day. I wanted her to be found. I felt real bad and afraid that I would be caught. But a man and a woman got blamed for it. My conscience is getting to me now. She was my first and I thought I would not do it again, but I was wrong.[8]

This document was followed shortly after by a third detailing the death of the Santa Nella Jane Doe, and spurring police to reopen their investigation:

My last victim was a street person. It was raining in Corning, California. She was wet and I offered a ride to Sacramento, California. I stopped at a rest area near Williams and had her. I put her body on or near a pile of rocks about 50 yds North [sic] of highway 152 westbound about 20 miles from Santa Nella. It was getting hard to trust my inner self. I kept arguing with my conscience. I had to get away from long haul trucking. Victims are too easily found. So I quit and found a good job driving where I am in the public eye and out of harms [sic] way. The truck has a bold name on the side so it is easily recognized. I got away from what became easy. I do not want to kill again and I want to protect my family from grief. I would tear it apart. I feel bad but I will not turn myself in. I am not stupid. I do know what would happen to me if I did. In a lot of opinions I should be killed and I feel I deserve it. My responsibility is mine and God will be my judge when I die. I am telling you this because I will be responsible for these crimes and no one else. It all started when I wondered what it would be like to kill someone. And I found out. What a nightmare it has been. I had sent a letter to Washington county judges criminal court taking responsibility, to # 1 (the Bennett murder). But nothing has been in your paper. This [sic] freedom of press you have the ball. I will be reading to find out. I used gloves and same paper as last letter "no prints." Look over your shoulder. I may be closer than you think.[9]

Each of the letters was signed by a smiling doodle, leading the press to dub their author "The Happy Face Killer." At last, poor berated little Keith was getting some of the recognition he knew he had always deserved.

TOO CLOSE FOR COMFORT

Keith Jesperson and Julie Winningham had first met at the Burns Brothers Truck Stop in Troutdale, Oregon, in 1994. About a year later, while spending a few days of relaxation at the same location, he ran into Julie and the two began to chat. Though he knew she was manipulating him for money, Jesperson decided to go along with it so that he could enjoy a good few nights of sex. He even agreed to marry her. But things came to a head when one afternoon in his truck she demanded $2,000 from him to pay off two DUI tickets because as an engaged couple they were supposed to "help each other out." When he refused, Winningham allegedly threatened to charge him with rape. Jesperson responded by choking her into unconsciousness, taping her arms, ankles, and mouth and driving east. As he forced her to repeatedly show "what her life was worth" by having sex with him, he described his previous murders to her in graphic detail. Once he had broken her psychologically, Jesperson introduced her to the Death Game, strangling her in out and of consciousness three to four times before finally finishing her. Later, he tossed her body over a fifteen-foot embankment on the Washington State side of the Columbia Gorge, across the river from where he had dumped Taunja Bennett.

Winningham's remains were discovered on March 10, 1995, and identified soon after. Detective Rick Buckner from the Clark County Sheriff's Department was assigned to the case, and, upon interviewing the victim's family, learned that she recently been spending a great deal of her time with her new fiancé, a towering trucker named Keith Jesperson. A background check revealed no criminal record, only a 1990 Yakima County divorce ruling from his wife Rose. Tracking Jesperson to New Mexico, Buckner and a handful of deputies arrested him at gunpoint on March 22 near the Las Cruces fairgrounds. Back at the police station, Jesperson steadfastly refused to answer any questions. When six hours of interrogation failed to break his resolve, they let him walk free after taking hair and blood samples.

Convinced he was about to be charged in the Julie Winningham murder, Keith Jesperson drove to a local truck stop where he purchased a package of Contac and sixteen extra-strength Tylenols to complement the Sudafed and Anacin he already had in the truck. Back in the sleeper cab, he washed them all down with a bottle of mineral water and waited patiently to die. Unsurprisingly, the little cocktail failed to kill the six-foot-six, 240-pound Jesperson. Always slow to learn, he tried again later, to no avail.

Driving to New Mexico, Jesperson vowed to forge ahead with his suicide plan, only this time he wrote a letter to his brother Brad, confessing to eight murders. After dropping it into the mailbox, he headed out to the foothills of the Chiricahua National Monument, parked, and set off on foot along a hiking trail. There, sitting on a rock overlooking the vast scrubland, he came to a decision. Hours later, at a restaurant pay phone in Arizona, Keith Jesperson dialled Detective Buckner's Clark County office, and confessed to the murder of Julie Winningham.

LOOK AT ME! LOOK AT ME!

With Jesperson's fate assured, Buckner decided to see what other mischief the murderous behemoth had been up to, requesting intel on unsolved homicides from sheriff's offices across the nation. In jail, "The Happy Face Killer" bragged about murdering Angela Subrize and was ratted out, leading to a jurisdictional debate as to whether she had been killed in Oregon or Wyoming. He also sent a letter to the *Washington Post*, claiming responsibility for the murder of Taunja Bennett, though this time, someone was listening. When Jesperson led investigators to the location of her previously undiscovered purse, it wasn't long before the wheels of justice began turning in Pavlinac and Sosnovske's favour. After four years behind bars, they were finally released on November 27, 1995. In addition, Jesperson would eventually confess to the cross-country murders of "Claudia," Cynthia Lynn Rose, Laurie Ann Pentland, Jane Doe, and "Susanna." Though convicted on several counts, he somehow managed to avoid the death penalty.

Over the next fifteen years, Keith Jesperson was rarely out of the public eye. A master manipulator and attention seeker, he once claimed up to 166 victims, a number he later recanted. At one point "The Happy Face Killer" convinced the notorious Sondra London (true crime writer and the so-called "Queen of the Serial Killer Groupies") to advertise a "Serial Killer Start-Up Kit" on her website. He also began a serial killer "Pen Pal Club," including such unsavoury members as John Wayne Gacy, Richard Ramirez, Danny Rolling, and "Railway Killer" Angel Resendez.

Locked in a cold cage in Oregon State Penitentiary, his first parole hearing is scheduled for March 1, 2063.

CHAPTER 12

THE ANGEL OF DEATH

Angels of Death are health-care workers who kill those entrusted into their care. Like the demons of Dante's *Inferno*, they take a number of twisted forms. Dorothea Puente, for instance, was an Angel of Death subtype of the hedonist-comfort killer, offing nine residents to fraudulently claim their monthly incomes. Such was the motive of Amy Archer-Gilligen, proprietor of Sister Amy's Nursing Home for the Elderly in Newington, Connecticut, responsible for forty-eight arsenic-related deaths from 1911 to 1916.

Power over life and death is probably the most common motive of the Angel of Death. When a seventy-seven-year-old patient begged Austrian nurse Waltraud Wagner to "end her suffering," she complied and became addicted to playing God, extinguishing a further forty-eight lives through drugs and drowning until her arrest on April 7, 1989. Britain's most prolific serial killer, Dr. Harold Shipman, decided to hang himself rather than explain his reasons for killing 215–250 of his elderly patients. Though he forged his last victim's will to leave him a small fortune, there was no evidence of financial motivation in any of the preceding deaths. Experts have since posited that Shipman murdered to feel "in control" of his otherwise pathetic life.

Then there are the attention-seekers. Possessing an insatiable need to be seen as a hero, Long Island nurse Richard Angelo employed Pavulon and Anectine to bring patients to the brink of death so he could revive them. Tragically, he misjudged the dosages often enough to become one of the worst medical serial killers in New York's history. A similar need for attention drove British nurse Beverley Allitt to murder four infants by potassium chloride injection between February and April 1991.

The motive behind American nurse Donald Harvey's murders of fifty to eighty-seven people through the seventies and eighties varied from wishing to end their pain to punishing them for causing him aggravation. Massachusetts Angel of Death Kristen Gilbert may have killed up to 350 men with epinephrine, often to impress her lover, a security guard at the hospital, by reviving them, but also for reasons as callous as wanting to get out of work early.

Of the Canadian Angels of Death we examine in this chapter, both **Dr. Thomas Neill Cream** and **Dr. Robert MacGregor** were partially motivated by financial gain. However, Cream's ineffective blackmailing scams seem to have been an afterthought. The true purpose of his killings was the sadistic delight he took in causing harm to women, and possibly, the power to hold their lives and deaths in his gnarled hands. Though a much better example of a profit-motivated Angel of Death, MacGregor's coveting of the Sparling family fortune was clearly equalled by his lust for its matriarch.

Dr. Thomas Neill Cream

The Lambeth Poisoner
7 Murders
London, Ontario/London,
England/ Chicago, United States

"I am Jack the ..."

A MAN OF WEALTH AND TASTE

Thomas Neill Cream was born on May 27, 1850, in Glasgow, Scotland, the first child of William and Mary Cream. Little is known about his formative years — he seems to have been a happy and healthy child in a stable and loving family. Four years after his birth, the Creams uprooted to Wolfe's Cove, Quebec. William found employment as a labourer at Gilmour & Company, a prestigious ship-building and lumber firm, soon working his way up to the position of manager. In time he would begin a lumber wholesale business of his own, employing several of his sons at the Cream Lumber Mill. His eldest boy, however, had loftier ambitions. In September 1872, Thomas Cream began studying medicine at Montreal's reputable McGill University, with the aim of becoming a doctor. Unfortunately, his discipline in academics did not extend to his sex life. Sometime during his studies he seduced a Miss Flora Brooks of Waterford, impregnating her. During one of his subsequent visits to her home, Cream convinced her to let him perform an abortion. Flora became so unwell as a result that her family brought her to see Dr. Phelan, the town physician. When they learned of Cream's trespasses they decided enough was enough. Shortly after his convocation in April 1876, Flora's father and brothers cornered him and forced him back to Waterford at gunpoint. He acknowledged his duty to marry Flora and the couple wed soon after. The next morning, the bride awoke to find her husband missing. In his place was a letter promising her he would keep in touch.

Cream re-emerged in October amongst the slums of London, England. At that time, Britain had the most highly respected medical schools in the world, and he was anxious to learn from them. He registered at St. Thomas Hospital in Lambeth with hopes of becoming a surgeon, but after six months of training, failed to meet the entrance requirements for the Royal College of Surgeons. Unperturbed, Cream continued his studies at St. Thomas, also finding time to work as an obstetrics clerk. He applied to the Royal College of Physicians and Surgeons in Edinburgh and was accepted. There he became a licenced midwife.

As Cream was leaving for Edinburgh in 1877, across the Atlantic his long-suffering wife Flora became violently ill. Struggling to understand her symptoms, Dr. Phelan asked her if she had been taking anything. She admitted that she had imbibed some medicine that her husband had sent her from England. Phelan asked her to abstain, and miraculously her symptoms seemed to disappear. Then in August she suddenly died. Though Phelan was never able to find any of the so-called "medicine" Flora had taken, he maintained until his dying day that Thomas Neill Cream had poisoned his wife.

A TALE OF THREE CITIES

For reasons unknown, Dr. Thomas Cream returned to Canada in late 1878. Whether it was the city's name or the opportunities afforded in this thriving logging community, he settled in London, Ontario, and soon began a medical and surgical practice. By May 1879, he had landed himself in hot water again. The corpse of Kate Gardener, one of his patients, was discovered in a woodshed behind Bennett's clothing store on Dundas Street. An autopsy revealed that the pregnant woman had died from chloroform inhalation. When questioned, Cream claimed that he had refused Gardener's request for abortifacients and had simply suggested suicide by chloroform as a possible alternative. Unfortunately, the absence of a chloroform bottle at the crime scene and markings on Kate Gardener's face suggested otherwise. Though Cream was never officially charged with her murder, word spread around London of the killer doctor. When things got hot, he did what he always did: he vanished.

Toward the end of 1879, Chicago police began to hear rumours that a Canadian immigrant who had passed his state health board exam and recently set up a practice at 434 West Madison was working after hours as an abortionist. Using midwives as go-betweens, Dr. Cream met his patients in the rooms of lodging houses, where he would conduct the terminations. In early 1880, he was brought before a jury charged with the botched abortion of Mary Ann Faulkner, a prostitute who had been discovered dead in a tenement flat. It was only the aptitude of Cream's lawyer which allowed him to escape a lengthy jail sentence, managing to convince the jury that a midwife was the responsible party and that Cream had merely shown up later in an attempt to resuscitate the victim. On another occasion he was linked to the poisoning death of Ellen Stack, who had ingested some of Cream's patented abortion pills, later found to be laced with strychnine. With insufficient evidence to charge him,

Cream evaded the law once again. However, he finally came undone selling another concoction of his own design — a popular epilepsy remedy whose effectiveness was known throughout Chicago. One of its adherents, railway agent Daniel Stott, often sent his wife to fetch his medication and soon the woman and Cream began an affair. When Stott voiced his suspicions, Cream spiked his medicine with strychnine, resulting in an agonizing death on June 4, 1881. In a foolish attempt to avoid suspicion, Cream wrote to the coroner, accusing the pharmacist of poisoning the formula. An exhumation and autopsy of Stott's body revealed a high level of strychnine in the dead man's blood. Suspicion fell on Cream rather than the coroner, and learning that a warrant had been issued for his arrest, the evil physician snuck back across the Canadian border. On July 27, 1881, he was captured in Belle River, Ontario, by a Boone County sheriff and taken back to Illinois. Mrs. Stott turned state's evidence against her former lover, and in November 1881 he was handed a life sentence at Joliet State Penitentiary. After spending ten years of his life seething in a cold prison cell, the ever-charming Dr. Cream managed to win a full pardon, partially through bribery, but also through the pleading of his brother, Daniel.

The balding, watery-eyed opium addict who shuffled out of the prison gates on July 21, 1891, however, bore little resemblance to the spry young doctor who had entered a decade before. Stopping off in Quebec to collect $16,000 of his father's inheritance, he departed for England in September of the same year. Among the baggage he brought aboard the S.S. *Teutonic* was a burning hatred for women.

A MURDER IN LAMBETH

Since the construction of the Waterloo bridge in 1817, the Lambeth area of East London had become a hotbed of vice and moral depravity, overflowing with pubs, music halls, and that most infamous of affronts to the pretensions of Victorian life: the prostitute. There were worse ways to make a living, really, at least in the experience of nineteen-year-old Ellen Donworth, who had quit the monotony of the fish cannery in exchange for the unpredictability of walking the streets. On the evening of October 13, 1891, Ellen met "a tall gentleman with cross eyes, a silk hat and bushy whiskers" at Waterloo Road's York Hotel. Though the exact nature of their meeting can only be guessed, at just after 7:00 p.m., a fruit vendor saw Ellen stumbling down the street alone. *Probably drunk*, he thought. Suddenly, she collapsed onto her face, squirming around on the cobblestones in agony. Not knowing what else to do, the fruit vendor helped her back to her boarding house where she began to convulse so violently that her landlady became terrified. Doctor's assistant John Johnson was summoned to the scene in time to hear Ellen gasp about a tall, cross-eyed gentleman in a silk hat who had let her drink out of a bottle with white powder in it. Rushed immediately to St. Thomas' Hospital, she died an agonizing death before reaching its doors. A subsequent autopsy confirmed Johnson's suspicions of strychnine poisoning, placing the matter in the hands of the London police. Then something peculiar happened: the East Surrey deputy coroner received a mysterious letter from an A. O'Brien offering to name Ellen's murderer for a sum of £300,000.

Five days after the Donworth poisoning, servant girl Lucy Rose found a letter addressed to Matilda Clover, a prostitute who occupied the Lambeth Road rooming house where Lucy worked. It was from a gentleman requesting that she rendezvous with him at 7:30 p.m. outside the Canterbury Music Hall. Matilda was escorted home later that evening by a tall, moustached man with gold-rimmed spectacles. Lucy heard Matilda shout "good night, Fred" to the departing gentleman, and then step back outside for a drink at her local. Hours later, Lucy and the landlady Mrs. Vowles awoke to blood-curdling screams from Matilda's room. They found her weeping in anguish on the bed, her body spasming uncontrollably. She claimed that Fred had given her two pills that had poisoned her. Despite their efforts to soothe her with tea and milk, Matilda vomited the contents up violently. A doctor's assistant was summoned, but foolishly dismissing the symptoms as drunkenness, left the dying woman with a bottle of medicine. Lucy could only look on helplessly as Matilda Clover's pretty feminine face blackened like a prune. By 9:00 a.m., she was dead. Unlike Ellen Donworth, doctors attributed her passing to a combination of bromide of potassium and brandy, and on October 27 she was filed away neatly into the sodden ground of Tooting Cemetery.

A second letter soon arrived at the office of M.P. Frederick Smith. Signed by an H. Bayne, it claimed to have evidence that incriminated Smith as the poisoner of Ellen Donworth and instructed him to place a poster in his shop window detailing when they should meet. The London police, who had received a similar letter, encouraged Smith to play along. There was no response to his poster.

Dr. William Broadbent, a physician at St. Thomas' Hospital, was the next recipient of a bizarre letter. This time it demanded a sum of £2,500 in return for destroying evidence that proved Broadbent had poisoned Matilda Clover. Upon consulting police, he advertised a potential meeting in *The Chronicle* as requested. Again, there was no follow-up from the elusive blackmailer.

TWO BIRDS WITH ONE DOSE

In the early morning hours of April 11, 1892, a horse-drawn carriage pulled up outside a Lambeth boarding house. While walking the beat, Constable George Comley heard screams coming from the windows and decided to follow the driver inside. He came upon the contorted bodies of twenty-one-year-old Alice Marsh and Emma Shrivell, eighteen, stretched across the floor in their nightgowns. Landlady Charlotte Vogt claimed to have been awakened by their screams and summoned the cab. She recalled that the two prostitutes had dined in their room with a mysterious doctor, offering him a meal of beer and tinned salmon in exchange for three pills to improve their complexions. Comley himself remembered seeing a man in dark overcoat and glasses leaving the residence around 2:30 a.m.

Alice, frothing violently from her mouth, died before arriving at the hospital. After receiving chloroform treatment, Emma battled courageously on for another six hours before eventually succumbing. Post-mortem examinations of the two women immediately dismissed any notions of bad salmon: they had been poisoned with strychnine.

Two weeks after the double-poisoning in Lambeth, a number of citizens received letters either offering information on the Marsh-Shrivell murders for a price, or threatening to blackmail them over their supposed involvement. Connecting the deaths through the mailing campaign, the London police ordered an exhumation of Matilda Clover's grave.

A Penny Dreadful cartoon depicting the crimes of "The Lambeth Poisoner."

CREAM RISES

Though it had been years since John Haynes had served as a police detective, he never truly lost the instinct. When the currently unemployed engineer befriended a bespectacled Thomas Neill Cream at a photographer's house, however, he didn't notice anything out of the ordinary. But when Cream showed him the homes of three poison victims he had known, Ellen Donworth, Matilda Clover, and Lou Harvey, Haynes began to suspect there was more to his cross-eyed companion's story. A brief investigation of the murders revealed that one of the women Cream claimed was poisoned, Matilda Clover, had died of alcohol poisoning. Stranger still, Haynes could find no record at all of a Lou Harvey.

When, on March 12, Constable Comley noticed a man watching prostitutes outside the Canterbury Music Hall who resembled the suspect at the Marsh-Shrivell murder, he was instructed to place him under surveillance.

By the end of May, an autopsy uncovered one-sixteenth of a grain of strychnine in Matilda Clover's digestive tract. It now seemed certain that the killer of Donworth, Clover, and the two most recent poison victims was the same fiend: a shadowy figure they had known only as "Fred." As Cream rose to prominence among a narrow field of suspects, Scotland Yard began to see the two entities as one and the same.

Elaborate efforts to trace Cream's movements since his arrival in London revealed that on October 12, 1891, the good doctor had purchased gelatin capsules from a pharmacy along with nux vomica, a medicinal compound of bromide and strychnine. Though he had spent much of his time in the company of prostitutes, Cream had also become engaged to a dressmaker named Laura Sabbatini in November of the same year. After travelling back to Canada the following January to take care of some business, he had purchased five hundred one-sixteenth grain strychnine capsules during a stopover in New York before returning to England on the second of April.

In order to buy some more time to collect evidence, Scotland Yard arrested Cream on June 3, 1892, charging him with blackmail. Fourteen days later, two witnesses, Eliza Masters and Elizabeth May, came forward with some startling information. On October 6 of the previous year, the women had attended a music hall in the company of a man who told them he was once a medical student at St. Thomas' Hospital. They arranged to reconvene three days later in the same area. While they were waiting, they noticed their gentleman friend courting a well-known prostitute, Matilda Clover, and followed the couple back to her boarding house. It was the last they ever saw of their suitor or Matilda Clover.

A subsequent inquest into the death of Matilda Clover provided the final nails in Thomas Cream's coffin. Most damning of all was the surprise appearance of prostitute Louisa Harris, who also went by the pseudonym "Lou Harvey." She testified that she had met Cream at the Alhambra Theatre on October 22, 1891, before sleeping with him that night at the Palace Hotel. The following evening on the banks of the Thames River, he had presented her with some pills for her complexion, which Lou pretended to swallow. Cream remarked that he had to get back to the hospital, and made plans to see her the following night, before scuttling off into the darkness. He failed to keep their appointment.

Charged on July 13 with the murders of Donworth, Clover, Marsh, and Shrivell, Thomas Cream was sentenced to die by Justice Henry "Hanging Harry" Hawkins after a sensational four-day trial. Before thousands of spectators, on November 13, 1892, he mounted the gallows outside Newgate Prison. His last words before plummeting through the trap were "I am Jack the ..."

Despite the persistence of urban legend, the fact that Cream was interred in Joliet Prison at the time of the Whitechapel murders immediately disqualifies him as a possible Jack the Ripper.

Dr. Robert MacGregor
4 Murders
Umbra, Michigan

"Kindly disrobe."

CURSED

Like deadly doctors Edward Rulloff and Thomas Neill Cream before him, London, Ontario's Robert MacGregor chose to establish his murderous practice south of the border. Working and residing in the tiny village of

Ubly, Michigan, one afternoon in January 1909, the tall, dashing thirty-year-old received a rather strange complaint from a Mrs. Carrie Sparling. The beautiful dairy farmer's wife and mother of four had been plagued by a terrible bit of dust in her left eye. MacGregor couldn't help but notice that his forty-five-year-old patient had kept herself in impeccable condition — in fact, if he hadn't known better, he would have guessed she was twenty years younger. After a thorough examination of Mrs. Sparling's naked form, he removed the dust from her eye, promising to check in on her the next time he was in the vicinity of her Sanilac County farm.

As luck would have it, a week later, MacGregor took the one-hour buggy journey to the Sparling home, introducing himself to Carrie's brawny husband John Wesley and sons Peter, twenty-four; Albert, twenty-three; Scyrel, twenty-one; and Ray, twenty. After shaking hands with the entire family, he took Carrie into the bedroom for an hour long "follow-up examination." Despite her youthful appearance, Carrie Sparling was evidently a very unhealthy woman, necessitating visits from Dr. MacGregor at least twice a month. Worse, MacGregor soon diagnosed her husband John with Bright's disease and despite the good doctor's continued treatment, he became bed-ridden and eventually died. The tragedy only further cemented his bond with the Sparling family, and, in light of their father's rapid decline and death, Dr. MacGregor advised the boys to take out life insurance policies. As luck would have it, MacGregor's father was an insurance agent and happily sold them Sun Life of Canada policies. It was a good thing, too, because less than a year later, eldest son Peter Sparling succumbed to acute pancreatitis and was buried beside his father.

Unable to maintain the farm in light of the two deaths, Carrie Sparling sold it, moving the family into a much smaller abode beside Dr. MacGregor's office in Ubly. Yet the coming of winter would bring only more tragedy to the Sparling household when the second-eldest son Albert took ill and died. MacGregor attributed his passing to internal injuries suffered when he had hefted a particularly heavy piece of farm machinery. As always, his good friend and newly appointed county prosecutor Xenophon A. Boomhower understood.

Soon after, Dr. MacGregor took his particularly unattractive wife on a motoring trip across Ontario. Upon returning, they discovered that

Carrie Sparling had invested in a second home just blocks away from MacGregor's office, and decided it would be a sound financial move to rent from her. Unfortunately, Mrs. MacGregor soon became violently ill, and, on the advice of her husband, returned to Ontario to rest up and visit with her family. No sooner had she left when Carrie Sparling began to spend her days at MacGregor's home, often staying until sunrise. The curse of the Sparlings struck again when Scyrel joined his father and brothers in the family plot. An autopsy, undertaken, of course by MacGregor, revealed the cause of death to be cancer of the liver.

DIAGNOSIS

In the rigid moral climate of the Edwardian era, the flagrant indiscretions of Robert MacGregor and Carrie Sparling were bound to attract attention. John Sparling, the venerable uncle of the late John Wesley, decided a little investigation was in order. Climbing a ladder to peak through MacGregor's window, he was shocked to discover the good doctor and his nephew's widow entwined in bed. Outraged, he took this information immediately to Xenophon Boomhower, who ordered Scyrel Sparling's body to be exhumed and his organs sent for examination at the University of Michigan. The results couldn't have been more clear: they were laden with arsenic. A subsequent examination of Albert Sparling's corpse revealed the same shocking detail.

Coincidentally, Dr. MacGregor soon approached Boomhower with the news that the last remaining Sparling son, Ray, had become bedridden with illness. Secretly, Boomhower visited Ray at the farm, and after divulging the truth to him suggested he save whatever medicine MacGregor had given to him for testing. As they suspected, analysis revealed traces of arsenic.

Charged with the murder of Scyrel Sparling, Robert MacGregor was found guilty in 1912 and sentenced to a life term in Michigan State Prison. Amazingly, Carrie Sparling's charges were dropped. However, Dr. Death still had a few tricks up his sleeve. Penning a letter proclaiming his innocence to Governor Woodbridge Fuller, the governor learned that evidence of Albert Sparling's poisoning had been allowed at the trial. When speaking with members of the jury, several admitted that if this evidence had not been present, they never would have convicted MacGregor of Scyrel's murder. After spending four years languishing behind bars, the foolhardy politician granted Robert MacGregor a full pardon. Unsurprisingly, MacGregor found that no one in the community wished to be his patient, let alone his friend. With little option, he successfully applied to be a physician at Michigan State Prison, spending the next twelve years caring for men that had once been his fellow prisoners. He died in 1928.

RIGHT UNDER OUR NOSES:

Colonel Russell Williams and the Writing of this Book, Part 3

Until Colonel Russell Williams's trial in October 2010, public knowledge of his crimes seemed to indicate an entirely different killer than the one who emerged during the proceedings. What *was* known was that on the evening of February 4, the forty-six-year-old Williams had been stopped at a police roadblock along Highway 37: a north-south road leading from his Tweed cottage, past Jessica Lloyd's house, on route to the Trenton air force base. When police checked the tires on Williams's Nissan Pathfinder, they discovered they matched impressions found in a field across from Lloyd's country home, and placed the colonel under immediate surveillance. Three days later, while staying in Orleans with his wife, Williams was summoned to an Ottawa police station to answer some questions. Under interrogation, he eventually confessed to murdering Marie-France Comeau and Jessica Lloyd, along with two sexual assaults and a rash of fetish burglaries in Tweed, and similar break-ins in Orleans. He subsequently directed police to Jessica Lloyd's body — dumped thirteen metres from Carry Road, near East Hungerford in Tweed.

With the limited knowledge I had at this point, I concluded that Williams was essentially a fetishistic rapist, killing solely to eliminate witnesses. Like **Angelo Colalillo** and **David Threinen**, he displayed mostly "organized" criminal traits, though leaned close to the "mixed" end of the spectrum. I also placed him, according to the Holmes-De

Burger classification system, under the power/control category of serial killer. Though sexual assault and lingerie fetishism seemed to colour his crimes, the "overkill" that typifies the hedonist-lust murderer was not present. If Williams had simply desired sex and the opportunity to snap a few pictures of women modelling lingerie, he could easily have found a prostitute to fulfill these desires. Rather, I believed he needed to psychologically dominate these women, forcing them to enact his fantasies of control. It is a view I hold to this day — though in the aftermath of his trial, I learned that Russell Williams was far more sadistic than I had initially imagined.

It seems Williams had first become acquainted with Corporal Marie-France Comeau while she was serving as flight attendant on one of his many voyages. Using his position of power on the base, he learned her home address in Brighton, Ontario, and broke in on several occasions to snoop around. On November 24, 2009, he decided to go a step further. Gaining access through the basement window, Williams hid behind the furnace while the unsuspecting Marie-France chatted on the telephone upstairs. When she descended into the basement to collect her cat, he ambushed her, smashing an aluminum flashlight against her skull. Stunned, with her head gushing blood, she attempted to flee her assailant, but Williams caught her near the top of the stairs and overpowered her. A true warrior, Marie-France Comeau continued to struggle as he bound her. Williams eventually managed to drag her into the bedroom where he blindfolded her and gagged her with duct tape. Once she was under his control, he switched on his video camera, filming himself repeatedly raping her over a number of hours. When Williams had finished, he suffocated her to death with duct tape, calmly recording as she thrashed around helplessly on the floor. He would later send an official letter of condolence to her family in his role as the head of CFB Trenton.

Unlike Comeau, twenty-seven-year-old Jessica Lloyd had been a total stranger to Williams. On January 27, 2010, he had spied the green-eyed beauty through her basement window, exercising on her treadmill. The next day he broke into Jessica's house to ensure she lived alone. Later that night, he entered through the patio door and crept into her bedroom with his flashlight to "subdue her." Before he had the chance,

Jessica awoke in horror to find a man standing over her bed. Terrified, she agreed to do whatever he wanted if he promised not to hurt her. Binding her and taping her eyes shut with duct tape, Williams forced Jessica to perform oral sex on him, and to pose for snapshots wearing a selection of undergarments, all the while meticulously documenting her ordeal with his digital video camera. At some point, he decided a change of venue was in order. Marching Jessica outside to his Nissan Pathfinder, Williams drove the frightened woman to his cottage in Tweed. There he forced her to shower with him, before continuing to sexually abuse and degrade her, cajoling her to smile as she modelled lingerie under threat of death. At 8:15 p.m. the following evening, he led her, still gagged and blindfolded, to the door of his cottage, ostensibly to set her free. With her guard down, Williams bludgeoned her from behind with the flashlight, strangling her unconscious body to death with a length of rope. Lloyd's corpse remained decomposing in the cottage's garage for three days before Williams finally drove out to deposit it at the entrance of his neighbour Larry Jones's hunting camp. The selection of this dump site was likely an attempt to frame Jones — the OPP had investigated him and, unbeknownst to the general public, cleared him as a suspect in two Tweed sexual assaults Williams had committed in late 2009. On September 17 of that year, the colonel had surprised a twenty-year-old mother in her home, striking her once to ensure her co-operation. Binding and blindfolding her with pillowcases, he made his frightened victim pose in lingerie for several hours, while he took photos. A similar attack occurred thirteen days later at the nearby residence of Laurie Massicotte. Williams escalated the level of violence, repeatedly punching and choking the mother of three, before cutting her clothes away with a knife. He briefly fondled the bound woman, but stopped himself when she complained. After three hours of humiliating photographs, Ms. Massicotte asked the masked intruder if he planned to kill her. Williams simply replied "no need for that."

Knowing that he had recorded the death of Marie-France Comeau on video camera greatly changed my perception of Williams's character. Even after spending over a year writing this book, I cringed when I read the headline: WILLIAMS VIDEOTAPED MURDER. If Williams had videotaped the rape and domination of his victims, it was undoubtedly because he intended to masturbate later while viewing the footage. His choice to keep the camera rolling while Marie-France Comeau suffered an excruciating death meant that Williams had actually incorporated murder into his fantasy life. This was not simply a perverse rapist who murdered out of necessity. Russell Williams experienced a sexual thrill watching an innocent woman's life slip away before his eyes. Even the infamous **Paul Bernardo** had switched off the camera for this final scene.

PART C

CATCHING SERIAL KILLERS IN CANADA

Understanding and classifying serial killers is not only fascinating, it is also crucial to solving their crimes. Where the previous chapters focused primarily on theories of serial murder, the remainder of this book will concentrate on the investigatory strategies Canadian law enforcement has applied in apprehending sexual predators.

In **Chapter 13**, we climb back inside the head of the serial killer as we look at the controversial art of criminal profiling, its implementation against **Brian Arp**, **Paul Bernardo**, and in the hitherto unsolved case of **The Edmonton Serial Killer.** After that, we move toward the hard sciences. **Chapter 14** looks at the colossal impact genetics has made in solving cold serial murder cases over the past twenty years. As it is beyond the scope of this book to delve into the finer points of forensics; finger, foot, and palm prints, fibre evidence et cetera, **Chapter 15** will examine only those techniques pioneered by Canadian scientists for the purpose of investigating local cases. These include ballistics location, bite-mark analysis, and, more recently, Kim Rossmo's revolutionary geographic profiling.

CHAPTER 13

NEW TECHNOLOGIES: OFFENDER PROFILING

On November 8, 1888, Dr. Thomas Bond put the finishing touches on a report for the head of London's Criminal Investigation Division regarding the probable occupation, income, motives, habits, and psychological disorders of Jack the Ripper. Though nobody realized its importance at the time, Bond's assessment would go down as the first criminal profile in history. Unfortunately, as the Whitechapel fiend was never apprehended, the accuracy of Bond's profile would never be tested.

Sixty-eight years later, in perhaps the most successful example of criminal profiling in history, New York's assistant commissioner of mental health, Dr. James Brussel, was solicited by police to develop a psychological portrait of the elusive "Mad Bomber," who had been detonating small explosive devices around the city for the past sixteen years. After reviewing the case files, Brussel predicted that the perpetrator was a middle-aged Roman Catholic of Eastern European descent, who suffered from paranoia. He was of medium build, unmarried, and living in Connecticut. Meticulous and conservative, he would probably be wearing a double-breasted suit at the time of his apprehension. When, with the aid of Brussel's profile, fifty-four-year-old George Metesky of Waterbury, Connecticut, was arrested, he matched the profile precisely. The Polish bachelor even took the time to change into a pin-striped, double-breasted suit before accompanying the police downtown.

One of the first criminologists to specialize in sex murder, Howard D. Teten, developed a system of profiling while studying at the University of California. After joining the FBI, he partnered with abnormal psychology expert Agent Pat Mullany in the creation of a federal behavioural science unit.

This age of criminal profiling began in earnest when, with the 1972 death of FBI head J. Edgar Hoover, psychology became an accepted part of the agency's curriculum. For years, the notorious bully had exercised absolute control, shooting down any idea that departed from his personal vision of what the bureau should be. Following Teten's retirement from the FBI, a team of enthusiastic young agents spearheaded by Robert Ressler and John Douglas set about interviewing a number of convicted sex killers from 1978 to 1983, whose crimes they reviewed in detail. Their results led to the development of the trichotomy outlined in Chapter 5.

In the years since, the effectiveness of criminal profiling has been a topic of immense controversy. The cases of the "Atlanta Child Murders," Robert Hansen, Larry Gene Bell, and the "Vampire of Sacramento," Richard Trenton Chase, are typically presented as evidence of the FBI's success. Yet there have also been some colossal failures, which have not only misled investigators, but also resulted in more tragic deaths: the "DC Snipers" John Allen Muhammad and Lee Boyd Malvo, Derrick Todd Lee, Henry Louis Wallace; and mailbox pipe bomber, Lucas Helder, to name a few.

The arrest of Prince George serial killer **Brian Arp** in 1993 is a prime example of how trained profilers can employ signature analysis to link two cases, solving them without even needing to create a profile.

Brian Arp
2 Murders
Prince George, British Columbia

SCATTERED

In mid-December 1989, a cross-country skier came across a human jawbone in a clearing ten kilometres from Prince George, British

Columbia. A police search of the area revealed further skeletal remains, scattered by animals. Dental records identified the victim as Marnie Blanchard: a twenty-something Caucasian woman missing since November 22. Last seen by a taxi driver, standing alone outside a bar in Prince George at 2:00 a.m., Marnie had climbed into a grey Nissan pickup driven by a man with shoulder-length dark hair. Though no cause of death could be found, the pathologist noted an absence of pre-mortem damage to the bones. Marnie's sweater, coat, and a length of nylon pantyhose were discovered in a nearby pile, along with other personal items and clothes strewn about the vicinity. Many of the articles of clothing, particularly the sweater, were severely cut or torn, though this may have been attributable to ravaging animals. What seemed undeniable was that the area between the skirt and camisole had been slashed with a sharp instrument. The circumstances of the discovery left little doubt — Marnie Blanchard's death was ruled a homicide.

Suspicion soon fell on local man Brian Arp. According to an acquaintance, Thorone Fontaine, he had gone out drinking with Arp one evening in November. Arp had dropped Fontaine at his residence, before speeding off downtown in the opposite direction from home. He stopped by Fontaine's the following day, explaining that he had driven a young woman to Vanderhoof the night before, and arrived home late. Apparently, his passenger had inadvertently left some of her jewellery on the dashboard. The next time Fontaine was in Arp's truck he noticed damage to the gear shift and the arm controlling the wipers and signal. Sharon Olson, another friend, claimed that around November 22, 1989, Arp bragged that after drinking with a friend, he had picked up a good-looking blonde, driven her home, and had sex with her in exchange for some of her jewellery, which his common-law wife had later been upset to discover in his pocket. On November 23, Arp also had told Arlene Spencer a similar version of the story.

Investigators searched Arp's pickup on April 18, 1990, discovering a four-inch double-edged knife in the driver's door, and a silver ring under the passenger seat. The ring would later be identified by Marnie Blanchard's friends as belonging to the deceased. Several fibres were also taken from the vehicle's carpet and sent to the RCMP laboratory in Vancouver. An expert confirmed that the samples were consistent with those found on Marnie's purple sweater, and on July 26, Arp was arrested for her second-degree murder. When twenty-five minutes of questioning failed to crack the suspect, detectives asked Arp for samples from his scalp and pubic hair in order to clear him. "That would be great with me," Arp replied, agreeing to submit to the procedure. A report from the forensic laboratory confirmed that his hair did not match any of the sixteen samples taken from Blanchard's coat, and after a preliminary inquiry, a provincial judge decided against trying Arp for the murder. On December 17, 1990, he was released from custody, and the slaying of Marnie Blanchard would remain unsolved for another two and a half years.

DISPLAYED

Theresa Umphrey, a Native Canadian woman in her thirties, came to Prince George on February 13, 1993, to have a good time. By around 3:00 a.m. on Valentine's Day, she was noticeably drunk and trying to score a ride outside a convenience store downtown. A group of men eventually obliged her, but after driving around for some time, Theresa could not remember where she lived and they dropped her back at the corner.

The next time Theresa was seen was at 2:30 p.m., her naked, half-frozen body posed atop a snowbank fifty kilometres southwest of the city. Scrapes on the corpse indicated it had been dragged across rough terrain, possibly behind a vehicle. Like Marnie Blanchard, Theresa's clothes where found nearby, tossed down an embankment. Her bra was discovered by the roadside 1.4 kilometres to the north, severed between the cups and knotted at the back. Her shoelaces had been similarly cut. A forensic pathologist listed the cause of death as both manual and ligature strangulation, marks from the latter consistent with the shoelaces found at the scene. As if that had not been enough, Theresa's skull had also been crushed, and a piece of her hair hacked crudely away. The presence of semen in her vagina pointed to her having had sexual intercourse sometime within twenty-eight hours before she died. Traces of sperm were also found on her sweater.

It's entirely possible that the murders of Marnie Blanchard and Theresa Umphrey would never have been linked if not for the acumen of RCMP investigator Ron MacKay. The first non-American to be trained by the FBI in the art of criminal profiling, MacKay noted in the Blanchard murder that an earring located by police in the opening to the clearing implied that Marnie's body had originally been displayed like Theresa's, but that it had been eaten by a lynx, and the bones eventually scattered. MacKay surmised this after having learned that lynx are known to nibble carefully around ear tags attached to caribou by wildlife preservationists. He thus linked the two slayings by the killer's signature: displaying the corpses of his victims.

Once again, Brian Arp found himself under intense police scrutiny, interviewed on numerous occasions. When he was informed that foreign traces of human tissue were found on Theresa's body and was asked for a DNA sample, Arp refused. Fortunately, he had left an ashtray full of cigarette butts in the interrogation room — a veritable goldmine of genetic information! When these cigarette butts were sent to the RCMP laboratory, along with the bodily samples offered by Arp during the Blanchard investigation, forensic biology specialist Barbara Fraser determined conclusively that they matched the semen from the Umphrey murder.

Brian Arp was rearrested on October 4, 1993, and charged with the two sex slayings. He was subsequently convicted of both. Though his defence attorneys appealed on the grounds that their client should have been tried separately for both cases, their attempts were ultimately unsuccessful.

———

Though behavioural scientists utilized a rudimentary signature analysis in the Arp murders, they would go to much greater lengths in their attempts to apprehend an even viler predator. During Paul Bernardo's 1987–1993 reign of terror over Ontario's Golden Horseshoe region, his crimes were profiled on three separate occasions: once as a rapist and twice as a murderer. We will now examine the implementation of profiling in the capture of Canada's most loathed serial killer.

Kay Feely.

Paul Bernardo

The Schoolgirl Murderer
3 Murders
Port Dalhousie, Ontario

"Tell my dick you love him!"

Paul Kenneth Bernardo. Shortly before his capture, he would change his name to Paul Jason Teale — a composite of the *Friday the 13th* slasher "Jason" and "Martin Thiel," a rich young serial killer portrayed by Kevin Bacon in the 1989 film *Criminal Law.*

THE SCARBOROUGH RAPIST

One December night in 1987, Vicky Cinq-Mars[1] stepped off the Lawrence Avenue bus and headed north along Centennial. Between the wind-swept snow dunes and endless suburban fencing, the streets of West Hill were deserted. She felt a shiver run down her spine. Given the choice, the pretty twenty-two-year-old would have preferred to take a taxi. Like every other woman in Scarborough, she had been made well aware of the sadistic sexual predator stalking their streets, but felt safe enough in her own neighbourhood, sticking to the well-lit half of the sidewalk. As she passed by the entrance to a townhouse complex, she heard something stirring in the bushes behind her. Before she could react, something slammed hard into her back, knocking her face first to the ground. Seizing her roughly, her attacker dragged her into the narrow space between two houses, pinning her arms at her side. Straddling her, he hissed menacingly into her ear: "Don't look at me or you're dead!"

Something struck hard into the side of her face, and for a moment her consciousness cut out like an unplugged television. Why had he punched her? She had done what he'd asked. The next thing she felt was a thick cord loop around her neck, constricting her windpipe. Immobilized, she could do nothing but gasp for air and pray as the ligature burrowed deeper and deeper into her skin. Like a mad beast, her attacker tore her pants and underwear down to her ankles. When he demanded she perform fellatio on him, she had little choice but to comply. After several minutes he withdrew from her mouth, and climbed behind to sodomize her.

"What's your name?" His breath was disgusting.

"Vicky," she sobbed.

"Tell me that you love me!" he demanded.

The words spilled emptily from her mouth. Vicky's one thought was that she didn't want to die like this: half-naked and strangled in the snow for all the world to see. Gritting her teeth, she tried to project her mind to a better place, away from the pain. Then, at once, he was finished. For what seemed like hours she kept her face buried, waiting to hear the sound of his footsteps beating a hasty retreat. But he wasn't leaving. Instead, to her horror, he circled back around to the front, thrusting his dirty penis toward her face.

"Don't look at me!" he repeated.

The assault continued for several more minutes before her mouth was filled with the foul taste of his ejaculate. She felt like vomiting. Dragging her toward a fence, he used her belt to bind her to a picket and began rifling through her purse. As he rose to leave, she felt a wave of relief come over her. It was over. Then, almost as an afterthought, her attacker whirled around and kicked her in the ribs. By the time she had recovered from the blow, he was long gone. Terrified, she waited several minutes before attempting to free herself. Her trembling hands made the task particularly difficult, though she wasn't sure if it was nerves or the cold.

THE GAME IS AFOOT

Just before Christmas, the man the media was now referring to as "The Scarborough Rapist" struck again. This time he crept up on his victim from behind, pressing a knife to her throat and threatening her with death. Herding her into the bushes, he tore down her pants and traced the blade across her anus before subjecting her to a horrific ordeal of rape and sodomy. When he had finished, he asked her to give him "one good reason" why he shouldn't murder her. Through a torrent of tears, the woman begged for her life. This time he decided to spare it, but only after warning that he had taken her ID: if she contacted the police, he knew where she lived. Before disappearing into the night he commanded her to keep lying face down for half an hour. When at least fifteen minutes had passed, the woman rose to collect her scattered clothing. Suddenly, her attacker charged from the bushes, striking her on the jaw. She collapsed onto the frozen earth where he screamed at her to "arch her back," before inflicting another gruelling anal assault. At one point she swore she heard him snarl something about his "fucking mother," before taking off, this time for good.

Following reports of a sixth and seventh attack in April 1988, the Metro Toronto Sexual Assault Squad sent the case files to the FBI's behavioural science unit in Quantico, Virginia. Renowned criminal profiler Gregg McCrary was assigned to the case, and, deciding that it merited a more hands-on approach, flew into Toronto with his colleague, maverick BSU pioneer, John Douglas. During the plane ride, McCrary had filled Douglas in on the specifics, both men agreeing that the offender or UNSUB (unknown subject) would already be familiar to police. Upon arriving, they were greeted with a tour of the rape sites, all occurring in Scarborough save for one in Mississauga, where he had broken the pattern by approaching his victim from the front. Due to the high volume of traffic in the areas, they concluded that the rapist must be a local man, as nobody had reported any strangers in the area. The next day, the two agents attended a conference where they presented their findings to a half-dozen Toronto investigators. McCrary's final profile of the Scarborough Rapist is included here.

F.B.I. Profile of Scarborough Rapist — November 17, 1988[2]

Victimology

We found nothing in any of these women's backgrounds or lifestyles that would elevate their risk of becoming victims of a violent crime and/or sexual assault. We consider all these victims to be low-risk victims. There are observable similarities in that the victims are white females 15–21 years of age, with six out of seven living in the Scarborough area and three of those living in extremely close proximity to one another ... The fact that four of the victims either travelled from or through the downtown area immediately prior to the attack is of note, but is not felt to be of significance in this analysis. If the offender was selecting his victims from a downtown location and surveilling them to their residential area for the attack, we would expect to see a far more random geographical pattern to the attacks than there is. With the exception of the Mississauga attack, all are clustered in the Scarborough area. Another notable similarity among the victims is their small physical stature, ranging from 5'1" and 93 lbs to 5'3" and 135 lbs …

Crime Analysis
We feel your offender uses bus stops for staking out points. He surveils streets rather than homes and does so at night. Some victims were victims of opportunity while others appear to have been previously targeted to a degree. We believe the offender has seen victims or potential victims in passing, but had no urge to attack and at other times has seen victims, had the urge to attack, but the moment was inopportune. The successful attacks occurred when the urge, opportunity and victim coincided. The victims are being targeted by the offender in the areas in which the attacks are occurring. He is following them short distances before attacking them.

The six victims in Scarborough were all approached from behind, while the victim in Mississauga was approached from the front. He gained control over all the victims by the immediate application of injurious physical force. He maintained control of the victims through the use of physical force and verbal threats of bodily harm and or death, all of which were often accomplished while brandishing a knife in a threatening and intimidating manner. All victims were attacked outdoors, while walking alone, near their residence during the hours of darkness. Typically, this type of offender starts his attacks in an area with which he is familiar. This familiarity is usually the result of the offender living or working in that area and gives him a sense of security and comfort as he knows the neighbourhood well, can plan escape routes, etc.

The behaviour exhibited by your offender is consistent with this premise. We believe your offender resides in the Scarborough area, specifically within walking distance of the first, second and fifth attacks. Because he lives in his attack area it is of utmost importance to him that the victims not see him. This is one of the reasons he prefers to approach the victims from the rear. Upon contact he forces them face down into the ground and/or demands they keep their eyes closed to ensure they do not see him. The victim in Mississauga was approached in a slightly different manner. After following her for a distance on foot, he approached her under the guise of asking directions. This approach allowed the victim to see his face, but was short in duration as the offender did not finish his first sentence before physically assaulting this victim and forcing her face down to the ground. It is our opinion that the offender was less concerned about being seen by his victim as he does not spend a great deal of time in the Mississauga area and believes that it is unlikely he would be recognized or seen there again. Another reason your offender approaches victims from behind is that he harbours some inadequacies. These inadequacies are further evident in his verbal behaviour as he scripts many of his victims to say, "Tell me you hate your boyfriend and love me" "Tell me you love me, tell me it feels good" and other ego-gratifying statements. Another indication of his inadequacies is evident in his victim selection. He selected victims that appeared non-threatening to him. As noted in the victimology section, the victims were physically small and could offer no real resistance to the attack. Each victim was walking alone at the time of the attack and was virtually defenceless. Anger, however, is the primary behaviour exhibited by your offender. His intent is to punish and degrade the victims as he is angry at all women. This is evident in the blitz style approach and the majority of his verbal behaviour as well as the type and sequence of sexual acts forced upon the victims in conjunction with the punishing physical force used against them. The typically profane verbal behaviour combined with scripting the victims to describe themselves as a bitch, a cunt, a slut etc., evidences his anger and his need to punish and degrade his victims. This anger is also apparent in the offender's sexual behaviour. By forcing the victims to perform oral sex on him after he has repeatedly vaginally and anally assaulted them he is punishing, degrading and humiliating them. The type and sequence of sexual assault is consistently observable in the series of attacks ... What is of concern is the escalation in violence observable in this series of attacks. He is using far more physical force against the victims than is necessary to control them. In addition to this, the offender has stuffed articles of clothing into the mouths of victims and in the case of the sixth victim, not only broke her collar bone, but poured dirt on her and rubbed it into her hair and onto her body. This is a symbolic gesture which expresses the offender's opinion of women. We do not believe the offender would attack a victim with a premeditated idea of murdering her. However, we would opine, based upon our research and experience, that if confronted by a victim who vigorously resists his attack, your offender is the type who would likely become so enraged he could lose control and thereby become capable of unintentionally murdering the victim ... when the victims either misunderstand a command or delay, even momentarily responding to a demand, the offender immediately becomes enraged and escalates the amount of violence directed at the victim. The offender's escalation in violence is observable also as the first three attacks could be seen as attempted rapes where no penile penetration occurred, while the rest of the attacks where successful rapes from the offender's viewpoint as he achieved penile penetration. This expansion of the sexual nature of the assaults was accompanied by an escalation in the verbal and physical violence directed at the victims. Also observable in the offender is the development of sadistic tendencies. He asked the seventh victim, should I kill you, thereby making her beg for her life. The sadist achieves gratification by the victim's response to his attempts to dominate and control her either physically or psychologically. He has shown adaptive behaviour, indicating he is becoming comfortable in committing the assaults and feels unthreatened and in control. This is exemplified in the sixth attack. While he was accosting the victim and attempting to gain control over her, a car pulls out of a driveway a few inches away and drives by them. He does not panic, but forces the victim into some bushes near a house and continues to assault her.

Offender Characteristics and Traits
Your offender is a white male, 18 to 25 years of age ... The behaviour exhibited throughout these assaults suggests a youthful offender rather than an older more mature one ... He is familiar with Scarborough, especially the initial assault sites, and, therefore, in all probability lives in the immediate vicinity of those first assaults. The offender's anger towards women will be known by those individuals who are close to him. He will speak disparagingly of women in general conversation with associates. He had a problem with women immediately before the onset of these attacks.

His anger would have been apparent not only for the particular women involved but those close to him. He is sexually experienced but his past relationships with women have been stormy and have ended badly. In all probability he has battered women he has been involved with in the past. He places the blame for all his failures on women. He is bright, but an underachiever in a formal academic setting. He is nocturnal and spends a great deal of time on foot in the target assault area. We believe your offender is single. His work record will be sporadic and spotty as he can not hold a job due to his inability to handle authority. He is financially supported by his mother or other dominant female in his life. He is a lone wolf type of person. He can deal with people on a superficial level but prefers to be alone. The personal property of the victims that your offender took from the assault scenes is being kept by him. These effects are viewed as trophies by the offender and allow him to relive the assaults ... The offender recognizes his inadequacies and attempts to mask them, but very often overcompensates ... Your offender harbours no guilt or remorse for these crimes.

PAUL BERNARDO: DEADLY INNOCENCE

The handsome young professional who would lead scores of women to proclaim he was "too good-looking to be a serial killer" was born a hideously ugly child at Scarborough General Hospital on August 27, 1964. When his mother Marilyn Bernardo first saw the black mark staining the left side of his face, she recoiled in disgust. Diagnosed as a large, transient blood clot, the deformity completely disappeared within six weeks.

Paul's father, Ken Bernardo, was raised by an abusive Italian orphan who went on to become successful in the marble and tile business. Graduating with a B.A. from Sir Wilfrid Laurier University in 1957, Ken soon found work as an accountant. In November 1955, he met Marilyn Eastman, an adopted child from a wealthy and prominent Toronto family and the two were married on May 20, 1960. Though Marilyn had some reservations about Ken, her father Colonel Gerald Eastman decided she should marry him over her other suitor, an uneducated labourer named Bill.

As soon as the newlyweds moved into their first apartment, the beatings began. With two children and a husband she was gradually beginning to hate, Marilyn sought comfort in the arms of her ex-lover. Furious at being cuckolded, Ken moved his pregnant wife and two children away to 21 Sir Raymond Drive in Scarborough's upper-middle-class Guildwood Village, far from Marilyn's lover.

In her earliest memories of her son, Marilyn recalled that baby Paul was unaffectionate, selfish, and stubborn. His health problems seemed endless; along with allergies to orchard grass, elm, poplars, cotton linters, and ash, by the age of three it was also clear that he was having trouble speaking. A trip to the doctors revealed that his tongue was connected to his palette by a webbing of skin; a deformity easily fixed by minor surgery. Freed of his communication handicaps, he grew to be an attractive and sociable adolescent, fawned over by girls and brimming with narcissism.

Where things seemed to be steadily improving for Paul, Ken and Marilyn Bernardo were deteriorating personally and maritally. Ken's frequent abuse combined with her ever-worsening thyroid malfunction, had profound physical and psychological effects on Marilyn Bernardo. She became angry and neglectful, refusing to cook meals for her children or even keep up with routine housework. Her body seemed to transform to match her temper: skin and hair coarsening, eyes and hands puffing like balloons, her once feminine body burying itself under a grave of obesity. Marilyn retreated into the basement — a world of darkness far from the ridicule of her husband.

For his part, Ken Bernardo took to creeping out at night to peer through the window of his neighbour's twenty-six-year-old daughter. Worse yet, he began to sexually abuse Paul's older sister Debbie. On Sunday nights it was routine for the Bernardo family to settle down in front of the television to watch *The Wonderful World of Disney*. While Marilyn sat with her boys, Ken would insert his fingers into Debbie's vagina. On occasion, Marilyn asked them what they were doing on the other side of the room, but though she must have harboured suspicions, never bothered to pursue the matter any further. Life was just too tiring.

One fateful day in grade ten, following a particularly nasty argument between Ken and Marilyn Bernardo, Paul's mother suddenly stormed into his room, tossed a photograph of an unknown man on the bed, and declared that this stranger, not Ken, was his real father.

"You're a bastard!" Marilyn glared into his baby-blue eyes. "You'd better get used to it!"

Right away, Paul knew she was telling the truth. He bore such a striking resemblance to the man in the photograph that they could have been twins. He decided that Ken was right — his mother was a bitch, and from that moment on he hated her with every inch of his being.

Despite their genetic differences, Paul and Ken Bernardo had another thing in common: they were both peeping Toms. On more than one occasion, the angel-faced teenager was caught peering through his neighbours' windows to watch their daughters undress themselves. At the age of sixteen, his voyeurism almost exploded into a street fight when a local man caught him masturbating in the bushes outside the bedroom of a young brunette.

Like many boys, Paul Bernardo developed a taste for pornography, starting with the lingerie sections of retail catalogues. The crucial difference was that some of the clippings he kept featured girls as young as ten. When he became a little older, he moved on to adult videotapes, favouring ones that emphasized bondage and simulated rape. In addition, he found he was increasingly aroused by scenes of urination and defecation. He began to seek out submissive or naive women whom he could browbeat into acting out his lurid fantasies. With his pretty-boy looks and irresistible charm, there was no shortage of teenage girls who would jump at the chance to shed their clothes for a winner like Paul Bernardo. If he made unusual demands of them like anal sex or binding their hands behind them with twine, it was worth it — there was just something about him that they couldn't help falling in love with. In one woman, however, Bernardo found his ideal partner: an attractive blond veterinarian's assistant who lived only to please him, complying with any demand no matter how painful, humiliating, or evil. Her name was **Karla Homolka**, and in the summer of 1991, she would become his wife.

Graduating from U of T Scarborough with a degree in Commerce and Economics, Bernardo would eventually blend effortlessly into the white-collar world, becoming a junior accountant for the Price Waterhouse firm. Like the character of Patrick Bateman in Brett Easton Ellis's cult classic *American Psycho*, his successful facade did more than enough to mask the evil oozing from his very being. By the time he was stalking the streets of Scarborough with a knife and electrical cord, he had spent most of his teens hiding his misogyny in plain sight. Yet in these first years of his terror campaign, none of his family or friends came forward to report him. Bernardo would later articulate this strange duality in some of the rap lyrics that he believed were going to make him famous:

> You think I'm innocent?
> But behind this, I'm packing a lot of deadliness
> So come at me, come at me
> I got a fucking nice face
> I look like a pretty boy …
> I'll kick your ass
> I'll kill your parents
> Then I'll shoot your girlfriend
> And fuck your wife,
> That's me, Deadly Innocence[3]

It was one victim's vivid recollection of this innocent face, replicated perfectly in a 1990 police composite, that would first lead police to Bernardo's door. On November 20, they questioned the genial young man with the bleached-blond hair about his whereabouts on May 26, the date of the latest savage rape. Though Bernardo admitted he couldn't remember, he did agree to provide a sample of his DNA for comparison. Unfortunately, it would be two years before it was processed.

LESLIE MAHAFFY: THE "BAD GIRL"

Fourteen-year-old Leslie Mahaffy had missed her curfew again. Friday, June 14, 1991, was a warm night and Leslie and her friends had gathered at "The Rock" — a local bush party spot — to share beers and mourn the passing of a close friend. Things in the Mahaffy home had been less turbulent lately, and, in light of the circumstances, Leslie's parents had permitted her to stay out past her 11:00 p.m. curfew on the condition that she phone to

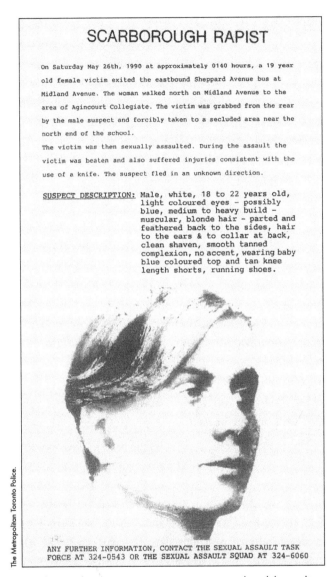

SCARBOROUGH RAPIST

On Saturday May 26th, 1990 at approximately 0140 hours, a 19 year old female victim exited the eastbound Sheppard Avenue bus at Midland Avenue. The woman walked north on Midland Avenue to the area of Agincourt Collegiate. The victim was grabbed from the rear by the male suspect and forcibly taken to a secluded area near the north end of the school.

The victim was then sexually assaulted. During the assault the victim was beaten and also suffered injuries consistent with the use of a knife. The suspect fled in an unknown direction.

SUSPECT DESCRIPTION: Male, white, 18 to 22 years old, light coloured eyes – possibly blue, medium to heavy build – muscular, blonde hair – parted and feathered back to the sides, hair to the ears & to collar at back, clean shaven, smooth tanned complexion, no accent, wearing baby blue coloured top and tan knee length shorts, running shoes.

ANY FURTHER INFORMATION, CONTACT THE SEXUAL ASSAULT TASK FORCE AT 324-0543 OR THE SEXUAL ASSAULT SQUAD AT 324-6060

The Metropolitan Toronto Police.

Scarborough Rapist composite poster circulated by police, pre-dating "The Schoolgirl Murders."

inform them where she was. Though the rebellious blonde had certainly intended to call, she had simply lost track of time.

When she finally left the party in the company of her friend Martin McSweeney, it was already past midnight. Not far from her home on upper-middle-class Keller Court, Leslie and Martin sat on a grassy hummock chatting and smoking cigarettes. Half an hour passed. When McSweeney finally escorted her to the side door of her house they found it locked. Leslie assumed she was going to be in trouble, but the thought didn't seem to bother her. The funeral was the next day, and though she expected a stern reprimand, there was no way Dan and Deborah Mahaffy were going to prevent her attendance. Saying goodbye to her friend, Leslie circled around to the front door to find it was also locked. The only option left was to ring the doorbell and wake her parents. Considering the circumstances, Leslie was in no mood for a lecture. Instead she decided to walk to a pay phone and call her friend Amanda Carpino to ask if she could spend the night. By then it was 2:00 a.m., and Amanda was surprised to hear Leslie was still out wandering the streets. Though she felt sorry for her friend, the last time the Carpinos had allowed her to stay, an infuriated Deborah Mahaffy had called to chastise Amanda's mother. Amanda reminded Leslie of this and tried to convince her to suck it up and ring the doorbell. The two chatted for twenty minutes or so before eventually saying good night.

"I'll see you tomorrow!" Leslie hung up.

But rather than following Amanda's advice, she returned to the backyard and seated herself on a picnic bench. Minutes later, a handsome man in a hooded jacket appeared from the shadows. When Leslie asked him what he was doing, he explained that he was casing homes to burglarize.

"Cool," she allegedly replied, going on to explain that she had been locked out of the house.[4] When she asked him for a cigarette, he was happy to oblige. The only problem was that they were in his car one street over. Naively, she followed him to the vehicle where he motioned for her to get into the passenger seat. Leslie knew the risks, but the man seemed friendly enough. Perhaps if she kept her legs outside the vehicle she would be able to run at the first sign of trouble. Climbing into the seat, she noticed that the dome light was out. The man handed her a cigarette and leaned over to light it for her. Leslie sucked the smoke deep into her lungs, turning her head to exhale out the doorway. The next thing she knew there was a knife at her throat.

"Get your legs into the car!" he hissed.

Terrified, she did as he asked. The man in the hooded jacket reached across the seat, wrenching the door shut. In one smooth motion he hit a lever by Leslie's legs, and the passenger seat collapsed backwards. Before she knew what was happening he had blindfolded her with a polo shirt and thrown a blanket over her. Tears began to stream down her cheeks as they sped into the night. To the rest of the world, Leslie Mahaffy had simply disappeared.

Thirty-two kilometres later, Paul Bernardo pulled his Nissan into the garage of 57 Bayview Road, the Port Dalhousie home he now shared with his fiancée, Karla Homolka. Threatening repeatedly to kill Leslie if she didn't co-operate, he helped her out of the passenger seat and led her into the living room. Still blindfolded, she could only guess at where he had taken her. Wherever it was, they seemed to have driven a long way. Bernardo switched on his video camera and pointed it at his trembling hostage.

"Here's what I want you to do. Unbutton your blouse and lift up your bra. Do as I tell you and you won't get hurt, okay?"

Leslie agreed to co-operate.

Over the next few hours the Burlington teen was subjected to a horrific ordeal, all captured on Bernardo's ever-present video camera. Forced to strip, she was led to the bathroom where he filmed her urinating, while masturbating with his free hand. Next stop was the bedroom where he commanded her to lie on the mattress, binding her hands to the bedposts with twine. Once she had been rendered immobile, Bernardo rushed upstairs to tell his fiancée the good news: he'd kidnapped a girl.

"Stay up here until I call for you," he instructed Karla. "Go back to sleep. We'll talk later."

Bernardo returned to find Leslie sobbing and pleading to be let go. When she was unable to comply with his order to stop crying he punched her in the face, splitting her lip. He raped her vaginally and anally before forcing her to perform fellatio. After he had ejaculated, he filled two glasses with champagne, one of which he also spiked with sleeping pills. This latter one he told her to drink. Next, he ordered her to masturbate for the camera and to flatter him with compliments, beating her if she misunderstood or was slow to comply. As the first rays of sunlight began to pour through the windows, they fell asleep together on the bed.

The humiliation continued when they awoke later that morning. Bernardo ordered Leslie into the shower where he videotaped her before taking her back into the bedroom and repeatedly raping her. Sometime after, Bernardo summoned Karla upstairs where she found Mahaffy sitting trussed and blindfolded against the couple's bed.

"Have you ever done it with three people?" he asked the frightened teen.

"No," Leslie began to sob, pleading to be set free.

When Bernardo explained that the third participant would be a woman, Leslie seemed to calm a little. Apparently the thought of being painfully raped by another man was too much for her to bear. With the video rolling, Bernardo ordered the women to simultaneously fellate him, before handing the camera to Karla to tape Leslie performing analingus while he moaned with pleasure. Next came sex with Karla before Bernardo returned to sodomizing Leslie.

As Leslie fell into another sleeping-pill-induced haze, Karla took her husband aside, reminding him that tomorrow her parents would be arriving for Father's Day dinner. Something would have to be done about the Mahaffy girl. They briefly debated letting her go, but after Bernardo quizzed his captive about what she knew, decided she could not be trusted to keep quiet and would have to be killed. While Bernardo prepared a black electrical cord in the basement, Homolka allegedly fed Leslie sleeping pills to render her unconscious. Then, cinching the ligature around her neck, Bernardo strangled her until blood streamed from her nose and ears, a pool of urine gathering at her feet. When Karla discovered to her shock that Leslie was still alive, Bernardo calmly resumed, jamming his foot in the small of her back for better leverage until he was certain the task was complete.

Later the couple were all smiles as they dined with the Homolka family and discussed plans for their upcoming wedding. In order to make it a perfect day, they insisted there would have to be a horse-drawn carriage and pheasant supper. Meanwhile, Leslie Mahaffy's strangled corpse lay cooling in the basement next to the laundry detergent and bags of potatoes they were eating for dinner.

The next morning while Karla comforted pained animals at the veterinary clinic, Bernardo dismembered Leslie's body with a power saw, encasing the parts in eight bags worth of quick-dry cement. When the concrete had hardened, he dumped five of the smaller blocks in Lake Gibson, a scenic reservoir eighteen kilometres south of Port Dalhousie where he and Homolka had once made love. After picking Karla up from work the following evening, the couple returned to the area. She stood guard while he threw two of the remaining blocks into the water off Beaversdam Road. At ninety kilograms, the section containing Leslie's torso was too heavy to dispose of in such a way, so they found a secluded bridge off Faywell Road on the western side of the lake. Hefting the block over the railing, they watched it plummet into the murky waters below. Neither of them suspected that the box had struck the bridge's billings, shattering the top and exposing Leslie's torso. In fact, it seemed like they had just committed the perfect murder.

Michael Doucette and his son squelched along the muddy banks of Lake Gibson, fishing rods in hand, to a tiny inlet off Beaverdams Road strewn with empty beer cans. As they prepared to cast out their lines, a man and woman launching their canoe nearby drew his attention to what appeared to be slabs of concrete sunken into the mud six metres from the shore. Rolling up his pants, Doucette waded out for a closer look, and on that June 29 afternoon in 1991, discovered the cement-encased remains of Leslie Erin Mahaffy.

PROFILING THE LESLIE MAHAFFY MURDERER

On April 14, 1992, Gregg McCrary held a conference call with one of lead investigator Vince Bevan's detectives, Sergeant Larry Maracle, to discuss his profile of Leslie Mahaffy's killer. McCrary expressed his view that the UNSUB was a Burlington resident who had either known Leslie or had seen a light on in her home. The murder, in his opinion, was secondary to a primary sexual motive, evidenced by the elaborate measures he took to dispose of his victim. As he had employed a power saw and concrete in the disposal, it was likely that he was a blue-collar labourer. The stress following the murder would manifest in visible changes to his behaviour, perhaps substance abuse or a sudden religious conversion. With the anniversary of Leslie's death approaching, he suggested that the police inundate the press with developments in their investigation to shake the killer's confidence. He believed that it would be a good idea to stake out Mahaffy's grave, as the UNSUB was the type who might return to it to relive his sexual fantasies.

Maracle had his reservations about McCrary's profile. In his view, the false power saw starts on the victim's body and poorly prepared concrete that had split on impact seemed to indicate somebody who was less than adept at using tools. The fact that McCrary assumed the killer lived in Burlington and had driven sixty-five kilometres to dump the four hundred kilograms of concrete in Lake Gibson because he was "comfortable with the area," didn't make much sense, either. Surely, it would have been safer to dispose of the body close to home rather than risking being caught on a long drive with human body parts in your vehicle. Considering that Burlington bordered Lake Ontario, that seemed like a much more obvious choice.

On the same April day when Maracle and McCrary were discussing the Mahaffy murder, a second schoolgirl abduction would shake the Niagara region. Unlike the previous abduction, this one would take place in the city of St. Catharines in broad daylight.

KRISTEN FRENCH: THE "GOOD GIRL"

"Excuse me," the blond woman called from the passenger seat of the gold sports car. "Can you help me with some directions?"

Fifteen-year-old Kristen French walked over to assist the attractive couple, the light rain flecking the empty parking lot of Grace Lutheran Church. Since the sex-slaying of Leslie Mahaffy, the A student and star athlete at Holy Cross Catholic school had been on her guard, but the couple seemed normal to her.

"Where are you going?"

"The Pen Centre."

Always eager to help, the pretty brunette began to explain the easiest route, but the woman in the car interrupted, asking if she could show her on the map. Stepping out of the vehicle she began to spread it across the roof. Before Kristen had time to notice it was a map of Toronto, the baby-faced man in the driver's seat appeared suddenly behind her, pressing a knife to her throat.

"You're coming with us!" he barked, pushing her toward the open passenger-side door. Kristen's shoulder slammed hard against the cold steel frame.

"You bastard!" the terrified schoolgirl screamed, but despite her fierce resistance he managed to force her into the seat, hitting the lever so it collapsed backwards out of sight.

"Hold her!" he ordered the blonde, who had now crawled into the back seat.

As always, Karla Homolka obeyed, seizing Kristen by the hair and pulling her head down to the carpet. Bernardo slammed the door shut, quickly circling to the front seat. He reminded his quivering victim that he had a knife and had no compunction about using it. By the time the vehicle pulled out on to the street, Kristen French had given up her struggle.

Minutes later, she found herself blindfolded with a polo shirt in the Bernardos' Port Dalhousie home. Thrown to her knees on the floor of her abductor's bedroom, she began to sob uncontrollably at the sound of a zipper opening. Slamming her head against the ground, Bernardo flipped up her skirt and tore her panties down to her knees. He raped her, first vaginally and then anally before ordering her to fellate him. Her lack of sexual experience only seemed to turn him on more, as in between moans he instructed her on the best techniques to pleasure him. Whenever she hesitated or resisted his commands, he simply battered her into compliance. As he finally ejaculated, he pulled her head hard against his groin, forcing her to swallow his semen. When he had finished, Kristen asked to use the bathroom. As he had done with Lesley Mahaffy, Bernardo followed her to the toilet, filming her vagina as she urinated.

After leading her back to the bedroom, he went downstairs to fetch the Halcion. Karla gently reminded him that the police would be able to link the crimes if they found traces of the drug in her system. Instead, she presented him with sleeping pills that he crushed into a drink before returning to the bedroom to feed his captive the concoction. Once again he demanded she perform oral sex, only this time he was going to videotape it. With the camera rolling, Bernardo began to "script" his victim telling her to say that she "loved his penis," "loved sucking dick," that she "wanted to make him happy." After filming her urinating again, he called down to Karla, ordering her to perform cunnilingus on Kristen. He concluded the attack by sodomizing her, demanding that she keep smiling through the agonizing pain and to repeat that she "loved him."

Downstairs, the three shared a chicken dinner before the exhausted Kristen passed out on their bed. Bernardo soon joined her. Karla was confined to the bedroom floor.

The next morning Kristen awoke feeling filthy from the previous night's ordeal, and asked permission to shower. Bernardo agreed, but first she had to listen to some of the lyrics he had written for his upcoming hip-hop album. He assured her it would eventually land him the record contract that would launch him onto the world stage. When the maestro had finished rapping about how cool he was, she was permitted to bathe. Naturally, the "white boy rapper" who was "neither fool nor toy" had to record it all on videotape, ordering her to continuously lather her buttocks with soap. As soon as she was clean, he prepared to dirty her again. Bernardo told Kristen that she and Karla were going to play "The Perfume Game" in which they would try on different fragrances and the one who smelled the worst was going to get "fucked up the ass." Even though Kristen won the competition, he explained that she was going to get it anyways as Karla was his wife and had earned "brownie points."

During another assault, he asked her if she had a boyfriend. She said that she did; his name was Elton Wade. Bernardo commanded her to say that she hated him, but here Kristen bravely drew a line in the sand. "Deadly Innocence" was forced to beat her twice as brutally before she finally relented. Then Bernardo decided to play mind games. Placing his knife on the floor in front of her, he dared her to pick it up and stab him. Kristen knew better than to try to take on a man thirty pounds heavier. Instead she refused, no doubt deciding to wait for the right opportunity to arise.

Her chance came at dinner time when she cleverly asked Bernardo if they could have McDonald's pizza. The trip would take him at least a half an hour, which would give her time to try and talk Karla into freeing her. Unfortunately, Karla had no such intentions, and Bernardo soon arrived home with the meal, which they ate in silence in front of the television.

When the movie ended, Bernardo decided it was time to film some of the lesbian sex scenes required for his collection. Undoubtedly reasoning it was still safer to co-operate and wait for a good chance to escape, Kristen participated in mutual cunnilingus and analingus with Karla, until Bernardo once again demanded fellatio. When he was satisfied, he drugged, bound, and handcuffed Kristen and placed her in the closet, telling Karla to stand guard. Nauseated by the sleeping-pill cocktails, Kristen threw up on the floor before being fed another knock-out mixture and passing out.

As in the case of Leslie Mahaffy, social obligations were now demanding that the Bernardos kill and dispose of their latest sex slave. Not only had they been out of contact with friends since Thursday, but Easter Sunday was coming, and the couple had arranged to dine with Karla's family. Wishing to keep Kristen around to satisfy his deviant sexual urges, Bernardo first suggested that they cancel Easter, but was reminded by Karla that it was the perfect alibi. Next he wondered if they could just leave her tied up in the closet. No, Karla reminded him, there was a massive search of the area planned that Monday, including their Port Dalhousie neighbourhood. Eventually, the two came to a consensus: Kristen would die soon, but not yet. Bernardo was simply having too much fun.

Having spent the morning and most of the afternoon working on his music, Bernardo asked Kristen what she would like for supper. This time she sent him to Swiss Chalet, a trip to the centre of the city that would take at least half an hour. Before he left, he bound her and stowed her in the closet. Karla was given a rubber mallet and instructed to keep watch while he was gone. What happened during his absence has long been debated. It has been posited that at this point, realizing she would never leave the Port Dalhousie home without a fight, Kristen convinced Karla to let her use the bathroom, attacking her once her legs were unshackled and prompting her blond jailer to beat her into submission. According to Karla, who had every reason to lie about the extent of her involvement, the two simply chatted until Bernardo came home.

Whatever occurred during that half hour, subsequent reviews of videotape evidence show a violent change in Bernardo's mood. Kristen was ordered to strip and climb into the couple's Jacuzzi bath where Bernardo filmed himself urinating on her because she "deserved it," even making a failed attempt to defecate on her quivering body. After allowing her to shower, he demanded more oral sex, but when Kristen refused he beat her and dragged her by the hair to the bedroom. There he attempted to scare her into compliance by showing her a videotape of a naked and blindfolded Leslie Mahaffy and threatening that she would meet the same fate if she continued to defy him.

"Some things are worth dying for," Kristen responded.

Enraged, he unleashed the worst beating on her yet until, broken psychologically, she agreed to go along with his plans. But this time, even when Kristen complied with his demands for oral sex, Bernardo seemed unsatisfied, constantly complaining that she wasn't doing a good enough job and losing his erection. In this angry state of mind, skin on skin contact couldn't get him off — instead, he needed to inflict maximum pain and humiliation over his victim.

Bernardo's sexual abuse persisted in a variety of forms throughout the evening, at one point committing his most vile act of torture yet: violently sodomizing Kristen with a wine bottle, before raping her as he strangled her with his signature black electrical cord. Throughout the ordeal he demanded that she repeat the words his twisted psyche so needed to hear:

> All the girls at Holy Cross want you … I'm glad you punished me. I deserved it … You're my master … You're the king … You're the most powerful man in the world … You're so nice, powerful, sexy. So much in control of everything. Nobody can overpower you … I want to line up all the girls' cunts when I get back … You're going to get them all to make you happy.

But it wasn't enough to save her life. Realizing now that no matter what she did, he was going to kill her, Kristen collapsed onto the floor and looked her captor in the eye one last time.

"I don't know how your wife can stand you."

"Just shut up, okay." Bernardo signalled to Karla to turn off the video camera.

Wrapping the electrical cord around Kristen's swollen neck, Bernardo strangled her to death on the bedroom floor. It took seven minutes.

With the Mahaffy dismemberment proving to be a total waste of time, Bernardo took a much more haphazard approach to disposing of Kristen's body. After enjoying Easter Sunday at the Homolkas, he and Karla painstakingly cleaned their Port Dalhousie home. He ordered Karla to cut off Kristen's pretty brown hair in case any carpet fibres had attached to it, and the two bathed the corpse in their bathtub to rid it of fingerprint evidence, before douching her vagina and anus. Burning her hair and clothes in the fireplace, they wrapped Kristen's body in a blanket and drove it out to Burlington. Bernardo reasoned that when police found it in the same city where Leslie Mahaffy had been abducted, they would assume the killer was a local. In a true testament to their sickness, they drove to the cemetery where Leslie's body was buried, planning to drape Kristen's corpse over the tombstone. Unable to find the grave, they settled for an embankment off Number 1 side road, covering the body with leaves before heading home.

On April 30, 1992, fourteen days after she had been snatched off the streets of St. Catharines, the well-preserved corpse of Kristen French was found by a man foraging for scrap metal outside Burlington's Halton Hills Cemetery.

PROFILING THE KRISTEN FRENCH MURDERER

Putting aside his skepticism of the Mahaffy killer profile, after a year of fruitless investigation, Vince Bevan instructed Sergeant Maracle to fly to Washington on Wednesday, April 29, 1993, to meet McCrary. The next morning, a group of FBI profilers agreed that despite the location of the bodies, the Mahaffy and French murders were probably committed by different individuals. Unlike the Mahaffy disappearance, there were witnesses who claimed to have seen two kidnappers at the site of French's abduction. The FBI concluded they were both men between twenty and thirty-five, who had difficulty socializing effectively with women. Judging by the fact that despite their numerical superiority, they had used a knife in the abduction, they made the assumption that both culprits had self-esteem issues.

The lengthy duration Kristen had spent in captivity seemed to indicate that the UNSUBs were utilizing a single family home either in the country or a residential area. There would be a dominant partner with a police record for sexual assaults, and a docile counterpart who would leave the area soon after French's body was found. The latter might have little or nothing to do with the murder, instead given the duty of caring for the victim. Kristen's hair had been cut off either as a trophy, to conceal her identity, or because her killers could not stand the smell of her perm. Recommendations were once again given to use the media to increase pressure on the perpetrators; this time the focus would be on Kristen's aborted sixteenth birthday.

Despite the FBI's insistence that the Mahaffy and French murders were not connected, Inspector Bevan remained unconvinced. For this seasoned detective, the bodies had been found too close to one another to be a coincidence. Though he had not been exposed to the intensive criminal-profiling seminars McCrary had at Quantico, time would prove Bevan correct. In the meantime, the wild inaccuracy of the two latest profiles would only serve to sabotage his case.

GUILTY INNOCENCE

In May 1992, Bernardo's friend and former neighbour Van Smirnis recognized his resemblance to the Scarborough Rapist composite, noting that the sexual assaults had stopped the year Bernardo relocated to St. Catharines. Smirnis spoke to the OPP about his suspicions, and his tip was filtered through various levels of bureaucratic machinery until it eventually reached the task force. Two agents arrived at 57 Bayview one afternoon in mid-May to interview Bernardo, who graciously invited them into his living room. When questioned if he had ever been involved with the police, he admitted to being a suspect in the Scarborough rapes and had provided a sample of his DNA in 1990. He remained calm through the twenty minutes of interrogation before the investigators finally decided he wasn't their man. They were looking for a suspect who drove a Camarro — Bernardo was a Nissan owner. Besides, he wasn't at all like the blue-collar sexual failure described in McCrary's profile; this guy was a charismatic accountant with a gorgeous blond wife and lakeside home. Instead, they decided to focus their energies on a more viable suspect. Fortunately, with a DNA sample sitting in a forensics lab waiting to be compared to that of the Scarborough Rapist's, it was only a matter of time before Paul Bernardo's mask of normalcy crumbled.

In late December 1992, Bernardo expedited his inevitable downfall with a second monumental mistake: he turned his accomplice against him. Two days after "The Ken and Barbie Killers" had spent Christmas together, the chronically insecure Bernardo asked his wife Karla why she no longer hugged him. When she failed to provide him with an answer, he flew into a tantrum, unleashing the worst beating she had ever received at his hands. The violence erupted again days later — this time he resented the way she had received a telephone message. Though Karla could normally cover up his abuse with makeup and lies, this time concerned co-workers placed an anonymous call to her parents, informing them that she had been badly hurt. Terrified for her safety, the Homolkas rushed to 57 Bayview, followed by two police cruisers and an ambulance. Neither Paul nor Karla was at home. Later that evening, the newlyweds returned from a cigarette-smuggling run, by which time the Homolkas and emergency crew had dispersed. That night, Bernardo smashed Karla's face repeatedly with a flashlight, sodomizing her while he strangled her with the same electrical cord he had used to murder Kristen French. When she showed up black and blue for work the next day, a fellow employee made a second anonymous phone call to the Homolka household, this time insisting that they come directly to the clinic because Karla's life was in danger. The moment Dorothy Homolka set eyes on her daughter's swollen face she knew that despite her assurances that everything would be okay, something had to be done. Along with Karla's sister, Lori, she drove to the Bernardo home later that day in an attempt to persuade Karla to leave. Eventually the two were forced to drag her from the house, driving her to St. Catharines General Hospital for medical examination. The doctor who treated her would later claim it was the worst case of spousal abuse he had ever seen. He immediately contacted the police. Paul Bernardo was arrested that same evening and charged with assault.

Over the next few days Bernardo repeatedly stalked and harassed the Homolka family in a vain attempt to locate his wife. When they refused to give in to his threats, he changed the locks on their Port Dalhousie home and cancelled Karla's insurance coverage on the Nissan. In the meantime, Karla was holed up in the apartment of her aunt and uncle, Patti and Calvin Seger, healing the immense physical damage inflicted upon her at the hands of her husband. The emotional and psychological damage, however, would not fade away so quickly.

Coincidentally, that same month, Detective Steve Irwin finally received the news for which he had waited six long years. After processing the genetic profiles of 229 suspects, forensics had determined the identity of the Scarborough Rapist: Paul Kenneth Bernardo.

In the **Karla Homolka** sub-section of Chapter 17 we will further explore the crimes, trials, convictions, and controversies of "The Ken and Barbie Killers," including the accidental death of Tammy Homolka and the infamous "Deal with the Devil," which continues to outrage the Canadian public to this day.

THE VERDICT ON PROFILING

As we have seen, the FBI formulated three separate offender profiles related to the crimes of Paul Bernardo. The first, focusing on the Scarborough rapes, correctly predicted his age and local residence, along with many of his psychological quirks and behaviours. Yet despite the accuracy of their appraisal, the profile played no role in the eventual apprehension of the suspect. Rather it was Bernardo's similarity to the composite drawing which led him to submit the DNA evidence that eventually damned him. Profiles 2 and 3, concerning the murders of Leslie Mahaffy and Kristen French, however, were wildly off the mark. Not only did they fail to link the crimes, a connection that Inspector Vince Bevan thankfully made in defiance of the FBI's advice, but they also were wrong on almost every account aside from the offender's inadequacies (which, incidentally, do nothing to help solve crimes). This begs the question: if criminal profiles are of limited use, but also frequently wrong, are they a help or a hindrance to an investigation?

Next we will look at a more succinct profile developed for the **The Edmonton Serial Killer**, arguably Canada's most notorious unsolved serial murder case. Hopefully, it won't be long before we are given a chance to assess the accuracy of this profile, and in turn, address the question of whether offender profiling should be continued in Canada.

The Edmonton Serial Killer (Unsolved)
0–31 Murders
Edmonton, Alberta

BURNED AND FROZEN

On Friday June 17, 2005, RCMP Constable Tamara Bellamy made a formal announcement: there was a serial killer operating in the Edmonton area. This was hardly news to the 730,000 citizens of Alberta's northern capital. Since 1983, the bodies of two-dozen sex workers had been found dumped in and around the city. Still, it was chilling to have their suspicions confirmed. Twenty-one-year-old Gail Cardinal's remains were the first to be found, ten kilometres south of Fort Saskatchewan. As time and scavengers had reduced her to a skeleton, no cause of death could be determined. On September 21, 1986, Melodie Joy Riegel was found lying dead in an Edmonton hotel bed. She had checked into the room with a mysterious man, whom nobody had reported seeing leave. The next victim, Georgette Flint, was recovered from Elk Island National Park on September 13, 1988. Once again, the cause of death could not be determined. Twenty-two-year-old mother of three Bernadette Ahenakew was pulled out of a ditch near Sherwood Park on October 25, 1989. Exactly one year later, the stab-wound-riddled body of Mavis Mason was found on a country road west of the city. That December, forty-six-year-old masseuse Lorraine Wray was murdered at her business, "West End Studio." She had been found manually strangled to death in the bathroom. In 1993, the rotting corpse of Elaine Ross was discovered wedged under a bed in a 183rd Street motel room. Joanne Ghostkeeper was the next to surface, strangled in her apartment on Christmas Day, 1996.

By 1997, the killings had begun to accelerate at a disturbing pace. On June 14, the body of Jessica Cardinal was found dumped behind a commercial building at 9325-111th, concealed behind some discarded furniture. Then Joyce Hewitt was murdered in Sherwood Park on October 19, the same area where in September the killer had dumped Cara King.

Despite the fact that something sinister was clearly happening in Edmonton before the turn of the century, all of these cases were to be overlooked in the RCMP's investigation, Bellamy explained. The real focus was on eight sex trade workers murdered since 1998. On January 27, 2001, the body of Kelly Dawn Reilly, twenty-four, was found behind a gravel pit near Villeneuve. Over a year later, the charred corpse of Edna Bernard was discovered on September 23, 2002, dumped in a field just east of Leduc. Farther south near Fort Saskatchewan, thirty-year-old Monique Pitre's frozen body was found on January 8, 2003, showing signs of extreme physical trauma. Four days later, and less than ten kilometres away, Melissa Munch, twenty, was discovered murdered in a wooded enclave west of Range Road, south of Highway 16. Former prostitute Debbie Lake, twenty-nine, was the next woman to appear on the coroner's table. Her skeletal remains were recovered near Miquelon Lake Provincial Park on April 12, 2003. Fellow sex-trade worker Katie Sylvia Ballantyne, forty, turned up dead twenty kilometres south of Edmonton in Leduc County. Ballantyne was the fifth female body in ten months to be recovered in the vicinity of the city.

Six more bodies were to appear between June 2004 and May 2006, beginning with the sexually mutilated remains of nineteen-year-old Rachel Quinney near Sherwood Park in June 2004. Samantha Berg's frozen body was found months later in a north side Edmonton parking lot, followed by the discovery of Charlene Gauld, twenty, charred and left in a field in Camrose, eighty kilometres southeast of the city. Ellie May Meyer and Bonnie Lynn Jack were both recovered in the same area of Sherwood Park in April 2005 and May 2006, respectively.

THE PROFILE

In response to the series of prostitute murders plaguing the city, the RCMP's Behavioural Science Unit constructed a profile of the predator, later disclosed to the public by Constable Bellamy. Though such information is typically kept secret, the Edmonton Serial Killer is believed to be known by multiple people in the area, probably even suspected by some of them. This concise profile focuses more on the UNSUB's transportation than his personal characteristics:

1. The suspect drives a truck, van, or a sport utility vehicle, and is comfortable driving in rural areas.
2. The vehicle is likely in good shape, with a significant amount of mileage.
3. The suspect may participate in outdoor activities such as hunting, fishing, camping, and uses his vehicle for them.
4. The suspect may have periodically cleaned the interior and exterior of his vehicle, perhaps at times that are unusual for this particular individual.
5. The suspect likely has a past or present connection to the areas south of Edmonton, perhaps Leduc, Camrose, New Sarepta, or the surrounding communities. He may have lived or worked in those areas, has family or friends in the area, or has used the area for recreational purposes.
6. Though there is a cooling-off period between murders, the time between killings is getting shorter.

Bellamy went on to disclose that though the RCMP believed one man was responsible for multiple offences, this did not necessarily include all of them.

Here is an exhaustive list of missing women and murdered sex workers in Edmonton from 1983 to the present. Both Thomas Svekla and Joseph Laboucan, convicted killers believed to have been involved in some of the slayings, are assessed as suspects in the following pages.

TABLE 4: MURDERED AND MISSING WOMEN OF EDMONTON

KEY: * = Svekla suspected of murdering

          ** = Svekla charged

          *** = Svekla convicted of murder

          Italics = Svekla in custody when body was discovered

          # = Joseph Laboucan and Michael Briscoe charged with murder.

          Bold = Laboucan/Briscoe in custody when body was discovered

VICTIM	AGE	STATUS	DATE FOUND	LOCATION	SEXUAL ASSAULT / ACTIVITY
Gail Cardinal	21	Murdered?	1983	10 kilometres south of Fort Saskatchewan	Unknown
Melody Joy Riegel	21	Murdered	Sept. 21, 1986	Hotel bed	Yes
Georgette Flint	20	Murdered?	Sept. 13, 1988	Elk Island National Park	Unknown
Bernadette Lynda Ahenakew*	22	Murdered?	Oct. 25, 1989	Ditch near Sherwood Park	Unknown
Mavis Mason	29	Murdered (stabbed)	Oct. 25, 1990	Rural road west of Edmonton	Unknown
Lorraine Wray	46	Murdered (manually strangled)	Dec. 21, 1990	Bathroom of her business at 15526 Stony Plain Road.	Yes
Elaine Ross	25	Murdered	Feb. 11, 1993	Under bed in motel room on 183rd street near Stony Plain Road	Unknown
Joanne Ghostkeeper	24	Murdered (strangled)	Dec. 25, 1996	Her apartment at 11925-34th Street East	Unknown

Jessica Cardinal	24	Murdered	June 14, 1997	In an alley behind a commercial building at 9325-111th Avenue behind discarded shelves	Unknown
Cara King	22	Murdered	Sept. 1, 1997	In a canola field in Sherwood Park	Unknown
Joyce Anne Hewitt	22	Murdered?	Oct. 19, 1997	In Sherwood Park near 17th Street and 89th Avenue	Unknown
Kelly Dawn Reilly	24	Murdered	Jan. 27, 2001	Behind a gravel operation 25 kilometres northwest of city	Unknown
Edna Bernard*	28	Murdered/ burned	Sept. 23, 2002	In a field east of Leduc	Unknown
Monique Pitre*	30	Murdered	Jan. 8, 2003	Fort Saskatchewan south of Range Road 22 and Township Road 540	Unknown
Melissa Munch*	20	Murdered?	Jan. 12, 2003	In a field south of Highway 16, west of Range Road 220	Unknown
Debbie Darlene Lake*	29	Murdered	April 12, 2003	Skull found near Miquelon Lake. Body still missing.	Unknown
Katie Ballantyne*	40	Murdered	July 7, 2003	South of Edmonton in Leduc country	Yes

Corrie Ottenbreit	27	Disappeared	May 9, 2004	118th Ave area	Yes
Delores Brower*	33	Disappeared	May 13, 2004	118th Ave and 700th Street, hitchhiking	Unknown
Rachel Quinney**	19	Murdered	June 11, 2004	In a grove south of Sherwood Park	Yes
Maggie Burke	*21*	*Disappeared*	*Dec. 19, 2004*	*Unknown*	*Yes*
Samantha Berg	19	Murdered	Jan. 25, 2005	Under snow in north side parking lot	Yes
Krystle Ann Knott Rene Lynn Gunning	16/19	Disappeared	Feb. 18, 2005	West Edmonton Mall	Unknown
Charlene Gauld	**20**	**Murdered/ burned**	**April 18, 2005**	**Oilfield by Camrose**	**Unknown**
Ellie May Meyer#	**33**	**Murdered**	**May 6, 2005**	**By Sherwood Park**	**Yes**
Theresa Innes*	**36**	**Murdered**	**Aug. 7, 2005**	**Killed by Thomas Svekla and stuffed in hockey bag**	**Yes**
Bonnie Lynn Jack	**Unknown**	**Murdered**	**May 19, 2006**	**East of Edmonton Near Sherwood Park**	**Yes**
Leanne Lori Benwell	**27**	**Murdered?**	**July 2007**	**Unknown**	**Yes**
Brianna Torvalson	**21**	**Murdered?**	**Feb. 2008**	**Strathcona Country**	**Yes**
Shannon Collins	**29**	**Murdered?**	**June 2008**	**Southeast of Sherwood Park**	**Yes**

Andre Kirchhoff.

Suspect: Thomas Svekla
The Bogeyman

"When I was abusing her, I thought if I did it more and pleasured her more, she would forgive me."

BIOGRAPHY OF A BUTCHER

George and Emily Svekla had always wanted a son. It wasn't that they didn't love their six daughters, but they were particularly proud in 1968 when baby Thomas was born. Big George knew he wasn't going to be young forever and needed help with some of the heavier tasks around the farm. Thomas also ensured that the Svekla name would live on. Unfortunately the rosy future they all dreamed of was not to be. In 1975, George drank the family farm away. The Sveklas stayed on as renters for a short period before picking up and moving to Fort Saskatchewan, where things went from bad to worse. An explosive drunk, George became universally feared in the family, even when he was old and feeble. So frequent and savage were the beatings that young Thomas actually considered committing suicide to escape them. It was not uncommon for the 280-pound George to whip his family with belts, choke them unconscious, and pummel their faces until they were dripping with blood. In her petition for divorce, Emily Svekla claimed that George threw chairs at her and kicked her in the back with steel-toed boots. She had required surgery as a result and was just recovering from the operation a few months later when he kicked her again in the same place. When Emily left him in 1980, George began harassing her friends and workmates for information: "Where does she live? Is she seeing anybody?" Eventually financial pressures caused her to drop the divorce and move back in with her husband. Her earnings working part-time at the Rivercrest nursing home simply weren't enough to sustain them, and when George promised he would seek treatment for his alcoholism, she forgave him. By the time Thomas was twelve years old, the Sveklas had moved to an acreage outside Fort Saskatchewan. For a short period everything was stable. Then George went back to the bottle.

While Svekla's father beat and terrorized him, his mother spoiled him rotten. During a subsequent interrogation, he would accuse her of being overprotective and guilting him into staying home to watch TV. Nor were sisters or ex-girlfriends exempt from blame. According to Thomas Svekla, all the women in his life rejected him and left him.

When he became a teenager, a retired farmer named Lawrence Jigolyk hired Svekla to help on the farm. He found the young man to be a polite and industrious worker and was surprised to hear later that he had been charged with murder. What Jigolyk did not know was that like his father, Thomas Svekla had a dark side. At first he expressed this in traditional teenaged forms of rebellion like binge-drinking at bush parties. When these weren't enough, he got his kicks fighting or stealing cars and crashing them. It is alleged that once he strangled a dog to death because it had foraged in his garbage.

One summer night when Thomas was seventeen, he knocked on the door of a friend's house and asked her to let him in. Noticing that his hand was bleeding, she showed him to the bathroom where he proceeded to rinse it under cold water. He claimed to have been hanging out smoking pot with her brother and to have accidentally struck a window during a fist fight. She kindly fetched him bandages from the kitchen, but upon returning, found his mood had become dark and nasty. Without warning he started to scream at her, telling her that it was her fault that he got into the fight. Terrified, she ran down the hall where Svekla caught her and pulled her to the floor. His powerful hands seized her neck, squeezing until her face went bright red and she started to wheeze. He told her that he could kill her if he wished, and that all he would need to do is squeeze harder. Grabbing her by the hair, he dragged her into the bedroom and began to fumble with her belt. She begged him not to rape her and informed him that somebody would be home at any minute. This seemed to snap him out of his murderous trance. Before taking off on foot, Svekla warned her that if she ever told anybody he would kill her. Later he would apologize, laying the blame on drugs and alcohol. Amazingly, she forgave him and the two even dated for a short time.

In 1987, things looked up for Thomas Svekla. Not only did he graduate from grade twelve at Sturgeon Composite, he had finally established a steady relationship with a girl. The couple dated for three years, but eventually parted ways when he attempted to choke her unconscious in a parking lot.

The next known incident of misogynist violence came in 1995 when Svekla was dating a divorcee and mother of four: two by blood and two foster children. First, he browbeat her into giving up the foster children, becoming jealous when she cried. The second major incident occurred when the couple made plans to move to a smaller community outside of Edmonton. Together they organized a garage sale to raise funds and rid themselves of any old junk they didn't need. On the night before, however, Thomas stayed out late drinking with a friend and fought with his girlfriend the next morning. Though he had promised to go around the neighbourhood posting signs, he argued that he was still too drunk to be of any use. When Svekla finally capitulated he accidentally left without the nail gun. Returning in a foul temper, he struck his girlfriend, knocking out her front tooth.

Despite the incident, the two followed through with their plans to move to the smaller community. Thomas settled down and found steady work at a gravel trenching company. The couple's first child arrived in 1998 — a boy. A year later, one of his girlfriend's former foster children accused him of molesting her. Despite his downplaying of the incident, the couple's relationship collapsed, and after a harrowing trial, he was sentenced to thirty months in jail. Svekla tried desperately to keep the mother of his child in his life by confiding to her that he was sexually abused as a child. It was useless. She had no sympathy left for him.

A GRUESOME DISCOVERY

In June 2004, Svekla contacted Edmonton police, claiming he had stumbled over a woman's body in a wooded area of Strathcona County. Apparently, he had driven out to the spot with a prostitute to freebase crack cocaine. The remains were later identified as those of nineteen-year-old sex worker Rachel Quinney. She had been horribly mutilated — her breasts removed and genitals carved out. However, when police looked into Svekla's story, it became obvious that something was amiss. Jolene Rea would later testify that she had accompanied Svekla to the dump site in 2004, and had seen no sign of a corpse. Another prostitute friend, Barb Card, reported seeing Quinney getting into a truck with a man who partly resembled Svekla on June 8, 2004. There had been a silver checker-plated toolbox in the back. Later that same day, Svekla's buddy Bradley Ludwik witnessed him remove an identical toolbox from his spotlessly clean vehicle before wiping the brown truck down with degreaser. In conversation, Svekla casually claimed to have tripped over the rotting body of a blond prostitute — an interesting account considering Quinney's hair was dark and she had decayed to the point where the police could not easily establish her sex. One victim who did have blond hair was Corrie Ottenbreit, who disappeared from the 118th Avenue area on May 9, 2004.

Perhaps the most damning evidence that Svekla had murdered Rachel Quinney was testimony from his sister, Donna Parkinson, that she had run into him on the night of the discovery and noticed scratches along his arms. Nervous and sobbing, he confessed to her that he had "done something terrible," but wouldn't specify what. It was the first time she had seen him in clean clothes in what seemed like an eternity. Amazingly, Svekla would not be charged with Quinney's murder until eight months after he had been arrested for an even more gruesome killing.

WORMS

One afternoon in May 2006, Thomas Svekla arrived unexpectedly at his mother's door in Edmonton, carrying a hefty hockey bag. It didn't take long before an argument erupted, prompting him to call his sister Donna and her husband to drive him back to their Fort Saskatchewan home. When Donna Parkinson inquired as to the contents of his luggage, Svekla explained that he was transporting $800 worth of compost worms as a favour to a breeder in High Level. Right away, Parkinson suspected he was lying — nobody in their right mind would entrust anything of value to her notorious brother.

Later, when Svekla had stepped out into the night, the Parkinsons decided to get to the bottom of his strange behaviour. Unzipping the hockey bag, they recoiled in horror. Inside were the dismembered remains of thirty-six-year-old Theresa Innes, wrapped in a shower curtain, air mattress, and several garbage bags, then bound together with wire. The Parkinsons contacted the RCMP immediately. Svekla was arrested and charged with murder. Subsequent research revealed that Innes was a prostitute and crack addict from High Level, Alberta, and was once considered to be Svekla's girlfriend. Eight months later, he was charged in connection with the murder of Rachel Quinney.

In June 2008, Judge Sterling Sanderman found Thomas Svekla guilty of the second-degree murder of Theresa Innes and committing an indignity on a human body, but acquitted him of any charges related to Rachel Quinney's death. Though Svekla had been sentenced to life for killing his lover, the horrific manner in which he attempted to dispose of Theresa Innes left many wondering if he was capable of more. He has repeatedly denied being a killer, despite hinting at other foul deeds he has committed, and claiming to have special insight into the mind of a serial murderer.

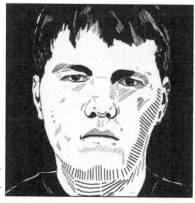

Suspects: Joseph Laboucan and Michael Briscoe

"I don't like hookers."

Kay Feely.

Kay Feely.

MALL RATS

For teenyboppers like thirteen-year-old Nina-Louise Courtepatte and her friend Kitty, fifteen, the West Edmonton Mall provided an affordable environment to socialize with people their own age. On April 3, 2005, the girls were sitting in the food court when they were approached by a blond-haired man named Joe, nineteen; and a girl, Stephanie, seventeen; who asked if they'd like to attend a two-hundred-person bush party on the outskirts of town. Also along for the ride were Mike, thirty-four; "Buffy," sixteen; and "Pyro," seventeen. The girls were flattered to have the older kids pay attention to them, and everyone seemed so excited about the party that they couldn't refuse the invitation.

Forty-five minutes later, as they coasted through the Alberta night, Joe and Nina began making out in the back of Mike's car. Throughout the trip, Stephanie continued to peer angrily at them from the front seat. It wasn't enough that Nina had landed a modelling contract, but now she was stealing her ex-boyfriend, too. Of course, Stephanie knew what lay in store for the vivacious thirteen-year-old. Having spent the previous day joking about hacking peoples' heads off with a machete and dumping them in the street, they had handpicked Nina to be their victim.

"Pull over and get the tools out!" Joseph Laboucan ordered the driver.

Though Mike Briscoe had fifteen years on his protegee, a breech birth had left him with a mental age of sixteen, making Laboucan the dominant male force that chilly April night. Briscoe complied, guiding his car to the muddy shoulder at the gateway to Edmonton Springs Golf Course. He later claimed he was oblivious to the carnage his friends were planning to unleash. Yet as they pulled over to retrieve a wrench and sledgehammer from the trunk, he must have known full well what they intended.

Nina, Kitty, and the other party-goers climbed out of the vehicle and started walking down a gravel path onto the fairway. The conversation between Joe and Stephanie began to veer in an increasingly bizarre direction as they discussed rituals of murdering somebody and bringing them back from the dead. Then without warning, Stephanie struck Nina from behind with a wrench. Stunned, the pretty thirteen-year-old toppled into the mud.

"What did I do?" she pleaded, blood streaming from her head. "How am I making you mad?" Clambering to her feet, she ran into Laboucan's open arms and he whispered something gently into her ear. Nina began to scream.

"No, don't do it! Please!"

Laboucan quickly silenced her, barring a cold wrench across her throat. Before she knew what was happening, Briscoe set upon her, pinning her to the ground as Laboucan loosened his belt, leering over her like a hungry jackal. Stephanie seized the fear-stricken Kitty by the arm and led her back to the car where she attempted to placate her with a cigarette and some CDs. Meanwhile, back at the fourth fairway, a stunned Nina could only squirm in horror as Joseph Laboucan, then Michael "Pyro" Williams raped her mercilessly. As she lay weeping in the mud, Laboucan hefted the sledgehammer. The sexual assault was merely an overture. Now it was time for the real show to begin.

When the rest of the ensemble returned to the car, a distraught Kitty asked what they had done with her friend.

"I beat the shit out of her and let her run home naked!" Pyro cackled.

Laboucan remained silent, washing the blood from his fists with a water bottle. Overwhelmed, Kitty didn't know what to believe — only that she would have to co-operate if she ever wanted to make it home alive.

On the way back, the six stopped to dine at a twenty-four-hour restaurant, running out on their bill. From there they took Kitty to a motel room, where they held her captive for four days. On two occasions they escorted her to the West Edmonton Mall, even buying her shoes. In the meantime, the hunt for Nina's killers was already well underway.

THE TRIAL

April 4, 2005: a cloudy day in Edmonton. At 3:30 p.m., an employee inspecting the fourth fairway at Edmonton Springs Golf Course happened upon a horrific sight:

Nina-Louise Courtepatte lay dead on a grassy patch — bludgeoned with a sledgehammer, stabbed with throwing knives, and choked with the handle of a wrench.

When Nina's parents reported their daughter missing two days later, they were taken to identify the body. Their worst fears were confirmed: the battered corpse lying on the slab before them was their daughter. Autopsy results revealed she had died from blunt-force trauma.

Within five days of the slaying, police laid first-degree murder charges against Joseph Laboucan, Michael Briscoe, Michael "Pyro" Williams, and Stephanie Bird. On April 14, a sixteen-year-old known as "Buffy" was similarly charged. Following a year and a half of legal wrangling, in January 2007 the Crown consented to allow the two adult offenders, Laboucan and Briscoe, to be tried before a judge rather than a jury. The *voir dire*, to determine which evidence was admissible, began on January 11. On the sixteenth, an undercover RCMP officer would testify that Briscoe told him he had only revealed 80 percent of what happened to the police.

The trial of Joseph Laboucan and Michael Briscoe began on January 22, 2007, with video footage shown of the fairway where Nina was found, along with that of her murdered body. Throughout the proceedings,

Kitty and the four accomplices focused the blame on Joseph Laboucan, while his defence team argued he was merely the fall guy for a cabal of teenaged girls who had killed Nina out of jealousy.

In its closing arguments on Monday March 5, 2007, the prosecution declared that it was inconsequential who delivered the fatal blow to Nina, as each of the five attackers was clearly complicit in planning and participating in the attack. Though the idea to murder Nina had been Laboucan's, the others had co-operated unquestioningly. Michael Briscoe had remained tellingly silent throughout the fated drive, never once asking Laboucan for directions to the killing ground. Though he later claimed he didn't want Nina to be killed, this hardly justified acquitting him of his role in her brutal demise.

On Friday March 23, 2007, Judge Brian Burrows found Joseph Laboucan guilty of the first-degree murder of Nina-Louise Courtepatte, sentencing him to a life term in prison, with the possibility of parole in twenty-five years. Astonishingly, Michael Briscoe was acquitted. Outside the courtroom Nina's mother would declare her outrage at the verdict: "Briscoe was just as involved as Laboucan. He was there."

His mother Violet professed a much different opinion: "My son didn't do it. He just stood there like a dummy."

WEST CANADA BOY

Joseph Wesley Laboucan was born the third of five children in Fairview, Alberta, on July 25, 1985. His mother, Elizabeth, left his volatile father, Daniel Jeffries, eight months later, and by the time Laboucan was a toddler they had settled into an apartment in Dawson Creek, British Columbia. There, Elizabeth married Lauren Johnson and the two began to run a work camp for oil and gas companies. Joseph pitched in whenever he could, becoming involved in a Baptist Church group that met on Friday nights. The group leader Kevin Throness viewed him as a gentle soul who would go to great lengths to win his peers' approval. Yet Joseph struggled to fit in, and had few close friends.

In the summer of 2000, Laboucan and his family relocated to Fort St. John, British Columbia. The sixteen-year-old did not adjust well to the change, and after failing several classes, was forced to attend a junior high school, which took a dramatic toll on his self esteem. This, along with his troubled relationship with his stepfather, led Laboucan to skip classes. Instead he spent his time hanging around the Totem Mall where he befriended thirty-year-old Adam MacKay, frequently sleeping on his couch.

Three years after moving to Fort St. John, Joseph was riding in a car to Edmonton with some friends when the driver, Donovan Chisholm, lost control of the vehicle, rolling it three times. Paramedics airlifted the unconscious Laboucan to a hospital where he eventually snapped out of his coma to find his upper back broken. A steel plate was inserted and he spent the better part of a year in a plastic body brace, earning him the moniker "Body Cast Joe." According to Laboucan's friends, his temperament became increasingly erratic after the accident. On one hand, he claimed to have "found God," falling in love with a girl from his church youth group. At the same time he became addicted to crystal meth, provoking violent confrontations for fun. His first criminal charge came in July 2004 when he broke into the AltaLink power substation facility in Breton, electrocuting himself in the process. Meanwhile, he began spending more and more time in Edmonton where he collected debts for the local Hell's Angels and Triads under the nickname "Snowman." Sporting two new tattoos, a flaming skull and Japanese symbol, he ensconced himself among the youths of the West Edmonton mall. In March 2005, Joseph Laboucan arrived in Edmonton to pick up an insurance cheque for his injury settlement, only this time he decided to stick around town a little longer. By now he was fantasizing about murder, and found a captive audience in his new mallrat companions.

MEYER

While Joseph Laboucan languished in his cell, a second charge of murder followed on September 11, 2008. The RCMP had learned of his intimate relationship with Ellie May Meyer, an 118th Avenue prostitute who had grown up with him in Fort St. John. Meyer's body had been discovered on May 6, 2005, bludgeoned to death in a field near the intersection of Township Road 540 and Highway 21, east of the city. The last time anyone had heard from the thirty-three-year-old mother was March 31, less than three days before the murder of Nina Courtepatte. Pursuing the lead further, the RCMP learned that DNA evidence found on Meyer's body belonged to Laboucan. Charges that Michael Briscoe had a hand in the murder were filed against him in April 2010. The Edmonton RCMP announced that this latest development was based on "hard evidence."

On Monday September 26, 2011, Joseph Laboucan stood trial for the murder of Ellie May Meyer. Stephanie Bird took the stand, testifying that on the night of March 31, 2005, she, Briscoe, and Laboucan had driven Meyer to a field near Fort Saskatchewan. Meyer had been the second prostitute Laboucan had enjoyed that night. Parking in the field, Bird and Briscoe exited the vehicle, leaving Laboucan and Meyer to have sex. Briscoe later returned to the car, and soon after, Bird saw a bloodied Meyer dashing across the field with the two men in hot pursuit. They eventually caught up with her, beating her to the ground. Incapacitated, Meyer begged them to spare her life, promising never to tell the police. At this point, Bird claimed to have left for the car. Laboucan returned carrying Meyer's severed pinky finger. Placing it in a bread bag, the two men kept the gruesome trophy inside a fridge at their motel room where, according to Bird, Laboucan would show the finger to visitors, bragging that it came from his "last victim." Sickeningly, Meyer had been alive during the amputation, and was seemingly left in the field to die.

At the time of this writing, Michael Briscoe's trial for the murder of Ellie May Meyer is still pending.

———

Though evidence indicates that Svekla and Laboucan/Briscoe were involved in the deaths of Edmonton-area prostitutes, neither party possessed the opportunity nor aptitude necessary to kill on a large scale. If the police profile is correct, it seems that the RCMP have nabbed some of the little fish. Meanwhile, a predator of greater proportions remains at large, trawling the streets of Canada's northernmost provincial capital. A reward of $100,000 for information leading to the arrest and conviction of the responsible party is being offered by Project KARE, an RCMP-led task force investigating the murders. Corporal Wayne Oakes had expressed his view that the RCMP would "love nothing less" than to be flooded by calls. Unfortunately, despite the reward and release of the profile, to this day there have been no strong leads in the Edmonton prostitute killings. In an effort to generate a list of suspects, Alberta justice minister Ron Stevens is attempting to pass a bill mandating all convicted johns to provide a sample of their DNA to the police. Ultimately, it was this irrefutable scientific approach, rather than profiling, which led to Bernardo's downfall. It is likely that, if the Edmonton Serial Murders are ever solved, DNA will also prove to be the decisive factor.

In the next chapter we will examine how DNA technology has recently been applied to close the books on three more of Canada's most notorious sex murderers.

CHAPTER 14

NEW TECHNOLOGIES: DNA

In the mid-eighties, the city of Leicester, England, gave birth to the most important crime-fighting technology in history. Molecular biologist Dr. Alec Jeffreys located the tiny percentage of human DNA responsible for individual variation, and in 1984 applied Restriction Fragment Length Polymorphism (RFLP) to resolve several important paternity and maternity tests. This meant the DNA of any two individuals, barring identical twins, could be compared and distinguished from one another. To use Jeffreys's own words he had discovered "genetic fingerprints."

In 1985, Jeffreys told a Leicester newspaper that it was possible to obtain a genetic fingerprint from even a minuscule amount of blood. When local police came across this information in 1986, they contacted the young scientist immediately. Three years prior, the body of fifteen-year-old schoolgirl Lynda Mann had been found raped and strangled on a footpath in nearby Narborough. The mystery remained unsolved in 1986 when the "Black Pad Killer" claimed another fifteen-year-old victim: Dawn Ashworth of Enderby. Police wondered if Jeffreys would analyze the semen found at both crime scenes to see if they matched. Furthermore, could he obtain a genetic fingerprint of the killer that they could compare to their prime suspect? Jeffreys gladly agreed to help and ran the samples through the RFLP process. It took weeks for the results to come back. When they did, they confirmed that the semen from the Mann and Ashworth crime scenes matched. More importantly, the police's main suspect was cleared of any involvement in the murders, becoming the first person in history to be exonerated by DNA evidence.

A decision was made to ask the men of Narborough and surrounding villages to voluntarily submit a blood sample for analysis. Those who did not donate would naturally be looked at closely by investigators. In the end over 4,500 men agreed, the majority being eliminated by simple, less-expensive blood tests. Eventually, a baker named Ian Kelly admitted that he had provided his own blood for a co-worker, twenty-eight-year-old Colin Pitchfork. Pitchfork crumbled in the confession room, admitting to both murders. When a sample of his blood was positively matched with the genetic profile of "The Black Pad Killer," he was convicted on both counts of murder and sentenced to two life terms. His conviction was the first ever secured by Jeffrey's revolutionary technique of genetic fingerprinting.

In the years since, the RFLP technique has closed countless cold cases. Let's take a look at some Canadian examples.

Michelle Chan.

Ronald Glenn West
The .22 Caliber Killer
2+ Murders
Gormley/Palgrave, Ontario

1995: COPS AND ROBBERS

In 1995, the communities between Sault Ste. Marie and Sudbury were plagued by a series of violent armed robberies. On June 7, a stocky man entered a shop in Sault Ste. Marie under the auspices of finding a gift for his wife. Tricking the clerk into a concealed area at the back of the store, he suddenly produced a black pistol and announced his intentions to rob her. Under threat of death, she was bound and thrust into a closet while the gunman rifled through her purse, making off with $480, several credit cards, and some inexpensive jewellery. It was a modus operandi that had been repeated successfully a number of times, but each new caper only cemented OPP Inspector Ed Pellarin's determination to bring the offender to justice. Nine days later, he struck again at a Sault Ste. Marie fur and jewellery boutique, escaping with $30,000 in merchandise. A stolen ring was later traced to a local pawn shop where the seller had been captured on security camera using his own identification. The name on the card read "Ronald Glenn West." A former Toronto policeman, West had evidently tired of playing "cops" in 1971 and by 1988 had switched emphatically to "robbers." Armed with the camera footage, Pellarin set up around the clock surveillance of the Blind River home West shared with his second wife, Reina Lacroix. They found various items reported stolen along with some latex gloves and rope that West had employed in the commission of his crimes. Faced with multiple charges of armed robbery and weapons offences, he plead guilty and was sentenced to eight years in Kingston's Collins Bay Penitentiary. Satisfied with the conviction, Ed Pellarin returned to policing the Sault, where there was never a shortage of despicable characters to collar.

1970: THE .22 CALIBER KILLER

Meanwhile, in southern Ontario, OPP Inspector Don McNeill was struggling to solve the murders of two housewives. The first incident had taken place twenty-five years earlier on May 6, 1970. Doreen Moorby had been busying herself with housework and attending to her twenty-one-month-old son, when she was disturbed by a knock at the front door. The former nurse would not have recognized the stocky, big-eared man standing on her porch, but somehow he managed to get inside. Perhaps he had been dressed as a police officer or had shown her a gun. What we do know is that the intruder brutally raped her before assuring her silence with five bullets to the head. Another two were retrieved from her back. In a tragic scene, schoolteacher Albert Moorby returned home to find his wife in a pool of blood on the kitchen floor, and his distraught infant son huddled by her body.

Investigating policemen discovered traces of semen at the crime scene, later determined to have come from a Type A secretor (a person with Type A blood who secretes blood into their other bodily fluids), which represented roughly one-third of the male population. Ballistics tests also revealed the murder weapon to be a .22-calibre revolver with a larger-than-normal ammunition chamber holding nine rounds — a rarity for 1970. Otherwise, the killer had been meticulous, wiping down surfaces to erase fingerprints, and even removing the shell casings from the crime scene. Albert Moorby lamented that the only thing that seemed amiss was that the front door was locked — in a sleepy, rural community like Gormley, such precautions were seen as foolish. Undoubtedly, the most disturbing element of the attack was its randomness. There was no evidence that Doreen Moorby had been stalked or harassed, nor did she have any enemies. By all appearances, the killer had simply waltzed up to the first house that caught his eye and hammered on the door.

Among those unsettled by the gruesome killing were Russell and Helen Ferguson of Palgrave, Ontario. Like the Moorbys, Russell was a teacher while Helen had been a nurse until she started having children. Naturally, Russell worried for his wife's safety, but the Moorby killing had occurred forty kilometres east of their home and they seemed to be more or less out of harm's way.

May 19, 1970, was a sunny spring morning. The Ferguson's oldest son Dale was home sick with the mumps when the doorbell unexpectedly rang. Figuring it wasn't for him, Dale carried on watching television while his mother Helen answered the door. She re-entered, followed by a man he had never seen before. Helen told him that the man had a sick child in his car and that she was going to give him directions to the hospital. They disappeared upstairs and Dale returned to his television program, forgetting the man was even there. About an hour later, he heard three loud bangs, which he dismissed as somebody playing with fireworks. Suddenly the stranger came racing across the hallway toward the door. When Dale saw him pause to wipe his fingerprints from the handle he realized something was wrong. Waiting until he heard the man's car back out of the gravel driveway, he called several times for his mother, but received no response. Nervous, he began to search the house. It didn't take him long to find her. Helen Ferguson lay in a pool of blood in the hallway — the horror of her final moments forever frozen on her face. Dale dialled 911. Around the same time, Russell Ferguson was arriving home from work to find his wife murdered and son inconsolable.

The OPP secured the scene and immediately began the painstaking process of searching for evidence. The crime scene bore a striking resemblance to Doreen Moorby's — Helen had been sexually assaulted, shot twice in the head and once in the back; the shell casings had been retrieved and there wasn't a single fingerprint. Post-mortem results would later confirm that Helen had been raped by a man with the same Type A secretor blood as Doreen Moorby's murderer. Slowly the realization that the OPP might be dealing with a disturbingly organized serial killer began to set in.

All was not lost. On this occasion, the police had a lead to follow, namely the eyewitness testimony of young Dale Ferguson. He described the man the press would soon dub "The .22 Caliber Killer"[1] as swarthy in complexion, between thirty-five and forty, medium height, and driving a 1964–65 beige Rambler. Having only seen him for a matter of seconds, Dale admitted that some of the details might be incorrect. Armed with this information and a sketch of the offender, the OPP set about organizing what was at that time the largest manhunt in Ontario's history. Yet despite receiving two hundred tips a day and investigating two thousand suspects, by the end of 1970, they were still no closer to catching the killer.

1995: A COLD TRAIL CATCHES FIRE

It was the close of 1995, and OPP Inspector Ed Pellarin was in southern Ontario for a standard yearly review of cases. By a stroke of luck, he ended up discussing the Ron West file with Inspector Don McNeill. Pellarin mentioned casually that following West's incarceration, his Blind River home had been sold, and that while renovating, the new owners had made a telling discovery. In a plastic bag behind the bathroom ceiling boards they found a permit to carry a special nine-shot .22 revolver made out in West's name and issued December 29, 1969. Interestingly, the weapon had been sold in 1972, right after he had quit the police force.

Deciding to dig a little deeper, McNeill learned that West had been off-duty at the time of both killings, and that he frequently vacationed in Doreen Moorby's area. Officers who had served with him in the 53 Division of the Metropolitan Toronto Police remembered him as a quiet, unremarkable fellow who got the job done, but did nothing above or beyond what was expected of him. Likewise, during his Northern Ontario stint as a miner in the eighties and early nineties, co-workers nicknamed him "the Ghost," as he was in the habit of disappearing after work. Certain that Ronald Glenn West and "The .22 Caliber Killer" were one and the same, McNeill held a six-member meeting to investigate him further. Naturally, Ed Pellarin was in attendance. After some discussion, they reached the conclusion that if West was indeed the man who had raped and killed Doreen Moorby and Helen Ferguson, then they could probably nail him on DNA evidence. The problem was in obtaining a sample of West's saliva. In a remarkable display of memory, Pellarin recalled that in 1995, West's wife Reina had turned over a letter from her husband to him, thinking that it might be of some use in the investigation. If forensics could salvage a sample of Ron West's saliva from the envelope, they could compare it to the semen found on the victim's clothing. Though the results were inconclusive, there was enough similarity between the two samples to obtain a blood warrant. Taken by surprise at Collins Bay Penetentiary, West denied committing the murders, but, with little option, agreed to have his blood drawn. This time, the results came back positive. Facing overwhelming evidence, on August 25, 1999 he plead guilty to the ".22 Caliber Killings" and was sentenced to life with the possibility of parole in ten years.

1972–1991

Following his conviction for the .22 Caliber Killings, police began to wonder what else Ron West had been up to since 1970. Two years after Helen Ferguson's death, the Palgrave area had been haunted by another .22 caliber killer. The body of twenty-two-year-old hitchhiker Janice Montgomery was recovered from a Georgetown field. She had been shot execution-style in the back of the head. True to West's MO, the shell casings had been removed, along with the labels on the victim's clothes. The following year, the bodies of Donna Sterne and Wendy Tedford were found killed in identical fashion in a Downsview field. Like Montgomery, they had recently been hitchhiking in the area.

Another case that stood out immediately was a senseless double homicide at a Blind River rest stop. On June 27, 1991, sixty-two-year-old Gord McAllister and his wife Jackie, fifty-nine, pulled their brand-new Winnebago into a scenic picnic area along the river. After a quick look around they decided to camp for the night. It was a warm summer's evening, the sounds of crickets lulling them to sleep. They woke to a loud hammering on their door.

"Open up! I'm a police officer," a stern-sounding voice declared. "You can't camp here. You're gonna have to move!"

Gord McAllister rubbed his bleary eyes and glanced at the clock. It was one in the morning. Half-asleep, Jackie pulled open the door when a man with stringy blond hair burst inside, holding a rifle in one hand and a shotgun in the other.

"I'm gonna rob ya first, and then kill ya," he sneered.

With little else they could do, the McAllisters hurriedly turned over their valuables. He thanked them by firing his .22 rifle into Jackie's chest. Adrenaline pumping, Gord rushed for the door and was grazed by a bullet. Falling outside, he rolled underneath the RV for cover, praying that the stranger would go away. At that moment, Brian Major pulled his car into the rest area to see what the commotion was about. Stepping out of the Winnebago, the stranger fired through his windshield killing him instantly. Gord waited until he heard the man drive away before staggering out to the highway to find help. Sadly, Jackie was dead by the time the ambulance arrived.

The double murder of Jackie McAllister and Brian Major remains unsolved to this day. Not only was Ron West living in the area at the time, his own wife is said to have remarked that the composite looked like her husband in a wig!

Gerald Archer
The London Chambermaid Killer
3 Murders
London, Ontario

"That's only the first strike against me. The ball game isn't over yet!"

They were all aging hotel chambermaids and one by one they walked blithely into his trap. What exactly the "London Chambermaid Killer" did to gain their trust, we will never know. Perhaps he claimed to be looking for a housekeeper or cleaners for his phony business. Maybe it was just his disarming smile. Whatever he did, it was enough to get himself past their front door. Once inside, he was free to unleash the ravenous beast raging under his skin. His first victim, sixty-year-old Jane Wooley was found beaten to death inside her York Street apartment on February 3, 1969. The investigating officers didn't need an autopsy report to know that she had already been dead for several days. They surmised by her partially clothed body that she was attacked while trying to defend herself against unwanted sexual advances. There was no evidence of penetration. Something else was shockingly apparent: she had invited her attacker inside. Jane was last seen on Dundas Street leaving the London House, where she earned $40 a week cleaning.

The beast was able to keep itself at bay for almost another two years before resurfacing in the fall of 1970 to claim fifty-seven-year-old Edith Authier. On September 5, the Kent County woman was found beaten and stabbed to death in her Merlin, Ontario, home. Unlike Jane Wooley, this time the killer managed to complete his sexual attack.

Four months later, Chatham chambermaid Belva Russell, also fifty-seven, became the third woman to be beaten to death. However, in this case, police were able to arrest, charge, and convict a thirty-nine-year-old petty thief with her murder. His name was Gerald Thomas Archer. There was one problem: they had failed to link him to the previous slayings. Subsequently, Archer was only ever charged with the murder of Belva Russell. When the jury returned a verdict of guilty, he cryptically shouted "That's only the first strike against me. The ball game isn't over yet!" Whatever game Archer was playing ended in 1995 when he died of a heart attack at the age of sixty-four. Paroled in 1985, he had spent his last ten years of freedom drifting aimlessly from town to town.

Following his death, Archer's wife and daughter approached police, claiming that he had confessed to the Authier murder in private. Armed with this new information, investigators were also able to connect him to the murder of Jane Wooley. Archer's body was exhumed in 2000 and a DNA sample confirmed his family's suspicions. After nearly thirty years, the identity of "The London Chambermaid Killer" had finally been resolved.

Allan Craig MacDonald
3 Murders
Dartmouth, Nova Scotia/Oxford County, Ontario

RED CHRISTMAS

It was two days before Christmas in Dartmouth, Nova Scotia, when Corporal Eric Spicer responded to a routine car break-in. An eight-year veteran of the force, there was little he hadn't seen, but when he stepped into that service station parking lot on December 23, 1975, he got more than he bargained for. Though there is some uncertainty about what happened next, it seems Spicer became embroiled in a scuffle with a car thief who managed to wrest his service revolver from his holster. Pointing the barrel at the officer's face he squeezed the trigger three times. Gunshots broke the winter silence and Spicer toppled backwards into the slush, dead. From his nearby taxi, cabbie Keith McCallum looked on in stunned horror. The murderer was turning toward him now, taking aim with the pistol. Another flash in the dark and suddenly there was blood everywhere, plastering his body like dark red molasses. By the time backup arrived, the gunman had long since fled. Keith McCallum was rushed to hospital where, after a courageous battle, he died as a result of his injuries.

Infused with the vengeful fervour that comes when a fellow officer has been gunned down, the Dartmouth police set out looking for their number-one suspect: twenty-two-year-old Allan Craig MacDonald. A native of Elmsdale, Nova Scotia, MacDonald was born illegitimate, and forced to live with his maternal grandparents until age thirteen when his mother and father were finally able to provide for him.[2] Unfortunately, he only resided with them for two years before quitting school to join a travelling carnival. During this period, the hulking MacDonald seems to have lived a solitary existence. Occasionally, he telephoned home or popped by for a surprise visit, but it was becoming increasingly obvious that family was not a priority.

Following a sweeping manhunt, MacDonald was apprehended on Christmas Day. His 1976 trial was a heart-wrenching ordeal. Corporal Spicer had been a father of two, and the first Dartmouth policeman to be killed in the line of service. MacDonald was convicted of both murders and sentenced to hang. For this future serial killer, however, the timing couldn't have been better. Shortly after his trial, capital punishment was struck from the Criminal Code of Canada and MacDonald's sentence was commuted to life. The judge inexplicably set his eligibility for parole at ten years and by 1989 this cold-blooded cop killer walked out of prison a free man. He didn't bother to notify his family, instead drifting west along the Trans-Canada Highway to eventually settle in a rooming house in Brantford, Ontario. MacDonald found a steady job working construction, and, for all intents and purposes, seemed to be putting his criminal past behind him. Or was he seeking a new hunting ground?

ENGINEER OF DEATH

On Sunday, April 15, 1990, Lynda Shaw, twenty-one, waved goodbye to her mother and climbed into the driver's side of her blue 1989 Dodge Shadow. Easter weekend in Huttonville had been relaxing, but the third-year engineering student had an exam to write on Tuesday and wanted to get back to studying in London. A bright and diligent woman, Lynda was attending the University of Western Ontario on a scholarship.

Heading onto the 401 she began to drive southwest. It was just past 11:00 p.m. and the highway was lit up like a lunar runway. After an hour on the road, Lynda started to feel hungry. By that time, she had reached Oxford County, an area northeast of London encompassing Woodstock, Ingersoll, and Tillsonburg. Pulling into a service centre Burger King just off the highway, she hurried inside and grabbed a Whopper and fries. She would never get to enjoy them.

The next morning, Lynda's car was found abandoned by the highway. Judging by the shattered rear window and flat front tire, she had almost certainly met a violent end. Police began a sweeping search of the area, but as the Easter weekend drew to a close, there was still no sign of Lynda. Privately, they suspected that while she was ordering food, somebody at the station had let the air out of her tire valve, then followed behind her for twelve kilometres until, forced to pull over, she inadvertently became a sitting duck.

People began to assume the worst when Lynda failed to show up for her Tuesday exam. She was simply not the type to up and vanish.

Then, six days after her disappearance, a farmer stumbled upon her charred body in the bushes, a few kilometers from where her car was found. Lynda had been brutally raped, beaten, and stabbed to death before the killer made a half-hearted attempt to cremate her. At the time, the presence of hair and semen at the crime scene excited police much less than a partially burned dark blue duffel coat found at the base of a nearby tree. They reasoned if they could identify its owner, they would find Lynda's killer.

Over the next few weeks, hundreds of tips flooded in as surrounding communities rallied to the investigators aid. Fear and paranoia were running rampant in Oxford County: if this could happen to Lynda Shaw, it could happen to anyone's daughter! Eyewitnesses claimed to have seen a mysterious automobile parked behind Lynda's car. One self-proclaimed car buff identified it as a 1970s Chrysler Newport. Next, an anonymous letter accusing a "bodybuilder" of the murder found its way into the hands of the police, but nobody recognized the penmanship. Three composites were drawn of the suspect according to eyewitness descriptions. Again, nobody reported knowing the killer's face.

CLOSURE

When OPP detective Sergeant Ray Collins took over the case in 2003, it was already twelve years cold. Time, however, was definitely on Collins's side. Advancements in DNA technology had yielded a genetic profile of Lynda's killer in 1995, which was subsequently compared to samples from over three hundred suspects, including **Paul Bernardo**, without a match. Collins's team decided to suck it up and start digging through the mountains of tips amassed over the last dozen years. Along the way, they submitted forty hairs taken voluntarily from criminals in the area for DNA analysis. In 1990, these hairs had been compared to those found at the crime scene, but genetic science was still in its infancy, and DNA testing had not yet been attempted on them. It was a long shot, but one with a shocking pay-off. Lynda's killer had been none other than Allan Craig MacDonald. Collins knew MacDonald well: he had been involved in a high-speed car chase with the colossal east coaster in 1994 around Woodstock, Ontario. Charged with dangerous driving and possession of a stolen truck, MacDonald was let out on bail. The following day, he walked into a phone booth and blew his own brains out with a shotgun.

The OPP went public with the news in the summer of 2005, admitting they had chased a number of false leads. Allan MacDonald had nothing to do with bodybuilding, dwarfed the parka, never owned a Chrysler Newport, and didn't resemble any of the composites. Still, there were suspicions that he had been helped by an accomplice, perhaps the true owner of these red herrings.

CHAPTER 15

CANADIAN FORENSIC INNOVATIONS

Every modern society that has produced serial murderers has been forced to adapt its police work in order to deal with them. From 1946 until 1990, Canada made several noteworthy contributions to international murder investigation while tracking depraved lust murderers through its streets. "The Fort Rouge Sex Maniac" **Michael Vescio** sodomized young boys at gunpoint in the back alleys of 1940s Winnipeg, pulling the trigger if they resisted his advances. When the idea of using a metal detector to find his bullets was successfully employed, the practice soon became standard worldwide. Twenty-five years later in Montreal, the dashing **Wayne Boden** found himself crossing the line from rough sex to murder. Dubbed "The Vampire Rapist," he left savage bite marks on his victims' breasts, becoming the first killer in North American history to be convicted by bite-mark evidence. More recently, the advent of geographic profiling by maverick investigator Kim Rossmo, would lead to his dismissal by the conservative upper echelons of the Vancouver police. History, however, has vindicated Rossmo with the conviction of **Robert Pickton**, and subsequently he has been acknowledged globally for the effectiveness of his system.

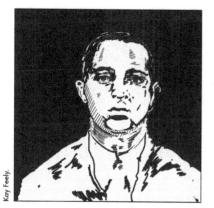

Kay Feely.

Michael Vescio
The Fort Rouge Sex Maniac
2 Murders
Winnipeg, Manitoba

"Shut up or I'll shoot!"

NO PEACE IN WINNIPEG

Donald Sherman Staley and Windsor's "Slasher" **Ronald Sears** weren't the only Canadian serial killers to ride in on the coattails of the Allied victory in the Second World War. Twenty days after the official surrender of Japan on the U.S. battleship *Missouri*, a short, olive-skinned man approached ten-year-old Halley Richardson as he was walking home from Winnipeg's Osborne Theatre. It was nearly ten at night on a Saturday and Halley had been to see a movie. The man seemed to be in something of a panic, pacing and endlessly running his fingers through his jet-black hair. He told Halley that his car had been stolen and asked the boy if he would help him look for it. In the days before widespread education about sexual predators, young Halley saw no reason not to help a stranger in need. The two walked from Warsaw Avenue in the Fort Rouge district up to Hugo Street where they entered St. Michael and All Angels Church. Inside, Halley's friend Rodney Fox greeted them warmly. They convinced Rodney to help them look for the missing vehicle. After searching for some time without luck, Rodney became bored and excused himself. Halley explained that he had to get going, too, and the stranger offered to walk him home. Cutting through an alleyway between Warsaw and Jessie Avenues, he suddenly seized the boy and ordered him to lie down. Terrified, Halley did as he was told, and continued to do so even when the man asked him to take his pants off. Helpless, he closed his eyes and thought of home as the man began to sexually assault him. Halley's attacker was not yet a murderer when the two crossed paths that cool

September night. He would remain that way for the time being. When giving a statement to police following the assault, Halley mentioned that the man might be German as he spoke with an accent and kept referring to "we Germans" and "you Canadian boys."

At the same time in the evening on Monday, November 19, the black-haired man fixed his sights on another victim. Ten-year-old Ronald Quick had returned to the corner of Hugo and Macmillan to look for a lost scarf when without warning he was grabbed by the collar from behind and forced between two garages. His dark-haired aggressor produced a pistol from the confines of his brown trenchcoat and promised him he wouldn't get hurt if he co-operated. His instructions were the same as they had been for Halley, however, when Ronald removed his pants, the stranger sodomized him. When he had finished, he fled into the night, leaving the boy feeling dirty, ashamed, and, thankfully, alive. Once again, Ronald recalled a short, black-haired man who spoke with a German accent.

SNOW ANGELS

A third attack followed on Christmas Eve. Donald Hewitt was returning home on McMillan Avenue after spending the evening delivering magazines. The eleven-year-old had just reached the foot of his apartment stairs when a man's voice called out to him. The dark complexioned stranger wanted to know if Donald would help him find a street — he wasn't sure if it was Belmont or Balmoral. Always eager to help, Donald agreed and the two spent several minutes searching the neighbourhood. Somewhere along Gertrude Avenue, the stranger suddenly explained that he was looking to rent a garage in the vicinity and led Donald into an alleyway. Once the shadows had engulfed them, the man drew a gun and raped him under threat of death.

Four days into the new year, Roy Ewen McGregor, thirteen, decided he would see the *Vote for George* and *Early Life* double feature with Ronnie Flowers instead of going to cadets. It was to prove a fateful decision. The film finished at 10:30 p.m., but as it was a warm Friday night, the boys caught a streetcar to the Dutch Maid ice cream bar on Osborne. At roughly 11:10 p.m., they reached the corner of Gertrude and Osborne, where they parted ways. Filled with sugar and visions of Hollywood starlets, Roy continued east for a block before crossing over to Wardlaw. Somewhere around the time the road began to turn left onto Clark Street, he came face to face with a young Mediterranean-looking man in a trenchcoat.

When Roy's mother glanced up from her ironing and saw that it was quarter to midnight, she began to panic. She called the Flowers residence and learned that Ronnie had arrived home some time ago. Roy's father and uncle set out to search the surrounding streets. Finding nothing by 2 a.m., they finally called the Rupert Street police station to report Roy's disappearance.

Across the street, Roman Klibak and Paul Ross arrived at Moore's Coal and Woodyard for their 8:00 a.m. shift. When Klibak turned on the yard lights, he was shocked to discover the body of a young boy secreted in a coal bin. Police noted that the child's pants had been pulled around his ankles, and the flap of his long johns opened. Stains around the flap seemed to indicate an attempted sexual assault. He had been shot twice: in the stomach and above the right ear, the second shot killing him outright. Death had occurred sometime between 10:00 p.m. and midnight. A trail leading from a nearby puddle of frozen blood to the coal bin also suggested that Roy had been killed near a boxcar and dragged to the dump site.

Now that "The Fort Rouge Sex Maniac" had escalated to murder, the police began a campaign of information aimed at the children of Winnipeg. Boys were cautioned to go out only in groups supervised by an adult. A composite of the killer along with a $1,000 reward for his capture was issued by the *Free Press*, though the picture bore no resemblance. Numerous theories as to who committed the murder began to circulate — one even pointed the finger at Ronnie Flowers. Others thought that this strange German rapist must have escaped from a nearby prisoner of war camp. The police were not convinced, in fact, given his dark hair and complexion, they doubted the killer was German at all.

On January 5, 1946, Winnipeg police began searching between the boxcar and coal yard. They had already recovered two empty cartridges, but in order to link the crime scene to a gun, they needed a bullet. Their solution, a metal detector, would change the course of forensics forever. Up until Inspector George Blow's suggestion, the device had never been used in a criminal investigation. It is now standard procedure. Two days of fruitless searching passed before a bullet was finally found buried beneath four inches of snow. The ballistic results came back from Regina at the end of February, confirming it had been fired by a Browning 9mm Fabrique International GP 35 automatic, a pistol manufactured by the John Inglis Company in Toronto and distributed to Canadian servicemen. Could "The Fort Rouge Sex Maniac" actually be a veteran and hero of the Second World War?

ACT TWO

Eight months after the murder of Roy McGregor, blue-eyed George Smith, thirteen, left for a local Scout meeting at Home Street United Church. It was a bleak night in Winnipeg, and, expecting a downpour, George had donned his skull cap and blue raincoat. His house was only three blocks from the church, but if there was one thing he had learned at Scouts, it was to be prepared. When the meeting ended at 9:45 p.m., George headed back with his friends Jack Brown, Albert Tait, and Bruce Leibrock. By ten o'clock, the other boys had filtered home, leaving George to walk the last block and a half alone. Unfortunately, he wasn't quite as alone as he thought.

When George hadn't arrived home by eleven o'clock, his parents contacted the Rupert Street police station and asked if there had been any accidents reported involving a young teenager. There hadn't. Anxious, Mrs. Smith began to phone friends and relatives. Her husband followed in the footsteps of Roy McGregor's father and went out in search of his son. When neither effort met with success, George's aunt called the police to report her nephew missing.

The following morning, as Frank Zehethofer eased out of his driveway into the alley between Home and Arlington, he thought he spotted something. Creeping closer, he discovered the crumpled body of George Smith, naked from the waist up and spattered with clay and blood. By 7:20 a.m., two representatives from the Rupert Street police arrived on the scene. Heavy rains had turned the alley into a veritable swamp, and the constables were literally up to their ankles in mud. The boy had been bound with a belt around the ankles and shot in the back. The absence of scorch marks on the body indicated that he had been killed from some distance. His torn blue raincoat, singlet, and skullcap were found within forty feet. Tire tracks in the clay indicated that someone had swerved their vehicle to avoid hitting the body. The coroner fixed the time of death at around 10:00 p.m., and although the butt of the pistol had been used to fracture George's skull, he believed the initial gunshot was the fatal blow. Sexual assault had likely been attempted, but George had fought his attacker so viciously that police put out an alert for a man with scratches on his face. This time the metal detector worked quickly, locating the bullet on the second day of searching. It wasn't long before ballistics confirmed it had been fired by the same pistol that killed Roy McGregor.

By now boys had taken to wearing hunting knives for protection and all evening sports activities were rescheduled for the daylight hours. At night, the streets of Winnipeg were empty. Additional RCMP officers were sent to the city to aid the investigation, as one by one every sexual deviant and pervert in Winnipeg was brought in for questioning. A $7,000 reward was offered for the apprehension of the "Fort Rouge Sex Maniac." The chief of police declared that all firearms in the city had to be registered, no easy task considering the recent war. Months passed as police registered and fired hundreds of 9mm pistols, but the one that had killed the two thirteen-year-olds continued to elude them.

Then on June 30, 1947, two masked gunmen held up the Port Arthur Palm Dairy in what is now Thunder Bay, Ontario, making off with $380. Within half an hour, police had three corresponding descriptions of the suspects and were watching every exit out of town. At 11:30 p.m., two suspicious-looking men were spotted lurking around the Port Arthur Canadian Pacific Railway station. Confronted by police, they identified themselves as twenty-two-year-old Michael Angelo Vescio and Frank George Guarasci, eighteen. They explained that they were waiting to board the midnight train to Winnipeg. Instead they were taken to the local police station and questioned. Still suspicious, the police escorted them back to the CPR station to inspect the locker where they were keeping their suitcases.

"There's something in there that doesn't belong to me!" Vescio announced suddenly. Intrigued, they opened the bags to find two pistols, one of which was a Browning 9mm FN GP 35 automatic. The suspects were arrested on the spot and taken back to the police station where, faced with overwhelming evidence, they confessed to the bungled robbery. Thanks to the memory of Chief George Taylor of the Port Arthur police, Vescio would eventually find himself confessing to much more. Taylor had remembered a secret bulletin sent out months earlier by Winnipeg's chief constable, asking them to keep their eyes open for a Browning 9mm FN GP 35 automatic pistol. He contacted the new chief constable in Winnipeg, who asked him to fire three shots from the weapon and forward it to the ballistics lab in Regina. Taylor was happy to oblige.

Vescio and Gaurasci plead guilty to armed robbery on July 12. The younger man, considered to be merely an accomplice, was sentenced to two years less a day at the Burwash penitentiary, while Vescio was packed off to Stony Mountain federal penitentiary for a three-year period. Within a week of his incarceration, ballistics results arrived in Winnipeg confirming that his Browning 9mm had been the same weapon used to kill Roy McGregor and George Smith. On August 8, two Winnipeg police officers met with Vescio at Stony Mountain where he confessed to both "accidents."

THE LIFE AND DEATH OF A SEX MANIAC

Born to an Italian-Canadian family in 1925 Port Arthur, Vescio had been the youngest of eight children. His mother died when he was very young, his father remarrying shortly after. Still traumatized by her death, Vescio resented every minute he spent under his father's roof. During this period, he had several minor run-ins with the law and spent as much time at his sister's house as possible. When he turned seventeen in 1942, he joined the army for no other reason than to leave home. There is no evidence that he ever left his post at Manitoba during his stint in the military. In 1945, Vescio stole a Browning 9mm pistol from a supply truck he was driving to the Grassmere Ditch POW Camp.

During the three years he boarded at 115 Rose Street, his landlords remembered him as a shy, quiet young man who never drank to excess or swore. An orderly sort, he left for work at 7:00 a.m.every morning and returned at 5:30 p.m. to clean himself up before heading to the Margaret

Rose Tea Rooms for supper. After he had dined, he would peruse the neighbouring book store for hours at a time. Later, the clerk would remember him as a polite, but taciturn gent who collected detective magazines. On Saturdays, Vescio went to the Fort Rouge Barber Shop for a shave and a haircut. The following morning was usually wiled away at the bookstore, though he dined with his landlords Sunday evenings. Monday nights were spent at the movies. Once in a while, Vescio would head out with friends to a hockey game or the tavern, but mostly he was a loner. Ironically, his army buddies had nicknamed him "Killer" in reference to his repeated overcompensation for his small size. His employers had a less than favourable opinion of him, alternately dubbing him "sly," "immature," and a "gun nut."

Between November 18 and 25, 1947, Michael Vescio stood on trial for the killing of George Smith. He claimed he had been drunk at the time and had asked George if he could use the telephone. When George replied that his father "would not want a drunk using his telephone," an enraged Vescio grabbed him and a scuffle ensued. Only when Vescio slipped in the mud did his pistol go off, tragically and "accidentally" hitting George in the process. Defence lawyer John L. Ross argued that the boy's rude response had provoked Vescio, and that the charges should therefore be reduced to manslaughter. Unfortunately, Ross didn't have a leg to stand on. If Vescio's account had been true, not only would there have been powder burns on the victim's body, there would also be no reason for him to be found half-naked. Instead the jury decided to believe prosecutor O.M.M. Kay's version of events in which Vescio lured Smith into the alleyway and attempted to undress him. Smith fought back and managed to break free, as evidenced by the torn singlet and raincoat, at which point Vescio shot him in the back to prevent him from reporting the assault. Uncertain if the boy was living or dead, he clubbed him across the head with the butt of the revolver and fled.

It took the jury just over half an hour to convict Michael Vescio of Smith's murder. Judge E.K. Williams sentenced him to death by hanging. On November 19, 1948 at 1:01 a.m., Michael Angelo Vescio became his own last victim.

Kay Feely.

Wayne Boden

The Vampire Rapist/Strangler Bill
4 Murders
Montreal and Calgary

Wayne Clifford Boden, born in Dundas, Ontario, near Hamilton.

LES BELLES FILLES

It is no secret that the ladies of Montreal are some of the most beautiful in Canada. Whether it's French flair or genetics, a summer stroll along St. Laurent Boulevard leaves even the most determined skeptics gaping. In this way, Wayne Clifford Boden was a lucky man. Tall and handsome with a beguiling smile, Boden was a regular in the local bar scene where he employed his considerable charm to bed an impressive array of Montreal beauties. Yet despite enjoying a sex life most men could only dream of, he was dissatisfied. Whereas many women expected their lovers to be gentle and considerate, Wayne Boden liked it rough.

On the evening of October 3, 1969, twenty-year-old Shirley Audette invited a charming stranger back to her flat in Anglophone Dorchester West. What passed between them during those hours is unknown. At some point Shirley called a friend telling her she was afraid, but refused to go into details. It would be the worst mistake of her life. The next morning Shirley's body was found sprawled at the bottom of her fire escape, fully clothed and barefoot. A single shoe lay in the courtyard. Judging by the abrasions around her nose, Audette had been strangled. Investigators determined that the killer had chased her out the apartment window and caught her on the fire escape. If she had cried out, then the slumbering tenants had not heard her, and when those powerful hands closed around her throat her screams became a death rattle. Before he fled, however, the killer left a single important piece of evidence at the crime scene: bite marks. In a sexual rage, he had gnashed his teeth savagely into Shirley Audette's breast. Since moving to the city from an east-end suburb, Audette had seen a number of young men. One by one, each of these would-be suitors was interrogated by police and eliminated from the list of suspects.

It would be over a month until the killer struck again. This time the victim was Marielle Archambault. Like Audette, she was twenty years old, new to the city, and living alone. The first sign that something was amiss came on November 26 when Marielle failed to show up for her shift at a nearby jewellery store. Concerned, her co-workers repeatedly called her apartment, but there was no answer. Finally, a custodian in Marielle's building was persuaded to check her flat. To his horror, he found the pretty bachelorette lying dead on her back across her sofa. Police noted teeth marks on her breasts and some bruising around the throat. The cause of death was ruled as strangulation, and this time there were clear signs of sexual assault. Friends informed police that Marielle had begun acting strangely in mid-November. She had become involved with a man named Bill, a relationship that she feared she "might not be able to get out of." Though nobody had ever met this Bill, one of the employees at the jewellery store claimed to have seen him briefly. When a search of Marielle's apartment yielded a photograph of an unidentified man, police showed the employee, who confirmed that the man in the picture and Bill were one and the same. Though pleased to have a break in the case, police were now faced with the troubling decision whether or not to release this picture of "Strangler Bill" to the public. After some deliberation, they decided to give it a green light. By January 1970, all of Montreal was abuzz with the news of the handsome stranger who stole hearts ... and lives.

Overnight, this carefree, swinging island became shrouded in suspicion. Police were inundated with phone calls from people claiming to recognize the man in the picture. Though many suspects bore a passing resemblance, they were each eventually eliminated, leaving the police in no better a position than before. Nor did greater public awareness help save lives.

On January 17, 1970, Newfoundland expat Jean Way entered a photographer's shop, complaining that a man outside had been bothering her. The clerk agreed to let her leave through the back door. At 8:15 that evening Way's boyfriend arrived at her apartment and rang the doorbell, but received no reply. Assuming that his girlfriend was simply running late, he had a drink at a nearby bar and returned shortly after. Still, there was no answer. Jean's boyfriend tried the door, and, surprised to find it unlocked, decided to check inside. He found her in the bedroom, lying on her back across the bed with a housecoat knotted around her neck. Her brassiere was ripped and she had been sexually assaulted, though there was no trace of bite marks. Unlike the previous crime scenes, the apartment showed signs of a struggle. Some among the police saw this as an indication that the increased publicity was forcing the killer to adopt different methods. They were right. After Jean Way's murder, the strangler never resurfaced and as the months passed without incident, the city of Montreal breathed a sigh of relief. "Strangler Bill" had seemingly moved on to greener pastures.

FLIGHT TO CALGARY

Four thousand kilometres west of Montreal in Calgary, Alberta, the last thing Elizabeth Portius expected was to run into a serial killer. For three years, she had worked as a school teacher, living alone in O'Neil Towers, a high-rise apartment building close to downtown. But in April of 1971, she had met a handsome stranger while on vacation in Banff. The two had shared drinks and swapped telephone numbers agreeing to meet up later in Calgary. They finally got around to their first date on May 17. The next morning, Elizabeth didn't show up for work. After several unanswered phone calls to her home, custodian Maurice Lutz and maintenance man Bill Moseley were asked to check on her. To their horror, the two men opened the door to discover the half-clothed Elizabeth lying spread-eagle in the centre of her living-room floor. Arriving within an hour, Detective Sergeant Ernie Reimer found her dress torn, the buttons left scattered about her body. Elizabeth's right breast had been bitten so savagely that the killer's lower teeth had actually punctured through the top. Post-mortem results showed she had been strangled, and a cufflink was embedded in her shoulder. It was suspected that she had fallen onto it during the struggle.

Some days after the murder, a schoolteacher told police that on May 17 he had seen Elizabeth in a car with a man in his mid-twenties. She had been wearing the same clothes she was found in. The car, a powder blue-green Mercedes with bobble-head dolls in the back window, became the focus of the investigation. Reimer put together a list of Mercedes owners in the area, tediously searching through records at the traffic office. One of the owners lived less than a block away from Elizabeth Portius. His name was Wayne Clifford Boden.

Upon approaching Boden's home, the first thing detectives noticed was a bobble-head doll gazing glassily back at them from the window. Certain this was their man, they knocked on the door and were greeted by a friendly, articulate young fellow who agreed to come back to headquarters to answer a few questions. In the interview room, Boden played it cool. He admitted to going on a date with Elizabeth Portius, but claimed she left his company safe and sound. When asked if he had lost anything, Boden indicated he had lost a cufflink — a damning admission, since he had not known it was found at the crime scene. Detectives immediately placed Boden under arrest, charging him with Elizabeth Portius's murder. Even this failed to ruffle his feathers. Boden confessed to having accompanied Elizabeth inside her apartment, where he lost the cufflink and left shortly after.

Though the cufflink blunder was enough to convince the detectives they had Elizabeth's killer, they realized they would need evidence directly tying Boden to the murder to win over a jury. In an unprecedented piece of Canadian forensic genius, the police enlisted orthodontist Dr. Gordon Swan to compare an X-ray of Boden's teeth to the marks on Elizabeth Portius's breast. At this point, bite-mark evidence had been used to convict in British murder cases, but was still untested on North American soil. While they waited for the results of the dental check to come in, detectives continued to press Boden for an admission of guilt. In the end, they concluded that it was useless; he was a remorseless psychopath who enjoyed playing cat-and-mouse. They would never get a rise out of him. Some of them had even begun to wonder if he was innocent. However, all that changed when a search of Boden's apartment revealed a button from Elizabeth Portius's dress. At the same time, Dr. Swan called to confirm that Boden's teeth matched the markings found on her body. Confronted by overwhelming evidence, Boden finally cracked. He admitted to going back to Portius's apartment after the date where he just "snapped." Furthermore, he also confessed to murdering Shirley Audette, Marielle Archambault, and Jean Way in Montreal. Reimer immediately contacted detectives in Quebec who flew in to question Boden about the deaths.

UNREPENTANT

Though Boden had confessed to murdering the three women in Montreal, police also suspected him in the murder of twenty-one-year-old Norma Vallaincourt. The young nurse had been found dead in her Hochelaga-Maisonneuve apartment on July 22, strangled and bitten several times on the breast. To their surprise, Boden denied any involvement in the slaying. In 1994, a man by the name of Raymond Sauvé would admit to the crime and be rewarded with a life sentence at a federal penitentiary.

On Valentine's Day in 1972, Wayne Clifford Boden was sentenced to life in prison for the murder of Elizabeth Portius. Three additional life sentences were added on April 12 when Boden plead guilty to the murders of the Montreal women. But the story of "Strangler Bill" wasn't over yet. While on a supervised day pass from his Quebec prison on May 4, 1984, Boden escaped through an adjoining door in a hotel restroom. When police finally caught up with him he was relaxing at a bar, chatting up a beautiful local woman. She would never know just how close she came to being the fifth victim of the infamous "Vampire Rapist." Boden succumbed to skin cancer at Kingston Penitentiary in 2006.

Andre Kirchhoff.

Robert Pickton

Pig Man
6–49 Murders
Port Coquitlam, British Columbia

"You're making me more of a mass murderer than I am!"

CRIES IN THE DARKNESS

What the hell? Lynn Ellingsen awoke to a strange clamouring noise from the slaughterhouse. The last thing the thirty-seven-year-old addict remembered was cruising downtown with her housemate Willie to pick up some cocaine and a hooker before returning to his Port Coquitlam farm. While Willie had his way with the woman on the other side of the trailer, she had returned to her room, where she figured she must have dozed off. That made sense — what didn't makes sense were the bizarre lights and activity in the abattoir at this ungodly hour. Lynn decided to investigate. Creeping out the front door, across the trailer's porch toward the slaughterhouse, she was suddenly assailed by the stink of offal. Surely Willie wasn't gutting hogs at this time of night? Peering through the slaughterhouse door, she recoiled at the sight of the blood-drenched pig farmer standing over a woman's body. Willie spotted Lynn, and dragged her screaming inside the building. Shaking with fear, her eyes struggled to comprehend what they were seeing. The woman's body was suspended from the ceiling by a chain; puddles of blood mellowed on a nearby table alongside clumps of black hair.

"If you don't keep yer mouth shut, you'll be right beside her," Willie cackled.

Lynn agreed, on the condition that he give her money for drugs, of course. Nobody was going to believe an addict over a respectable member of the community, anyway. As she hopped into the back of the taxi to head downtown, one image lingered in her mind's eye: ten little toes lacquered with red polish hanging at eye level. Lynn Ellingsen had never needed a hit so badly in her life.

THE GEOGRAPHY OF MURDER

The ten blocks of seedy hotels and pawn shops comprising Vancouver's downtown east side is arguably the most derelict area in Canada. With a population of up to ten thousand down-and-outs, the streets are strewn with used condoms and syringes. At the core of "the Low Track" is the intersection of Main and Hastings, dubbed "Pain and Wasting" by locals for the legions of emaciated heroin and crack addicts who call it home. It was here in 1983 that prostitutes began to vanish without a trace.

After years of ignoring the demands of community activists to investigate the disappearances, in 1998, the Vancouver police formed an official task force. Among those most convinced that a serial killer was operating on the Low Track was Detective Inspector Kim Rossmo. Throughout the eighties, Rossmo had been engineering CGT (Criminal Geographic Targeting), a computer program that analyzes the proximity of crime scenes in order to find the killer's base of operations. To assess the reliability of his new system, Rossmo ran tests on previously solved murders. After feeding geographical data related to the **Clifford Olson** slayings into CGT, Rossmo was astonished to find the program had highlighted the four-block squared area where Olson resided. In another case, Rossmo was able to pinpoint the exact basement where a serial rapist lived. As there were no body dump sites associated with the Low Track disappearances, Rossmo focused instead on the areas where the missing women were last seen. Although there was insufficient information to generate a usable geographic profile, the system did determine the presence of serial prostitute murderer on the Low Track. When Rossmo presented his findings to the chief homicide detective, however, he was shocked to be greeted with overwhelming denial and hostility. Resenting Rossmo's swift promotion from constable to detective, the upper echelons of the Vancouver police hierarchy decided he lacked "real" investigatory experience. Deeming his pioneering work of little use, they opted not to renew his contract. Insulted, Rossmo turned down their offer of a lower-paying position, and found employment at the University of Texas's Geographic Profiling Unit. In the years since, he has garnered international recognition as the founding father of the world's first geographic profiling system. He has also been proven correct in his sinister appraisal of the Low Track disappearances. If the Vancouver police had taken his findings more seriously, they may have caught "The Pig Man" years earlier, possibly sparing the lives of up to twenty women.

PIGLET

None of the other Port Coquitlam children liked the Pickton boys. Most were the offspring of workers at the local insane asylum, raised in sterile, middle-class backgrounds. David and Willie Pickton, on the other hand, were the sons of an aging hog farmer, forced to slop pigs and clean sties until dusk. To their detriment, their domineering mother Louise was nowhere near as strict about their personal hygiene and, to put it frankly, the boys stank. Willie was even known to hide in gutted hog carcasses when he wanted to be left alone. This abysmal hygiene, exacerbated by a pathological fear of showers, lasted into his adulthood. A female friend took on the role of notifying Willie when his stench reached an unbearable level, at which point he would meekly retreat to the bathtub.

Always more intelligent and confident than his older brother, Dave Pickton eventually fell in with a gang of good old boys and took to drinking and hellraising. Sometimes they let Willie hang out with them, but inevitably he became the butt of their jokes. Never one to make trouble, he shrugged it off with a toothless smile. But behind the manure-caked overalls and timid demeanor lay a land of violent fantasy where Robert William Pickton was king. It was a place where nobody called him stupid; where instead of laughing at him, the girls shrieked and cowered in his mighty shadow.

This violent streak ran in the family. A story circulating in Port Coquitlam held Louise Pickton responsible for the 1967 death of Timothy Barrett. According to local legend, on October 16 of that year, Dave Pickton was driving his father's truck east on Dominion Avenue when he hit the fourteen-year-old Tim. Horrified, Dave scrambled out of the truck to see Barrett's broken form lying unconscious in the road. Not knowing what else to do, he sped home and informed his mother of the accident. The two returned to the scene where, after checking the boy's condition, Louise allegedly rolled him off-road into a nearby marsh. The next morning, Barrett's father found his son lying in a pool of filthy water ten feet from the road. The cause of death: drowning. Though Barrett had sustained a fractured skull and dislocated pelvis, none of these injuries had been sufficient to kill him. Louise was never charged with his murder. Officially it was ruled accidental, and sixteen-year-old Dave Pickton was stripped of his licence for two years. We can only wonder what moral lessons the Pickton brothers drew from their mother's example. Another story Willie often repeated was his horror at discovering his parents had slaughtered a calf he had raised since its birth. If there was one thing he learned growing up, it was that life was cheap.

The boys' father Leonard, a venerable Englishman, has been alternatively described as distant and abusive, especially toward Willie, though sister Linda has consistently spoken fondly of him. Of the two,

Willie was undoubtedly closer to his mother, although the relationship was not a positive one. When Louise Pickton died several years after her husband in 1979, Willie was shocked to learn that unlike Dave and Linda, who would receive their $86,633.33 inheritance immediately, he would have to wait ten years for his share in the estate. Though he was paid $20,000 in trust, this meant he would be bound to a life of drudgery on the farm until he turned forty.

With his self-esteem in ruins, Willie reinvented himself as a caregiver, providing poor women in need of money, drugs, or food a place to stay. Their presence on the Pickton farm undoubtedly made him feel like less of a loser, and he enjoyed having them around to cook and clean. Though he wanted the relationships to be sexual, the women always refused, forcing him to seek comfort in compulsive masturbation or the life-sized inflatable doll he had purchased at a local sex shop. Of course there were always the women of the downtown east side, who needed money so badly they could not afford to refuse him. Sadly, it would be these women, the only ones willing to have sex with him, upon whom the "Pig Man" would unleash his boundless anger.

STENCH OF DEATH

The first time Robert "Willie" Pickton's name arose in connection with the missing downtown east side prostitutes was in 1998 when Bill Hiscox, a thirty-seven-year-old worker at the Pickton Brothers' salvage company in Surrey, told police of a "creepy" Port Coquitlam pig farm thirty-five kilometres outside of Vancouver where he went to pick up his pay cheques. A six-hundred-pound boar patrolled the grounds with a pack of dogs, reportedly charging and biting at trespassers. The owners, Dave and Willie Pickton, were known for hosting debauched parties on the property featuring Hell's Angels, copious amounts of alcohol, pig roasts, and entertainment from downtown east side prostitutes. Willie, in particular, was a habitual john and had even been charged a year earlier with the non-fatal stabbing of sex worker Wendy Eistetter. A quiet sort who seemed uncomfortable in the company of men, his pride and joy was a converted bus with tinted windows. Willie's brother Dave Pickton had also been charged with sexually assaulting a woman in a trailer there in 1992, and was fined $1,000, spending thirty days on probation. Most damning of all was Hiscox's claim to having seen numerous IDs and items belonging to the missing women on the Pickton farm. Armed with this information, police searched the area on a total of three occasions but were unable to find any evidence linking the property to the missing women.

Four years later, the Pickton farm came back into focus when police informant and former drug addict Scott Chubb tipped off the authorities that unlicensed firearms were being stored on the premises. A warrant was obtained to scour the property, and though no illegal guns were found, in the bedroom area of Willie's trailer, searchers stumbled upon an asthma inhaler prescribed to one Sereena Abotsway, a working girl who had disappeared from the downtown east side on August 19, 2001.

Spurred on by Wells's discovery, more members of the missing women task force convened upon the seventeen acres, dividing it into 216 twenty-by-twenty-metre search grids. Layers of dirt were excavated and sifted by archaeologists and anthropologists along one of two conveyor belts. After several weeks of fruitless searching, two policemen decided to investigate a rancid stench emanating from a meat freezer in the workshop garage. Inside they discovered two buckets, each containing a human head that had been sliced in half and stuffed with pairs of hands and feet. These skulls, later identified as belonging to Sereena Abotsway and missing prostitute Andrea Joesbury, showed bullet holes from a .22-calibre weapon. Forensic analysis revealed they had been sawed partway through with a handheld reciprocating saw, then manually pulled apart. This method of dismemberment bore a chilling resemblance to the body of a Jane Doe that had been recovered from a swamp near the Pickton property in 1995.

Two months after the discovery of Abotsway and Joesbury, a bullet-holed skull belonging to another member of the missing person's list, Mona Wilson, was recovered from a garbage pail near the pigpen. True to the killer's modus operandi, a pair of skeletal hands and feet had been stowed inside the bisected skull.

Meanwhile, the sifting team had made some gruesome finds of its own: a woman's jawbone with three teeth was later identified as belonging to Brenda Wolfe. A mother of two who had been forced to beg government assistance because she had spent her last penny on Christmas presents, Wolfe had disappeared from the Low Track in February 1999. The jawbone of vanished streetwalker Marnie Frey was similarly discovered in a cistern. Fourteen hand bones, one of which was linked to missing prostitute Georgina Papin, were retrieved from a rat's nest under the pigpen. Also uncovered were several human toes, a heel, rib bones, tufts of human hair, victims' clothing, and a condom.

PIG IN THE PEN

By October 2002, fifteen charges of first-degree murder had been laid against Pickton, prompting his defence lawyer Peter Ritchie to publicly announce he would quit the case due to its excessive workload unless the Crown facilitated some kind of funding arrangement. So far, over ten thousand pieces of evidence had been logged. Preliminary hearings related to the counts began in January 2003, and on July 23, Pickton was ordered to stand trial on fifteen counts of first-degree murder. Four months later, police finally wrapped up their year-and-a-half search of the Port Coquitlam farm, having collected 150,000 swabs of DNA and identified the remains of thirty-one women, twenty-seven of whom were on the task force's missing persons list: Brenda Wolfe, Andrea Joesbury, Mona Wilson, Sereena Abotsway, Marnie Frey, Georgina Papin, Cara Ellis, Kerry Koski, Andrea Borhaven, Wendy Crawford, Dawn Crey, Yvonn Boen, Tiffany Drew, Sarah de Vries, Cynthia Feliks, Angela Jardine, Diana Melnick, Debra Jones, Jacqueline McDonnell, Diane Rock, Heather Bottomley, Jennifer Furminger, Helen Hallmark, Patricia Johnson, Heather Chinnock, Tanya Holyk, Sherry Irving, Inga Hall, and three Jane Does. Unfortunately, just because their DNA placed them on the property, it did not constitute enough evidence to merit charges of murder.

In another twisted development, British Columbia's health officer Dr. Perry Kendall proclaimed in March 2004 that human remains may have been mixed with pork products sold from the Pickton farm, but that these were chiefly given only to close friends and neighbours, and if cooked properly bore little health risks for their consumers. It was little consolation to those that had eaten them.

Jane Wolsak

Courtroom sketch of Pickton appearing via video-link at his 2005 pre-trial.

The Pickton case was delayed again in May 2005 with the Crown's announcement that they were laying twelve new charges of first-degree murder, for a total of twenty-seven. The following month, British Columbia Supreme Court veteran Justice James Williams was appointed to hear the case. The Pickton trial opened with a *voir dire* in January 2006, a hearing where Williams would assess what evidence was admissible in court. Three months later, he ruled that the remaining Jane Doe murder charge would be thrown out due to lack of evidence, bringing the total to twenty-six. Then, on August 29, he further narrowed the trial to focus solely on the deaths of Abotsway, Frey, Papin, Joesbury, Wilson, and Wolfe. Williams reasoned that given the trial was already slated to last two years, it would "pose an unreasonable hardship on the jury" to weigh all twenty-six counts of murder. Instead, the remaining twenty would be tried at a later date.

Thanks to Justice Williams's wise decision-making, the Robert Pickton trial finally began in December 2006. Two videotapes shown to the jury revealed the various faces of the defendant; the first, an eleven-hour police interview portrayed an innocent Pickton who called himself "just a plain farm boy" and denied any involvement in the British

Columbia prostitute murders. A second video taped in his cell, however, revealed him confessing to an undercover RCMP officer that he had aimed to kill fifty women, but had only reached forty-nine. He had used a nearby rendering plant to dispose of his victims, but had "gotten sloppy." After reaching his goal, he planned to take a break before slaughtering an additional twenty-five and at one point claimed he was "bigger than the Green River killer."

For the most part, Pickton spent the trial behind a box of protective bulletproof glass, looking bored by the proceedings and doodling on a notepad. During an analysis of the reciprocating saw used to bisect the skulls, however, he was seen to smile.

The only .22-calibre weapon to be found on the property was a revolver with a dildo fixed over the barrel, containing biological evidence pertaining to Pickton and Mona Wilson. The gun had not been fired while the dildo was attached. Bloodstains on a mattress in Pickton's mobile home were linked through DNA to Mona Wilson. Forensic chemist Tony Fung also acknowledged that a chemical substance found in a hypodermic needle in Pickton's office contained methanol, a common component in windshield-wiper fluid. Toxicology tests conducted on tissue samples retrieved from the farm revealed no traces of methanol, but all contained cocaine along with methadone and Valium.

Scott Chubb, the police informant who had originally directed them to the farm, appeared as a key witness for the prosecution. According to his testimony, Pickton had confided in him that he routinely murdered prostitutes by injecting windshield wiper fluid into their veins. As most of the women were drug users, police would simply dismiss their deaths as an overdose. This admission, when combined with the discovery of the syringe, proved to be damning evidence. Chubb also revealed that Pickton had asked him to "speak with" Lynn Ellingsen, a term which he took to mean murder her, because she was "costing him a lot of money."

Pickton divulged another of his favourite murder methods to witness Andrew Bellwood one night over a pork supper. While engaging in sex in the doggy-style position, Pickton would handcuff them to the bed and gag them, strangling them to death with a wire ligature. He would then dispose of the bodies by hacking off parts and feeding them to his pigs, mixing the rest with barrels full of offal to be shipped off to a disposal plant.

Another witness, Gina Houston, who had been a friend of Pickton's for over ten years, claimed that while police were searching the farm two days before his arrest, Willie confided in her that he was aware of numerous corpses on the farm, including six behind the barn in the piggery. He lamented that he was to blame, and admitted that he was contemplating suicide. Strangely, when she had asked him if he had killed the women, he denied it, placing the blame for three or four of the deaths on prostitute Dinah Taylor. In an interesting twist, DNA tests on items belonging to some of the victims actually linked them to Taylor. Houston also testified that on an earlier occasion in November 2001, she had been speaking on the phone to Pickton when she heard signs of a struggle accompanied by a woman's screams in the background. Pickton later told her that the woman "didn't make it" and identified her as "Mona."

After nine days of jury deliberation, on December 9, 2007, Robert William Pickton was convicted on six counts of second-degree murder, and sentenced to life imprisonment without the possibility of parole for twenty-five years. The fact that the convictions were in the second-degree possibly reflects the jury's feelings that Pickton did not plan the murders or commit them alone.

At one point during his initial interrogation, Pickton had been accused of murdering sixty-seven women, prompting him to exclaim, "You're making me out to be a bigger mass murderer than I am!" The most likely number who met their end on the Pickton farm (though not necessarily at the hands of Willie himself) is thirty-one, as represented by the DNA samples found on the property. However, Pickton once bragged to his cellmate, an undercover RCMP officer, of slaughtering forty-nine sex workers. This should be taken with a grain of salt. Serial killers routinely boast of committing more murders than they are actually responsible for, but the idea that Pickton would brag about killing less is incomprehensible. Even if "The Pig Man" did kill forty-nine downtown east-side prostitutes, this still leaves twenty-one unaccounted for. Fortunately, there has been no shortage of viable suspects passing through the Vancouver area in the past few years. At the forefront are convicted serial killers **Gilbert Paul Jordan**, **Keith Jesperson**, and Scott William Cox (an Oregon trucker); Frank Roy, slayer of eleven-year-old Alison Parrott; sadistic rapists Ronald McCauley, Barry Niedermeyer, and Michael Leopold; and even Robert Pickton's own brother, David, convicted of sexual assault in 1992. It is entirely possible that the **Edmonton Serial Killer** and the perpetrators of the prostitute murders in Calgary, Winnipeg, and other parts of British Columbia may also have claimed victims along the Low Track.

TABLE 5: 70 MISSING AND MURDERED WOMEN FROM VANCOUVER'S EAST SIDE (1978-2001)

Names in **bold** indicate the six victims Pickton was convicted of killing.

NAME	AGE	LAST SEEN	REPORTED MISSING	RESULT
GILBERT PAUL JORDAN ACTIVELY KILLING PROSTITUTES IN VANCOUVER				
Lillian O'Dare	34	Sept. 12, 1978	Sept. 12, 1978	
Wendy Louise Allen	33	March 30, 1979	April 5, 2002	
Rebecca Guno	23	June 22, 1983	June 25, 1983	
Yvonne Abigosis	26	Jan. 1, 1984	May 22, 2002	
Sherry Lynn Rail	27	Jan. 30, 1984	Jan. 3, 1987	
Linda Grant	31	Oct. 1984	Feb. 2, 1996	
Sheryl Donahue	21	May 30, 1985	August 31, 1985	
Laura Mah	42	Aug. 1, 1985	Aug. 3, 1999	
Elaine Allenbach	20	March 15, 1986	April 11, 1986	
GILBERT PAUL JORDAN IS ARRESTED FOR MURDERS IN 1987				
FRANK ROY ARRIVES IN VANCOUVER, ROUGHLY MID-1988				
Teressa Williams	15	July 1, 1988	March 17, 1999	
Elaine Dumba	34	1989	April 9, 1998	
Ingrid Soet	30	Aug. 28, 1989	Dec. 1990	
Gloria Fedyshyn	27	Jan., 1990	July 2002	
BARRY NIEDERMEYER FIRST KNOWN TO BE IN VANCOUVER				

KEITH JESPERSON AND SCOTT WILLIAM COX BEGIN PROSTITUTE MURDERS				
Mary Lands	28	1991	2004	
Nancy Clark	25	Aug. 22, 1991	Aug. 23, 1991	
FRANK ROY LEAVES VANCOUVER, SOMETIME BEFORE END OF 1991				
Kathleen Wattley	33	June 6, 1992	June 29, 1992	
Elsie Sebastien	40	Oct. 16, 1992	May 16, 2001	
SCOTT WILLIAM COX IMPRISONED FOR TWO PROSTITUTE MURDERS				
Sherry Linda Baker	24	1993	2004	
Teresa Triff	23	April 15, 1993	March 21, 2002	
Leigh Miner	35	Dec. 12, 1993	Feb. 24, 1994	
Angela Arsenault	17	Aug. 19, 1994	Aug. 29, 1994	
RONALD RICHARD MCCAULEY PAROLED				
Catherine Gonzalez	26	March 1995	Feb. 7, 1996	
KEITH JESPERSON ARRESTED FOR MURDERS				
Catherine Knight	25	April 1995	Nov. 11, 1995	
Dorothy Spence	33	Aug. 30, 1995	Oct. 30, 1995	
Diane Melnick	20	Dec. 27, 1995	Dec. 29, 1995	Pickton initially charged, dropped
Dawn Cooper	32	1996	June 26, 2002	
Cara Louise Ellis	25	1996	Oct. 2002	RP initially charged, dropped
MICHAEL LEOPOLD ARRESTED IN 1996 FOR RAPE				
Francis Young	36	April 6, 1996	April 9, 1996	
Tanya Marlo Holyk	20	Oct. 26, 1996	Nov. 3, 1997	Pickton initially charged, dropped
Olivia Gale Williams	21	Dec. 6, 1996	July 4, 1997	
Stephanie Lane	20	Jan. 11, 1997	March 11, 1997	
Sharon Ward	29	Feb. 14, 1997	March 1997	

BARRY NIEDERMEYER LEAVES VANCOUVER SOMETIME IN 1997

Andrea Borhaven	25	March 1997	May 18, 1999	Pickton initially charged, dropped
Sherry Irving	24	April 1997	March 21, 1998	Pickton initially charged, dropped
Kellie Little	28	April 23, 1997	April 30, 1997	
Janet Gail Henry	36	June 26, 1997	June 28, 1997	

FIRST PICKTON MURDER THAT WAS PROVEN IN COURT

Marnie Frey	**23**	**Aug. 1997**	**Sept. 4, 1998**	**Pickton convicted in second-degree murder**
Helen Hallmark	31	Aug. 1997	Sept. 23, 1998	Pickton initially charged, dropped
Jacqueline Murdock	26	Aug. 14, 1997	Oct. 30, 1998	
Cindy Louise Beck	32	Sept. 30, 1997	April 30, 1998	
Cindy Feliks	39	Nov. 26, 1997	Jan. 8, 2001	
Tania Peterson	28	1998	2003	
Ruby Hardy	33	1998	March 27, 2002	
Tammy Fairbairn	27	1998	Dec. 2004	
Kerry Lynn Koski	38	Jan. 7, 1998	Jan. 29, 1998	Pickton initially charged, dropped
Inga Monique Hall	46	Feb. 26, 1998	March 3, 1998	Pickton initially charged, dropped
Sarah deVries	28	April 14, 1998	April 21, 1998	Pickton initially charged, dropped
Sheila Egan	19	July 14, 1998	Aug. 5, 1998	
Julie Louise Young	31	Oct. 1998	July 6, 1999	
Angela Jardine	27	Nov. 20, 1998	Dec. 6, 1998	Pickton initially charged, dropped
Tanya Emery	34	Dec. 1, 1998	March 13, 2002	
Michelle Gurney	19	Dec. 11, 1998	Dec. 22, 1998	

Marcella Creison	19	Dec. 27, 1998	Jan. 11, 1999	
Jacqueline McDonnell	23	Jan. 16, 1999	Feb. 22, 1999	Pickton initially charged, dropped
Brenda Wolfe	**30**	**Feb. 1, 1999**	**April 25, 2000**	**Pickton convicted in second-degree murder**
Georgina Papin	**34**	**March 2, 1999**	**March 14, 2001**	**Pickton convicted in second-degree murder**
Wendy Crawford	43	Nov. 27, 1999	Dec. 14, 1999	Pickton initially charged, dropped
Jennifer Furminger	28	Dec. 27, 1999	March 30, 2000	Pickton initially charged, dropped
Tiffany Drew	24	Dec. 31, 1999	Feb. 8, 2002	Pickton initially charged, dropped
Sharon Abraham	35	2000	2004	
BARRY NIEDERMEYER ARRESTED IN APRIL FOR ASSAULTING 7 PROSTITUTES				
Dawn Crey	42	Nov. 1, 2000	Dec. 11, 2000	
Deborah Jones	42	Dec. 21, 2000	Dec. 25, 2000	
Patricia Johnson	24	March 3, 2001	May 31, 2001	
Yvonne Boen	33	March 16, 2001	March 21, 2001	
Heather Chinnock	30	April, 2001	June 19, 2001	Pickton initially charged, dropped
Heather Bottomley	34	April 17, 2001	April 17, 2001	Pickton initially charged, dropped
Angela Joesbury	**22**	**June 6, 2001**	**June 8, 2001**	**Pickton convicted in second-degree murder**
Sereena Abotsway	**29**	**Aug. 1, 2001**	**Aug. 21, 2001**	**Pickton convicted in second-degree murder**
Diane Rock	34	Oct. 19, 2001	Dec. 13, 2001	Pickton initially charged, dropped

Mona Lee Wilson	26	Nov. 23, 2001	Nov. 30, 2001	Pickton convicted in second-degree murder
LAST PICKTON MURDER TO BE PROVEN IN COURT				

TRIMMING THE MEAT FROM THE FAT

On September 2, 2006, the *Vancouver Sun* published two letters sent by Pickton to twenty-seven-year-old warehouse worker Thomas Loudamy of Freemont, California. Loudamy had first written Pickton in early February 2006, pretending to be a troubled woman named Mya Barnett and had received a reply in March. A second letter was sent in early August, to which Pickton responded a week later. As there was publication ban on the trial, and the contents of the letters would have assuredly influenced the jury's opinion, incriminating sections were omitted from the September 2 publication. After the trial ended, on December 10, 2007, the *Sun* released the previously censored material. At last, the world had a glimpse inside the mind of the man who had committed some of the worst atrocities in Canadian history:

> I know I was brought into this world to be hear [*sic*] today to change this world of there [*sic*] evil ways. They even want to dis-re-guard [*sic*] the ten command-ments [*sic*] from the time that Moses in his day brought in power which still is in existence today … You can be sure that no immoral, impure or greedy person will in-herit [*sic*] the kingdom of God … Don't be fooled by those who try to excuse these sins, for the terrible anger of God comes upon all those who disobey him … [1]

In the letters, Pickton referred to himself as "a condemned man of no wrong doing" and offered an interpretation of Acts 14:22: "In each city they helped Christians to be strong and true to the faith. They told them that we must suffer many hard things to get into that holy nation of God."

Robert Pickton's religious zeal may have certainly been a motivation for his crimes, but more likely it was a convenient means of justifying them.

RIGHT UNDER OUR NOSES:

Colonel Russell Williams and the Writing of this Book, Part 4

The apprehension of Colonel Russell Williams will likely go down as one of the most successful serial killer investigations in Canadian history. In this instance, luck, as well as Williams's sloppiness, certainly favoured the police. Still, we should not lose sight of the many wise proactive decisions applied by investigators: behavioural science at its best. Having reasoned that the killer probably travelled regularly down Highway 37, the choice to stop vehicles and inspect tires at a routine roadblock resulted in the identification of Williams within less than two weeks of Jessica Lloyd's disappearance. Furthermore, the interrogation strategy employed by OPP Detective Sergeant Jim Smyth not only netted a speedy confession, but put Williams in a mindset to co-operate with the police and court systems indefinitely. Smyth's brilliant questioning was eventually released to the public and broadcast on televisions across the nation.

The following is a partial transcript of the interview, edited extensively for the reader's convenience. Please note that before Williams was brought in for interrogation, the OPP's behavioural science unit met to devise the best strategy for cracking Williams psychologically. Knowing that despite his antisocial tendencies, the killer colonel had spent his entire life in highly structured institutions (private school, university, the military), they agreed that Smyth should establish a sense of camaraderie with Williams, as if the OPP investigator were a friendly schoolteacher, fellow military officer, or co-pilot. At the same time, they would refer to him as "Russell" rather than "colonel," denying Williams any sense of control or the notion that he was being deferred to.

After some casual bantering to establish rapport, and an explanation of Williams's rights, Smyth began to focus on the questions concerning the Lloyd/Comeau murders along with the two sexual assaults in Tweed. This is a transcript of the conversation:

> **SMYTH:** Okay, those four cases are a concern to us and, you know, you've kind of almost hit the nail on the head about some of our issues that kind of make us want to talk to [you] Russell. [Be]cause essentially there's a connection between you and and all four of those cases. Would you agree? Geographically?

> **WILLIAMS:** And that I guess I drive past, yes ... I would say there's a connection, yes.

> **SMYTH:** Yeah and ... that's why I'll be quite frank with you. That's why things kind of evolved when the officers talked to you on Thursday night. We kind of went from there because ... you discussed ... the fact that you were a colonel at the base ... So essentially then the connection with Miss Comeau ... was made and I believe you're a door or two down from one of those two incidents ... in Tweed.

> **WILLIAMS:** Three doors down yeah ...very close, absolutely.

At this point in the interview, Williams's guard still seemed to be down. However, when Smyth began to foray into the world of forensics, the colonel's manner and body language changed subtly, showing signs of apprehension.

SMYTH: So the next thing we need to cover is, well, I'll just ask you this straight out: given the types of crimes we're investigating, do you get much chance to watch television shows? *CSI* and things like that?

WILLIAMS: I prefer *Law and Order* but I do watch *CSI* occasionally, yes.

SMYTH: Okay, so you have an idea of obviously the forensic capabilities … that are out there.

WILLIAMS: Mm-hmm.

SMYTH: What would you be willing to give me today to help me move past you in this investigation?

WILLIAMS: What do you need?

SMYTH: Well do you want to supply things like fingerprints, blood samples?

WILLIAMS: Sure.

SMYTH: Things like that?

WILLIAMS: Yeah.

SMYTH: Okay, footwear impressions?

WILLIAMS: Yeah. [NOTE: Here Williams glances nervously at his shoes]

SMYTH: … Alright I think that's what we're going we're going to ask you to do.

WILLIAMS: Okay.

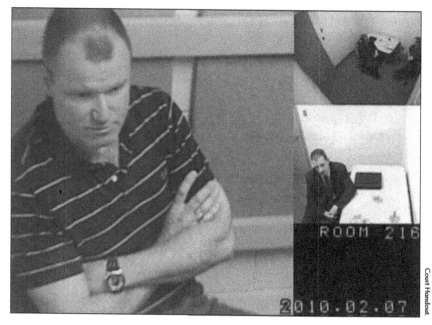

Court Handout

Camera footage of Williams in the OPP interrogation room with Smyth.

Shortly after, Williams provided the OPP with blood samples and fingerprints, along with photographs of his boot soles. When he and Smyth resumed their interrogation, however, Williams began acting cagey, asking the investigator if he was "going to be discreet," and voicing concern over how the base could be negatively affected if the public learned he was a suspect. Assuring him that they would be as prudent as possible, Smyth moved onto the issue of the tires on his Pathfinder.

> **SMYTH:** Just want to make sure I'm covering all the bases here, okay? What kind of tires do you have on your Pathfinder?
>
> **WILLIAMS:** I think they're Toyo.
>
> **SMYTH:** Okay ... I'll read this off to you. See if it rings a bell ... You ever heard of ... Toyo Open Country HTS?

WILLIAMS: That sounds right.

SMYTH: Would it surprise you to know that when the CSI officers were looking around her property that they identified a set of tire tracks to the north of her property ... as if a vehicle left the road ... and ... drove along the north tree line of Jessica Lloyd's property? They... examined those tire tracks ... and they have contacts in the tire business obviously ... Tire tracks are a major source of evidence for us ... Shortly after this investigation started, they identified those tires as the same tires on your Pathfinder.

WILLIAMS: Really?

SMYTH: Yeah ... Okay one of the other ... things that they do to try and identify the type of vehicle that may have those tires ... well, they do two things: they talk to witnesses. Okay, there was a female police officer that actually drove by that location that evening and recalls seeing an SUV-type vehicle in the field up to the north of Jessica Lloyd's house consistent with a Pathfinder ... What they also do to try and identify the type of the vehicle, is they look at what they call the "wheelbase width" ... Okay, [be]cause different vehicles [and] different makes' models have wheelbase width so ... they can take those two sets of tire tracks and measure the distance between them ... and determine ... what the width is ... and then they can enter that into a vehicle data base and it will spit out the types of vehicles.

WILLIAMS: Yeah.

SMYTH: Okay, your Pathfinder's wheelbase width is very very close to the width of the ... tires that were left in that field.

WILLIAMS: Mm-hmm.

SMYTH: Okay, do you have any recollection at all of being off that road?

WILLIAMS: No, I was not off the road, no.

At this point, Williams had not only categorically denied driving into the field beside Jessica Lloyd's house, but also ever having had consensual sexual relationships with any of his victims. Though he was trying to distance himself from the crimes, in reality, Williams was actually tightening the noose around his own neck. Now there could be no excuses why his tire tracks, boot prints, and DNA matched those at the crime scenes. If the pieces fit, then Russell Williams must be guilty. The next time Detective Sergeant Smyth entered the room, he began moving in for the kill.

SMYTH: I told you when I came in here that I'll treat you with respect and I've asked you to do the same for me. We talked about the whole idea of how we've approached you here, okay — the trying to be as discreet as possible ... But the problem is Russell, is every time I walk out of this room there's another issue that comes up, okay? And it's not issues that point away from you, it's issues that point at you ... and I want you to see what I mean ... [NOTE FROM AUTHOR: Smyth begins showing photographs of boot prints to Williams] All right, this is the footwear impression of the person who approached the rear of Jessica Lloyd's house ... on the evening of the twenty-eighth and twenty-ninth of January ... Now I want you to keep in mind that this is slightly smaller than scale okay? If you look here on the ruler you'll see that one inch is just slightly smaller than an actual inch, but this is the way it prints off on your computer ... I'll move this over so you can see what I mean. Essentially, when you're dealing with footwear impressions, we have a gentleman on the OPP who's basically world-renowned. His name is John Norman ... Footwear impressions are very much like, uh, like fingerprint comparisons ... You take a look at this print ... There's several different prints to compare. So we're going to get features off of one print to compare features off another print.

WILLIAMS: Yep.

SMYTH: These are identical, okay? Your vehicle drove up to the side of Jessica Lloyd's house. Your boots walked to the back of Jessica Lloyd's house on the evening of the twenty-eighth and twenty-ninth of January. You want discretion? We need to have some honesty, okay, because this is getting out of control really fast Russell, okay? Really really fast.

WILLIAMS: (*sniffs*) hum (*sighs*).

SMYTH: This is getting beyond my control, all right? I came in here a few hours ago and I called you today [be] cause I wanted to give you the benefit of the doubt. But you and I both know you were at Jessica Lloyd's house, and I need to know why.

WILLIAMS: Well I don't know what to say. It's, um ...

SMYTH: Well you need to explain it, because this is the other problem we're having Russell ... right now ... there's [a] warrant being executed at your residence in Ottawa. So your wife now knows what's going on. There's a search warrant being executed at ... the residence in Tweed and your vehicles [have] been seized, okay? You and I both know they're going to find evidence that links you to these situations ... You and

I both know that the unknown offender male DNA on Marie-France Comeau's body is going to be matched to you, quite possibly before the evening's over. This is a major investigation. The centre of Forensic Science is on call twenty-four hours a day helping us with this. Your opportunity to take some control here, and to have some explanation that anybody's going to believe, is quickly expiring.

WILLIAMS: Mm-hmm.

Here, the dialogue between Smyth and Williams reads like something from a Tom Clancy novel. By emphasizing the fact that things were "getting beyond my control," Smyth was intentionally playing into Williams's Air Force psychology, as if the OPP investigator were a desperate military adviser looking to a senior officer during a time of imminent crisis. He also added Williams's wife into the equation — an invaluable emotional stronghold that had now come under threat. When it became obvious that Williams was still unwilling to break down, Smyth began to appeal to the colonel's need to salvage another important base: his reputation.

SMYTH: ... Russell ... listen to me for a second, okay? When that evidence comes in and that DNA match[es]. When that phone rings and somebody knocks on this door ... your credibility is gone, okay? Because this is how credibility works ... and I know you're an intelligent person and you probably don't need to hear this explanation, but I also know your mind's racing right now, okay? The bottom line is that as soon as we get that piece of evidence that solidifies it ... DNA, okay, as soon as the expert in footwear impressions the expert in tire impressions calls me "yes, I examined those and they're ... a match," ... it's all over. Because as soon as that happens, where's your credibility? Where's your believability?

WILLIAMS: Mm-hmm.

SMYTH: Russell, what are we going to do?

WILLIAMS: Call me Russ, please.

SMYTH: Okay. What are we going to do, Russ?

WILLIAMS: (*sighs*)

SMYTH: Is Jessica somewhere we can find her easily? Like, is it something where I can make a call and tell somebody to go to a location and they're going to find her, or is this something where we have to go and and take a walk? Which direction are we heading in here? Can you tell me what the issue is you're struggling with? What's the use of you struggling now?

WILLIAMS: (*sniffs*) It's hard to believe this is happening.

SMYTH: Where do we go, Russ? Is there anything you want from me? Is there anything you want me to explain? Is there something missing you're struggling with that I can shed some light on for you? Russ, what are you looking for?

WILLIAMS: I'm concerned that they're tearing apart my wife's brand-new house.

SMYTH: So am I. But if nobody tells them what's there and what's not, they don't have any choice. [NOTE FROM AUTHOR: Some time passes] Computers have been brought to Microsoft in California ... They'll be picked apart. You can't erase ink from computers, it doesn't happened [*sic*] ... That's pretty common knowledge these days ... They sell programs that ... try and help people clean their computers and stuff, and our guys are pulling that stuff out all the time … This investigation will end up costing no less than ten million dollars, easy … Any requests this major case manager makes, they've already been told it's approved. So what am I doing, Russ? I put my best foot forward here for you, bud … I don't know what else to do to make you understand the impact of what's happening here. Do we talk?

WILLIAMS: I want to minimize the impact on my wife.

SMYTH: So do I.

WILLIAMS: So how do we do that?

SMYTH: Well, you start by telling the truth.

WILLIAMS: Okay.

D/SGT. SMYTH: All right so where is she?

WILLIAMS: Got a map?

Finally, after hours of careful, effective interrogation, Russell Williams's defences crumbled and he began his long confession. The man who had once taken such perverse pleasure in humiliating his victims would now be humiliated for the whole world to see. Hundreds of photographs recovered from Williams's Orleans home were presented as evidence at his trial, invariably depicting the stony-faced colonel modelling bras, panties, and pajamas stolen during his rash of fetish burglaries. Some of the undergarments belonged to girls as young as eleven. When coupled with the adolescent pornography recovered from Williams's computer, it left little doubt — Russell Williams was a pedophile.

On October 21, before a packed Belleville courtroom, Justice Robert F. Scott convicted Williams on all eighty-eight charges, including two counts of murder, two of sexual assault, two of forcible confinement,

Court Handout.

Underwear stolen from victims of Williams's home invasions. Note the meticulous arrangement, which was accompanied by a deranged cataloguing system.

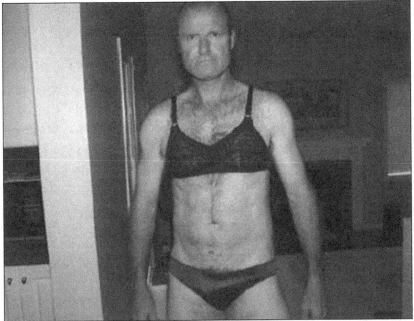

Court Handout.

Williams in one of his "self portraits." He derived sexual pleasure from donning the undergarments of female residents during his many home invasions.

and eighty-two charges of breaking and entering. Sentenced to two concurrent life terms in Kingston Penitentiary, it is unlikely he will ever walk this earth as a free man again. Publicly disgraced, Williams was stripped of his rank and military medals, and released from the military for "service misconduct." Any wages earned since his February arrest were revoked, and he was denied severance pay, though legally there seems to be no way to halt his military pension. As Williams's name had been stitched into his Air Force uniform, the clothing was burned, symbolically eradicating any connection he once had with the Forces. He may be the most despised Canadian in recent history. To quote Jessica Lloyd's mother Roxanne McGarvey: "… I have heard that people should be forgiven for their sins … but I can honestly say I hate Russell Williams … There's no punishment that can make this better."

———

I've decided to focus on the recent success of the Williams investigation, not only because it merits applause, but because it provides a ray of hope. If future Canadian serial murderers are confronted with the kind of professionalism shown by the OPP and the Belleville police, then I believe the public can breathe a sigh of relief. Unfortunately, not all serial murder investigations have been as successful — in fact, there have been numerous cases where prevailing social attitudes, police procedure, and the criminal justice system have worked to the detriment of Canadians. The final section of this book examines some of the worst instances of this. Though it is necessarily critical (and unapologetic), it has been written solely to prevent such issues from reoccurring. It is reassuring to note that many of them are already being addressed, at least to a greater extent, by both the Canadian public and its government. Hindsight certainly is 20/20, however, its lessons should not be ignored. By learning from our past mistakes, Canadians can and *should* prevent further unnecessary loss of life both at present and in the future.

OUTRAGE AND CONTROVERSY

In order for a murderer to become a serial killer, he must outwit the authorities on at least one occasion. This does not necessarily imply an error on behalf of the Canadian justice system. Still, throughout the last two centuries, there have been numerous incidences of blatant negligence resulting in otherwise preventable deaths. Nowhere is this clearer than the "devil may care" attitude shown to Canada's most vulnerable social groups: Native women and sex-trade workers. The gruesome crimes of **The Edmonton Serial Killer** and **Robert Pickton** in the last section are merely a starting point. In the next chapter, we examine four comparable cases spanning western Canada from Victoria to Niagara Falls.

Where Native Canadians and prostitutes have suffered chiefly from the indifference of authorities, the deaths of many of the "respectable" middle-class citizens in **Chapter 17** also reveal a high degree of systematic and/or procedural incompetence.

The final case in this section illustrates the worst example of Canadian judicial dysfunction, combining police negligence towards sex-trade workers with a series of inept parole board decisions. A sadistic rapist, **Gilbert Paul Jordan**, was repeatedly released from prison to commit more heinous crimes. Inevitably, he would make the transformation from sex offender to serial killer. Even after being charged for the slayings of seven Vancouver-area prostitutes and convicted on one count, Jordan was released in 2004, immediately violating parole. At the time of his reapprehension, he appeared well on his way to committing another murder.

CHAPTER 16

CANADA'S MOST DANGEROUS PROFESSION

In a nation dominated for the past three hundred years by middle-class Christian white men, it is unsurprising that two of the groups most neglected by the Canadian legal system are Native women and prostitutes. Unfortunately, as victims of serial killers, they are often one and the same. For decades, poor indigenous girls have fled the monotony of life on alcohol-ravaged reservations, only to fall into similar patterns of addiction that ruined their homes. Locals call them "Twinkies": naive young women lured by the bright lights and excitement of Western Canadian cities such as Vancouver, Edmonton, Calgary, Saskatoon, and Winnipeg. Of course, there is an ample supply of women from other races and cultures who, often through drug dependency, also fall into the dangerous lifestyle of prostitution. **The Hemlock Valley Murders**, for example, involved the slayings of three women of varying ethnicities. The same can be said of the other three cases we will study in this chapter: **The Calgary Prostitute Murders**, **The Prostitutes-in-the-Lake Killings**, and **Niagara's Prostitute Murders**.

The Hemlock Valley Murders (Unsolved)

3 Murders
Hemlock Valley, British Columbia

TRIPTYCH

In July 1995, just under a year after he was paroled on charges of rape, Ronald Richard McCauley (a "Low Track Slayer" suspect mentioned in the **Robert Pickton** case), pulled up outside Vancouver's infamous Astoria Hotel to let a streetwalker into his truck. Driving her out to Hemlock Valley, ostensibly on a car date, he ended the evening by brutally battering and raping her before shoving her from his vehicle. Unfortunately for McCauley, the prostitute would survive the attack to incriminate him. That September, he was arrested on charges of rape and attempted murder, and was convicted a year later. By the time he was in custody, however, the bodies of two sex workers had appeared in the Hemlock Valley, making McCauley a prime suspect.

The first to be found was thirty-year-old Tracy Olajide, a black mother of one and intravenous drug addict who dabbled in crack cocaine. At the time of her death, she was rumoured to have given up prostitution, though she was still heavily involved in narcotics. Tracy's nude body was discovered on August 12, 1995, fifteen kilometres north of Lougheed Highway 7 in Harrison Mills. Last spotted two days earlier near Vancouver's Waldorf Hotel on Franklin and Commercial, she had been dumped on a wooded trail beside the Morris Valley logging road.

A mere twenty-one days later, Tammy Lee Pipe, known on the street as "Starr," was found five kilometres south of Olajide's body on the road to a hang-glider launch area on Mount Woodside. Like Olajide, the twenty-four-year-old was stripped of her clothing. She was last seen alive on August 29 in Vancouver at the Cobalt Hotel on Main Street. An unusual brand of sex worker, Tammy sometimes supported her cocaine habit by performing nude interpretive dance routines, though she relied mainly on prostitution, plying her trade on Hastings, Victoria, and Franklin.

A third victim, Victoria Lynn Younker, thirty-five, was discovered in a state of semi-decomposition on October 21. As the condition of her nude body made it difficult to determine whether she had been killed before or after McCauley was in jail, he also became a suspect in her death. A prostitute and petty thief, she was known to walk the streets between Main and Victoria, disappearing on September 11, 1995. Victoria's corpse was discovered laying eight metres down an embankment off Sylvester Road, thirty-six kilometres north of Lougheed Highway 7 in Mission. A nearby logging spur road culminated in a dead end. In a strange twist, discarded pieces of her identification were retrieved from a Dumpster near the Vernon Rooms Hotel in Vancouver.

Though the police were certain that McCauley was their man, in 2001, DNA evidence cleared him of any involvement in the Hemlock Valley murders. The case remains unsolved to this day.

The Calgary Prostitute Murders (Unsolved)
5 Murders
Calgary, Alberta

LADIES OF THE NIGHT

Jennifer Janz, sixteen, was not one to be fooled easily. Having spent the better part of her life on the streets of Calgary, Alberta, she had developed a keen sense of who not to trust. Still, despite her experience, on July 12, 1991, she disappeared only to turn up on August 13 in a shallow grave in the city's Valley Ridge district off Highway 1. The condition of her body has been described as "battered," with death coming from internal injuries following a massive blow to the chest.

On August 30, seventeen-year-old Jennifer Joyes was reported missing. A shallow pit containing her body was found just a mile south of Janz's on October 6. Twenty-two-year-old former cocktail waitress Keely Pincott disappeared three months later, and was also found in the same area on March 11, 1992; her skeletal remains laid out in a similarly haphazard grave. The final two victims, Tracy Maunder and Rebecca Boutilier, twenty, disappeared in October 1992 and February 1993, respectively. Unlike the previous three, these women were found in fields to the east of the city. Both Maunder and Boutilier had succumbed to multiple stab wounds.

Then, as soon as the killings had started, they stopped. Police suspect the killer may have been jailed for another crime. One common thread linking the five victims is that just before their disappearances, each had made an earnest attempt to leave behind the lifestyle; Janz, for instance, had attended a Bible school in Texas to help find the necessary resolve, while Pincott had begun to look into the possibilities of a life as a makeup artist. With this in mind, it is possible that the Calgary Prostitute Killer may in fact be a jealous pimp or customer, whose inability to relinquish control over the girls led him to murder.

Aside from the five victims commonly attributed to the suspected serial killer, there are an additional six unsolved female murders in the city from July 1991 to March 11, 1993.

The Prostitutes-in-the-Lake Killings (Unsolved)
3–5 Murders
Toronto, Ontario

LADIES IN THE LAKE

Between the summer of 1994 and fall 1997, three Toronto sex workers were sexually assaulted with a foreign object, strangled unconscious, and dumped in Lake Ontario to drown. The first to be discovered was Julianne Middleton, a twenty-three-year-old Parkdale prostitute and known crack cocaine addict. Naked save for a bra, the African-Canadian's lacerated body was found in the Sunnyside pool near Lakeshore Boulevard on July 7, 1994. By October 28, a second victim, sex worker Virginia Coote, was found under similar circumstances less than one hundred metres away, behind the Palais Royal. A blond Caucasian, the thirty-three-year-old had been stripped nude below the waist. Three years passed before, on October 29, 1997, the corpse of recovering crack addict Darlene McNeil joined the list of female prostitutes to be found strangled and drowned in Lake Ontario. All three women's clothes had been found neatly folded nearby with their shoes placed on top. For thirteen years, the murders sat in the cold case department of the Toronto Metropolitan Police. Then, on October 28, 2010, all of that was to change.

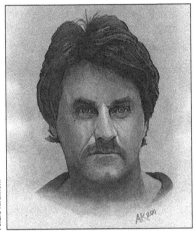

Andre Kirchhoff.

Suspect: Peter Dale MacDonald

THE RED DIRT RAPIST

Peter Dale MacDonald first appeared as a suspect in the Toronto Stranglings in 1994, allegedly due to his reputation for violence. The fourth of five children, MacDonald had grown up in the tiny Prince Edward Island community of Carleton Siding, where his parents ran a general store and potato warehouse. Known to be a hard-working and decent lot, the MacDonald siblings would grow to have careers and families of their own. All except for Peter. A habitual troublemaker, those close to him maintain that his personality changed for the worse after he struck his head falling from a moving pickup truck around the age of eleven.

Tremendously strong, and aggressive while under the influence of alcohol, the teenaged MacDonald soon developed a reputation as somebody who was not to be messed with. Despite his high IQ, MacDonald was bored by school, dropping out in grade nine to spend his time hanging around the streets of nearby Summerside and Borden. He fell into a criminal lifestyle, his offences increasing in violence each time he returned to jail.

Following his eighteenth birthday, he landed a two year sentence at Dorchester Penitentiary in New Brunswick. Upon his release, MacDonald briefly tried his hand in the auctioneering business, but was fired and relocated to Charlottetown where he began to dabble in drugs and prostitution. Two more stints in jail did little to alter his behaviour — MacDonald repeatedly attempted to escape, once by tunnelling through the wall under his bunk. Eventually he drifted southwest to Hamilton where he netted an eleven-year sentence on multiple counts of robbery. During the time of the Toronto prostitute stranglings, MacDonald had been staying at a halfway house on Keele and Dundas, just north of Parkdale, where the victims worked as streetwalkers. It would be sixteen years before the Metropolitan Police would lay charges against him for the murders of Middleton, Coote, and McNeil.

WINDSOR

The case that inevitably brought Peter Dale MacDonald to justice would do so in ways nobody would ever have imagined. While living in Windsor some years later, MacDonald became the prime suspect in the murder of a forty-year-old woman. Michelle Charette was reported missing by her father on July 31, 2000, after he had twice visited her apartment to find the door locked, windows open, and mail pouring out of the letterbox. Her semi-clad skeletal remains were discovered by employees of the Ford Motor Company that August on an abandoned property overgrown with weeds. MacDonald was charged with her murder on July 4, 2001, following a tipoff by an anonymous informant. After a preliminary trial in 2002, the Crown suddenly dropped the charges against him. Police continued to trace MacDonald, clandestinely retrieving DNA samples to test against evidence found on Charette's body. Though the results were inconclusive, they did link MacDonald to the April 2000 Toronto slaying of James Campbell. The retired sixty-three-year-old meat plant worker had been murdered by an unknown assailant in his Parkdale apartment. Investigators learned that MacDonald had met Campbell in a local park and gone back to the other man's residence where he strangled him to death during consensual sex. Convicted of second-degree murder in 2004, MacDonald was sentenced to life imprisonment in Kingston Penitentiary without the possibility of parole for thirteen years.

On Thursday October 28, 2010, Toronto police announced they had charged fifty-two-year-old Peter Dale MacDonald in the murders of Julianne Middleton, Virginia Coote, and Darlene McNeil. At the time of this writing, they have not revealed what led them back to MacDonald. Windsor authorities have also charged him for a second time with the 2000 slaying of Michelle Charette.

Niagara's Prostitute Murders (Unsolved)

2+ Murders
Niagara Falls, Ontario

BODIES

Once upon a time, the vanishing women of Vancouver's lower east side were Canada's darkest secret. With the subsequent publicity following the Pickton trial, the legacy of prostitute murder in the Niagara-Hamilton area may now be the strongest contender. Pregnant sex worker Dawn Stewart, a mother of two boys, was the first to disappear from her Niagara home in September 1995. Her fate remained a secret until March 31, 1996, when her skeletal remains, along with those of her six-month-old fetus, were found in the woods near Centre Street in Pelham.

On May 8, 1999, two cyclists along Victoria Avenue spied an almost nude corpse lying in a ditch, just south of Vineland close to Eighth Avenue. The victim was soon identified as twenty-six-year-old Nadine Gurczenski. Known by the stage name "Sammy" at Marilyn's, the Mississauga strip club where she was employed as a dancer, Nadine was a mother of two who had moved from her birth country of Jamaica in 1992 to marry and live in Toronto. When her marriage dissolved she had relocated to St. Catharines. Along with sustaining numerous internal injuries, her neck had been broken.

Niagara Falls' Diane Christina Dimitri, alternately listed as twenty-eight and thirty-two years of age, was the next prostitute to be found discarded in a ditch on August 9, 2003. Partially decomposed, she had been dumped at the corner of Darby and Grassy Brook, on the outskirts of Niagara Falls. The mother of four had been a happily married woman until one morning in 2001, when she woke to find her husband and soulmate Angelo dead of a heart attack. This caused her to lapse into a crippling depression.

In a case that may be unrelated to the prostitute murders, on July 9, 2004, the body of local Margaret Jeannette Jugaru was found kneeling in the parking lot of a Niagara Falls elementary school on Culp Street.

The sex worker slayings resumed in 2005, with the disappearance of Cassey Cichocki, a Port Colborne resident, reported missing by her family on December 10. By Thursday, January 19, 2006, Niagara police announced the establishment of a special twelve-man task force to look for patterns in the murders. The team would work side by side with a crime analyst from the Ontario Provincial Police's Behavioural Science Unit, who, if necessary, would formulate both offender and geographic profiles.

Five days later, the discovery of the twenty-two-year-old Cichocki's body near the Niagara gorge gave the task force their first new piece of information. In the vicinity of Church's Lane and Whirlpool Road, a Niagara resident was strolling along a hydro right-of-way and spotted the body wrapped in a blanket and secreted in some bushes. The prevalence of trash strewn across the area left no doubt as to what the killer thought of his victim. An exotic dancer, Cassey had been found just a few blocks away from where she worked. Autopsy results revealed she too had died from physical trauma.

HAMMER/FALLS

Niagara Falls is no anomaly when it comes to south-western Ontario prostitute murder. From November 2002 to 2003, Hamilton's Project Advocate examined a series of murders and attacks on local sex workers but uncovered no significant connections. Thirty-nine-year-old Susan Gourley vanished in November 2001 followed by the September 2002 disappearance of fifteen-year-old Felicia Floriani. Kimlyn Judy Tolgyes, nineteen, was found naked and bludgeoned to death in Burlington's Kerncliff Park in August 2002. In 2007, representatives from Project Advocate met with the Niagara task force to compare notes. Earlier in the year on January 7, a Hamilton exotic dancer and mother, thirty-five-year-old Cynthia Watson, was discovered in a forested area off Copetown's Powerline Road. An employee at a Brantford Strip Club, her autopsy revealed no cause of death.

Kay Feely.

Suspect: Michael Durant

PRIME SUSPECT

To most people, there was nothing unusual about Michael Durant. A thirty-three-year-old labourer, in June 1999 he had married a woman named Dana, and moved into a house owned by her parents on Toby Crescent, where together they had a daughter. By the summer of 2004, however, their marriage was on the rocks, and the couple separated. Custody of the child was awarded to Dana, with Durant given visitation rights and ordered to pay $100 per month. He moved into a deserted shop at 4670 Queen Street in Niagara Falls, continuing with his more or less unremarkable existence.

But on January 30, 2006, Niagara police suddenly arrested Durant and charged him with the second-degree murder of Cassey Cichocki. Rumours began to circulate as task force members swarmed Durant's home along with a boarded-up Canadian Tire several blocks away on Victoria Avenue. The building had traditionally been a magnet for the local homeless population, converting briefly to an antique shop, before being overrun again following a 2005 relocation.

More charges followed on June 5 in the first-degree slaying of Christine Dimitri. Simultaneously, Cichocki's murder was upgraded to first degree. As of this writing, Durant's case still lies in the hands of the courts.

CHAPTER 17

NEGLIGENCE: WHEN THE SYSTEM FAILS

Serial murder cases are undeniably the toughest to crack, violating all known rules of homicide investigation. Normally, detectives begin searching for suspects among the victim's friends, family, and lovers, as they are more likely to possess the necessary motive. Aside from the **Hedonist-Comfort Killer** (Chapter 8), however, the vast majority of serial homicides target strangers, leaving a pool of suspects that is infinitely larger and a case which is increasingly complex. That said, the investigation into "The Schoolgirl Murders" perpetrated by **Paul Bernardo** (Chapter 13) and **Karla Homolka** remains one of the most shocking incidence of widespread police incompetence in Ontario's history. Fixated on the notion that his suspect drove a cream-coloured Camaro, Inspector Vince Bevan and the Green Ribbon Task Force sunk millions of dollars into tracking vehicles, discovering later that Bernardo had, in fact, used a Nissan 240 SX. When the Metro Toronto rape squad handed Niagara police the killer on a silver platter, they somehow managed to bungle searching his home. By the time they were finished scouring the property, six hours of incriminating video tape remained undiscovered behind a lighting fixture in the upstairs bathroom — hardly the final resting place of the Holy Grail. Bevan's worst mistake, however, was his premature judgment of Karla Homolka as just another victim, an error that would lead to the most controversial plea bargain in Canadian history.

Andre Kirchhoff.

Karla Homolka
3 Murders
St. Catharines, Ontario

"Enough has been said about Kristen and Leslie ... if I do ever decide to 'tell my story' ... it will only be a story about the abuse I endured."

Note to the reader: In order to grasp the full scope of the Homolka controversy it is necessary to first review the case of Paul Bernardo (Chapter 13: Offender Profiling), which details the Mahaffy/French killings, and the Scarborough rapes.

A WOMAN SCORNED

"Do you know why we're here?

Behind the raccoon ringlets left by the flashlight beating, Karla Homolka's eyes shone with fear. This had to be it — they knew everything. When Niagara police contacted her, requesting an interview in February 1993, she assumed it was related to the abuse she had suffered at the hands of her estranged husband, Paul Bernardo. Yet as four officers identifying themselves as representatives of Metro Sexual Assault Squad and Project Green Ribbon stepped into her aunt and uncle's apartment, she realized at once their true intentions. .

"Have you ever cut anyone's hair?"

How could Karla forget shearing Kristen French's brown locks hours before dumping her down that leafy embankment? Though she did her best to play it cool, the detectives kept turning up the heat. Now they were on to the Scarborough rapes. What kind of sex life did she and Paul have? Was he into anal sex? Had she ever been to Grace Lutheran Church? For hours, Karla maintained her poker face amidst intense police scrutiny. The moment they left the apartment, however, she broke down and tearfully confessed to her Aunt Patti what she and Paul had really done. They had abducted, raped, and murdered Leslie Mahaffy and Kristen French.

First thing the next morning, Karla Homolka contacted criminal counsellor George Walker. Bit by bit, she revealed the gruesome details of the schoolgirl murders, while Walker struggled to remain professional against feelings of intense revulsion. When she had finished, he contacted Ray Houlahan, the local Crown attorney, to negotiate a plea bargain. Owing to the high-profile nature of the case, Houlahan referred him to the foremost judicial authority in Ontario, the ministry of the attorney general. Walker stated that his client was willing to plead guilty and file divorce proceedings against her husband so that she could testify against him in court. In return, Karla expected total immunity from prosecution. The infamous "Deal with the Devil," outlined below in Walker's "Plea Resolution Authorization," rejected this demand, instead reducing Karla's charges from sexual assault and second-degree murder to manslaughter:

I, Karla Leanne Homolka, of 61 Dundonald St., St. Catharines, Ontario, do hereby authorize and instruct my counsel, George F. Walker, Q.C., to continue towards finalizing my plea bargain arrangement with Murray Segal, Esq., of the Ministry of the Attorney General of Ontario.

I understand that I must co-operate fully with the investigating officers, be truthful and frank in providing answers to all questions asked, and to provide full details of my knowledge and/or participation in the Mahaffy and French investigations and any others. That I will provide induced statements to the investigators at a time and place convenient to the officers.

I understand that I will be called upon to testify against my husband at his trials and I hereby agree to do so. That this agreement is null and void if I commit perjury. I understand that I will enter a plea of guilty to

1 count manslaughter, vis-a-vis, Mahaffy, and 1 count manslaughter, vis-a-vis, French and at least one other charge in relation to each victim.

That I am to receive sentences totaling 10 years in custody.

That the Crown will not seek an increase in the period before parole eligibility.

That the Crown will write to the Parole Board, will include a record of my trial proceedings, will indicate my co-operation, remorse etc. and will indicate on behalf of the police and the Crown that they will leave the matter of when releases and/or parole should commence, up to the Parole Board without further comment.

That my counsel and the Crown will go before the Justice before hand to ensure the terms of the agreement are acceptable.

That when charged I will go before a Provincial Court Judge, waive my preliminary hearings, be brought before a Justice, enter my pleas of "guilty" and be released pending sentencing.

That the Attorney General's office will indicate to the Federal Correctional Authorities and Provincial Authorities that they are not opposed to the offender being transferred from a Federal to a Provincial Institution to serve my sentence.

That I have had all my rights explained to me by my counsel and have been advised that I am free to contact another lawyer for another opinion but have advised my counsel that I fully understand and wish to proceed with the agreement forthwith.

DATED at the City of Niagara Falls this 26th day of February, 1993.
Witnessed by Karel and Dorothy Homolka.
Notarized by Geoffrey Hadfield.
Signed, *Karla Leanne Bernardo*[2]

After Paul had been taken into custody, Homolka admitted herself to Northwestern Hospital's psychiatric ward where she spent the better part of two months in a Valium-induced haze. The realization that she would soon be imprisoned for a significant portion of her life was certainly difficult to deal with, but it was not chief among her concerns. Instead, it was that one little secret she held on to, that deadly morsel of information that could turn her family against her along with the rest of the world. It was during this internment at the hospital that she finally summoned up the courage to face the inevitable. Putting pen to paper, she began to write:

> Dear Mom, Dad and Lori,
> This is the hardest letter I've ever had to write and you'll probably all hate me once you've read it. I've kept this inside myself for so long and I just can't lie to you anymore. Both Paul and I are responsible for Tammy's death. Paul was "in love" with her and wanted to have sex with her. He wanted me to help him. He wanted me to get sleeping pills from work to drug her with. He threatened me physically and emotionally abused me when I refused. No words I can say can make you understand what he put me through. So stupidly I agreed to do as he said. But something — maybe the combination of drugs and the food she ate that night — caused her to vomit. I tried so hard to save her. I am so sorry. But no words I can say can bring her back. I have thought many times of killing myself, but I couldn't put you through the pain of losing another daughter and sister again. I don't blame you all if you hate me. I hate myself.
>   I live with the pain of knowing I unintentionally killed my baby sister every day. I think that's the real reason I put up with Paul's abusive behavior — I felt I deserved it for allowing him to drug and rape my beautiful baby sister. I loved her so much and never wanted to do anything to hurt my "Tamsikins," please

believe me. I would gladly give my life for hers. Nothing I can do or say can bring her back. I don't expect you to ever forgive me, for I will never forgive myself.
Karla[3]

MERRY CHRISTMAS, PAUL

December 23, 1990. Tammy Homolka felt like such a grown-up. A few years earlier, the twinkling Christmas lights and tinsel adorning the basement rec-room would have filled her with holiday magic. Tonight, however, as she sat up sipping daiquiris with her big sis and Karla's super-cool boyfriend, Paul, she felt the gateway to the adult world swing wide open to welcome her. Dorothy Homolka had instructed her to go to bed, but Tammy had insisted on staying up to watch the movie Paul and Karla had rented: *Lisa and the Devil*. Outside a snowstorm was raging, but the warm crackle of the fireplace made her feel safe and secure. Lulled by the flicker of flame and television, her eyelids began to weigh heavier and heavier.

It wasn't long before Tammy had passed out in the big comfy chair. Karla crept over to the sleeping beauty and prodded her, but she didn't stir. The Halcion pills they had crushed into her drinks had done the trick. The couple exchanged knowing glances before lifting her from the chair to lay out like a present by the Christmas tree. Paul eagerly unwrapped his gift and set up the video camera while Karla left to get the Halothane (an anesthetic). When she returned, she poured the substance onto a rag and held it over her sister's face to keep her under. Paul switched the video camera on and began to film himself applying lubricant to Tammy's vagina. Then he entered her.

"Hurry up!" Karla hissed nervously.

"Shut up," he replied. He had been waiting a long time for this moment and wasn't about to let Karla spoil the best Christmas present ever. As he began to near climax, Karla begged him to put a condom on, but he ignored her.

"Suck on her breasts," he ordered. By now, Tammy's sweater was bunched up around her neck. Karla complied, as Bernardo withdrew his penis to change the camera angle. Now he commanded that she go down on her sister.

"Put out your tongue. Probe. You're not doing it."

413

"I am so," Karla whined.

"Do it. Lick her cunt ... lick her clean," Paul continued. "Put your fingers inside."

Karla refused at first, but as always, broke down when he repeatedly insisted. Soon she had jammed all three fingers of her hand into Tammy's vagina. Whether it was the girl's broken hymen or the beginnings of her period, Karla's fingers were wet with blood.

"Taste it."

"I did."

"... inside and taste it. Quick."

"No."

Seconds later, she was licking blood from her fingers.

"Taste good? Not bad, eh?" Paul asked.

"Fucking disgusting," Karla rubbed her lips on the sleeve of her white turtleneck.

As Karla went to check on Tammy's breathing, Paul slid his penis into the unconscious girl's rectum and began to sodomize her. Suddenly, he withdrew. Something was wrong. Tammy's body lurched, showering vomit over the floor. Panicked, Karla turned her sister upside down the same way they did with the animals at the clinic. Paul tried desperately to clear her throat. No luck. With their minds near the breaking point, they dragged Tammy's body across the carpet into Karla's room, hurriedly dressing it to cover up the sexual assault. As Paul attempted mouth-to-mouth resuscitation, Karla dialled 911, then frantically scrambled around the house, pouring the Halothane into the sink and hiding the empty bottle and Halcion pills in the laundry room. The rest of the Homolka family awoke to the sounds of emergency vehicles pulling up outside their home. Tammy was whisked immediately to hospital, as a stunned Karel and Dorothy Homolka followed in bleary-eyed pursuit

Constable David Weeks of the Niagara police was suspicious. The first thing he noticed was the strange red burn mark around Tammy's mouth. According to Paul and Karla, the three had been watching a movie downstairs when Tammy began to complain that she was having trouble seeing. Later they awoke side by side to the sound of her vomiting. Paul had tried to revive her with mouth-to-mouth, but had ultimately failed. Though still a rookie, Constable Weeks knew bullshit when he heard it. This story didn't account for why Tammy had been found in Karla's bedroom, let alone the markings. He wondered if the fifteen-year-old had overdosed while freebasing crack with the older couple, scorching herself in the process.

With the elder Homolkas detained at the hospital, Weeks decided to question Paul and Karla in the basement rec room. When he raised the issue of the suspicious red mark, Bernardo hypothesized that Tammy must have received rug burns from being dragged across the carpet. Seconds later, Weeks answered a call from St. Catharines Hospital. The news was terrible — Tammy had officially been pronounced dead. Distraught, Lori Homolka raced upstairs to telephone her ex-boyfriend, Mike. Concerned and somewhat suspicious, Weeks followed after her. Upon returning to the basement, he found Karla casually loading Tammy's vomit-soaked bedsheets into the washing machine, and stopped her immediately. Despite his heightened suspicions, separate questioning of Bernardo and Homolka back at the station revealed no inconsistencies in their story. The decision was made not to pursue the matter any farther.

On December 27, 1990, mourners gathered at Tammy Homolka's funeral to pay their respects to the fifteen-year-old star athlete who had died so suddenly and unexpectedly. Gazing down into her open casket, they must have silently wondered about the strange raspberry-coloured mark on her face. Except Paul Bernardo and Karla Homolka, of course.

TRIAL BY DARKNESS

Karla Homolka's trial began on June 28, 1993, in a tiny St. Catharines Courtroom built to seat 160. Following three days of controversial discussion, the proceedings were ruled subject to a publication ban. Bernardo would be going to trial after Karla, and Crown prosecutors reasoned that dissemination of any details revealed in Homolka's case would jeopardize his right to a fair hearing. Not only did most Canadian media outlets oppose the ban as a violation of the principles of the justice system, even Bernardo's own legal team denounced it, claiming it portrayed Karla as a victim rather than an accomplice.

Throughout the proceedings, the twenty-four-year-old Homolka sat motionless behind a screen of bulletproof glass, showing emotion only when Deborah Mahaffy and Donna French read victim impact statements to the court. Many in attendance concluded that she was heavily sedated. During the trial, the few reporters allowed inside were shocked to learn not only of her roles in the abduction and disposal of Leslie Mahaffy and Kristen French, but also that while drugging her sister Tammy with sleeping pills and Halothane, she had accidentally killed her in the process. Pleading guilty on two counts of manslaughter in the deaths of Mahaffy and French, on July 6, Karla Homolka was sentenced to two concurrent twelve-year sentences in Kingston Penitentiary, with the possibility of parole in four. Before sentencing, Crown prosecutor Murray Segal addressed the perceived leniency of the charges by explaining that Homolka was trying to redress some of the pain she had caused by pleading guilty, and had been coerced into the murders by her physically and emotionally abusive husband. Even Judge Kovacs felt the need to expand on this point, claiming that Homolka was a passive person suffering from battered-wife syndrome, and that considering her lack of prior criminal record was unlikely to reoffend. Of course, neither had been privy to the contents of the couple's sex tapes. In fact, there was only one man in the courtroom who knew the truth about the depth of Karla Homolka's depravity, and for now, Bernardo's lawyer Ken Murray wasn't talking.

THE RAPE TAPES

On May 6, 1993, Ken Murray had arrived at 57 Bayview Drive, Port Dalhousie, with specific instructions from his client — behind the light fixture in the upstairs bathroom lay the infamous videotapes that, if discovered by police, would damn him in a court of law. Under the auspices of clearing out the property, Murray entered the home and found exactly what he was looking for. Not long after, he rented the necessary equipment to transfer the contents of the 8mm tapes onto VHS. What he would eventually witness on that six and a half hours of footage would convince him beyond a shadow of a doubt that Karla Homolka was every bit as complicit in the Schoolgirl Murders as his client. Unfortunately, the tapes also offered irrefutable proof that Bernardo had repeatedly raped and tortured both Leslie Mahaffy and Kristen French. This put Murray in a difficult position, legally and morally. He had sworn two seemingly conflicting oaths: to uphold the law, and, to the best of his ability, defend Paul Bernardo. Eventually, he sought the advice of The Law Society of Upper Canada, a confidential three-member committee devoted to ensuring proper legal conduct and standards. They advised Murray to turn the tapes over to the court, an approach that would necessitate him testifying against his client. Legally, this meant he would no longer be permitted to defend Paul Bernardo. With police repeatedly questioning him as to whether he possessed any additional evidence, Murray began to suspect he was under surveillance. There was no denying it — this case had turned into a full-fledged nightmare.

At a crowded St. Catharines courtroom in May 1994, Paul Bernardo pleaded not guilty on nine charges, including two counts of murder and the Scarborough rapes. That same day, an additional charge of manslaughter was added for his part in the death of Tammy Homolka. Amazingly, though Karla had acquired and applied the chemicals that resulted in her sister's death, she had escaped any responsibility for her crimes by way of the infamous plea bargain.

Three months later, Ken Murray, complaining of an overwhelming workload, stepped down as Bernardo's attorney, unburdening the case on veteran defence lawyer John Rosen. A month later, he finally turned over the missing six videotapes to the police. Now, with almost seven hours of graphic footage compared to the paltry two minutes screened at her trial, the world took a first shocking look at the real Karla Homolka. Gone was the portrait of a psychologically shattered woman portrayed by Vince Bevan and his supporters. Instead, the extent and enthusiasm with which Karla carried out her sexual assaults hinted at a darker creature lurking behind the falling mass of blond hair: one that had just pulled off the greatest swindle in Canadian judicial history.

THE PAUL/KARLA WHODUNNIT?

On May 3, 1995, twelve jury members were drawn from a pool of one thousand to assess the most psychologically disturbing trial in Canadian history. Realizing that it was useless to fight the rape charges, Bernardo's new defence team opted for a strategy that would implicate Karla Homolka as the murderer. Rosen reasoned that if he could create doubt that Bernardo had killed the two girls, it might spare his client a lifetime behind bars. Besides the horrific screening of the videotapes, the most dramatic moment of the Bernardo trial came on June 25, when Karla Homolka took the stand to testify against him. Throughout nine days of questioning, she remained expressionless, her voice monotone as she clarified her torturous role in the video footage: "Well, I'm performing cunnilingus on her, and then I'm inserting a wine bottle into her anus." It wasn't until defence attorney John Rosen addressed the issue of her sister Tammy that Karla showed even a hint of emotion; still, she was far from breaking down.

During cross-examination, Rosen reconstructed a highly believable narrative of the Schoolgirl Murders in which Karla, not her husband, was the sole killer of Leslie Mahaffy and Kristen French. The strength of his argument was owing to forensic evidence that seemed to contradict her accounts of the slaying as depicted in **Chapter 13**. In the case of Leslie Mahaffy, Karla testified that she and Bernardo had agreed Leslie would have to be murdered because the Homolka family was coming for dinner. While Karla comforted Leslie, feeding her sleeping pills to ensure she would be unconscious at the time of her death, Paul had gone to the basement to fetch the black electrical cord with which to strangle her. Yet, as Rosen pointed out, the ligature is clearly shown lying around the master bedroom on the video footage. If Karla had lied about Paul's foray into the basement, then why? Even more suspicious was that a post-mortem examination of Leslie's body revealed no signs that she had been beaten or strangled. What they did find were two internal bruises on either side of her spine, marks which Rosen concluded were the size of Karla's knees. Rather than Bernardo strangling Leslie to death with the black electrical cord, Rosen theorized that his client had wanted to "let her go," as he had done many times in the past. Fearing that their captive had seen too much, Karla decided to prevent her release by kneeling on Leslie's back and forcing the unconscious girl's face into a pillow, suffocating her to death. She had then aided Bernardo in dismembering and disposing of the body in Lake Gibson.

Nor, according to Rosen, was his client responsible for the French murder. On the final day of Kristen's young life, Bernardo handed Karla a rubber mallet and advised her to guard their prisoner while he left to pick up Swiss Chalet. During his absence, Kristen asked Karla if she could use the bathroom, attempting to escape when the bonds had been removed from her legs. Frantic, Karla responded by battering her to death with the rubber hammer. This accounted for traces of blood Kristen had aspirated into her lungs before she died, as well as internal hemorrhaging above both ears, which Rosen claimed was too deep to be caused by fists. Ultimately, Kristen French had died from a combination of blunt-force trauma and choking on an intricate restraint system fastened around her body and neck.

Despite Rosen's brilliant performance in court, the jury failed to accept his theories and on September 1, Paul Kenneth Bernardo was found guilty on all nine counts and sentenced to life imprisonment. He is currently incarcerated in a specially built 4'x8' cell in Kingston Penitentiary, where he is kept in total isolation.

Immediately after testifying, Karla was returned to her cell in the segregation unit of Kingston's Penitentiary for Women where she prepared to wait out her late twenties and early thirties behind bars.

FREE AS A BIRD

After twelve years of incarceration, on July 24, 2005, Karla Homolka was smuggled in secret from Sainte-Anne-des-Plaines prison to the downtown office of the SRC, while camped-out reporters scattered in pursuit of decoy vehicles. There, at the French-language arm of the CBC, Homolka and her attorney Sylvie Bordelais granted an interview to Joyce Napier, in hopes of putting the Canadian public at ease regarding her release. Speaking in French, Homolka acknowledged that she wished to restart her life in Quebec, claiming that she had a support system there and that the news media was less sensational. When asked if she had repaid her debt to society, Homolka answered that legally she had, but still owed something socially and emotionally. She claimed to experience intense remorse, frequently crying and feeling as though she did not deserve to be happy. Though refusing to talk about her friends in prison, Homolka was more than willing to elaborate on the death threats she had received while locked in penitentiaries in Kingston and later Saskatchewan. She confirmed that despite her complicity in the death of her younger sister Tammy, she maintained a good relationship with her family, who forgave her for what she did.

Following the interview, Homolka vanished. Unbeknownst to the Canadian public, in August 2005, she had moved into a low-income apartment in the Montreal suburb of Longueuil and found work as a trainee clerk at a Rona hardware store. For a time she managed to avert media attention, dyeing her hair and hiding behind thick sunglasses. Shortly after, however, her boss, thirty-nine-year-old Richer Lapointe was charged with attacking his ex-wife. In light of his crimes, police declared Lapointe an unsuitable employer for Karla and she quit the next day. Unfortunately for her, this newfound attention had blown her cover. Thrust into the media spotlight, Richer Lapointe boasted of secretly taping Karla confessing to breaching her parole conditions. The flame-scarred businessman alleged she had visited her former prison lover, convicted murderer Jean-Paul Gerbet, bringing him cooked meals. Later, a spokesperson for the Laval prison where Gerbet is incarcerated responded that it was technically impossible to bring food into the prison. Lapointe also claimed that Karla had babysat his nine and fourteen-year-old sons without informing him she was prohibited by court order from associating with children under the age of sixteen.

Unfortunately, these allegations seem to have been nothing more than a lonely, pathetic man's bid for attention. A statement from the Quebec justice department on November 3 clarified that Homolka had not breached her release conditions, and therefore no charges would follow.

Twenty-seven days later, Quebec superior court judge James Brunton overturned fourteen conditions on Homolka's release, citing a lack of evidence to justify them. The depraved woman who had participated in the deaths and rapes of multiple underage girls was now free to enjoy their company.

On February 2, 2007, rumours began to surface that the thirty-six-year-old had given birth to a baby boy in a Montreal hospital. The Canadian public was still struggling to digest this unsavoury development when French-language television station TVA announced that Homolka and her new husband, Thierry Bordelais, had uprooted to an unspecified island in the Lesser Antilles in hopes of providing a normal existence for their son.

Tensions flared again when in the spring of 2010, Karla Homolka became eligible for a full pardon, spurring frustrated Prime Minister Stephen Harper to enact immediate reforms to the criminal justice system.

THE TRUTH ABOUT KARLA

But how dangerous is Karla Homolka? Given her past crimes against the young, should she be entrusted to raise a child of her own? The true nature of her character, labelled by some psychiatrists as a "diagnostic mystery," has been the most pervading enigma of the Schoolgirl Murders.

Born by Caesarian section on May 4, 1970, to taciturn Czech immigrant Karel Homolka and his attractive Canadian wife, Dorothy, Karla Leanne Homolka was the first of three beautiful blond girls in a household that would come to be dominated by women. A dealer of kitsch trinkets in nearby Niagara Falls, in 1975 Karel moved his family into a trailer park at 241 St. Paul Street West in St. Catharines. Karla began kindergarten at Westdale Public School that September, where she was immediately recognized as a bright, hard-working, and popular student. When Karel Homolka decided to start selling lighting fixtures instead of glittery junk, the family's profits soared, allowing them to move into a townhouse at 64 Foster Street. The trade-off was that he spent more and more time on the road, leaving Karla without a strong male presence in her life. She was also extremely asthmatic, hospitalized on at least twelve occasions from 1976 to 1978. It is interesting to note that these attacks would often be brought on by changes in Karla's routine, such as beginning or ending school, her father's comings and goings, or the excitement of holidays such as Christmas or birthdays. Under the guidance of her fastidious mother, she became obsessed with eliminating dust and dirt from her home, developing a meticulousness and predilection for chemicals that would serve her well in the future.

By 1978, the family relocated again to a larger semi-detached home at 61 Dundonald Street across from Victoria Lawn Cemetery. With four storeys, and an inground swimming pool, the Homolkas' star seemed to be rising. Though Karla switched schools frequently, she continued to display high competence in English and the arts, but was forced to work a little harder at math and science. Completing grade eight with an 83.9

percent average, she was subsequently tested as having a 131 IQ. By now her asthma had all but disappeared.

The first signs that Karla Homolka was anything but a keen and glowing addition to the status quo came when she began attending Sir Winston Churchill Secondary School. Faced for the first time with a population of pretty blond princesses to compete with, her character began to take on darker overtones. She started dyeing her hair compulsively, dressing in black, and applying dark mascara. Her reading habits focused increasingly on thrillers and occult books such as *Michelle Remembers* and *Brainchild*, and she began to conduct candlelit seances, the air perfumed by a blanket of burning incense. One of Karla's favourite hobbies was to descend into "The Screaming Tunnel," a five-metre-high train underpass on the outskirts of St. Catharines. Local legend had it that a girl had burned to death in the tunnel, and that by lighting a match inside you could hear her eternal screams of agony. Karla swore this had happened to her on every occasion. She also began to self mutilate, carving strange symbols into her arms and filling them in with makeup. Frequently, she threatened suicide. Casual acquaintance Lyn Cretney was more than a little shocked when Karla wrote "Remember: Suicide kicks and fasting is awesome. Bones rule! Death rules. Death kicks. I love death. Kill the fucking world!" in her yearbook.

Along with high school friends Debbie Purdy and Kathy Wilson, Karla formed the Exclusive Diamond Club, a three-person sisterhood devoted to marrying older, attractive men, getting a diamond ring, and settling down to a life of domestic luxury. When, at the age of seventeen, she met boyishly handsome yuppie Paul Bernardo at a Howard Johnson, she became the first member of the EDC to fulfill their collective dream. The boost to her fragile ego must have been so significant, that she clung to the tenets of the EDC, even as her dream slowly descended into the realm of nightmare.

DIAGNOSES

The first psychological assessment of Karla Homolka, ultimately exonerating her in the Mahaffy/French killings, was conducted by esteemed FBI profiler Roy Hazelwood. With Paul Bernardo already labelled a classic sexual sadist, Hazelwood found Homolka's psychological condition in keeping with a "compliant victim of a sexual sadist," a phenomenon he had once explored in an academic article co-authored with Janet Warren and California forensic psychiatrist Park Dietz. The basis for the article was Hazelwood's interviews with seven women who had participated in their partner's sexually sadistic crimes. Three such women had been wed to their partner, their marriages varying from two to thirteen years in duration, while the remaining four had dated them exclusively from a period of three to eighteen months. In all seven cases, the women had been subject to physical, sexual, and psychological abuse; though mistreatment was nothing new for them. Growing up, four had been abused sexually, two physically, and six psychologically, though only one claimed not to be "sexually naive," and none had any prior experience with sadomasochist practices. Another common thread was that despite hailing from middle- and upper-middle-class backgrounds, they all had notably low self-esteem. They had aided their partners in rape and murder, but only while suffering from post-traumatic stress disorder (PTSD), which negated their ability to break psychologically free from masculine coercion. Of the sixteen mental health professionals who have examined Karla Homolka over the years, the majority have found themselves in agreement with Hazelwood's diagnosis.

When examining the following chart: Karla Homolka vs. Hazelwood's Compliant Victims, it is easy to note the many similarities between Homolka's treatment at the hands of Paul Bernardo and the seven women in the study. The main departures lie in Karla's upbringing — while all the women had been subjected to some form of childhood abuse, Karla seems to have enjoyed a rather prosperous and carefree development. More to the point, as the author Stephen Williams explains in his twin exposés *Invisible Darkness* and *Karla*, there are several key differences distinguishing her from the traditional battered-wife PTSD sufferer. Rather than being subject to her boyfriend's unrelenting tyranny, Karla still lived with her parents during the drugging, rape, and manslaughter of her sister Tammy. Bernardo's workload was so substantial during this period that the only time the couple saw each other was on weekends. Nor was Karla isolated from outside influences. Even as late as the Kristen French murder, she held down a regular nine-to-five job, mingling happily with her co-workers at the veterinary clinic.

TABLE 6: KARLA HOMOLKA VS. HAZELWOOD'S COMPLIANT VICTIMS[4]

	KARLA HOMOLKA	7-WOMAN SAMPLE	MATCH?
Childhood			
Physically abused	No	2/7	N/A
Psychologically abused	No	6/7	No
Sexually abused	No	4/7	No
Sexually naive	Arguable**	6/7	N/A
Low self-esteem	Yes	Yes	Yes
Background	Middle class	All middle class	Yes
Professionally successful	Yes	6/7	Yes
Partner is charming and thoughtful at first	Yes	7/7	Yes
In Relationship			
Physically abused	On at least one occasion	7/7	N/A
Verbally abused	Yes	7/7	Yes
Strangled during sex	Yes	4/7	Yes
Bondage	Yes, but suggested it first	7/7	No
Forced oral sex	No, submitted willingly	7/7	No
Anal sex	Yes	6/7	Yes
Slave contract	No	3/7	N/A
Held captive	No	3/7	N/A
Sexually photographed	Yes	4/7	Yes
Scripted	Yes	6/7	Yes

** Until sleeping with Paul Bernardo on the night they first met, Karla Homolka had only a brief sexual relationship with an ex-boyfriend named "Doug." It is doubtful that Karla and Doug had the opportunity to try anything other than "vanilla sex," but this does not necessarily imply that Homolka was sexually naive. At an early stage in her relationship with Paul, she had introduced handcuffs to their lovemaking, demonstrating at least a playful knowledge of sadomasochistic practices.

Stephen Williams has not been alone in rejecting the compliant victim/ PTSD explanation for Homolka's crimes. One, Dr. Hubert Van Gijseghem, criticized previous diagnoses as not explicitly stating the trauma that led Karla to develop PTSD. He posited that potential psychopathic and narcissistic personality disorders might have gone undetected by existing tests. On a previous exam to determine the presence of anti-social personality disorder, Karla had scored five, a paltry sum compared with the minimum twenty points required to diagnose psychopathy. For what it's worth, many of Karla's harshest detractors have condemned Van Gijseghem's findings as nonsense.

Perhaps the most plausible counter-depiction has come from Dr. Graham Glancy, a forensic psychiatrist hired by Bernardo's attorney, John Rosen. Glancy diagnosed Karla as a "histrionic hybristophile" — an excessively emotional and egotistical attention-seeker turned on by a partner who rapes and dominates other women. As the hybristophile is not masochistic (she doesn't like to experience pain herself), the relationship with her lover is only successful as long as his aggressions are focused on a third party. The moment the violence is directed at the hybristophile, as it was in January 1993, the female partner typically dissolves the partnership.

If we are to trust the opinion of the majority of mental health experts who have assessed Karla, then there is little to no chance of her re-offending. To her credit, the most respected and qualified psychologists and psychiatrists have tended to fall on this side of the argument. Yet if Dr. Glancy is right, and Karla found herself in a relationship with another violent man, she could easily become his willing accomplice, perhaps even goading him on. As a hybristophile, she might consciously or unconsciously seek out such a partner. Her correspondence with convicted spouse-strangler Jean-Paul Gerbet indicates that prison life has done little to curb her tastes. In the end, regardless of what path her future takes, the Canadian public is unlikely to forget or forgive the crimes of Karla Homolka.

———

NEGLIGENCE: PAROLE BOARDS

The foolhardy releases of **Bruce Hamill**, **Peter Woodcock,** and **Doug Moore** are merely a glimpse at a history of long-standing parole board incompetence that has resulted in preventable murders. It was not always so: according to an article in the *Ottawa Citizen*, between 1970 and 1982, 307 convicted murderers were paroled and none committed a second homicide.[5] In the mid-eighties, something went drastically wrong. Despite evidence of ritualistic sex murder in their previous crimes, between 1985 and 1989, **Allan Sweeney**, **Melvin Stanton**, and **Paul Cecil Gillis** were each released into Ontario communities with appalling consequences to the young women they encountered. **Michael Hector** made a similar transformation from armed robbery to murder. Fortunately, the incompetence of Corrections Canada seems to have been remedied by the twenty-first century. For Celia Rugrok, Tema Conter, Robert McCollum, Kevin Solomon, and Blair Aitkens, these changes would be too late.

Kay Feely.

Allan Sweeney
2 Murders
Sault Ste. Marie/Ottawa,
Ontario

THERE GOES THE NEIGHBOURHOOD

A recent graduate of Carleton University's criminology program, twenty-one-year-old Celia Ruygrok accepted her part-time position at Ottawa's Kirkpatrick halfway house because she wanted to help people. When parolee Allan James Sweeney came stumbling back drunk and past curfew at 1:00 a.m.on July 6, 1985, she followed protocol, informing him of his infractions and telephoning her supervisor to report his strange behaviour. She was advised to simply write a report. The next day, Celia's corpse was found wrapped in a carpet, wedged between boxes and upholstery material in a locked basement storage room. She'd been beaten, raped, mutilated, and ridden with multiple stab wounds. Sweeney, then thirty, was arrested and charged with her first-degree murder later that same day. Eventually convicted, he earned himself an additional life sentence without the possibility of parole for twenty-five years. During sentencing, Ontario Supreme Court Justice David Watt expressed his astonishment that Sweeney had been released at all, citing a total lack of "reason and logic" on behalf of the parole board and the John Howard Society for accepting him into their halfway house. What went wrong?

In its defence, the John Howard Society claimed it was made unaware of the details of Sweeney's criminal background, and had the extent of his depravity been known they never would have accepted his residency. They had not even been informed that his first victim was a woman.

A native of Sault Ste. Marie, Ontario, in 1975, the mentally ill nineteen-year-old broke into his neighbours' home in the early morning hours, raping Margaret Donovan at knife-point while her husband Jim toiled at St. Mary's Paper Mill. Locked in their bedroom, the couple's nine-year-old daughter Lisa and son Raymond, eight, were forced to listen helplessly for ninety minutes. At one point they heard their mother ask Sweeney whether he was going to kill her. Later that morning they received their answer; Margaret was found stabbed to death and stuffed into a sleeping bag, her corpse hideously mutilated.

Apprehended within twenty-four hours, Allan James Sweeney was found by the court to be mentally ill, but legally sane. A psychiatrist testifying at his trial dubbed him a "sexual sadist" and warned that, if given the chance, Sweeney would kill again. Sentenced to life imprisonment in 1975, it would take five years before prison staff requested information regarding his crime. When scant details came back from the police and trial judge, rather than pushing the matter, simply believed Sweeney's account that a routine house burglary had gotten out of control. Nine years later, he was granted a six-month parole due to his record of good behaviour and positive psychological reports. Over the next two years, he had been given escorted and unescorted temporary passes without any problems. As a result, his parole was made full on April 5, 1985. When, in a month, it became apparent that the convicted murderer couldn't handle his new-found freedom, this privilege was quickly suspended. Sweeney's girlfriend had reported his chronic use of alcohol and drugs to his parole officer, along with a particularly insidious incident were he had broken into her home, and used a knife to stab a threatening note to her kitchen table. Though his parole had been temporarily revoked, no charges were laid against Sweeney, nor was the parole board informed of his threatening letter. Incredibly, on June 21, full parole was reinstated on the condition that Sweeney resume his residence at the little red-brick halfway house on MacLaren Street. Two weeks later he lost control, murdering Celia Ruygrok in a predictable act of sexualized rage.

The fallout of the Sweeney case was overwhelming. Within days of the murder, the John Howard Society revised its policy ensuring that:

- No female employees be permitted to work the overnight shift.
- The Kirkpatrick house would no longer house men who required psychiatric help.
- The staff would learn how to respond to a hostile resident.

Celia Ruygrok's father filed a $400,000 lawsuit against the parole board, but dropped it when his recommendations for change were met. At a subsequent inquest, a jury advocated sweeping improvements to the gathering and sharing of information among police, Crown counsel, corrections, parole, and voluntary agencies. In the case of a parolee who poses a significant danger to others, all confidentiality should now be put aside for the greater public good. As the following cases will demonstrate unfortunately, these changes were still insufficient to prevent further mayhem.

Melvin Stanton
2 Murders
Toronto, Ontario

OUT OF CONTROL

Melvin Stanton grew up amidst an atmosphere of physical abuse and neglect in northern Alberta. Sent to a juvenile detention centre at the age of twelve for theft and drug use, he was repeatedly raped by older inmates, leading him to develop an overwhelming desire to take revenge on society. Stanton was released on a day pass at age fourteen, at which point he sniffed nail polish remover, entered a downtown Edmonton apartment complex, and raped the custodian's sixty-two-year-old wife in a restroom. Awaiting trial at a juvenile court for the attack, four months later, Stanton escaped and escorted his girlfriend to a park where they both dropped LSD. When the fourteen-year-old girl allegedly questioned his sexuality, he flew into a rage, battering her to death with a rock.

Sentenced to six years at a federal penitentiary for manslaughter, Stanton was incarcerated at Drumheller Institution on his fifteenth birthday: March 17, 1971. During a psychiatric assessment at Alberta Hospital, he flew the coop once more, breaking into a private dwelling, starting a fire, and ultimately adding a further five years to his sentence. Lest there be any doubts that the prison system reformed young Melvin, in 1978, while out on day parole from a prison in Mission, British Columbia, the twenty-four-year-old raped a second woman and was given an additional six-year sentence. A third rape occurred a year later, when Stanton escaped Vancouver's Riverview Hospital by driving a stolen pickup truck through the fence. This time, his victim was a pregnant woman working as a school janitor. In 1980, he was convicted and sentenced to eight additional years for the crime, the judge recommending that Stanton be transferred to a psychiatric hospital following the conclusion of his prison term. Though he was supposed to receive counselling at Warkworth Institution over the next few years, psychologist Robert Cannon later admitted that he and the only other practicioner at the institution were so bogged down in paperwork that it was impossible to provide regular treatment to the five hundred inmates assigned to them. Unsurprisingly, during his time at Warkworth, Stanton's behaviour remained impulsive and violent; in March 1985, he trashed his cell, threatened suicide, and was caught spying on the women's staff washrooms through a vent.

Eventually he received treatment at Kingston Penitentiary, but the initial positive effects dwindled when he returned to Warkworth. In 1987, at age thirty-one, Stanton brandished a knife at a fellow inmate, threatened to murder a staffworker, and was discovered smoking marijuana. When he finally came up for review with the parole board near the close of that year, he was determined to be suicidal. Astonishingly, as nobody in the prison system wanted to deal with a suicidal inmate, the National Parole Board actually encouraged Stanton's gradual release. In January 1988, he was given six forty-eight-hour day passes.

INEXCUSABLE BEHAVIOUR

Released into Montgomery House, a private Toronto halfway house with a questionable reputation under contract from the Correctional Service of Canada, Stanton began his gradual reintegration into society (as if he had ever been integrated in the first place). He decided to prove his worth on June 27, 1988, when around suppertime, he ambushed twenty-five-year-old fashion buyer Tema Conter in the corridor of her upscale Balliol Street apartment. Forcing the dark-haired beauty back into her twenty-second-floor home, he beat her unconscious, stripped her naked, bound and gagged her before subjecting her to a brutal rape. Paramedics would later find her body lying face-down on the bed, perforated by eleven stab wounds. The murder had taken place a mere thirty-six hours after Stanton had checked into the halfway house. Three days later, police tracked Stanton down and arrested him for the killing. He was eventually convicted. One of the paramedics, Vince Savoia would become so disturbed by the event that he could not bear to let his wife leave the house, even to go to the corner store. Despite eight years of therapy, he was forced to eventually quit his chosen profession due to the memory of Tema Conter's anguished face. He has since founded a memorial trust in her name (*www.tema.ca*).

A subsequent inquest into her death revealed widespread incompetence; extending to staff at the penitentiary, the National Parole Board, and Montgomery House, none of whom were sufficiently aware of Stanton's criminal past or wanted to deal with him. Instead, a dangerous and unstable man was passed off onto the Canadian public by the same institutions entrusted to protect them. This behaviour is inexcusable.

Paul Cecil Gillis
3–9 Murders
Midland, Ontario/British Columbia

UNDER THE BRIDGE

It had been twelve years since Paul Cecil Gillis last wandered unsupervised through the community. In the early seventies, he had raped and viciously slaughtered two Vancouver-area teens, Barbara Statt and Robin Gates, before hitchhiking east. Mark Bourrie, author of the classic *By Reason of Insanity*, attributes a further six British Columbia sex slayings to Gillis. Arriving in Ontario, the twenty-five-year-old drifter continued to ply his dark trade. In 1974, at a park near Parry Sound, Gillis raped, murdered, and mutilated Laverne Merle Johnson, stowing her body under a bridge. He was only caught when he couldn't resist dropping hints to the volunteer search party about the location of the dump site. Found not guilty by reason of insanity, Gillis was institutionalized for an indefinite period. Now after a dozen years holed up in various mental hospitals, the ripper was being allowed out on day passes from a medium-security prison in St. Thomas. Accompanying him on his outings was fellow triple-murderer Robert George Abel, a hulking psychotic who had slaughtered his wife and two children. They had found work at the Sparta Mercantile factory, where Gillis had eventually saved enough money to buy a car.

On Thursday, March 31, 1988, the twisted duo informed their boss that they were skipping out early to go drinking and get laid. Finding a liquor store, Abel purchased a jug of Kelly's, and the two men settled beneath a tree in a nearby park. As they sat guzzling booze with a third mental patient, Gillis's conversation began to increasingly focus on sex. He kept insisting how badly he needed to "get laid," the details of his fantasies becoming more graphic and lurid with each sip. That two multiple murderers would be allowed out on unsupervised day passes where they could drink and were allowed access to a car may seem like a serious breech of common sense, but apparently the good doctors at St. Thomas felt they knew better.

Soon Gillis and Abel were driving to London. At 6:45 p.m., the drunken Abel announced he was going to vomit, so Gillis pulled the car over in a residential neighbourhood. As his burly protege emptied the contents of his guts onto the asphalt, Gillis spied an adolescent girl waiting at a bus stop. Pulling into a nearby driveway, he exited the vehicle and started toward her. Sensing that something was wrong, the fourteen-year-old began to run, but lost her footing and tripped in the middle of the street. It was just the opportunity Gillis needed. Seizing her violently, he threatened to kill her if she didn't get into the car. Terrified, the poor girl obeyed. He forced her between himself and Abel, who, on the verge of unconsciousness, thought his friend had picked up a hooker. Unfortunately, to a sadist like Gillis, sex and violence were inseparable. When Abel passed out again, Gillis snarled that if his captive didn't "behave herself" he would hurt her. It was a lie — he planned to hurt her anyway.

At this point, Gillis made the strange decision to return to his workplace in St. Thomas about thirty kilometres south of the city. As Abel remained unconscious in the car, he marched his quivering captive into one of the empty offices, forcing her to strip before raping her vaginally, orally, and anally. On the way back to the car, he suddenly seized her from behind and choked her until her body went limp and collapsed on the pavement. Gillis carried her body to the back seat of the car, telling Abel, who had awakened and resumed drinking, that she was dead. They drove out to Catfish Creek near the psychiatric hospital, where, despite Abel's pleas not to hurt her, Gillis tossed her crumpled form over a bridge twenty-three feet into the shallow waters below. Certain that she was dead, he returned to the car where he grabbed Abel by the arms, threatening to do the same to him if he ever told anyone. Though twice his size, Abel had been too drunk to intervene. Returning late to St. Thomas hospital, the two men signed in and went to their respective rooms, falling into deep sleeps.

"DANGEROUS" OFFENDER?

Little did they know, their victim was tougher than they had anticipated. Revived by the cold water, the teen began to crawl up the bank, blinded by blood, but determined to reach safety. Amazingly, she made it to a nearby farmhouse and staggered inside only to find it empty. Fading in and out of consciousness, she staggered from room to room, turning on lights, before her own lights finally went out. An hour later, the owners of the property returned to discover her, and immediately called the police.

Though she was to spend the next three weeks in hospital undergoing plastic surgery and a skull graft, she would survive her ordeal.

The next day, Paul Cecil Gillis awoke to find her story in every newspaper in the province. For once he did the smart thing and turned himself in. Hours later, Abel was arrested. On February 20, 1989, Gillis plead guilty to aggravated sexual assault and attempted murder. The trial lasted only a matter of minutes. That same month, charges against Robert Abel were dropped. In June, Gillis was declared a dangerous offender, and transferred to a maximum-security institution in Kingston. If being a serial killer does not get one immediately labelled a dangerous offender, perhaps the criteria should be expanded. With the blood of at least three butchered women already on his hands, how much more dangerous could Paul Cecil Gillis get?

Michael Hector
3 Murders
Thunder Bay, Ontario

EX-CAR THIEF

Michael John Hector used to be a thief. According to his parole officer, Ambihapathy Chinniah, executive director of Thunder Bay's John Howard Society, Hector had been a member of a Winnipeg stolen car ring. In actuality, Hector's criminal career was far more extensive.

Convicted of armed robbery at the age of eighteen, Hector had served a paltry jail sentence, continually violating the terms of his parole following his release. He had been twenty-three when on September 28, 1987, he robbed a Thunder Bay credit union with a sawed-off .22-calibre rifle, making away with $18,000. Just over a month later, Hector had convinced an accomplice to employ the same MO to hit another Thunder Bay credit union. Already suspected of the previous crime, he had intended to provide himself with an alibi, simultaneously attending a therapy session. However, his accomplice had lost his nerve during the getaway and capitulated to the police, giving them impetus to arrest and convict Hector for the first robbery. Sentenced to four years, he had served less than half that time before being granted full parole on October 20, 1989. When Hector had been charged with conspiracy to commit robbery on March 5, 1991, this had been suspended. Two months prior, he had robbed Hull's Food Store in Winnipeg of an excess of $12,000, for which he had been convicted and handed a ten-year sentence, reduced to eight and a half on appeal.

Of course, by April 28, 1995, Hector had been released on full parole again. Yet to Ambi Chinniah, the charming Michael Hector who stood before him dreaming of marrying, buying a house in Newfoundland, and embarking on a career was no more than an ex car-thief. "Michael keeps me informed of all his problems and has been very frank about his future plans," Chinniah wrote of their relationship. Hector had simply neglected to mention the double murder.

HAVING A BLAST

On January 9, 1997, Michael John Hector was hanging out at the home of Robert McCollum, a drug dealer with known ties to the Hell's Angels motorcycle club. When McCollum refused to sell him an ounce of cocaine for less than $2,000, Hector waited until the dealer leaned over the kitchen counter to snort a line, aimed his .38 Enfield revolver, and shot him through the chin and right eye. He then proceeded to the bathroom where McCollum's friend Kevin Solomon was showering, blasting him through the face before turning off the tap and leaving with the cocaine.

The next to die was gas station pump attendant Blair Aitkens on February 3. After robbing the Can-Op gas station of $944, Hector led him to the back of the garage and shot him twice through the head. Discovered by a customer within ten minutes, Blair was rushed to hospital where he was placed on life support.

Having heard about the robbery and attempted murder, Hector's brother Jim was eager to broach the subject when the two bumped into each other the next day at Victoriaville Mall. But Hector refused to believe that Blair Aitkens was still fighting for life. "One in the back of the head, one in the ear," Hector said incredulously. "That kid is not alive." Prophetically, Aitkens died soon after.

Convinced his brother was responsible for the murder, Jim wrote a sworn statement to local police, detailing the conversation in the mall. The following day, Michael Hector was arrested and charged with possessing an unregistered restricted firearm. Eventually charged with all three murders, Hector plead guilty on May 5, 1997, receiving concurrent life sentences without the possibility of parole for twenty-five years. Considering that Hector was already on parole for armed robbery, a special inquiry was launched by Correctional Service of Canada and the National Parole Board to examine their failures. These results have been kept hidden from public scrutiny.

Just over a year after his murder convictions, Hector was transferred to medium security at Winnipeg's Stony Mountain Institution. Notified by Blair Aitkens's father, an outraged Leo Toneguzzi, chief of the Thunder Bay police, wrote to the CSC, condemning their decision.

In the end, Hector was remanded to New Brunswick's Atlantic Institution where he later married and enjoys conjugal visits.

Andre Kirchhoff.

Gilbert Paul Jordan

The Boozing Barber
8–10 Murders
Vancouver, British Columbia

"Down the hatch, baby! Twenty bucks if you drink it right down."

NATURAL BORN BOOZER

Gilbert Paul Elsie was born on December 12, 1931, in Vancouver. By the age of sixteen, he was a severe alcoholic, consuming three bottles of vodka a day. Dropping out of high school, he soon ran afoul of the law, garnering arrests for theft, car theft, assault, and the possession of heroin. Around this time, he also developed an insatiable taste for drunken sex. Elsie later explained that sober people wouldn't go out with him so he was left without any other option. He estimated that he had slept with around two hundred women a year, the majority being Aboriginal prostitutes from Vancouver's east end. In 1961, police found Elsie with a five-year-old Native girl in his car and he was charged with abduction, but acquitted. In December of the same year, he threatened to commit suicide by jumping off the Lion's Gate Bridge, causing a massive traffic jam in the process. Charged and brought to trial in North Vancouver, he gave the "sieg heil" salute to the judge and was found in contempt of court. Two years later, he lured two women into his car where he reportedly raped and robbed them. He was convicted of the latter and sentenced to hard time.

While in prison, he learned hair-dressing skills, and, upon his release, opened Slocan Barber Shop on Kingsway Avenue's east side and began to invest in the stock market. Despite this facade of normalcy, the "Boozing Barber" continued to have drunken sex with prostitutes. In 1965, Elsie checked into a cheap motel room with English-born switchboard operator Ivy Rose Oswald. Her naked corpse was found there the following day. A subsequent autopsy revealed a blood alcohol level of 0.51 — death by alcohol poisoning normally occurs at 0.4. Either Ivy had a liver of steel, or somehow she had managed to keep drinking after she had fallen unconscious. Nevertheless, her death was ruled accidental. Meanwhile, her killer changed his surname from Elsie to Jordan. Unfortunately, his habits remained consistent. Over the next five years, he logged numerous arrests for drunk driving, even managing to be charged twice in one day in 1969. A 1971 charge for committing lewd acts in a public place was dismissed, but two years later, he was convicted of indecent exposure in Mackenzie. Jordan finally managed to land himself back in prison in 1974 when he was found guilty of indecent assault in Prince George. He was sentenced to two years less a day. Though the Crown petitioned to have him declared a "dangerous offender," Jordan's lawyer was able to block the manoeuvre. A year later, he was paroled. It wasn't to last. After kidnapping two women from a mental institution in 1975, Jordan returned to prison for twenty-six months. This time, he would emerge a monster. Between July 1982 and June 1985, three alcoholic prostitutes were found dead in the Slocan Barbershop. Amazingly the police never linked Jordan to their deaths. They might have reasoned that as he had reported them, it must have been a gruesome coincidence. Perhaps they were simply too lazy to radio in a criminal record check.

Then on October 11, 1987, twenty-seven-year-old prostitute Vanessa Lee Buckner booked into Vancouver's inexpensive Niagara Hotel, accompanied by a balding middle-aged man. The next morning, an anonymous phone call drew police to the hotel room where Vanessa Lee's naked body lay dead. Though known to be a moderate drinker, her blood alcohol level tested 0.91. The call was traced to a room at the nearby Marble Arch Hotel, registered to a Gilbert Paul Jordan. When prostitute Edna Shade was found dead of alcohol poisoning in November, police matched fingerprints found at the scene to Jordan. At long last, they decided to put the Boozing Barber under surveillance. Over the next fifteen days, police interrupted him trying to poison women on four different occasions. Each attempt occurred at a downtown east side motel room. He was finally arrested when he was caught attempting to pour vodka down an unconscious woman's throat.

"Have a drink, down the hatch, baby, twenty bucks if you drink it right down," Jordan was heard to say. "See if you're a real woman. Finish that drink, finish that drink, down the hatch hurry, right down … you need another drink. I'll give you fifty bucks if you can take it."

HAIR OF THE DOG

Eventually, Gilbert Paul Jordan would be linked to ten alcohol-related deaths in the Vancouver area, and charged with seven. At his 1988 trial, he confessed to the slaying of Vanessa Lee Buckner, calmly explaining how he had observed black fluid trickling from her nose and mouth before he left her to die. He showed no remorse: "They were all on their last legs. I didn't give a damn who I was with, we were all dying sooner or later." Convicted only of the Buckner slaying, he was sentenced to fifteen years, which was then reduced to nine when appeals changed his sentence from murder to manslaughter. In a travesty of Canadian justice, Jordan was released after serving only six years of his original fifteen-year sentence. Justice Sam Toy justified his release in the following statement:

> Although the appellant has left a trail of seven victims, the last was the first occasion when persons in authority, in a forceful and realistic manner, brought to the appellant's attention the fact that supplying substantial quantities of liquor to women who were prepared to drink with him was a contributing cause of their deaths, for which he might be held criminally responsible.[6]

In essence, Toy claimed that Jordan had no idea his drinking games were responsible for the seven deaths. Now that "persons in authority" had informed him of the perils of alcohol, he deserved a second chance. It's hard to understand how a government official could consciously make such a foolish decision. Unreformed, Jordan went on to commit several smaller offences and soon found himself back inside. Once again, he attempted to change his name in 2000, but backed down when the authorities learned of his plan. He was released again in 2004 on the condition that he remain on Vancouver Island. Naturally, he disappeared and a Canada-wide alert was issued. Two days later on August 11, Jordan, now seventy-two, was arrested at a hotel in Winnipeg. After spending two more years in and out of jail for parole violations he died on July 7, 2006, in Victoria, British Columbia.

CHAPTER 18

CONCLUSION

Over the course of this work we have examined a total of sixty serial murder cases. There have been approximately five hundred known victims of Canadian serial killers, including American murderers who crossed the border to claim Canadian lives. The victims of the solved cases total somewhere in the area of 375. Of these killers, the ones with the highest body counts tend to have claimed the majority of their victims in the United States. Americans William Dean Christensen and Earle Leonard Nelson may have killed up to fifty-two people between them, yet only four of this number were on Canadian soil. Comparatively, Canadian serial killers seem to claim fewer victims than their neighbours to the south. As previously mentioned, baby farmers William and Lila Young currently hold the record for most prolific Canadian serial murderers — though their victims perished mainly due to negligence. By all accounts, the Youngs did not actively seek to cause the deaths of the women and children in their care — they were simply callous and unaffected. With between thirty-one and forty-nine victims, Robert Pickton stands out as the second highest-tallying Canadian serial murderer of all time, a number comparable to infamous Americans Ted Bundy (31–36+), Gary Ridgway (48+) and John Wayne Gacy (33). Yet the next highest, Michael McGray, reached a total of only seventeen. Perhaps Canadian law enforcement deserves a pat on the back for thwarting the nation's worst offenders before they could reach the astronomical levels seen south of the border. Then again, we must also consider the cases Canadian authorities have failed to solve. A similar number of women have succumbed to a predator or predators stalking British Columbia's legendary "Highway of Tears," and though they predate the comparable Green River Murders of Washington State, unlike Gary Ridgway, the perpetrator(s) remain(s) at large.

———

Despite my intentions to make *Cold North Killers: Canadian Serial Murder* exhaustive, there were several cases in which available information was so scant, I was unable to include them. For example, thirty-four-year-old **Noel Winters** who gunned down two friends, a father and son, in a fit of alcohol-induced rage in 1984 New Brunswick. Remembered primarily for his grisly body disposal, Winters dismembered both men with a saw, secreting their remains in garbage bags, which he then discarded at the local dump. Convicted of these crimes, he later committed suicide in Dorchester Institution, hanging himself with a bedsheet. That same day, the bodies of a French Canadian couple who had rented Winters's Saint John-area cottage were unearthed from a metre-deep grave on the property.

In December 1987, thirty-seven-year-old Burnaby, British Columbia, cabinetmaker, **Allan George Foster**, beat his common-law wife to death with a hammer before murdering her daughter and daughter's friend, both aged twelve, and sexually assaulting their bodies. Having already served time for the rape and murder of his eighteen-year-old sister-in-law, Foster promptly turned himself into police. He committed suicide two weeks later by stabbing himself in the heart with two ballpoint pens.

North Ontario ne'er-do-well **Paul Alan Hachey** admitted to the 1994 slaying of a homosexual Toronto man following his arrest for the murder and post-mortem rape of twenty-year-old Sarah Whitehead in North Bay. Hachey attacked Whitehead while she was taking a shortcut home from the mall along a footpath on August 7, 1997. In addition to his two murders, he was also convicted of three Edmonton sexual assaults and is currently serving a life sentence.

Astonishingly, a halfway house administered by the John Howard Society in Vernon, British Columbia, is directly linked to two little-known serial murderers. In 1996, the institution released sex slayer Raymond Russell back into the community, where he began renting a room from Mrs. Darlene Turnbull. Russell eventually murdered his new landlady, who was blissfully uninformed by the parole officer that a depraved killer was living under her roof. Four years later, another convicted killer and resident of the halfway house named Donald Falkner brought further shame upon the building. Though the body of Falkner's girlfriend Karen Miller has never been found, the amount of blood in her trailer left little doubt as to her fate, and he was convicted of her slaying. According to Karen's sister Kendra, the only information the Miller family received regarding Falkner's prior conviction was that the murder "happened at the wrong place, at the wrong time." In reality, he had stalked his wife's family before brutally slaying his mother-in-law in her Calgary home. Amazingly, the same halfway house would release spree killer Eric Norman Fish four years later.

More recently, **Davey Mato Butorac**, twenty-nine, of Aldegrove, British Columbia, was charged with the deaths of two prostitutes in January of 2010. Butorac first came to police attention during their investigation into the murder of fifty-year-old Langley sex worker Sheryl Lynn Korroll. Having recovered DNA evidence from the suspect's car, they were shocked to find a match to yet another unsolved prostitute murder, that of forty-six-year-old Gwendolyn Jo Lawton, whose body was discovered on March 13, 2007, in Abbotsford.

In Ottawa, **Camille Cleroux** confessed to killing his upstairs neighbour, Paula Leclair, sixty-four, leading police to her body in the old Walkley trainyards in the summer of 2010. Suspicion had fallen upon the fifty-six-year-old drifter, when Leclair's son was greeted at her apartment door unexpectedly by a dishevelled Cleroux. He claimed that Paula had won $50,000 on the lottery and was off celebrating at Disneyworld. A former dishwasher at a ByWard Market diner, Cleroux is also charged with murdering his former wife, Lise Roy, who disappeared in 1990, and common-law spouse Jean Rock, missing since 2003. Like **Sam Pirrera**, Cleroux allegedly hired a woman in his building to write letters to Rock's family, pretending to be from her. The woman claimed he told her he had kicked his wife out when he had caught her in bed with another man.

Even as this book entered the editing phase, two more suspected serial killers appeared in the Canadian press, prompting me to wonder if the project would ever satisfactorily end. In November 2010, country boy **Cody Legebokoff** was charged with the murder of Loren Leslie, a near blind fifteen-year-old from Fraser Lake, British Columbia. By later October 2011, the twenty-one-year-old Legebokoff made headlines nationwide when he was linked to the slayings of three additional women in the Prince George area. If convicted, he will become the youngest known serial killer in British Columbia history. Simultaneously, **Mark Garfield Moore**, a twenty-seven-year-old Torontonian, was charged with the random shooting deaths of four men, along with fifty other charges, including armed robbery and attempted murder. Though Moore reportedly fantasized about life as a gangster and rapper, in reality he seems to be nothing more than a deluded, psychopathic loner.

Notes

PREFACE

1. John E. Douglas, Ann W. Burgess, Allen G. Burgess, and Robert K. Ressler, *Crime Classification Manual: A Standard System For Investigating and Classifying Violent Crimes — Second Edition* (San Francisco: Jossey-Bass, 2006), 96.
2. Though this definition was first given in Ramsland's *The Human Predator*, I discovered it in one of her subsequent works: Katherine Ramsland, *The Devil's Dozen*. (New York: Berkley, 2009).

CHAPTER 1: THE FIRST CANADIAN SERIAL KILLERS

1. This fact relies on the assumption that Wilson has not overlooked any British serial killers in his work.
2. In *The Collected Works of Max Haines Volume 2*, Haines pegs the year of Rulloff's birth as 1819.
3. In *The Collected Works of Max Haines Volume 2*, Haines lists this date as August 21, 1870, which would fall on a Sunday. As it is unlikely the two clerks would be working on a Sunday night, Haines's date is likely an error.
4. In *The Collected Works of Max Haines Volume 2*, Haines lists the date of execution as May 17, 1871 — one day before.
5. French Canadians may be interested to know that rather than referring to LaPage as a "Canadian," the *New York Herald* repeatedly labelled him a "Frenchman."
6. A description of LaPage given by a Pembroke resident during his first trial.

7. Virginia A. McConnell, author of *Sympathy for the Devil: The Emmanuel Baptist Murders of Old San Francisco*, has pointed out that 40 percent of survivors suffered lasting brain damage — a potential reason for Theo's subsequent lack of impulse control.

8. The authoritative voice on Northcott, James Jeffrey Paul repeatedly states his belief in *Nothing Is Strange with You* that George Northcott was a passive man dominated by his wife and son. He points out that such aggressive behaviour seems contrary to the character of the man as gleaned from historical records. Paul believes the family ascribed abusive behaviour to George as a sympathy plea to the jury at Stewart's trial.

CHAPTER 2: NATURE, NURTURE, OR NEITHER?

1. The coincidences in childhood behaviour (strange noises and walking, inexplicable fear) exhibited by Shawcross and Peter Woodcock, detailed later in this chapter, are startling. Could there be some common psychiatric disorder linking the two? It is also noteworthy that both men began by killing children, moving on to adults as they reached middle age.

2. This does not mean that Olson's parents were necessarily saints. In her *Youthful Prey: Child Predators Who Kill*, Carol Anne Davies claims that Clifford Sr. was once found guilty of "breach of the peace." After moving to Richmond, he became a bingo caller and was investigated for fraud.

3. Christopher Berry-Dee and Steven Morris have written a fascinating book on the subject. I highly recommend *How to Make a Serial Killer*, despite some errors in the final assessment of Harold Shipman (he *was* a drug addict and had an unhealthy relationship with his mother).

4. The case for Woodcock possessing a "demon seed" partially because his birth mother was a prostitute is, of course, debatable. I included it to show that he had blood relatives who willingly violated the law and cultural norms. I do not wish to compare prostitution to murder in any other way.

CHAPTER 4: VICTIMOLOGY

1. Wilson notes that the majority of victims are women, though surprisingly he does not create a special category for this demographic.

RIGHT UNDER OUR NOSES: COLONEL RUSSELL WILLIAMS AND THE WRITING OF THIS BOOK, PART 2

1. I made this assumption based on similar behaviour displayed by known American transvestite killers Jerry Brudos and Dennis Rader. When photographs of Williams dressed in women's clothes began to surface during his trial, I learned that some of the clothing actually belonged to pre-pubescent girls.

CHAPTER 5: ORGANIZED/DISORGANIZED/MIXED

1. This chart is an amalgamation of the charts shown on pages 122 and 123 of *Sexual Homicide: Patterns and Motives*, printed in 1992.
2. It may already be obvious to the reader that Carl was mixing up the details of his two murders, which can be explained by his confused mental state at the time, a true hallmark of a "disorganized" offender. In Carl's case, his use of crack cocaine may have caused temporary psychosis, causing him to misremember significant events. There is also the chance that he is blatantly fabricating certain elements of the story in order to make himself look better.

CHAPTER 6: THE VISIONARY KILLER

1. According to the crime scene characteristics outlined in *Serial Murder: Second Edition*, by Ronald M. Holmes and Stephen T. Holmes.

CHAPTER 7: THE MISSIONARY KILLER

1. According to the crime-scene characteristics outlined in *Serial Murder: Second Edition*, by Ronald M. Holmes and Stephen T. Holmes.
2. Patrick Brode, *The Slasher Killings* (Detroit: Painted Turtle, 2009), 24.
3. Brode, 36.
4. Brode, 63.
5. Brode, 88.
6. Brode, 90.

CHAPTER 8: THE HEDONIST-COMFORT KILLER: BLACK WIDOWS, BLUEBEARDS, AND BABY FARMERS

1. According to the crime-scene characteristics outlined in *Serial Murder: Second Edition*, by Ronald M. Holmes and Stephen T. Holmes.
2. They did, however, discover a life insurance policy on Dhillon's niece, again naming him the beneficiary.

CHAPTER 9: THE HEDONIST-LUST KILLER

1. According to the crime-scene characteristics outlined in *Serial Murder: Second Edition*, by Ronald M. Holmes and Stephen T. Holmes
2. See *www.ctv.ca/CTVNews/2/20060204/mad_slasher_060204/* (accessed December 27, 2010).
3. When Oak Ridge patient Paul Cecil Gillis was granted day passes so that he could work, he used the opportunity to get drunk, sexually assault and attempt to murder a teenage girl. Peter Woodcock's day-pass murder of Dennis Kerr occurred shortly after. In the years since, the public has wisely demanded more transparency from the review boards who make these decisions.

4. See *http://tocrime.blogspot.com/2006/01/killers-eyes.html* (accessed December 27, 2010).

CHAPTER 10: THE HEDONIST-THRILL KILLER

1. According to the crime-scene characteristics outlined in *Serial Murder: Second Edition*, by Ronald M. Holmes and Stephen T. Holmes.

CHAPTER 11: THE POWER/CONTROL KILLER

1. According to the crime-scene characteristics outlined in *Serial Murder: Second Edition*, by Ronald M. Holmes and Stephen T. Holmes.
2. Possibly a pseudonym.
3. There is really no clearer evidence of Snow's obsession with power and control than this particular ego-reinforcing form of psychological torture.
4. Doctor Zoffman's assessment of David Snow was located in Allison Shaw's *A Friend of the Family* (Toronto: Macfarlane, Walter & Ross, 1998), 213–216.
5. Roger Sasaki's assessment of David Snow was located in Shaw, 217–218.
6. The accounts of Jesperson's childhood and murders in this chapter are primarily drawn from the killer's own recollections in Jack Olsen's compelling *"I": The Creation of a Serial Killer*. As the reader will undoubtedly note, a majority of his victims seem to have treated Jesperson unfairly and used him, as if provoking him to murder them. Though it is impossible to know if Jesperson's narratives are true, in light of his unabashed lying and legendary manipulation of the press, the reader is advised to consider that the victims may simply have been painted in a bad light by a man who wished to minimize his responsibility in the crimes.
7. Jack Olsen, *"I": The Creation of a Serial Killer* (New York: St. Martin's, 2002), 159.
8. Olsen, 160–161.
9. Olsen, 161–162.

CHAPTER 13: NEW TECHNOLOGIES: OFFENDER PROFILING

1. A pseudonym.
2. Gregg O. McCrary, "F.B.I. Profile of the Scarborough Rapist" in Doug Clark's *Dark Paths, Cold Trails* (Toronto: HarperCollins, 2002), 61–67.
3. Nick Pron, *Lethal Marriage* (Toronto: Seal Books, 1995), 60.
4. The only account of Leslie's seemingly bizarre reaction is Bernardo himself, a notorious liar.

CHAPTER 14: NEW TECHNOLOGIES: DNA

1. West was the first of many serial killers to bear this moniker. Twenty years later, the Florida press would attach it to the crimes of Aileen Wuornos, and

later still it would become the nickname for Spokane prostitute murderer Robert Lee Yates.

2. Let it never be said that MacDonald's parents didn't care for him. They married shortly after his birth and regularly travelled the 320 kilometres to visit him as he was growing up.

CHAPTER 15: CANADIAN FORENSIC INNOVATIONS

1. See *www.canada.com/topics/news/national/story.html?id=758d4b02-2cc7-451a-9b3d-e15db3d16f2e* (accessed December 27, 2010).

CHAPTER 17: NEGLIGENCE: WHEN THE SYSTEM FAILS

1. Abby Deveney, "Dead Woman's Father Wants Parole Review," *Ottawa Citizen*, December 11, 1986.

2. Stephen Williams, *Karla* (Toronto: Seal Books, 2004), 209–211.

3. _____, *Invisible Darkness* (Toronto: McArthur & Company, 1999), 457.

4. Based on information provided in the article *Compliant Victims of the Sexual Sadist* by Hazelwood, Warren, and Dietz.

5. Abby Deveney, "Dead Woman's Father Wants Parole Review," *Ottawa Citizen*, December 11, 1986.

6. See *www.firstnationsdrum.com/2009/april/gpj.html* (accessed December 19, 2009).

Bibliography

GENERAL

Berry-Dee, Christopher. *How to Make a Serial Killer.* Berkeley: Ulysses Press, 2008.

Douglas, John E. *Crime Classification Manual: A Standard System for Investigating and Classifying Violent Crimes — Second Edition.* San Francisco: Jossey-Bass, 2006.

Godwin, Maurice. *Tracker: Hunting Down Serial Killers.* New York: Avalon, 2005.

Holmes, Ronald M. *Serial Murder: Second Edition.* Thousand Oaks, CA: Sage, 1998.

Norris, Joel. *Serial Killers.* New York: Doubleday, 1989.

Ressler, Robert K. *Sexual Homicide: Patterns and Motives.* New York: The Free Press, 1992.

Wilson, Colin. *The Serial Killers: A Study in the Psychology of Violence.* London: Virgin, 1990.

Wilson, David. *A History of British Serial Killing.* London: Sphere, 2009.

Vronsky, Peter. *Serial Killers: The Method and Madness of Monsters.* New York: Berkley Books, 2004.

SERGE ARCHAMBAULT

Clark, Doug. *Dark Paths, Cold Trails.* Toronto: HarperCollins, 2002.

TELEVISION

"The Butcher of St. Eustache." *Crime Stories.* History Television.

GERALD THOMAS ARCHER

Pron, Nick. "Three Unsolved Murders Linked to Serial Killer; But Suspect Died Several Years Ago Sources Say." *Toronto Star*, February 15, 2000.

Pron, Nick. "30-Year-Old Murders; Petty Thief Confessed Before He Died 5 Years Ago." *Toronto Star*, February 16, 2000.

DONALD ARMSTRONG

Mitchell, Bob. "Killer's Move to Quebec Angers Families: Transferred from Ontario Prison Before His Release. Attempt to Avoid Publicity Cited by Prison Officials." *Toronto Star*, June 1, 2006.

Mitchell, Bob. "Peel Murderer Back in Tougher Jail; Fury Greeted Move to 'Cottage.' Danger to Any Community." *Toronto Star*, March 7, 2003.

Mitchell, Bob. "Victim's Sister Fights to Keep Killer in Jail." *Toronto Star*, May 18, 2006.

BRIAN ARP

Clark, Doug. *Dark Paths, Cold Trails*. Toronto: Harper Collins, 2002.
WEB
http://csc.lexum.org/en/1998/1998scr3-339/1998scr3-339.pdf (accessed November 2, 2011).

PAUL BERNARDO

Anderson, Diane. *Bloodstains*. Calgary: Detselig, 2008.

Boer, Peter. *Canadian Crime Investigations: Hunting Down Serial Killers*. Edmonton: Folklore, 2002.

Clark, Doug. *Dark Paths, Cold Trails*. Toronto: HarperCollins, 2002.

McCrary, Gregg O. *The Unknown Darkness: Profiling the Predators Among Us*. New York: HarperTorch, 2004.

Pron, Nick. *Lethal Marriage*. Toronto: Seal Books, 1995.

Williams, Stephen. *Invisible Darkness*. Toronto: McArthur & Company, 1999.

WAYNE BODEN

"The Vampire Rapist." *Crime Stories*. History Television.

THE CALGARY PROSTITUTE MURDERS

Cawthorne, Nigel. *The Mammoth Book of Killers at Large*. Philadelphia: Running Press, 2007.

WILLIAM DEAN CHRISTENSEN

"American Ripper? Convicted Killer Suspect in 15 Other Slayings." *Pittsburgh Post-Gazette*, February 18, 1985.

Duggan, Paul. "Maryland Court Adds 40 years to Murderer's Life Term." *The Washington Post*, August 25, 1989.
"Man Convicted of Slaying." *Pittsburgh Post-Gazette*, August 6, 1987.

ANGELO COLALILLO
Hanes, A. "Killer's Grim Trail of Horror Laid Bare." *The Montreal Gazette*, January 11, 2006.
"Lawyer Wants Charges Dropped." *Montreal Gazette*, October 9, 2002.
WEB
www.cbc.ca/canada/story/2003/11/20/probation031120.html (accessed September 2009).
http://lcn.canow.com/lcn/infos/faitsdivers/.../20040507-191943.html (accessed September 2009).

JOHN MARTIN CRAWFORD
Boer, Peter. *Canadian Crime Investigations: Hunting Down Serial Killers.* Edmonton: Folklore, 2002.
Goulding, Warren. *Just Another Indian.* Calgary: Fifth House, 2001.

DR. THOMAS NEILL CREAM
Boer, Peter. *Canadian Crime Investigations: Hunting Down Serial Killers.* Edmonton: Folklore, 2006.
WEB
Geringer, Joseph. "Dr. Thomas Neill Cream," at *www.trutv.com/library/crime/serial_killers/history/cream/index_1.html*.

SUKHWINDER DHILLON
Wells, Jon. *Poison.* Toronto: John Wiley & Sons, 2008.

LÉOPOLD DION
www2.canoe.com/cgi-bin/imprimer.cgi?id=127221 (accessed June 26, 2010).

THEO DURRANT
McConnell, Virginia A. *Sympathy for the Devil: The Emmanuel Baptist Murders of Old San Francisco.* Lincoln: University of Nebraska Press, 2005.
WEB
www.trutv.com/library/crime/serial_killers/history/theo_durrant/index.html (accessed October 8, 2011).

THE EDMONTON SERIAL KILLER
Boer, Peter. *Canadian Crime Investigations: Hunting Down Serial Killers.*

Edmonton: Folklore, 2002.

WEB

"Edmonton's Missing and Slain Women," May 28, 2008. Located at *www.cbc.ca/news/background/svekla-thomas*.

MELISSA ANN FRIEDRICH

Leydon, John. "Internet Black Widow 'Stalked Pensioner on the Net.'" January 13, 2005, *www.theregister.co.uk/2005/01/13/internet_black_widow* (accessed May 5, 2010).

"Melissa Friedrich: Internet Black Widow." March 14, 2005, *www.cbc.ca/news/background/crime/friedrich.html*.

Thompson, Jamie. "Police Say Woman Victimized Companion." January 12, 2005, *www.sptimes.com/2005/01/12/Tampabay/Police_say_woman_vict.shtml* (accessed May 5, 2010).

WILLIAM FYFE

Clark, Doug. *Dark Paths, Cold Trails.* Toronto: HarperCollins, 2002.

TELEVISION

"The Killer Handyman." *Crime Stories.* History Television.

PAUL CECIL GILLIS

Adamick, Paula. "Trial Ordered for Inmate on Abduction, Assault Charges." *Toronto Star*, August 24, 1988.

Bodnaruk, Fred. "Letter to the Editor: Why Was Three-Time Murderer Freed?" *Toronto Star*, April 20, 1988.

Bourre, Mark. *By Reason of Insanity: The David Michael Krueger Story.* Toronto: Hounslow Press, 1997.

Henton, Darcy. "Three-Time Killer Pleads Guilty to Sex Assault on London Teen." *Toronto Star*, February 21, 1989.

JAMES GREENIDGE

Hoshowsky, Robert. *Unsolved: True Canadian Cold Cases.* Toronto: Dundurn, 2010.

CARL HALL

Wells, Jon. "Witness: A True Crime Story" *Hamilton Spectator*, available online at *www.thespec.com*.

BRUCE HAMILL

Bourre, Mark. *By Reason of Insanity: The David Michael Krueger Story.* Toronto: Hounslow Press, 1997.

MICHAEL HECTOR

Harris, Michael. *Con Game: The Truth About Canada's Prisons.* Toronto: McClelland & Stewart, 2003.

THE HEMLOCK VALLEY MURDERS

Cawthorne, Nigel. *The Mammoth Book of Killers at Large.* Philadelphia: Running Press, 2007.

Kines, Lindsay. "Jailed Rapist a Suspect in Murders, Disappearances." *Vancouver Sun, www.missingpeople.net/vancouver_fears_serial_killer.htm* (accessed December 27, 2010).

WEB

www.rcmp-grc.gc.ca/cc-afn/index-eng.htm (accessed September 12, 2010).

THE HIGHWAY OF TEARS

Cawthorne, Nigel. *The Mammoth Book of Killers at Large.* Philadelphia: Running Press, 2007.

WEB

www.ctv.ca/CTVNews/MSNHome/20071012/highway_oftears_071012 (accessed August 8, 2011).

www2.canada.com/nanaimodailynews/news/story.html?id=2334742 (accessed August 8, 2011).

www2.canada.com/nanaimodailynews/news/story.html?id=2331959 (accessed August 8, 2011).

KARLA HOMOLKA

Pron, Nick. *Lethal Marriage.* Toronto: Seal Books, 1995.

Williams, Stephen. *Invisible Darkness.* Toronto: McArthur & Company, 1999.

Williams, Stephen. *Karla: A Pact with the Devil.* Toronto: Seal Books, 2003.

WEB

www.trutv.com/library/crime/serial_killers/notorious/bernardo/index_1.html (accessed April 2010).

Hazelwood, Roy. "The Disturbed Mind: Compliant Victims of the Sexual Sadist." at *www.canadiancrc.com/Newspaper_Articles/FBI_USA_Disturbed_Mind_-Compliant_Victims_of_Sexual_Sadist.aspx* (accessed April 2010).

KEITH JESPERSON

Boer, Peter. *Canadian Crime Investigations: Hunting Down Serial Killers.* Edmonton: Folklore, 2006.

Olsen, Jack. *"I: The Creation of a Serial Killer."* New York: St. Martin's Press, 2002.

RUSSELL MAURICE JOHNSON

Jones, Frank. "A Strangler So Gentle." In *Trail of Blood: A Canadian Murder Odyssey.* Toronto: McGraw-Hill Ryerson, 1981.

TELEVISION

"The Bedroom Strangler." *Crime Stories.* History Television.

GILBERT PAUL JORDAN

Donnelley, Paul. *501 Most Notorious Crimes.* London: Bountybooks, 2009.

WEB

www.firstnationsdrum.com/2009/april/gpj.html (accessed December 19, 2009).

CHARLES KEMBO

Hall, Neal. "Jury Hears Chilling Recording at Kembo Trial." *Vancouver Sun,* November 11, 2009.

Hall, Neal. "Kembo Killed Mistress, Crown Alleges Body of Sui Yin Ma Found Stuffed in a Hockey Bag Near George Massey Tunnel, Trial Hears." *Vancouver Sun,* October 15, 2009.

Hall, Neal. "Trial of Charles Kembo, Who Is Accused of Four Murders, Adjourned to Oct. 13." *Vancouver Sun,* September 21, 2009.

"Kembo Gets Life for Killing Family, Friend." *National Post,* June 12, 2010.

Makwana, Dharm. "Crown's Opening Arguments in Kembo Trial." *Vancouver 24 hours,* October 13, 2009.

Mulgrew, I. "Charles Kembo: I Am Not a Serial Killer." *Vancouver Sun,* July 29, 2006.

JOSEPH LABOUCAN AND MICHAEL BRISCOE

"Briscoe Charged in Alberta Prostitute's Death." *www.cbc.ca/.../edmonton-briscoe-ellie-mae-meyer-charged-murder.html,* April 30, 2010.

Iltan, Cigdem. "Hearing Begins for Convicted Murderer." *Edmonton Journal,* March 9, 2010.

"Laboucan Charged with Second Murder." *Edmonton Journal,* September 13, 2008, *www.canada.com/vancouversun/news/story.html?id=b03e448b-40f9-45ac-9c18-d33617ec636d.*

"Laboucan's Life a Ride from Hell." *Edmonton Journal,* September 13, 2008, *www.canada.com/vancouversun/news/story.html?id=2bd677c7-90b7-4bd2-8f23-bcf83f40876e.*

"Laboucan Was 'Fall Guy' in Murder." *Edmonton Journal,* March 8, 2007, *www.canada.com/edmontonjournal/features/stolenyouth/story.html?id=fbd7126c-48cc-4d7b-8db7-f87efcde8f00&k=87254.*

"Laboucan Was Friends with Slain Prostitute." *Edmonton Journal,* September 15, 2008, *www.canada.com/edmontonjournal/news/story.html?id=dc0d1b88-3c9d-4fd7-b261-f572703f871c.*

Noel, Alyssa. "New Trial in Nina Courtepatte Slaying." *Edmonton Sun, http://cnews.canoe.ca/CNEWS/Crime/2009/01/07/7942511-sun.html.*

Payton, Laura. "Top Court to Rule on Appeals in Courtepatte Murder." April 6, 2010, *www.torontosun.com/news/canada/2010/04/06/13488986-qmi.html.*

"Timeline of Events." *Edmonton Journal,* January 22, 2007, *www2.canada.com/edmontonjournal/features/stolenyouth/story.html?id=f403cbd9-6ad6-4f60-97e4-9f8f0ff0ea41.*

JOSEPH LAPAGE

"Executed on the Gallows." *New York Times,* March 16, 1878.

"The Langmaid Tragedy; A Conclusive Show of Evidence against LaPage — His Conviction Almost Certain." *New York Times,* November 2, 1875.

The Trial of Joseph Lapage, The French Monster. Philadelphia, 1876.

ALLAN LEGERE

Boer, Peter. *Canadian Crime Investigations: Hunting Down Serial Killers.* Edmonton: Folklore, 2006.

Haines, Max. *The Collected Works of Max Haines Volume 6.* Toronto: Penguin, 2008.

Maclean, Rick. *Terror.* Toronto: McClelland & Stewart, 1990.

CHRISTIAN MAGEE

Haines, Max. *The Collected Works of Max Haines Volume 2.* Toronto: Toronto Sun, 1991.

Pron, Nick. "'Flat-Out Victory' for Serial Killer; Tribunal Rules 'Mad Slasher' be Moved to Toronto Facility Centre That's Held Him for 30 Years Might Face Contempt." *Toronto Star,* May 12, 2006.

WEB

www.ctv.ca/CTVNews/2/20060204/mad_slasher_060204/ (accessed December 27, 2010).

ALLAN MACDONALD

Duncanson, John. "Killed Cop, Cabbie but Escaped the Noose." *Hamilton Spectator,* August 13, 2005.

De Almedia, Jacquie. "Killer's Mom Haunted By Shaw Murder; Woman Struggles to Understand the Son She Never Really Knew." *Hamilton Spectator,* August 16, 2005.

WEB

www.ctv.ca/CTVNews/WFive/20060210/wfive_murder_060211/ (accessed December 28, 2010).

MICHAEL MCGRAY
"The Homicidal Drifter." *Crime Stories*. History Television.
WEB
www.cbc.ca/news/story/2000/03/20/nf_mcgray000320.html (accessed November 14, 2009).
http://news.sympatico.cbc.ca/local/bc/serial_killer_charged_with_killing_cellmate/0f6fcc27 (accessed May 31, 2011).

DR. ROBERT MACGREGOR
Haines, Max. "Darling Mrs. Sparling." In *The Collected Works of Max Haines Vol. 2*. Toronto: Toronto Sun Publishing, 1991.

DOUG MOORE
Donovan, Kevin. "The Making of a Monster." *Toronto Star*, July 10, 2004.
Donovan, Kevin. "A Pedophile Turns to Murder." *Toronto Star*, July 11, 2004.

EARLE LEONARD NELSON
Haines, Max. *The Collected Works of Max Haines Volume 6*. Toronto: Penguin, 2008.
Newton, Michael. *The Encyclopedia of Serial Killers*. New York: Checkmark Books, 2000.
Schecter, Harold. *The Serial Killer Files*. New York: Ballantine Books, 2003.
Wilson, Colin. *The Serial Killers: A Study in the Psychology of Violence*. London: Virgin, 1990.

NIAGARA'S PROSTITUTE MURDERS
Burman, John. "Murder Squad Gets New Info on City Killing." *Hamilton Spectator*, February 9, 2006.
Clairmont, Susan. "Second Charge in Sex Worker Killings; Labourer Faces Two Counts of First-Degree Murder." *Hamilton Spectator*, June 6, 2006.
"Falls Man to Stand Trial in Killings." *Hamilton Spectator*, February 13, 2008.
Morse, Paul. "A High-Risk Lifestyle." *Hamilton Spectator*, March 5, 2007.
Pron, Nick. "Man Charged with Murder; Accused, 33, Is 'Known to Police.' Police Probe Links to 4 Other Slayings." *Toronto Star*, February 1, 2006.
Pron, Nick. "Second Murder Charge Laid; Man, 33, Now Accused of Killing Two Area Women." *Toronto Star*, June 6, 2006.
"Police Charge Man with Murder of Exotic Dancer; Lobby Group Accuses Niagara of 'Indifference' to Killings of Five Women." *Hamilton Spectator*, January 31, 2006.
"Man Faces Second Charge in Niagara slayings; Police Task Force Trying to Determine if There Is a Connection with Three Other Homicides in Niagara Region." *Guelph Mercury*, June 6, 2006.

GORDON STEWART NORTHCOTT

Paul, James Jeffrey. *Nothing Is Strange with You.* Philadelphia: Xlibris, 2008.

BRAEDEN NUGENT

Gomes, Julio. "Dead Con Didn't Do Drugs, Inquest Was Told." *Chronicle Journal,* April 6, 2006.

Gomes, Julio. "Dead Inmate was 'Serial Killer in the Making.'" *Chronicle Journal,* March 30, 2005.

Gomes, Julio. "'Serial Killer in the Making' Died of Overdose." *Chronicle Journal,* October 26, 2005.

CLIFFORD OLSON

Boer, Peter. *Canadian Crime Investigations: Hunting Down Serial Killers.* Edmonton: Folklore, 2002.

Clark, Doug. *Dark Paths, Cold Trails.* Toronto: HarperCollins, 2002.

Davis, Carole Anne. *Youthful Prey: Child Predators Who Kill.* London: Pennant, 2008.

Holmes, W. Leslie. *Where Shadows Linger: The Untold Story of the RCMP's Olson Murders Investigation.* Victoria, B.C.: Heritage House, 2000.

WEB

www.trutv.com/library/crime/serial_killers/predators/olson/1.html (accessed January 29, 2010).

www.montrealgazette.com/news/canada/Canada+infamous+serial+killer+Clifford+Olson+dead/5488179/story.html (accessed October 4, 2011).

ROBERT PICKTON

Boer, Peter. *Canadian Crime Investigations: Hunting Down Serial Killers.* Edmonton: Folklore, 2002.

Cameron, Stevie. *The Pickton File.* Toronto: Alfred A. Knopf, 2007.

Cawthorne, Nigel. *The Mammoth Book of Killers at Large.* Philadelphia: Running Press, 2007.

Culbert, Lori. "Pen Pals from Prison." *Vancouver Sun,* September 2, 2006.

"Exclusive Pickton Letters." *Vancouver Sun,* December 10, 2007.

Ramsland, Katherine. *The Devil's Dozen: How Cutting-Edge Forensics Took Down 12 Notorious Serial Killers.* New York: Berkley Books, 2009.

WEB

Newton, Michael and Katherine Ramsland. "Robert Pickton: The Vancouver Missing Women" at *www.trutv.com* (accessed August 28, 2009).

SAM PIRRERA

Wells, Jon. *Vanished: Cold-Blooded Murder in Steeltown.* Toronto: John Wiley & Sons, 2009.

THE PROSTITUTES-IN-THE-LAKE KILLINGS

www.cbc.ca/canada/toronto/story/2010/10/28/macdonald-murders.html
(accessed November 2010).

www.cbc.ca/canada/windsor/story/.../pei-peter-dale-macdonald-584.html
(accessed November 2010).

www.thestar.com/news/crime/article/882276. "Man Charged in Parkdale Prostitute Murders" (accessed November 2010).

EDWARD RULLOFF

Bailey, Richard W. *Rogue Scholar: The Sinister Life and Celebrated Death of Edward H. Rulloff.* Ann Arbor: University of Michigan Press, 2003.

Haines, Max. "Teacher, Doctor, Killer." In *The Collected Works of Max Haines Volume 2.* Toronto: Toronto Sun, 1991.

WEB

www.trutv.com/library/crime/serial_killers/history/john_rulloff/1_index.html
(accessed September 26, 2011).

RON SEARS

Brode, Patrick. *The Slasher Killings.* Detroit: Wayne State University Press, 2009.

DAVID SNOW

Shaw, Allison. *A Friend of the Family.* Toronto: Macfarlane Walter & Ross, 1998.

TELEVISION

"The House Hermit." *Crime Stories.* History Television.

MELVIN STANTON

Growe, Sarah Jane. "Murder Scene/Murder Seen; Ex-paramedic Still Suffers Trauma from What He Experienced 13 Years Ago in Slain Woman's Bedroom." *Toronto Star*, May 13, 2001.

McDermid-Gomme, Ian. *The Shadow Line: Deviance and Crime in Canada.* Toronto: Harcourt, Brace & Jovanovich, 1993.

Marshall, W.L. *Criminal Neglect: Why Sex Offenders Go Free.* Toronto: Doubleday, 1990.

Ware, Beverley. "Gone But Not Forgotten — Metro Fundraiser Dinner to Honour Memory of MD's Murdered Sister." *Chronicle-Herald*, March 24, 2010.

DONALD SHERMAN STALEY

"Jury Names Staley Killer." *Calgary Herald*, August 22, 1946.

"Staley Witness Guilty of Theft." *Calgary Herald*, September 23, 1946.

"Say Staley Read Reports of Murder." *Edmonton Journal*, October 2, 1946.

"Sentence Insanity: Confessed Murderer Gives 13 Points in Plea." *Calgary Herald*, October 29, 1946.

"Staley 'Felt Bad' Over Killing Boy." *Edmonton Journal*, October 4, 1946.

"Staley on Stand Tells Court of Early Troubles." *Calgary Herald*, October 3, 1946.

"Verdict in Goss Murder Case is Expected this Afternoon." *Calgary Herald*, October 5, 1946.

"Vet Admits Goss Slaying to Face Murder Charge Here." *Calgary Herald*, August 19, 1946.

THOMAS SVEKLA

Boer, Peter. *Canadian Crime Investigations: Hunting Down Serial Killers.* Edmonton: Folklore, 2002.

WEB

"Thomas Svekla's Secret Life." *The Edmonton Journal*, June 8, 2008, *www.canada. com/edmontonjournal/news/story.html?id=e4e51ac2-82c2-48c3-b833-84dde0e23c1a.*

ALLAN SWEENEY

Barron, Sherri. "Halfway House Death Prompts Rule Changes." *Ottawa Citizen*, December 10, 1986.

Deveney, Abby. "Dead Woman's Father Wants Parole Review." *Ottawa Citizen*, December 11, 1986.

Evanson, Brad. "Residents Stop Group Home Plan." *Ottawa Citizen*, December 13, 1986.

"Lessons from a Senseless Death." *Ottawa Citizen*, December 11, 1986.

Marshall, W.L. *Criminal Neglect: Why Sex Offenders Go Free.* Toronto: Doubleday, 1990.

"Paroled Murderer Gets Life for Halfway-House Slaying." *Montreal Gazette*, December 10, 1986.

Provencher, Norman. "Slain Woman's Husband Wants No Parole for Killer." *Ottawa Citizen*, December 10, 1986.

WEB

www.npb-cnlc.gc.ca/about/hist-eng.shtml (accessed February 2010).

DAVID THREINEN

"4 Children's Bodies Found in Canada." *Pittsburgh Press*, August 13, 1975.

"Saskatoon Man Held for Murder of Two Children." *Leader-Post*, August 13, 1975.

"Man Held in Slayings of Children." *Sarasota Herald Tribune*, August 14, 1975.

TORONTO'S GAY VILLAGE MURDERS

Hoshowsky, Robert. *Unsolved: True Canadian Cold Cases*. Toronto: Dundurn, 2010.

MICHAEL VESCIO

Anderson, Diane. *Bloodstains: Canada's Multiple Murderers*. Calgary: Detselig, 2006.

RON WEST

Duncanson, John. "Elusive Killers Leave Cold Trail for Police." *Toronto Star*, April 2, 1992.

TELEVISION

"The .22 Caliber Killer." *Crime Stories*. History Television.

HENRY WILLIAMS

Haines, Max. *The Collected Works of Max Haines Volume 6*. Toronto: Penguin, 2008.

Haliechuk, Rick. "How Parole Board Decides Who Gets Pass." *Toronto Star*, February 28, 1987.

Haliechuk, Rick. "Killer-Rapist Denied Pass from Prison." *Toronto Star*, October 5, 1988.

COLONEL RUSSELL WILLIAMS

Appleby, Timothy. *A New Kind of Monster*. Toronto: Random House, 2011.

Ontario Provincial Police. "Transcript of Taped Interview" at *www.cbc.ca/news/pdf/edited-williams.pdf* (accessed December 2010).

WEB

www.cbc.ca/news/canada/story/2010/10/18/col-williams-court-1018.html (accessed October 24, 2010).

www.cbc.ca/news/canada/story/2010/10/19/russell-williams-day-2.html (accessed October 24, 2010).

www.theglobeandmail.com/news/national/colonel-russell-williams-is-a-man-no-one-really-knew/article1463964/ (accessed February 11, 2010).

www.theglobeandmail.com/news/national/colonel-russell-williams-the-making-of-a-mystery-man/article1537412/ (accessed November 1, 2010).

www.thestar.com/news/canada/article/877044--day-in-court-ends-with-details-of-assault, accessed (October 18, 2010).

TELEVISION

"Above Suspicion." *The Fifth Estate*. CBC Television

"The Confession." *The Fifth Estate*. CBC Television.

DANNY WOOD

Duncanson, John. "New Witnesses Emerge After Story on Decade-Old Northern Slayings." *Toronto Star*, October 31, 1991.

"Family Hopes Death Will Finally Be Solved." *Hamilton Spectator*, October 16, 1991.

French, Janet. "Lawyers to Take on Fight of Wood Murder Conviction. New Evidence Witness Hints at Wrongful Conviction." *Star Phoenix*, February 18, 2005.

"Judge Orders CBC to Pull Program on Convicted Killer." *Toronto Star*, January 7, 1986.

"North Bay Family Hopes '80 Murder Will be Solved." *Waterloo Record*, October 16, 1991.

PETER WOODCOCK

Bourre, Mark. *By Reason of Insanity: The David Michael Krueger Story.* Toronto: Hounslow Press, 1997.

Vronsky, Peter. *Serial Killers: The Method and Madness of Monsters.* New York: Berkley Books, 2004.

LILA AND WILLIAM YOUNG

Cahill, Bette L. *Butterbox Babies.* Halifax: Fernwood, 2006.

Newton, Michael. *The Encyclopedia of Serial Killers.* New York: Checkmark Books, 2000.

Index

Of Related Interest

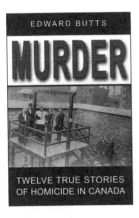

Murder
Twelve True Stories of Homicide in Canada
by Edward Butts
$24.99
978-1554887620

Who committed Toronto's Silk Stocking Murder? Why did a quiet accountant in Guelph, Ontario, murder his wife and two daughters? How did an American confidence man from Arizona find himself facing a murder charge in Cape Breton, Nova Scotia? These questions and more are answered in this collection of thrilling true Canadian crime stories from colonial times to the twentieth century. Butts also profiles the investigators who tracked the killers down, and in some cases sent them to the gallows in this collection of true tales that range from shocking and macabre to downright weird.

Justice Miscarried
Inside Wrongful Convictions in Canada
by Hélèna Katz
978-1554888740
$24.99

Behind the proud facade of Canada's criminal justice system lie the shattered lives of the people unjustly caught within its web. *Justice Miscarried* tells the heart-wrenching stories of twelve innocent Canadians, including David Milgaard, Donald Marshall, Guy Paul Morin, Clayton Johnson, William Mullins-Johnson, and Thomas Sophonow, who were wrongly convicted and how the errors in the nation's justice system changed their lives forever.

Unsolved
True Canadian Cold Cases
by Robert Hoshowsky
978-1554887392
$24.99

Despite advances in DNA testing, forensics, and the investigative skills used by police, hundreds of crimes remain unsolved across Canada. With every passing day trails grow colder and decades can pass before a new lead or witness comes forward ... if one comes forward. In *Unsolved*, Robert J. Hoshowsky examines twelve crimes that continue to haunt us. Some cases are well-known, while others have virtually disappeared from the public eye. All of the cases remain open, and many are being re-examined by police using the latest tools and technology. Hoshowsky takes the reader through all aspects of the crimes and how police are trying to solve them.

WALKING ----➔
BROOKLYN

MAR 1 8 2019